信仰与社会

——全球化时代的精神反思

Faith and Society

张志刚 严 军◎主编
方 文 王锁劳◎副主编

北京论坛秘书处
北京大学宗教文化研究院 编

宗教文化出版社

图书在版编目（ＣＩＰ）数据

信仰与社会：全球化时代的精神反思/张志刚、严军主编. －北京：宗教文化出版社，2013.10

ISBN 978 － 7 － 80254 － 771 － 1

I. ①信... II. ①张... ②严... III. ①宗教社会学 － 文集 IV. ①B920 － 53

中国版本图书馆 CIP 数据核字（2013）第 238093 号

信仰与社会
——全球化时代的精神反思
张志刚　严　军　主编

出版发行：宗教文化出版社

地　　址：北京市西城区后海北沿 44 号　　（100009）

电　　话：64095215（发行部）　64095234（编辑部）

责任编辑：霍克功

英文审读：刘洪宇

版式设计：高秋兰

印　　刷：北京柯蓝博泰印务有限公司

版权专有　　侵权必究

版本记录：787×1092 毫米　16 开本　30.75 印张　350 千字
　　　　　　2013 年 10 月第 1 版　　2013 年 10 月第 1 次印刷

书　　号：ISBN 978 － 7 － 80254 － 771 － 1

定　　价：78.00 元

作者简介

特稿作者

王作安,中国国家宗教事务局党组书记、局长

托尼·布莱尔(Tony Blair),英国前首相,中东问题四方小组特使,托尼·布莱尔信仰基金会创始人,北京论坛国际顾问。

卓新平,中国社会科学院学部委员,世界宗教研究所所长、研究员,中国宗教学会会长。

张志刚,北京大学哲学系、宗教学系教授,外国哲学研究所研究员,北京大学宗教文化研究院院长,中国宗教学会副会长。

第一部分作者

迪特里希·荣格(Dietrich Jung),南丹麦大学当代中东学中心主任、教授。

王宇洁,中国社会科学院世界宗教研究所伊斯兰教研究室主任、研究员。

阿德尔·萨布里(Adel Sabry),埃及《华夫脱报》主编。

杰里米·顾恩(T. Jeremy Gunn),摩洛哥艾赫韦恩大学国际关系副教授。

阿尔贝托·托尼尼(Alberto Tonini),意大利佛罗伦萨大学政治学副教授。

王凤,中国社会科学院西亚非洲研究所副研究员。

斯蒂芬妮·拉克瓦(Stephane Lacroix),法国巴黎政治学院教授。

王锁劳,北京大学国际关系学院中东研究中心主任、副教授。

第二部分作者

菲利普·高斯基(Philip S. Gorski),美国耶鲁大学社会学系教授。

居拉伊·蒂尔克曼-德尔维什奥卢(Gülay Türkmen – Dervişoğlu),美国耶鲁大学社会学系教授。

方文,北京大学社会学系教授,北京大学宗教与社会研究中心主任,北京大学宗教文化研究院副院长。

梁景文(Graeme Lang),香港城市大学亚洲及国际学系教授。

刘金光,中国国家宗教事务局政策法规司副司长。

李向平,华东师范大学宗教与社会研究中心主任,社会学系教授。

赵星光(Hsing – Kuang Chao),台湾东海大学社会学系教授。

周越(Adam Yuet Chao),英国剑桥大学东亚系讲师。

高卉,新疆石河子大学政法学院副院长、讲师。

卢云峰,北京大学社会学系副教授,北京大学宗教与社会研究中心执行主任。

第三部分作者

赵敦华,北京大学哲学系、宗教学系教授,外国哲学研究所研究员,教育部哲学学科教学指导委员会副主任,中华外国哲学史学会理事长。

斯图尔特·布朗(Stewart Brown),英国爱丁堡大学神学院院长、教授。

阿尔贝托·梅洛尼(Alberto Melloni),博洛尼亚若望二十三世宗教学研究所主任、教授。

蜂屋邦夫（Hachiya Kunio），日本东京大学名誉教授。

吉原浩人（Yoshihaya Hiroto），日本早稻田大学文学学术院教授。

黄保罗（Paulos Huang），芬兰赫尔辛基大学系统神学与比较宗教研究员。

张桥贵，云南民族大学副校长、教授，中国宗教学会副会长。

陶飞亚，上海大学宗教与中国社会研究中心主任、教授。

王晓朝，清华大学人文学院哲学系教授，中国宗教学会副会长。

序 言

本书可谓《信仰与责任——全球化时代的精神反思》(宗教文化出版社 2011 年)的"姊妹篇",是对前书研讨内容的拓展与深化。本书的内容,主要选自国内外专家学者提交给北京论坛(2012)的分论坛"信仰与社会——全球化时代的精神反思"的 40 篇论文;排在前面的四篇特稿,一是国家宗教事务局王作安局长专为本书撰写的,一是英国前首相、北京论坛国际顾问托尼·布莱尔(Tony Blair)在北京大学讲演(2012 年 12 月 1 日)的英文稿,随后两篇是卓新平教授和张志刚教授专为本书提供的。

北京论坛是经中国教育部批准,在北京市政府的指导与支持下,由北京大学、北京市教育委员会和韩国高等教育财团联合主办的国际性学术论坛。该论坛创办于 2004 年,每年秋季举办一次,总主题为"文明的和谐与共同繁荣"。北京论坛(2012)的大会主题为"文明的和谐与共同繁荣——新格局·新挑战·新思维·新机遇",共设八个分论坛:(一)反思资本主义——后危机时代世界面临的挑战,(二)信仰与社会——全球化时代的精神反思,(三)世界经济变化中的教育发展——质量、公正与效率,(四)世界城市精神传承——经验与创新,(五)文明的建构——语言的沟通与典籍的传播,(六)社会化媒体时代的创新与变革,(七)全球经济新格局下的社会企业与企业家责任,(八)共同的世界,不同的视角——德国、欧洲、中国。两年前举办的北京论坛曾设专场研讨"信仰与责任",此次分论坛(二)题为"信仰与社会",其学术立意主要如下:

全球化时代的到来,使我们深切地感受到,不同的社会、民族、国家或文明具有不同的信仰,而人类的信仰之所以是多元化的,就是因为人们在不同的历史、文化和社会背景下形成了不同的世界观、价值观和人生观。因而,要理解全球化时代的新格局,便不能不认知不同社会的信仰者;要回应全球化时代的新挑战,也不能不相遇不同社会的信仰者;要抓住全球化时代的新机遇,更不能不携手不同社会的信仰者。一言以蔽之,在全球化时代,要实现各民族、国家和文明的和谐相处与共同繁荣,就不能不从现实社会层面上来促进多元化信仰之间的交流、理解与对话。这是我们对全球化时代的多元化信仰所应抱有的精神反思维度。

基于上述立意,我们广邀海内外的 40 位资深专家和学界新秀,围绕"信仰与社会"的关系问题,展开了如下三场跨文化、多学科的专题讨论:(一)多元信仰与社会变迁,主要议题为(1)中东北非变局中的宗教、政治与社会,(2)全球化时代的伊斯兰化思潮,(3)各大信仰传统的政治观与社会观;(二)多元信仰与社会治理,主要议题为(1)多元信仰与社会行为,(2)多元信仰与社会法治,(3)多元信仰与社会公益;(三)多元信仰与文化建设,主要议题为(1)当代宗教冲突与宗教对话研究,(2)东西方信仰传统的比较与对话,(3)各大信仰传统与当代文化建设。本书所划分的三部分内容,便是上述三场专题讨论的主要成果,但此次正式出版的论文均在会后经过各位作者的修改完善。

在本书编辑过程中,两位副主编,北京大学社会学系方文教授和北京大学国际关系学院王锁劳副教授,分别精选了他们所负责主持的两场专题讨论的论文;沈满琳博士仔细整理了托尼·布莱尔的讲演稿"全球化背景下的挑战与合作",并协助两位主编做了大量辛苦的编辑工作。在此,我们连同全书的所有作者一并致谢。

北京大学宗教文化研究院院长 张志刚
北京论坛秘书长 严 军
2013 年初夏记于北大燕园

目 录

特 稿

发挥宗教界在生态文明建设中的作用

王作安

宗教思想中包含丰富的生态保护内容,宗教界也具有珍惜自然的优良传统。贯彻党的十八大关于加强生态文明建设的部署,要动员宗教界人士和信教群众参加生态文明建设,为建设美丽中国做出积极贡献。

一、宗教主张尊重自然和保护环境

佛教认为,人与环境是有机统一体。佛教讲业报轮回,认为人身是正报,环境是依报,二者密不可分,都是主体的业力所为,因此要像对待自身一样对待环境。佛教主张众生平等,佛经说:"一切众生,悉有佛性。""青青翠竹,尽是法身;郁郁黄花,无非般若。"大自然的一草一木都是佛性的体现,都有其存在的价值。慈悲为怀,善待生命,是佛教的基本伦理。《大智度论》说:"诸余罪中,杀业最重;诸功德中,放生第一。"佛教的高僧大德都追求物我相融的境界,无论深山僻壤,还是城郭闹市,举凡佛寺所在,大都树木葱茏,鸟语花香,环境很好。

崇尚自然,保护生态,是道教的核心理念。《道德经》认为,道生一、一生二、二生三、三生万物;人法地、地法天、天法道、道法自然。就是说,天地万物同出于道,强调求道者必须达到"天地与我并生,而万物与我为一"的境界。庄子也主张,"人兽不乱群,入鸟不惊飞"。在对待人与自然的关系上,道教主张知常、知和、知止、知足,"知常"就是懂得天地万物和谐自然之常,"知和"就是懂得人与自然和谐相处之道,"知止"就是要把握好利用自然之度,"知足"就是要少私寡欲、避免贪婪过度。

伊斯兰教也有丰富的生态伦理。《古兰经》认为,大自然是真主对人类的恩赐,爱护大自然不仅是"善行",而且是衡量是否顺从主命的标准。《古兰经》说:"天地万物,只是安拉的。安拉是周知万物的。"反复倡导对动物植物及一切自然物都应存仁爱之心,禁止随意宰杀砍伐。伊斯兰教认为,社会发展须以人与自然的和谐为前提。人类是真主委以管理自然界的"代治者",保护环境、爱护自然、维护社会安宁,是真主赋予人类的神圣职责。

天主教和基督教都很重视保护生态。《圣经》认为,人类可以支配利用自然,同时也要善待自然。所谓"主上帝把那人安置在伊甸园,叫他耕种,看守园子",就是强调人有责任像园丁一样保护所有受造物,认为上帝为人类创造了适于居住和生存的世界,也把管理和保护的责任托付给了人类。人类有支配自然的权力,但没有破坏自然的权力。

二、宗教界为保护环境做了许多有益工作

以道教为例。道教对生态保护特别关注,近 20 年来一直在进行有益探索。上世纪 90 年代初,中国道教协会号召全国道教徒"植树造林,美化环境",并对先进个人进行表彰。1995 年,中国道教协会参加在英国召开的世界宗教与环境保护会议,发表了《中国道教关于生态环境保护的宣言》。2003 年,中国道教协会在甘肃省民勤县建立"中国道教生态林建设基地",10 年来海内外道教界持续捐款建设"道教生态林"工程,在防沙治沙方面收到很好效果。2006 年至 2008 年,中国道教协会联合学术机构和企业,先后召开 3 次"中国道教宫观生态保护论坛",提出了"生态道观"项目,要求各地道观"建立健全生态保护和宣传教育的规章制度,大幅度提升住观道众的生态环保意识,最大限度地采用节能技术和材料,形成与周边自然环境和社区人群相协调的良性生态圈。"此举得到联合国开发署的关注,并得到有关国际环境组织的支持。2009 年,中国道教协会制订了《中国道教界保

护环境的 8 年规划(2010－2017)纲要意见》,要求各地道教协会、宫观将生态保护纳入创建和谐宫观目标,为建设生态道观、保护生态环境作出新的贡献。在 2011 年召开的国际道教论坛上,各国各地区与会代表共同探讨道教生态思想的现代意义,并盛赞中国道教界在生态保护方面所做出的贡献。

其实,不仅是道教,我国各宗教都在环境保护方面做了许多有益工作。2011 年 1 月 28 日,我国五大宗教全国性团体发表的《倡导宗教和谐共同宣言》提出:"尊重自然,保护生态,追求健康生活方式,树立可持续发展理念,促进人与自然和谐相处。"这一《共同宣言》,表明我国各宗教在生态保护方面形成了牢固共识,对我国各宗教共同致力于生态保护事业起到了有力促进作用。

三、发挥宗教界在生态文明建设中的作用

建设美丽中国,实现中华民族永续发展,关乎人民福祉和民族未来,必须全民动员投身生态文明建设。宗教界参加生态文明建设,有信仰基础,有历史传统,有自觉意识,有社会公信,可以发挥独特作用,是一支重要力量。总结近年来宗教界保持环境方面的实践,应支持宗教界重点做好以下四个方面的工作:

弘扬宗教生态伦理思想。近年来,党和政府支持我国各宗教开展宗教思想建设,挖掘和弘扬宗教教义、宗教道德、宗教文化中健康文明的内容,跟上社会发展和时代进步,走与社会主义社会相适应的道路。在这一过程中,各宗教开始重视宗教生态思想的阐释和研究。当前和今后一个时期,要按照党的十八大精神,支持宗教界在宗教思想建设中更加重视整理和挖掘宗教生态理念,进行符合现代要求的阐释,形成与社会主义生态文明建设相适应的宗教生态观,加大宣传和培训力度,提高宗教界人士和信教群众的生态文明素养,更加自觉地珍爱自然,更加积极地保护生态,与全国各族人民一道努力,共同走向社会主义生态文明新时代。

重视开展环保类公益活动。改革开放以来,我国各宗教本着慈悲济

世、服务人群的优良传统,积极从事公益慈善活动,其中包括保护环境的活动,产生了良好社会影响。2012 年,国家宗教局会同有关部门联合制定《关于鼓励和规范宗教界从事公益慈善活动的意见》,把环境保护列入重点支持的非营利活动,为宗教界从事生态保护提供了重要的政策保障。各宗教要把生态保护放到从事公益活动的重要位置上来,在宗教界人士和信教群众中普及环境保护和生态建设基本知识,树立尊重自然、保护自然的生态文明理念,在日常生活和修行实践中身体力行。各宗教要根据自身传统和特点,在植树护林、保护动物、旧品回收、节电节水、理性消费、健康饮食等方面,积极行动起来,打造环保类公益活动品牌。

建设环境优美的宗教活动场所。寺观教堂既是实践宗教生态理念的重要基地,也是展示宗教生态建设的重要窗口。特别是许多佛教寺院和道教宫观,环境优美,庄严清静,成为我国宗教尊重自然、保护生态的生动例证。2009 年发起开展的和谐寺观教堂创建活动,对宗教活动场所建设起到积极推动作用,今后要把生态保护列入重要的创建标准,倡导植树栽花,倡导文明进香,倡导低碳生活,倡导科学放生,把宗教活动场所建设成为生态保护示范基地,推动宗教界的生态文明建设。另外,在国务院公布的七批全国重点文物保护单位中,宗教活动场所占有一定比例,宗教界要切实担负起保护职责,处理好保护与利用的关系,坚决防止"被上市"、"被承包"、"被拆迁"等乱象。

开展生态保护方面的国际交流。我国道教界在生态保护国际合作方面已经迈出了重要一步,积累了重要经验,可供其他各宗教借鉴。要把生态保护列入宗教方面对外交流的重要内容,拓展宗教对外友好交流的领域。通过同相关国际组织和其他国家宗教界的交流,介绍我国节约资源和保护环境的基本国策和具有中国特色的生态文明发展道路,介绍我国宗教尊重自然、保护自然的文明理念,介绍我国宗教界在生态保护方面所做出的贡献,同时学习借鉴国外宗教界在生态保护方面的有益经验,为建设美丽中国和美丽地球家园而共同努力。

Challenges and Cooperation in the Context of Globalization

Tony Blair

2012.12.1,*Peking University*

Ni-hao！

Thank you very much, Vice President and professors. Thank you for having me back here to Peking University. It's a great honor and a great pleasure to be here again.

This year, we had the Olympics in London. And, because you did so well in 2008, we had to do something spectacular in 2012. I don't know if any of you came, but it was a great party. So, it is a wonderful thing to be back here again.

I am going to talk to you today about globalization and its challenges, and after that we will have some time for questions and answers.

One of the things I've been able to do since I stopped being Prime? Minister is to see much more of the world. I think this is my 28th visit to China in the last few years. But I've also been able to see many other countries and even continents, like Africa. This helps me have a better picture of the world today.

The world is driven by this force called globalization. There is a lot of misunderstanding around globalization. Sometimes people think globalization is a policy that is adopted by governments, whether the Chinese government, or the British government, or the American government. But, globalization is a force driven by people, and particularly in my view, people allied to technology. This is what is changing the world today. The debate around whether globalization is good or bad is a debate that is almost irrelevant, because globalization is a fact and it's only going to get stronger. It changes profoundly the way the world is.

First of all, globalization produces challenges that are global in nature. Take the global economy today. If you look at what's happening in Europe and in the United States, you have a major issue around fiscal positions, which are going to have to be resolved in a few weeks. And here in China, you have a new leadership with a very big ambition to double the size of your economy in the years to come. But it is harder to do growth in the economy as the economy grows.

If you take for example, the RMB and the dollar, what happens to the RMB affects America and what happens to the dollar affects China because cause you have so many reserves in dollars. So the point is the impact of China on America, or America on China, is big today. And the impact of Europe on the world economy is big. That is how today's world is. We have a situation where the global economy is more interdependent and integrated than it has ever been in human history.

Then, if we look at migration, the movement of people across the world, again today as a result of globalization, this is happening in a way that is unprecedented. The estimates are that at any one time in the world today, any moment in time, around 200 million people are on the move, moving across national boundaries. In virtually every Western country today, immigration is a big, big, hot politic issue, because this is a process again that globalization is driving.

And then there is the development of social media. As I come in here, I see lots of people with mobile phones. When I was at your age, as a student, we didn't have mobile phones. I know it sounds strange. It sounds like we were back in the Stone Ages then. Just in the last few years, you can look at the IPad, Google, social media-Twitter, Facebook, and the Chinese equivalents. Hundreds of millions here in China, and hundreds of millions elsewhere are now part of this revolution.

Social media in itself is changing the world. Things people hadn't even heard of twenty years ago are now producing momentous social and political changes across the world. What people call the Arab Spring are actually the Arab revolutions: upheavals, out in the Middle East. I think social media was itself a major dimension to those events. So what it means is that as globalization continues, the world becomes more interconnected than ever before economically, but also physically, and online, through technology.

Therefore, what rises out of this? Politics finds it difficult to catch up, and to keep up, with the events that are happening in the developments of globalization. The result is that if problems and challenges are increasingly global, the solutions need to be global. These solutions need to be based on some common values. Otherwise, how do people reconcile their different interests?

People themselves have to be more open to other people because they are mixing with other people more than ever before. When I was growing up in the north of England in the 1960s and 1970s, everyone was kind of the same. I actually remember the day, because I was 12 years old, when I met my first black person. It was the first time I had ever seen someone of a different color than me. That's the world I grew up in, one of small communities. Today, the world my children are growing up in is a world where people of different colors, and races, and faiths, and cultures mix together as a matter of course. And, even if they are not mixing physically, they'll be mixing with them through technology and social media.

Therefore, we have to co-operate and work together on an unprecedented scale, in ways that are deeper, more effective, more integrated, and where we recognize that difference and diversity are not things we should be scared of, but things we need to welcome and embrace. In other words, we have to create societies of harmony between people of different cultures and different faiths. If we don't, and we are all pushed together and mixing more together, then we are going to end up in a situation where there is conflict. If you look around the world today, probably over half the conflicts going on have a strong faith or cultural or religious dimension to them.

So what are the things we need to work on together? I would suggest there are four major areas, where we should work together today, in a way that is different from many things we have done before.

The first is on the economy. We are going to have to work to keep the world's markets open and trade flowing. The great risk in this time of economic crises is economic nationalism, protectionism, and markets closing down, when actually markets need to keep opening up. Take the case of China. How has China come from where it was a few decades ago to where it is today? By opening up. What is happening in your country is the single biggest advance in terms of lifting people out of poverty, the single biggest advance human history has ever known. It's an extraordinary thing. In 2000 we set a series of millennium goals for the world, called the United Nations Millennium Development Goals. The one that could be met is the reduction of poverty, and would be met because of China, essentially. And how did that happen? It happened because China opened up. We forget that at the time that was a contested policy, but it has worked, and there is a lesson for the world there. We have to carry on opening up.

But I see big dangers in Europe, in America, elsewhere, of us closing down in the face of economic crisis. We are going to have to find ways of globally cooperating to make the economy work on a global scale. When I was Prime Minister, the G8, was still the major international gathering. Now it's the G20. That's happened in just a few years and for very obvious reasons. People recognize that without China, India and the large emerging markets of the world, it is absurd to have a discussion about the global economy without their presence. So that's the first thing. We have to keep the global economy open and moving. And I mentioned Africa just a short time ago. China is now going to invest more in Africa next year than the whole of the World Bank programs put together. So we need to keep these investment flows going and we need to keep world trade open.

The second area is climate and the environment. This is very tough, because there are some people who say that because the economic crisis we should postpone actions on the environment. I think it is increasingly clear that if this generation does not take strong action to protect our environment, then we will be acting in a way that is totally irresponsible toward the generations to come. But it is going to be hard because you have to be able to grow and the West is going to want to carry on with a high stand of consumption and a high stand of living. The answer, in my view, is the development of science and technology so that we consume differently. We have to put massive efforts into this and into trying to secure an international agreement that allows us to share technology, to be able to deal with specific issues like deforestation, and frankly at the moment, in the international apparatus for negotiating this, it is quite hard to see it working.

It is very important that in your recent party congress, your leadership made it clear that the environment and the issues to do with the climate are actually central, to the development of China. But again, this can't happen properly unless it happens worldwide because you need to carry on growing, and the world needs to carry on growing. We all share an interest in developing the science and technology of the future. So that's the second area, in which global cooperation is going to have to become deeper and more effective.

There is the third area, which is very obvious. When I am out in the Middle East, I see a need for the East and West to come closer to each other to try to understand each other's perspective and work together, to resolve some of these fundamental questions that have the potential to impact far beyond the particular region where any conflict is located.

If you take the Israeli-Palestinian issue, it has the ability to reverberate and impact, throughout the world. Because it impacts Islam, it also impacts on Western policy. So again, one consequence of the world today, is that the impact of disputes very rarely remains in their own location. The impact spreads fast, across national boundaries, and of course the new media and technology multiplies the impact of this. One of the things that have changed most since the time I came into politics is that real, live events get recorded and transmitted around the world as they are happening. In fact, even when I was Prime Minister, sometimes we would switch on the television to get the latest information rather than from our own government services. This means that very quickly events influence thinking, sentiments and emotions across the world. So for us to be able to cooperate on security questions is very important, because if we fail to cooperate, we get increased instability and chaos and disorder that is fundamentally dangerous. That's the third area of cooperation.

The fourth area is the one that my foundation focuses on and the reason for the partnership with this great university. That is this idea of how people of different cultures also understand each other better and learn to live with each other. My theory here is very simple. I think where there is ignorance, there is often fear, and where there is fear, there is often conflict. On the contrary, where there is understanding, there is more likely to be harmony, because the knowledge about the other person reduces the prospect of conflict. So if it is true that the world is moving closely together, and people have to mix with each other across the divide of nations, and culture, and faith, then we have to learn about each other. We have to be able to understand each other. Again, when I was brought up, I was brought up in a Christian setting, in a Christian way of life. It never occurred to me that there was any other. It is just the way it was. Now today I know that I can't understand the world, unless I understand not just different faiths or religions, but different cultures.

One of the single most important things is bringing about greater understanding about China, because the rise of China is having such an impact on Western thinking right now. Sometimes I think maybe it's hard to understand. All the history I was taught in school, all the big events that I read about, learnt about when I was your age, they were all totally Western dominated. We lived in a world that was dominated by the West. We set the terms at the debate, we sort of wrote the history. And now people are realizing that this isn't true. We can't operate this way.

Actually in any event in the 21st century, you're seeing the power shifting East. At the very least, this power is going to have to be shared between East and West in the future. Sometimes when you try to understand a country, you can't do that just by having political leaders talk to each other. You have to have people begin to understand each other. This is why it's so important that we create platforms of understanding and dialogue so that we can understand each other better. So that we understand for example in the West, that yes modern China was created 60 odd years ago, but China has a history, a rich tradition of philosophy and culture that we need to understand and be comfortable with. The more we do understand it, the more we will find there are all sorts of things that are in common between the cultures.

One of the things that fascinates me about religious faith is that what often happens is that religious faith becomes manifested in doctrines, in dogmas, in rituals, in practices, in all sorts of institutions, but actually the basic religious teachings of most religious faith is essentially about love and compassion for your neighbor. There is actually a famous Rabbi who had someone make a bet with him. That person said to the Rabbi, "I will convert to Judaism if you can stand on one leg and recite the whole of the Torah." So the Rabbi stood on one leg and he said, "Love your God and do to your neighbor as you would have him do unto you. That is the Torah. Everything else is commentary. Now go and do it." And so most of the faiths have that in common, but you don't see that and understand that until you start to explore those faiths and get behind the dogma and ritual.

My final point is this that when you have the force of globalization, and it's changing the world that it offers us the opportunity to create a platform of understanding. So we actually have the means within our hands, to communicate with each other, and cooperate with each other, and work with each other, and learn about each other, learn to live with each other. The challenge is for us to do it, and this has to be worked on. The reason why the partnership between my Foundation and Peking University is important consists in the fact that there isn't a better place to do it than here in China. There is no better way to do it than within a university with you students, because you are going to be the future of our world. One day you'll be decision makers, like I was a decision maker, or still am in some ways. Then it will be your responsibility, and how your minds develops now, how you learn to think about the world, and judge the world, analyze it, will be an important part of whether we bring peace and harmony to our world.

So thank you all for having me here today, it's a great pleasure to be back at Peking University. And I want to say what an inspiration the university has been to me. So it's great honor to come back and share my thoughts with you. Thank you.

关注中国宗教的文化战略意义

卓新平

　　在贯彻执行中国共产党的十八大精神,努力构建中国和谐社会的当代发展中,文化问题凸显,并已引起人们的高度重视。在我们关注我国的文化发展和文化繁荣时,自然会思考什么是信仰、什么是宗教、什么是文化、什么是文明这些问题。一方面,人们深感当前社会建设、尤其是文化建设在中国改革开放的深化时期已经处于急迫需要的状况,社会需要一种中华文化精神的重振,否则整个社会发展会因这一"短板"而受到巨大影响。但另一方面,人们在信仰、宗教、文化等问题上有着思想上的混乱、观点上的分歧,很难在目前多元认知的情况下达到"求同"、"共识"。虽然我们在制定政治、经济等发展战略上占有明显的优势,已经有了颇为强大的"硬实力",而在文化精神的弘扬、文化战略的制定上却显得尚未到位,其结果是在文化"软实力"上很难与政治、经济的"硬实力"相平衡,人们已很难找回中华民族以往曾有的文化精神,而在铸就新的文化精神上却尚未达成共识。如果这一问题不能得到妥善的解决,那么我们当前的改革发展就会像一个"跛足"的巨人,在整体格局中出现"短板",归根结底会制约、影响到我们的可持续发展。因此,我们今天在加强文化"软实力"的建设时,应该从文化战略的意义上特别注意宗教、信仰等涉及我们精神深层次的问题,认识到这一问题的理想解决是中国当代社会可持续发展的关键因素之一。

　　应该承认,我国宗教发展正处于最好的时期,有人将之称为"黄金时期"。一方面,我们的社会对宗教的理解已经有了很大的进步;另一方面,我们的政府对宗教的生存与发展提供了在许多国家都根本不可能的有利条件。最近国家宗教事务局、中共中央统战部等联合颁发了《关于鼓励和规范宗教界从事公益慈善活动的意见》,肯定我国宗教界在公益慈善福利事业上有着积极地参与,承认其爱心、善举受到了社会的普遍好评,并通过相关文件和政策来使宗教界更好地参与社会公益慈善活动,使之有着制度上的保障。宗教界这种积极的社会参与,开始使中国社会及广大民众重新认识宗教的意义、审视以往关于宗教的形象。不过,这种社会层面的认知突破和政策举措,并不真正意味着对宗教的客观认识及正确理解问题已经得到根本解决;从当前文化战略的意义上来看,正确解决这一问题已十分必要和迫切。

经过30多年的改革开放,中国社会已经进入到改革深化、社会转型的关键时期,其确保可持续发展也已经处于攻坚战的阶段。目前国际环境已发生重大变化,国内各种矛盾亦有趋于恶化的态势,尤其是民族、宗教问题因为理论及实践上的新情况而变得更加复杂。人们对之众说纷纭,难达统一;而我们现行的一些理论与实践在其内在逻辑上也出现自相矛盾、相互掣肘或实际对立的现象;不少"知"与"行"既不符合中国的真实国情,也与马克思主义经典作家的理论精神和科学方法相违背;一些教条主义、形式主义的提法及做法正在损害马克思主义的声誉,影响我们宗教信仰自由基本方针的贯彻执行,也破坏了我们国家社会和谐、民族团结、宗教适应、基层稳定的努力。一些人仍习惯于"拿来主义",在许多关键的理论认知和实践指导上只是沿着西方各种理论学说来"跟着说",充其量也只有简单的"接着说",却没有独立自主、体现创新、开拓的"自己说"。针对这一状况,我们有必要对我们的思考、理论及相关政策加以冷静、科学的分析,进行必要的澄清、梳理、调整和完善,争取在这一社会转型的关键时期也能完成我们理论形态、思想认知、实际政策上的相应转型或提升,有着必要且必须的观念改变。在这些方面,我们应该有适合中国国情和现实"世情"的当代马克思主义理论发展,应该尊重历史发展、现实存在的客观规律,应该建立起系统的、创新的中国特色社会主义理论体系及其核心价值观,应该形成有利于中国可持续发展的和谐文化战略及其科学部署;这些都需要我们解放思想、转变观念。面对紧迫的现实需求,这种具有战略意义的调整和转型实际上已是刻不容缓,我们必须认真对待,有所作为。

在今天的文化创新中,制定相应的文化战略至关重要。我们的社会主义文化强国建设,核心在于形成能够振奋全民族的文化精神,而不是单纯在于文化产业的发展。在我们"大力弘扬民族精神和时代精神","丰富人民精神世界,增强人民精神力量"时,信仰及宗教是可以发挥作用的,至于能够发挥什么样的作用,则在于信仰及宗教与我们的当代社会究竟能够如何双向互动、形成呼应,也在于我们的社会民众今天能如何理解信仰及宗教。如果中华民族的文化发展要想获得一种光明的前景,真正做到以"美丽心灵"来实现"美丽中国"的景观,给世界树立当代中国的美好形象,则必须"建设优秀传统文化传承体系,弘扬中华优秀传统文化",其中不可避免地要包括信仰及宗教因素。过去我们太多强调自己的传统文化和宗教的负面意义及作用,使之成为精神负担而压得我们自己喘不过气来,也影响到我们真正树立中华文化的正面形象和确立我们中国人的文化自觉与自信。这种状况应在尽可能短的时间中彻底改变,而且越快越好。同世界其他伟大民族一样,我们必须站在自己文化传统的厚重实地上来挺直腰板,抬起头来,为我们的文化自豪,让我们的文化得以实实在在的传承和弘扬。同理,我们也理应将中国的宗教视为中国普通百姓安身立命的一种正常方式,视为中国人精神生活有机而鲜明的构成之一。为此,必须经常强调,"宗教作为政治力量应该成为我们自己政治力量的组成部分;宗教作为社会系统应该成为我们当今和谐社会的有机构建;宗教作为文化传承应该成为我们弘扬中华文化的积极因素;宗教作为灵性信仰应该成为我们重建精神家园的重要构成"。文化建设是一个整体工程、系统工程,当人们无视其核心或破坏其局部,则无法真正对之有效、可靠地加以构建。人类绝大多数民族都承认并肯定其宗教在自己民族文化中的重要地位和战略意义,他们的文化建设与宗教的有机整合是一体的,自然的,并没有像我们那样产生根本性疑虑。所以,让宗教"脱敏",不再把宗教视为我们今天中国社会的"另类",应该是我们当前中华文化重建中的重要思路之一。宗教作为精神文化现象是全人类的普遍现象,也是世界文明历史的重要构成,我们有着悠久文明传统的中华民族没有必要在宗教问题上跟全世界过不去,也更没有必要跟我们自己的宗教文化传承和当今社会现实过不去。如果宗教认知的问题不能得以解决、中国人的信仰情结不能得以肯定,任何文化建设都只能取得表面的成功,其所能呈现的也只是短暂的辉煌。回归中华文化上下五千年的文明历程,宗教的呈现及贡献占有很大比重。因此,这种因排拒宗教、使信仰与中华民族性脱节而积淀了百年的心结应该解开了,好迎接我们中华民族和谐通融的全新发展。这种跟宗教"拧着"的神经也应该放松了,好使广大普通民众能够轻松、自由地享受其精神生活和保持其文化民俗。

诚然,宗教因与政治的复杂关联而有其社会问题,要根本解决这一问题绕不开过去百年的政治发展,包括"新文化运动"对宗教的否定性认知,对中华文化数千年传统的反思和批判,以及在引进并接受马克思主义之后对宗教的政治理解。但与政治相关的社会现象非常之多,政治势力本身就有正邪之区分,我们没有必要单独将宗教凸显出来作为进行"政治斗争"的考量,不能让宗教变得似乎比政治还敏感,由此避免陷入"制造敌情"、"扩大敌情"的发展怪圈和恶性循环。也就是说,对宗教问题应从整个社会进步、民族和谐、文化发展和走向世界的视野来认识,积极引导和疏导,而不必"草木皆兵"、过度紧张。其实,在过去的五六十年来,我们对政治本身的认识也已经发生了很大变化,政治层面的宽容、包容、团结合作也是今天社会所鼓励的。因此,即使在宗教与政治的关系上,我们也应该有更为积极、更加和谐的举措。在约百年前中国"新文化运动"的启蒙中,我们对世界宗教及中国宗教的认知曾陷入过误区,从而使我们民族的文化发展受阻,忽视了我们自己的文化"软实力",结果尚未建立起真正能够自立于世界文化之林的"新文化"。当我们从西方引进的"革命文化"在今天的对外交流中遭冷落、被边缘化、"妖魔化"时,我们中国自己的传统文化却迄今仍对世界各族有着无限的魅力和吸引力,并通过民间的方式、自然的过程而传向世界,影响到众多国家和地区;而在这种传播方式中,中国的传统宗教文化起到了很大的作用。由此可见,"新文化"不是建立在"虚无"之上,也不是纯为"拿来主义"的从外引进,而必须是基于我们自己文化传统的弘扬与创新。从这一意义上,我们对自己的文化、尤其是宗教文化的认识有必要经历一种"再启蒙"的洗礼,以便能够摆脱虚无主义、空想主义、绝对拿来主义的缠绕,重新回到我们的社会文化现实,站立在中华文化坚实的大地上。当然,对我们自己的传统文化也必须自我反思和反省,在批判性审视上使之脱旧更新,达到其创造性、重建性复新,而不是简单的复旧、复古。包括中国的各种宗教,同样离不开其自我革新、改进,以便适应时代发展和中国现实国情的发展经历。这也是我们今天的政治文化必须要认真思考的。对于宗教等诸种精神问题的探究,过去人们曾长期在黑暗中摸索,看不到一线亮光,而在今天拨乱反正的进程中,当突然有一道亮光闪现在面前时,已经习惯于黑暗的人们却会又感到它过于耀眼,不愿正视,不敢相信它是真的,从而会错过走出黑暗、迎来光明的机遇,结果又重新回到黑暗之中。今天中国的民族振兴、文化复兴乃千载难逢,世界整体形势也对我们比较有利,但这种机会也可能会稍纵即逝,故此我们必须当机立断、抓住机遇,留着并扩大这道亮光,不可再犹豫彷徨、坐失大好时机。过去我们曾因政治的考量而对宗教有过警惕及防范,但同样也对之有过团结及统战的举措。今天,从政治意义上也更需要我们团结宗教,使宗教在加强我们的文化软实力、建设及巩固我们的精神家园上起积极作用。其实,政治也应"攻心"为上,我们应以对宗教的同情性精神理解、积极的社会评价来使宗教成为我们的同路人、一家人。否则,光靠经济利益的驱动或行政手段的强势压力,而没有心境上的沟通和共鸣,对解决民族宗教问题的作用会微乎其微。对此,古今中外的经验教训,我们一定要认真研究,方法于未然。

文化战略旨在动态的文化发展、文明进程,是一种对未来发展的考量。文化是一种进行时,而不是一种静态。文化不只是保持传统的责任,而更是发展、创新的任务。正是在这种文化的行进中,我们必须有所作为,从而能更新、发展和创造。当然,这种文化思考有着整体关联,应将相关文化进程的过去及现在串起来考虑,才可能以历史视域的洞若观火来展望未来发展。对当代中国来说,文化战略所思考的也是一种具有重要意义的战略转折,从而使中国文化具有能动、富有活力的可持续发展。这在信仰、宗教等精神意义的理解上尤为重要。因此,我们的文化战略理应将中国文化发展作为从古到今一条动态的连线来考量,对其中的文化本真及其历史发展规律,以及对其中宗教的发展变迁及其与传统文化和当代社会的关系,都应该有辩证发展的认识。

　　由此观之,中国的文化战略也必须注意到其时代性和开放性。而这种关注首先就应该看到并承认文化的多样性和精神世界的多元性,人类文化的趋向统一也只能是一种多元的共在,恰如中国文化传统所体验的"多元求同"、"多元通和"那样。世界多样性的存在或共在,人类多样性的统一,已经成为当代人的共识。在我们所面临的这一重要时代机遇和战略转折期,正视并巧妙地处理好这种多样性的共在,达成多样性的统一,是一种政治睿智。在政治、文化、精神及信仰上仍想奢求一种"一元的独在",已是一种僵化的思想和不明智的选择。向多样性开放并从这种多元中学得自身发展的最佳可能,才是当代文化的可行之途。在国际社会共在的努力中,我们倡导一种"人类命运共同体意识";而在我们的文化共建中,我们也必须要有"精神"、"信仰"共同体的思考。其实,中国当代改革开放以来,中国社会在经济文化上已有很大的开放和很多的吸纳,不过,我们不能够仅满足于物质技术和经济模式及其游戏规则的吸纳,也不能仅是看到"可口可乐文化"或"好莱坞文化"在我们社会市场的风行;为了防范我们的当代文化变得流俗和肤浅,我们也必须注重精神文化的开放性和多样性,必须在信仰、宗教等精神深层次的认识上具有开放性、时代性和深刻的体悟及把握。由于对信仰的认识不清、对宗教的把握不准,我们的社会文化正潜藏着深层面的精神危机,我们的民众在诚信、忠义的持守上也出现了巨大的滑坡;而消除这种危机,制止这种滑坡,理顺我们社会的精神信仰关系,在今后五到十年则极为关键。我们社会的稳固、民族的和谐,不仅需要政治制度及法律体系的外在约束,同样也应有中国传统中曾起到重大作用的内在信仰层面"举头三尺有神明"这种"天命"般的道德"绝对命令"之警示,以及由此而能达到的自律、自责和自觉。当政治信仰在某些层面"失效"或成为仅为少数社会精英的持守时,宗教信仰对普罗大众的积极影响和正面作用则不能轻看或忽视。所以,当代中国文化的动态发展及其战略转折,需要我们从文化战略的意义上认真思考并梳理我们对信仰、宗教的认知及态度。

　　中国人的信仰与宗教之有无或是否可以缺失,这是当代中国社会及其理论界、学术界颇为纠结的一个问题。人们究竟有没有信仰、需不需要信仰? 这也是在公众讨论中认识不清、争议很多的一个焦点。其实,信仰是人类本性的内在构成,与人类从古到今的发展密切交织。信仰之所以成了问题,乃是中国近现代发展中出现的社会及认识问题,是中国人在其精神生活中显现出的某种识别迷惘和方向感的迷失。不可否认,信仰问题已经成了制约当前中国可持续发展的关键问题之一,信仰缺失或扭曲在当今公众社会生活中也是一个不争的事实。这已经在很大程度上影响到中国人的精神家园的构建和其人格心性的塑造,因此,对这一问题的探讨具有现实意义和思想意义,很有必要对之加以认真梳理和透彻澄清。有些人只是从负面来看信仰,认为共产党不需要有信仰,也不应该提信仰;而中国共产党的十八大报告则明确肯定了对信仰、信念的正面表述;所以说,我们党和国家的发展、中华民族的振兴,是需要信仰的指导和支持的。

　　同样,宗教是什么?中国人有没有宗教、需不需要宗教?这也是人们仍在争论、难达统一的问题。尤其是对社会主义社会的宗教应该怎样看,对当今中国社会主义社会的宗教应该如何定位,都是目前在理论上和实践上都没有解决的问题。由于对宗教的理解涉及到对其政治及社会评价,非常敏感,故此人们也极少或难以从文化层面对宗教加以较为透彻的评说。这里,除了对宗教的价值判断及社会定位之外,人们至少在两个问题上还存在着明显分歧,一是当今世界的宗教发展究竟是"复兴"还是"衰落",二是当前中国的宗教存在究竟是较为普遍的现象还是个别地区、少数人群的现象,中国的宗教是否因"恢复"而出现了迅猛发展的"复兴"。实际上,国际舆论已经关注到西方宗教的衰落和东方尤其是中国宗教的崛起这一反差,并预示当中国宗教在未来世界中的作用及影响势必扩大之态势。这种对国际国内宗教现状的判断,在很大程度上也涉及到对宗教的理解问题。其实,对宗教如何理解,已直接影响到我们文化战略的思考和制定。特别是在未来世界的竞争中,宗教在中国综合国力的构成中究竟是起着积极或消极的作用、是正能量还是负能量,关键就在于我们当今社会对宗教的认识和引导。由于目前我们的文化战略中尚没有宗教文化的地位,我们的文化"软实力"构成中没有考虑宗教的因素,在世界范围的文化战略、文化博弈、文化浸润中,我们的文化"走出去"仍处于弱势,我们的宗教文化所发挥的作用也仍然微乎其微。而中外关系上"黄金纽带"的维系、"丝绸之路"的开拓,都与宗教相关。所以说,我们必须从世界范围,特别是从中西交往与对峙、周边国家与中国的关系及对中国的影响等方面来认真考虑宗教与文化战略的关系问题,并把重点放在中国宗教与文化战略的基本构思和实施上。现在世界的局势发生了根本变化,我国周边环境也在恶化,其主要原因并不是意识形态上或社会制度上的,而更多是民族利益、国家利益的竞争。在这种竞争中,文化因素特别是宗教因素也能够为之加分或减分,因为这种文化的环境、宗教的气场已经跨越了国家、民族之界,它们可以形成各种各样的重新组合,从而可以增加或减弱相关国家及民族的国际竞争力。于此,我们的视野必须开阔,我们的举措必须得力,已经不能允许我们有太多的误解或太大的失误,我们绝不能在这新一轮竞争中自己就输在起跑线上。

宗教作为一种信仰体系,其突出特点是其信仰会影响到信仰者的社会存在及社会行为,形成其社会凝聚力或破坏力。这样,在社会层面就有一个如何管理或治理社会中的宗教组织及宗教行为问题。特别是在中国这一具有各区域共构"大一统"的政治传统、各民族共聚"大家庭"的文化传承中,对宗教的社会审视就显得格外重要,我们的政治考量也理应谨慎和周全。对于宗教必须有一种根本性的认知和客观真实的评价,而不能满足于对宗教实用性、功利性、随意性的掌控和利用。具有中国特色的社会主义"和谐社会"的建设,需要我们欢迎宗教积极参与,而绝不能轻率地排拒宗教。所以说,我国宪法保障的宗教信仰自由是对所有真正的宗教开放的,应该让任何有宗教信仰的人们都能在"在阳光下信仰",公开、光明正大地表述并持守自己的宗教信仰。如果继续保持对宗教的政治敌意和社会歧视,那么我们自己的文化体系就肯定会出问题,而我们在国际舞台上和世界文化交流中也会陷入孤立、无友的尴尬。当然,任何势力如果借"宗教"之名来行"政治"之实,对其态度和举措在对等意义上也只能是"政治"的,从而在根本上已彻底脱离宗教的范畴。在此,政治与宗教也不能相混。基于当前"全球性"的视野,我们对宗教的看法及处理故而必须慎之又慎,必须要有正确的选择。

在当前新的国际环境和国内形势下,我们理应理论创新,尝试对我们社会存在的宗教和信仰现象重新加以客观、真实、正确的说明。信仰、宗教都涉及到人类的精神文化问题,所以我们在涉及这些精神领域时应该要有文化意识,要从世界文明的包罗万象、中华文明的源远流长上来看待人的信仰及宗教。关心、重视文化和精神发展,也是中国共产党的十八大所特别强调的。习近平同志在谈及全面贯彻落实党的十八大精神时曾指出,"我们要继续坚持走中国特色社会主义文化发展道路,推动社会主义文化大发展大繁荣,深化文化体制改革,提高国家文化软实力,加强社会主义核心价值体系建设,丰富人民群众精神文化生活,增强人民精神力量。"只有文化的健康发展才能真正保障相关社会的可持续发展,作为中华民族精神家园的文化共同体存在乃是我们政治主张得以畅行和持久的重要基础和前提条件。精神文化是我们社会的灵魂所在,也是我们发展的活力所依。所以,我们必须要有保障文化发展、形成文化软实力的文化战略及相关举措。对此,理解文化的本质及其基本构成要素,就有其独特的意义及价值。

文化战略的思考首先就必须基于对文化的理解、判断和把握,也就是说,思考者应该"有文化"、"讲文化"。从这一意义上,我们一定要走出仅从"产业"、"产能"、"产销"及"产效"来衡量文化、利用文化的狭隘境界,而必须把重点放在文化精神的塑造及弘扬上,让当代中国人真正讲文化、有文化,体显我们中国作为文化大国、礼仪之邦的精神风采和悠久传承。诚然,文化包括宗教文化会影响到经济的发展,可以为经济实业的开创营造一种有利或良好的氛围;但宗教的本真追求在根本上却不是经济利益,而我们对文化的现实需求首先也并不是文化"产业"或文化"产品",不是也要把文化染上"商气",即不是让精神"下海"、流俗。文化最重要的是对我们社会精神、对我们民族灵魂的铸就,所以我们要把文化作为"事业"、"使命"来抓。这自然会涉及到文化领域中的宗教、信仰等方面。同样,我们对宗教也应该有文化的审视和考量,不能只想到"宗教经济"、"宗教市场",把宗教仅仅作为可能赢利的产业或商品,更不能让宗教成为追求经济利益的工具或诱饵。从某种意义上,没有信仰的文化乃是一种空洞、虚弱、失魂的文化,其肤浅使之没有可持续发展的动力及能力,使我们的社会缺少潜在的精神力量。这种浅薄的文化形式虽然能热闹一时,达其轰动效应,却不可能持久,而只会如过眼烟云、昙花一现。我们决不可陶醉于这种表面看似"繁荣"的文化泡沫,在其短暂的五颜六色面前感到眼花缭乱、随之失去理智,而必须有着清醒的文化思考、冷静的文化分析、睿智的文化决策。从精神文化的现状来看,中华民族的确已经到了发展的关键时期,时不我待,须争朝夕。从这一意义上,信仰、宗教、文化这三大范围正是我们思考宗教与文化战略的基本定位,也是需要我们解决其根本问题的主要领域。

Re-understanding of the Social Role of Religion

Zhang Zhigang

I. Theoretical Problems that this Article Reflects on

I had been responsible for a significant issue "Research on Contemporary Religious Conflicts and Dialogues," one of the "Chinese Ministry of Education's Key Projects of Major Subjects of Philosophical and Social Sciences" (2003 – 2008). After these five years of progressive research, I not only deeply felt that this topic was extremely crucial, but I also perceived a number of questions on the theories of religious studies that were worth pondering over. If these questions were integrated as one point, that would be how one re-understands the social role or cultural functions of religion under the background of "globalization" or "global village," especially under the reorganization of international politics, economics and cultural structure in the post - Cold War era. Let me first explain briefly my comprehension on the above two questions: First, the comprehension of the important practical problem raised by this issue which I was responsible for. Second, the comprehension of the theoretical problem of religious studies that I have perceived through the probing of this important issue.

1. Important Practical Problems

One year prior to the September – 11 Attack (9/11), Mr. Qian Qichen, Vice Premier of China, and concurrently holding the position as the dean of the School of International Studies (SIS) of Peking U-niversity, pointed out that religious and ethnic issues have stood out after the Cold War. Many international hot issues are mostly related to religious and ethnic problems. The religious issues after the Cold War have the following characteristics: (a) Religion is often associated with ethnic issues. (b) Freedom of religion is often associated with human rights issues. (c) Religion is often associated with fundamentalism or terrorism. (d) Religion is often associated with the political situation of the state, the problem of ethnic division or unity. (e) Religious identity often cuts across national and ethnic boundaries. Therefore, we must study religious issues attentively.[①]

After the world-shaking 9/11 incident, the importance and seriousness of religious problems has aroused the universal concern of the international community. This prompted many experts and scholars in China and abroad to reflect on the great changes of international situations before and after the Cold War, and re-think the extensive influence of religious factors on the various international hot problems and major conflicts. As one expert on international issues pointed out, the following series of political, economic and military conflicts; such as the conflicts of Bosnia-Herzegovina, Northern Ireland, the Molucca Islands and Aceh province in Indonesia, the disputes over Kashmir, and etc., contain ever-complicated and ever-increasing religious factors. "We can say that rapidly change of international situation could not be separated with religions. After the 9/11 Attack, religious and

---

① See Qian Qichen: Some Key Problems in the Study of Today's International Relations, *Journal of World Economics and Politics*, 2000, No. 9.

ethnic problems have been important driving force in international politics and caused the convulsive fluctuation in the world situations. "①

This poses a important practical problem upon us: why do religious factors cause such extensive and heavy impact on the various international hot issues and major conflicts after the Cold War?

2. Some Theoretical Problems of Religious Studies

(1) Formulation of "religious conflict" is relatively simplistic.

After the Cold War, although "religious conflict" has become the most frequently used keyword in domestic and foreign media, if studied closely, "simple or direct religious conflict" is rare, small and has little effect. This signifies that, what is known as "religious conflict" would usually appear in a more complex and intricate form. Actually, the fact many domestic and foreign theorists pay attention to is that almost all international hot issues or major conflicts in the post-Cold War consist of religious factors or are on the basis of religious background that cannot to be ignored.

(2) Current religious views or concepts of religious studies are also relatively simplistic.

How does one explain the extensive influence of religious factors or backgrounds toward international hot problems or major conflicts after the Cold War? The following viewpoints are commonly found in the related study results: Firstly, they are " in the coat of religion ", "under the banner of religion " or "took advantage of religious faith" and others. Secondly, the so-called "benefit-ism"; attributing religious influence or role to this or that benefits, such as economic benefits, political benefits, military benefits, benefits for an ethnic group

---

① See Lu Zhongwei: Religious Factor in International Conflicts, 世界宗教问题大聚焦(*The Focus of World Religious Issues*), ed. Center for Ethnic and Religious Studies in China Institute of Contemporary International Relations (CICIR), Beijing: Shishi Press, 2003, "Preface", pp. 1 –2.

or a nation. Thirdly, the "combination-of-factors theory" (theory of synthetic factors); the international hot issues or major conflicts are generally made of many interwoven factors, such as territorial disputes, struggle for resources, security issues, political interest, ideologies, religious beliefs, racial or ethnic discord, and so forth.

With regards to the former two viewpoints, anyone who researches on some major religious traditions and not looks upon them as "fraudulent matters", will then find easily these two views are simplistic and superficial. As for the third viewpoint, more explanation is required. This view was proposed by "war and conflict" researchers, and has become a common methodology in this field. [1] This methodology seems to be comparatively comprehensive and have "taken every aspect into consideration". However, in my opinion, this view on religion is still simplistic. That is, it put the religious factor in the same category with various factors or causes of the economy, politics, military, races or ethnic groups. This view apparently ignored the uniqueness of religious phenomena, and this cannot explain the mutual interaction of "religious faith factor" with the other factors, and its complicated influence. The above views have been prevalent mainly in the studies of international politics and international relations.

Religious academic world has been ever-changing over the past century, nevertheless, some theoretical viewpoints are still holding dominant positions, such as theories on the decline and fall of religion; separation of government and religion; personalization of religion; secularization of religion; marketization of religion; and so

---

① Kalevi J. Holsti, Canadian renowned scholar in international politics pointed out: "Investigators of conflicts, crises, and war reached a consensus years ago that monocausal explanations are theoretically and empirically deficient.", *Peace and War: Armed Conflicts and International Order*, 1648 – 1989, Cambridge: Cambridge University Press, 1991, p. 3. The author refered to the Chinese translation by Wang Puqu and others, Beijing: Peking University press, 2005.

forth. Do these viewpoints suffice to explain the fore-mentioned important practical problem? Here the question first, then I will review and
comment.

It is precisely because the above theories are insufficient in general, I consider, through probing the fore-mentioned important practical problem-why does religious factors cause extensive and significant
influence to the many international hot issues and major conflicts after
the Cold War-we will likely be able to achieve a breakthrough in the
theory of religious studies in order to understand more comprehensively and deeply the complicated characteristics of religious phenomena
and its social role or cultural function. Following is a brief report of
my theoretical attempt in recent years. The main method is to grasp
the "religious factor" as the keyword of the aforementioned important
practical problem, then explain it emphasizing the four complexities
influenced by it. I named them as "nature of accumulation", "nature
of permeation", "nature of infiltration" and "nature of depth".

II. Accumulation Nature of Religious Factors and Its Influence

After the Cold War, a number of many international hot issues
and major conflicts have been increasingly and deeply affected by religious factors. This is a new problem arising from new circumstances.
However, first we need to be aware of is the fact that religion is an
ancient, universal social and cultural phenomenon. Precisely because
of the long and profound relationship of religion with human society or
cultural activities, thinkers dedicated to cultural history or civilization
history researches, mostly put emphasis on the social role or cultural
function of religious traditions. Due to the limited space of this arti-

cle, we can only review on the inspiring studies of Toynbee (Arnold Toynbee) and Dawson (Christopher Dawson) on the social role or cultural function of religious traditions.

According to the great work of comparative history of civilizations *"A Study of History"* (1934 – 1961), Toynbee's plan to interpret history he had studied with great concentration, is the systematic categorization of the relationship between religious traditions and social civilizations (culture in a broad sense) and comparing of the 26 social civilizations in order to reveal the basic model of transformation of human civilization. He investigated deeply into the important social and historical role of religious traditions in the process of civilization's birth, growth, breakdown, and disintegration. He considered that religious belief as a fundamental attitude of human life could be said as "source of life" or "spiritual bond" of each social civilization, and that once a certain social civilization lost its traditional spiritual belief, it was bound to decline until replaced by a new form of civilization. Why did he say this? Toynbee believed that for hundreds and thousands of years, various major religious traditions were able to attract many followers because they responded respectively to some major psychological types of humankind, and satisfied the emotional needs of each type of believers experienced under different forms of civilizations. Therefore, all activities of civil society including politics, economy and culture have maintained by the way of life which each religious belief explained. As a result, when he overviewed the transformation process of civilization, he kept paying attention to the deep impact of the different religious traditions towards the cultural mentality or cultural sub-consciousness under different forms of civilizations. Such investigation and analysis permeate the entire volume of the *"A Study of History."*

Same as Weber (Max Weber), Christopher Dawson, the renowned cultural historian and philosopher of history, also investigated the origins of modern Western culture from the aspect of religious traditions. But when compared with Weber, Dawson's theories hold a broader view. Weber's research was strictly limited to the affinity between Protestant Ethic and the Spirit of Capitalism. Dawson's investigation was on the historic connections between the religious tradition and the evolution of Western culture. In his opinion, to reveal the causes of modern Western culture, one must not overlook the historical process of accumulation of traditional religious culture. In particular one must not underestimate the period which was the threshold to the modern age, because the spiritual creative power which was necessary to the modern culture, even to the pioneers of modern culture, was all bred and formed during this period.

Basing on the comprehensive investigation of Western cultural history, especially the Medieval cultural history, Dawson pointed out something which gave one much to think about. What is known as a religion is not an abstract ideology, and it is not merely a kind of an ancient spiritual resource, but is mainly continuous cultural traditions and cultural customs that exerted its subtle influences in history. Yet, previous researchers often concentrated on the "high-level issues", that of political, ideological, intellectual and so on, they were not aware that these issues made just a very small portion of the long course of history. In fact, the greatest influence on the common people and social life still comes from the cultural customs or religious traditions. [1]

Summing up the study results of the above two eminent scholars, we can obtain the following points:

---

[1]   For more information on Dawson's viewpoint, refer to *Progress and Religion*, *Religion and the Modern State*, *Religion and Culture*, *Medieval Essays*, *Religion and the Rise of Western Culture*, and many other works. Readers can also refer to my book《宗教文化学导论》*An Introduction to Religious Studies*, Beijing: Orient Press, 1996, Chapter 4. "道森的文化史学"(Dawson's Cultural History).

（1）If we can say that only a broad view of the evolution process of human history or culture, instead of a certain period of time in history or culture, make us possible to study and discuss the social role or cultural function of religious traditions comprehensively and deeply, then, the currently existing religious factors in the human society or cultural activities should mainly be regarded as the result of historical accumulation. This is the point that I would like to stress first from the standpoint of methodology. This point allows us to reflect upon ourselves as follows: the fore-mentioned modern theoretical views on religions, theory on the decline and fall of religion; separation of government and religion; personalization of religion; secularization of religion; marketization of religion and so forth, are the views mainly limited with "Western Modernization," a particular space and time and cultural stage. If we stretch the meaning of this interpretation, why cannot we say that it impedes our comprehensive and profound understanding of the social role or cultural functions of Eastern and Western religious traditions?

（2）As a result of historical accumulation, religious factor and its influence usually don't surface, rather be stored up in the depth of society or cultural activities. In other words, like the cultural traditions, cultural customs, cultural psychology or social sub-consciousness that the fore-mentioned two scholars investigated, the influences of religious factor mostly work in a subtle manner.

（3）Although "in a subtle manner" may be comprehended as a normal form of religious factors and its influence, people always review and reflect on their history or cultural tradition in one way or another, especially when in the historical turning point, corresponding to the challenge of time. In this crucial moment of history, the most religious factor and its influence will be clearly reflected and strongly affected.

I think this historical characteristic will help us to understand the background of evident increase of impact of religious factor and its influence after the Cold War. However, it is worthy to take note that the obvious influence of religious factors on many international hot issues and major conflicts of today emerge not only from the new situation, that is, the realignment of international political structure, but also from the historical background of "globalization" or "global village". This has provided us an unprecedented "theoretical opportunity" in order to re-understand the social role or cultural function of religion from the global viewpoint.

Ⅲ. Permeation Nature of Religious Factors and Its Influence

The accumulation nature mentioned previously is mainly probed and illustrated from the historical point of view on religious factors and its influence. When we look back to the present reality, the permeation nature of religious factor and its influence is another characteristic that should not be neglected. The permeation nature of religious factors derives from the wide spreading of religious phenomena. To understand this is not difficult at all. Let us go over the following statistics first:

It was estimated that up till 2001, the world population was about 6.128 billion, among which 2.024 billion Christians, 1.213 billion Muslims, 363 million Buddhists, 823 million Hindus, 14.552 million Jews, and about 23.68 millions Sikhs, 1.03 billion were followers of all other new religions. [1]

---

① *International Bulletin of Missionary Research*, January, 2001.

The above statistics show clearly that most believers in the world still subscribe to several traditional religions. This fact proves the former characteristics, that is, the religious factor and its influence should mainly be regarded as the results of the historical accumulation. More thought-provoking fact is that even in the present hi-tech era, the believers account for 80% of the world's population.

This huge figure awakens us that: (1) Such widespread religious phenomena are not illusion, but a true reflection of the situation of faith and most people's way of life in the world. (2) Although the objects of worship of various religions are all "transcendent, sacred and even mystified", all believers have explained "the ultimate meaning of life" and also set their "rule of earthly life" basing on such beliefs.

One of the founders of modern sociology of religion, Durkheim (Emile Durkheim), pointed out long ago, "A religion is a unified system of beliefs and practices relative to sacred things."[1] Sociologist of religion Yinger (John Milton Yinger) also stressed that: "Religion, then, can be defined as a system of beliefs and practices by means of which a group of people struggles with the ultimate problems of human life."[2] In the recent three or four decades, one of the most influential concepts in international study of religion is "Ultimate Concern." This concept includes an attempt to grasp the nature and function of various religious beliefs by the method of comparison with cross-cultural and cross-age concepts. Its advocate Tillich (Paul Tillich) considered that: "Religion, in the largest and most basic sense of the world, is ultimate concern ··· Religion is the substance, the

---

① Emile Durkheim, *The Elementary Forms of the Religious Life*, New York: The Free Press, 1965, p. 62.

② J. Milton Yinger, *The Scientific Study of Religion*, New York: The Macmillan Company, 1970, p. 7.

ground, and the depth of man's spiritual life. This is the religious aspect of the human spirit."[1] Such views are designed to show that: for the broad masses of believers, religion is not just a world and life view, neither is their standard of value. It is the lifeway to which they are devoting themselves. Or one can say, religious belief is in fact the lifestyle that certain types of believers acquired through their ultimate concern. Therefore, we can determine that the so-called religious factors are bound to permeate and influence the spiritual activities and material life of followers.

We can recognize the breadth of religious phenomena caused by permeation nature of religious factors, as well as from the viewpoint of the relationship between religions and ethnic groups. Broadly speaking, there are over 2,000 ethnic groups, large and small, which spread out in more than 200 countries and regions. Until now, no ethnos or country is found without any religious phenomena. The religious beliefs of most ethnos are multiplied and diversified. But some ethnos have embraced their common religious tradition. For example, almost all Arabs are Muslims, almost all Jewish are Jews, most Indians are Hindus, and so forth. Accordingly, we can judge that: religious factors permeate and influence all ethnos, countries and regions. The religious atmosphere is strong, especially where the majority of the population are religious believers. Therefore, the social influence or cultural function of the religious factor particularly cannot be ignored. For example, this is the case with the so-called "Christian World" and "Islamic World".

---

①   Paul Tillich, *Theology of Culture*, Oxford: Oxford University Press, 1959, pp. 7 – 8.

Ⅳ. Nature of Infiltration of Religious Factors and Its Influence

The fore-mentioned permeation nature of religious factors means that religious factors have a very strong nature of infiltration. In other words, religion can infiltrate and affect several major factors of human social activities, such as politics, economy, culture, and so forth. The term "nature of permeation" is used to graphically show that religious factors are distributed throughout the entire social life in tangible or intangible ways. Like this, "nature of infiltration" can explain that the religious factors can penetrate into all the other factors of social activity obviously or obscurely, resulting that the religious belief as the view of the world, life values, and the way of living is infused together with the other factors such as politics, economy and culture. Then they become inseparable, functioning together and causing influences. When one is aware of this complex feature of religious factors, this enables us to think further into how religious factors have affected the many post-Cold War international hot issues and major conflicts.

As previously mentioned, many Chinese and foreign scholars believe that major international hot issues and conflicts are not caused by "one single cause", but are the result of various factors of economy, politics, military, culture, ethnos and religions interwoven together. If so, why do I consider this type of research concept is too simple or even too superficial to understand religions? The main reason is that this type of concept still remains in "the mere recognition of surface phenomenon", simply explaining religious factor as a kind of relatively independent phenomenon which can be discussed on the same plane as factors of economy, politics, military, ethnos and nations. Yet, is this true in reality? This is the problem. Let us see with two examples.

As commonly known, the root cause of the Palestine-Israel conflict, which is also the deadlock of the problem, is the territorial dispute, particularly on Jerusalem. This dispute is connected with the struggle for survival and development of both. Therefore, it entirely affects the various benefits of the two conflicting parties; such as the political, military/security, economical and cultural benefits. However, the more complicated is that it is the continuing territorial dispute emerged in religious backgrounds. Most Palestinians are Muslims, while the majority of Israelites are Jewish, and Jerusalem is the holy place that is never to be lost in the hearts of both parties. Just as Huntington (Samuel Huntington) wrote, "Once the conflict becomes focused on religious issues, it tends to become zero sum and difficult to compromise: ⋯ either Jews or Muslims control the Temple Mount. "①

The above analysis clearly states that in such an uncompromising territorial dispute between Palestine and Israel, the so-called religious factor does not appear singularly and not play a partial role; instead it creates "the specific atmosphere" in the entire conflict. This atmosphere envelopes all the other conflicting factors, such as territorial issues, ethnic contradictions, economic benefits, political divergences, cultural differences and so forth. These factors are inevitably infiltrated and conditioned by the heavy influence of religious factor to a certain degree. If we can regard the Palestine-Israel territory dispute as a typical case, would the "infiltration nature of religious factors and its influence" assist our further and deeper understanding on the influ-

---

① Samuel P. Huntington: *Who are We? The Challenges to America's National Identity*, New York: Simon & Schuster, 2004, p. 357. The author refered to the Chinese translation by Cheng Kexiong, Beijing: Xinhua Press Agency, 2005.

ence of "the religious background or atmosphere" towards international hot issues and major conflicts? To prove this point, let us take a look at the following example.

Is America, as Bush (George W. Bush) claimed, entrusted with a special mission from God-to spread freedom and democracy to the whole world? This is the question Albright (Madeleine Albright) intended to pursue in her recent book *The Mighty and the Almighty*: *Reflections on America*, *God and World Affairs* (2006). She, former United States Secretary of State, examined and analyzed this problem through various angles; such as the impact of religious traditions towards America's view, the effect of the Christian Right on U. S. policies, the Bush administration's success and failure in responding to 9/11, the challenges posed by the war in Iraq and the importance of understanding Islamic World. She came to the following conclusion: U. S. policy-makers must understand the power and role of religion in motivating others or coloring how American actions are acceptable. Religion and politics are not only inseparable, but when the two are joined, if utilized appropriately, can be a force for justice and peace. [1]

Schroder (Gerhard Schroder), former chancellor of Germany, looking back his many meetings with President Bush after 9/11, recalled that President Bush time and time again said he is a devout believer, he only obeys the highest authority-God's will. In President Bush's speech on January 29, 2002, he used many words from the Bible to declare that Iraq, Iran and North Korea are "Axis of evil", and they are next U. S. military targets. Schroder pointed out that, if a devout believer determines his behavior through prayers in his per-

---

[1]　See Madeleine Albright, *The Mighty & the Almighty*: *Reflections on American*, *God and World Affairs*, New York: Harper Collins Publishers, 2006, Abstract.

sonal life, it is understandable. However if in the political decision-making, its legitimacy is from God's will as President Bush claimed, it would be problematic; because it would not allow any criticism, and less likely to make changes through exchanging views. Schroder reflected on this and said, that all of them (mainly refers to state leaders of the European Union) underestimated the role of religions and ethical teachings in America; the political group formed by neo-conservative intellectuals and Christian fundamentalists had great influence on U. S. domestic politics and on President, but "personal demonization of Bush" had hindered them from analysing this political group critically. [1]

V. Nature of Depth of Religious Factors and Its Influence

Regarding the religious influence on the depth of culture, Paul Tillich pointed out years ago that: "Religion as ultimate concern is the meaning-giving substance of culture, and culture is the totality of forms in which the basic concern of religion expresses itself. In abbreviation: religion is the substance of culture, culture is the form of religion."[2] He explained that all religious act, not only in organized religion but also in the most intimate movement of the soul, are culturally formed. In other words, there is no cultural activity without an ultimate concern expressed in it, be it from the theoretical function or practical function of human spirit.

---

① See Gerhard Schroder: *Entscheidungen. Mein Leben in der Politik*, Hamburg : Hoffmann und Campe, 2006. The author refered to the Chinese translation by Xu Jinghua, Li Yueyi, Shanghai: Yilin Press, 2007; mainly pp. 91, 110,113.

② Paul Tillich, *Theology of Culture*, p. 42.

On the research of cultural meaning and social function of religious traditions, the most important theoretical result in the last 30 years is probably the "Thick Description: Towards an Interpretive Theory of Cultures" by Geertz (Clifford Geertz). Based on solid fieldwork and thorough case studies, this theory explains more concretely and deeply how "religious tradition as a system of symbols" is accumulated and forms the worldview and the sense of values in a certain cultural region; how the tradition subtly influences the psychological tendency and the motivation of action in a certain ethnos or social grouping. Geertz defines "religion" as (a) a system of symbols which acts to (b) establish powerful, pervasive, and long-lasting moods and motivations in men [and women] by (c) formulating conceptions of a general order of existence and (d) clothing these conceptions with such an aura of factuality that (e) the moods and motivations seem uniquely realistic. [1]

Even though the achievement of these studies may not be perfect, or even, have a certain kind of deviation such as "religious determinism", however they have undoubtedly reasonable and inspiring contents. From the perspectives of these fundamental theories-the "nature" and "function" of religious belief, we can deepen our understanding of religious factors and their impacts. The foregoing discussion shows that the so-called religious factors do not only refer to a particular religion itself, but generally refer to the reflection or embodiment of various religious beliefs in the human culture and the social living realm. The effects of the religious factor mainly mean the cultural function or social role of religious belief. Speaking academically, the function or role of a matter depends on its essence or its na-

---

[1] Clifford Geertz, *The Interpretation of Cultures*, New York: Basic Books, Inc., Publishers, 1973, p. 90.

ture. The religious factor in the social life should also be the case. Therefore, on comparison studies we can define "religious belief "as "ultimate concern", or in the more common concept it refers to the world and life view or values with some ultimate, absolute, or sacred characteristics. Then, it is not difficult for us to comprehend the depth nature of religious factors and its influence that we are probing here.

Here I use the phrase "the depth nature", mainly because I want to emphasize the following: religious factor is the reflection of religious belief in the real life or the social embodiment of the belief, for this reason it contains in the depth the world and life view or values of various religions. Therefore, from deep or the most fundamental level, religious factor exercises huge influences on the political, economic, and cultural activities of humankind, especially on social organizations, party groupings, races, ethnos, international associations or organizations and so forth, which are social activity bodies possessing deep religious traditions and strong atmosphere of faith. If we acknowledge this nature of depth, we can comprehend more accurately how and why the religious factor and its influence have the aforementioned three kinds of characteristics, namely, the nature of accumulation, nature of permeation and nature of infiltration, at the same time we can get a better understanding where the influences of religious factor are coming from towards the post-Cold War international hot issues and major conflicts.

VI. A Brief and Immature Conclusion

For the past 20 years, I was mainly followed two lines of research, the theory and method of religious studies and religious philosophy. As a result, I held a general interest, or one should say, a strong theoretical interest to explore the above four characteristics. In my opinion, if these four characteristics can be established, then this theoretical idea may help us to reflect methodologically upon such long-term popular religious viewpoints; as theories on the decline and fall of religion, separation of government and religion, personalization of religion, secularization of religion, marketization of religion and so forth. This is because these viewpoints not only could not explain the immense influence of religious factor towards the post-Cold War international hot issues and major conflicts, but also made people underestimate and even ignore the social role or cultural function of religious beliefs for long periods of time.

This brief report is no more than an immature theoretical attempt. I would appreciate any comment and criticism from experts and scholars.

（本文曾发表于 *The Journal of Oriental Studies*, Vol. 20, 2010, 由 Cheng Mei Kee Janet 翻译为英文, 此次发表略经修改）

第一部分

◎ 多元信仰与社会变迁

Islam and Modernity: The Myth of Muslim Exceptionalism

Dietrich Jung

Introduction

Why does an introduction into the modern politics of the Middle East start with a cursorily description of the life of Prophet Muhammad?[①] A neo-orientalist answer would be that Muhammad as a prophet and a "statesman" represents the trans-historical model for Islamic politics. Considering Islam as the independent variable in the understanding of the political, economic and social history of the Middle East, the orientalist tradition has ascribed the Muslim world an exceptional role in world history. Orientalist scholars perceive the separation between the modern state and religion as incompatible with Islamic culture. According to them, only a radical farewell to the heritage of Islamic traditions would offer an entrance ticket to a modern world whose culture and institutions have been fundamentally shaped by the historical experiences of the Enlightenment and the Christian reforma-

---

① An example is the otherwise very good introduction to the political history of the Middle East by Mehran Kamrava (2011).

tion. Bernard Lewis, for instance, once asserted that with the establishment of the Islamic Republic in Iran, an "unnatural aberration" of the separation of religion and politics in this country had come to an end (Lewis 1988:2). In a similar vein, Bassam Tibi has repeatedly put forward the argument of a fundamental incompatibility between Islam and modernity. In his eyes, modernization, secularization and westernization are synonymous developments that render all attempts irrelevant to propose the rise of Islamic modernities (cf. Tibi 2009).[1]

Turning toward Muslim intellectual traditions, we find strong parallels to this essentialist concept of western orientalism in the broad range of so-called Islamist or neo-fundamentalist ideologies.[2] Since the early twentieth century, the development of Islamist ideologies has revolved around the very same themes of difference to the West and of an intrinsic unity of religion and politics in Islam. In line with orientalist scholars, Islamist intellectual have framed Islam as being more than a mere religion, as representing a holistic civilization. While orientalist scholars reserve the property rights of a social order that is characterized by functional differentiation to the West, Islamist intellectuals interpret instances of the functional separation of social realms

[1] This general conviction of Tibi also drives his analysis of reformist parties with an Islamist background such as the Justice and Development Party (AKP) in Turkey.

[2] I apply the term "Islamist" instead of the also frequently used term "fundamentalist", which serves much more comparative purposes than the first. Looking at one of the many definitions of fundamentalism, the definition given by the *Fundamentalist Project*, it is clear that both concepts overlap. In particular the "selective retrieval" and re-interpretations of "doctrines, beliefs and social practices of a sacred past" are a core feature of both Islamist ideologies and fundamentalist religious interpretations. Furthermore, similar to the fundamentalist movements in the studies of the *Fundamentalist Project*, Islamist movements attempt the reorganization of society according to the norms, rules and values of their religious identities (cf. Marty and Appleby 1994: 1). However, other definitions of fundamentalism do not specifically refer to political action and reserve the term to the confines of religious belief systems and thus not to political but theological disputes. This form of religious fundamentalism is also observable in the Muslim world and, in this sense, a Muslim religious fundamentalist may be but is not necessarily an Islamist.

in Muslim societies as a cultural assault by the West. Translated into the theme of a confrontation between Islam and the West, these intertwined perceptions found their most audible echo in Huntington's scenario of a clash of civilizations and in the ideologies of militant transnational Islamists such as Osama bin Laden.

This paper will challenge both neo-orientalist and Islamist discourses on Muslim exceptionalism that basically exclude Islamic history from the master narratives of modernity. In focusing on the relationship between religion and state, I shall present a counter-narrative that makes the history of Islamic institutions and Muslim people part of an emerging global modernity. Informed by contemporary discussions in social theory, my counter-narrative builds on the assumption that social change in Muslim societies should be understood as an integral part of a larger process of socio-cultural evolution toward functional differentiation. Modern systems theory understands the emergence of modern society as a non-teleological process in the course of which functional differentiation becomes the dominant mode of social differentiation. In structural terms, modernization replaces the primacy of segmentation and stratification as the ordering principles of pre-modern forms of the social by social systems based on functional differentiation (Luhmann 1981, 187).

From this evolutionary perspective, modern systems theory has conceptualized modern society as an all-encompassing system of communication. In principle, therefore, modern society is "world society". Society is further differentiated by functionally defined, equally self-referential subsystems such as politics, economy, law, education, science or religion. The self-referential logic of these subsystems is based on specific binary codes, deciding about the compatibility of communications. The legal system, for instance, operates with the code legal/illegal, science with true/untrue, religion with transcendent/immanent and economics with to have/to have not. It is by these codes through which functional systems draw sharply differentiated boundaries to their environments (Luhmann 1986). The selective mechanism of binary codes transforms contingency into order by auton-omously defining elements of a regulated systemic communication. This mechanism guarantees the operational closure of function sys-tems-that communication is identified as juridical, scientific, religious or economic-through a sharp distinction between systemic communica-tion and communication in its environment (Luhmann 1986, 124 and 183).

Given their relative autonomy and operational closure, the rela-tionships among function systems are characterized by a clear separa-tion between system and environment. For the system of politics, for instance, the economic system is beyond its boundaries of communica-tion and economic interferences into politics have to be translated into the particular systemic communication of the political system and its medium power. Otherwise, external communications remain to be "white noise". Following their own specific modes of communication, none of these societal subsystems is any longer able to represent socie-ty as a social whole. In the theoretical framework of systems theory, therefore, the convenient fusion of society and national states clearly becomes obsolete.

I develop my counter-narrative in two steps. First, I present a critique of orientalist and Islamist representations of Islam in questio-ning their mutually shared holistic image of Islam as a total system by a brief sketch of the social diversity that we actually can observe in the Muslim world. This sketch addresses both the complexities of "Is-lamic ways of life" and the varieties of institutional arrangements that characterize the relationship between state and religion in Muslim countries. Then, I briefly analyze specific periods and institutions in

Islamic history which often have been taken as evidence for the alleged unity of religion and politics in Islam. In this second section, I shall argue that we can observe various tendencies toward functional differentiation in Islamic history, not only caused by colonialist interventions, but also as a result of indigenous social transformations with their institutional expressions.

Holistic ideals and realities of Muslim life

The continuing influence of the orientalist tradition in western representations of Islam and its mirror-image in Islamist ideologies becomes utterly puzzling when we turn to the empirical reality of Muslim life-worlds and the institutional make-up of Muslim states. Both micro-sociological walks of life and macro-sociological institutional arrangements of state and religion in Muslim countries show a high degree of diversity. In each domain we can observe multiple instances of counter-factual evidence to the above-described essentialist images of Islam. We first sketch out diversity by some anecdotal evidence for the complexities of "Islamic ways of life" from the capitals of three Muslim countries: Malaysia, Egypt and Turkey. Then, we give a brief overview over the factual variety of structural arrangements that has characterized the relationship between state and religion in the Muslim world.

My sketch of Islamic lifeworlds begins in Malaysia's capital Kuala Lumpur. To the surprise of most visitors, a form of traditional Malay village life seems to have survived in the midst of Kuala Lumpur. Surrounded by the high-rise symbols in steel, glass and concrete of Malaysia's rapid economic development, Kampung Baru represents on the surface an "idyllic" place. Only one metro stop from Kuala Lumpur's bustling city center (KLCC), the dwellers of Kampung Baru follow a lifestyle in which Malay folk traditions and a conservative interpretation of Islam appear to be the core identity markers. Hereditary ownership of houses and land has so far prevented this place from being sucked into the city's commercial drive. In political terms, the specific situation of Kampung Baru is reflected in the strong support which Malaysia's Islamist opposition party PAS (*Parti Islam Se Malaysia*) finds in this area. [1] In sharp contrast to the slow, traditional, and modest way of life in Kampung Baru, the KLCC symbolizes the energetic capitalism that has become an essential part of modern Malaysia. In the conceptualization of Malaysia's previous Prime Minister Mahatir Muhammad, it is precisely this merger of capitalism and Islam that makes the country to a model of his vision of a modern Islamic state. In particular the Suria Shopping Center at the feet of the Petronas Twin Towers is an incarnation of this modern feature of the country. There, the consumptive patterns of second modernity clearly determine the pulse of life. Muslims from all parts of the world engage together with non-Muslims in the pleasures of modern consumerism, united by the attractions of our increasingly commoditized world. [2] The modern social order of Malaysia combines Islamic traditions with a state-driven capitalization of society.

These features of the lifestyle of global Neoliberalism have also left their imprint on city life in Cairo, although in different forms and to much less a degree than in Malaysia. After decades of dilapidation,

---

[1] The electoral strongholds of PAS are in the northwestern provinces Kelantan and Terrenganu, where the party was able to form regional governments.

[2] Observing the scenery at KLCC, I must cast doubt on Bryan Turner's assumption that Islamic fundamentalism could be best understood as a consequence of the global "proliferation of consumer lifestyles" and its destructive impact on religious beliefs and values (1994: 90). In the various shopping complexes in Muslim countries like Malaysia, Saudi Arabia, or the United Arab Emirates the observer can record a host of evidence that consumerism and conservative or fundamentalist attitudes to Islam are not mutually exclusive phenomena.

the facades in Cairo's city centre have received a new face. Walking from tahrir square along talat harb street to the north, the observer could almost get the impression that the policies of economic liberalization, initiated by the late President Anwar al-Sadat in the 1970s and continued under the Mubarak regime, have finally succeeded in shaping a vibrant Egyptian middle class. On a Thursday night, at least in this area, one will meet a critical mass of youth and young families, who, equipped with mobile phones and higher middle-class cars, launch into the Muslim weekend with happy consumerism. Yet, only a few hundred meters away, to the east of Opera Square or at Ramses Railway Station, these signs of economic prosperity and consumptive culture reveal themselves to be the same kind of illusion that the fresh painted facades of Cairo's city centre actually are. Indeed, only at first glance are the latter able to deceive the observer with regard to the disastrous condition which in fact characterizes the colonial architecture of the city. For the overwhelming majority of Egyptians, this happy Thursday-night consumerism remains nothing more than a fata morgana. Within a short walking distance from talat harb Egyptian life-worlds undergo dramatic changes and the consumptive environment of second modernity quickly dissolves into living conditions that rather reminds us to the social hardships of early industrial society.

A similar impression of radically changing life-worlds is provided by a stroll through the centre of Turkey's capital Ankara leading from the gecekondu Altindag via Ulus along Atatürk Boulevard to the fancy residential area of Cankaya. [1] There is no doubt that this walk does

---

① A *gecekondu* is a squatter settlement and the name indicates that its houses have been erected "over-night," thereby enabling the authorities to move its squatters out by force. Since 1945, Turkish cities have faced dramatic growth of population with more than 50 percent of the new residents finding their homes in a *gecekondu* (Wedel 1996).

not rank prominent among Turkey's numerous tourist attractions. On the contrary, the functional architecture of first modernity that forms the backdrop for most of this walking tour seemingly corroborates the negative image which most travel guides usually paint of the Turkish capital. Indeed, many buildings in Ankara's city centre symbolize the Kemalist ideal of a state-dominated organized Turkish society in stone. Yet Ankara is not as bad as this image purports. In fact, making this tour through central Ankara offers a multiplicity of insights into the various lifestyles which actually characterize contemporary everyday life in Turkey. The simultaneity of headscarf and mini-skirts with poor street vendors and shiny fashion stores are some cases in point. Moreover, the view from the hisar, the old castle that meanwhile is populated by rural migrants, with the huge Kocatepe Mosque to your left and the Anıtkabir, the classicist mausoleum of Mustafa Kemal Atatürk, to your right, gives a petrified image of the two essential ideational forces that in various ways have molded Turkey's different individual walks of life. For the careful observer, this walking tour through Ankara is not only an encounter with Turkey's petrified history but also with the country's lively and multifaceted society and with its peculiar merger of Kemalism and Islam. [1]

Turning to the institutional arrangements of state and religion in Muslim countries, the macro-sociological reality of the Islamic world seems as diverse as the picture presented above of collective and individual Muslim lifestyles. The supposedly fixed image of a unity of religion and state in Islam is far from historical reality. Since the dawn of decolonialization, the political landscape of the Muslim world has been shaped by the emergence of formally sovereign and territorially

---

[1] For an excellently written account of the contradictory features of Turkish society and history, see the book *Crescent and Star* by Stephen Kinzer (2001).

demarcated national states (Piscatori 1986). The history of Muslim politics is an inseparable part of the narrative of modernization as modern state formation with all it historically diverse institutional facets.

Looking at the 57 member states of the Organization of Islamic Conference, ranging from the Kingdom of Morocco in the West to the tiny but rich Sultanate of Brunei Dar-us-Salam in the East, it becomes apparent that these national states look back on very different paths to modern statehood, thus displaying a broad variety of institutional and legal arrangements organizing the political and the religious spheres. Whereas republican Turkey has been characterized by the rigid rules of Kemalist secularism, the clerical leadership of the Islamic Republic of Iran is legitimizing its political order by means of a specific interpretation of the traditions of Shiite Islam. Both states, however, implemented republican principles based on the modern concept of popular sovereignty and the formal distribution of powers. The majority of OIC member states consider themselves as republics which distinguish them sharply from Muslim monarchies such as Brunei, the Gulf States, Jordan, Morocco or Saudi Arabia. Yet looking at concrete patterns of rule, these republics in fact expose a wide range of political systems from the one-person dictatorship of Turkmenistan to the representational democracy of the EU candidate Turkey, thoroughly reforming its political and legal institutions according to the liberal framework laid out in the "Copenhagen Criteria". [1]

The most populous Muslim state, Indonesia, added a religious

---

① The Copenhagen Criteria are the political and economic benchmarks with which the European Union is measuring whether an EU membership candidate is eligible to take up accession negotiations with Brussels. They were agreed upon at the EU summit in Copenhagen 1993, and they refer in political terms to normative standards in the fields of democratic governance, rule of law, human rights, and the protection of minorities, whereas in the economic realm they require a functioning market economy.

component to its declaration of independence, though not an explicitly Islamic one. As one of its five principles, the concept of the Pancasila stipulates monotheism as a constitutional element of the Indonesian state, defined in a way that subsumes all five officially accepted religions in Indonesia under this category, namely Islam, Catholicism, Protestantism, Hinduism and Buddhism (Arenhövel 2005). In South Asia, the communal conflict among India's elite led to a two-state solution at independence. With the foundation of India and Pakistan in 1947, South Asian state formation attained a particularly religious connotation. Yet this transformation of religious into political boundaries has not solved the conflict. On the contrary, the communal tension has been elevated to the inter-state level, resulting in a series of wars between the Indian and Pakistani states. Furthermore, the religious definition of Pakistan's identity as a modern national state could not prevent the secession of Bangladesh (1971), nor the dangerous political fragmentation of what remained of Pakistan. Since the establishment of two Muslim states in South Asia, they have both constantly been faced with severe domestic conflicts, which, in the case of the Pakistani provinces of Sind and Belujistan, have assumed war-like forms (Jung *et al.* 2003: 215 – 23). These historical experiences of South Asian state formation alone are proof to the fact that also in the Muslim world religious identities do not necessarily correspond to political loyalties.

Against the evidence of these micro-and macro-instances of diversity, orientalist scholars and Islamist ideologues have put forward a number of historical and principal arguments which should substantiate their propositions of an inherently inseparable link between religion and politics in Islam. The following sections will discuss four points in this defense of the holistic nature of Islam. First, I examine the nature of the "community of Medina", which often serves as an ideal historical example of the "organic" unity of state and religion in Islam. Then, I shall ask whether the revealed religious sources can provide us with clear guidance for the establishment of Islamic rule. Thirdly, I will selectively examine the political history of Islam from a comparative perspective, pointing to both similarities and differences with regard to processes of state-building and institutional differentiation in western and Muslim societies. Finally, we shall deal with the relationship between Islamic law and political authority in the light of contemporary debates about the "implementation of the *sharia*." Do we find Islam's social order in religious law?

Medina and the Ideal of an Islamic State

It is not surprising that the life of the Prophet Muhammad plays a central role in the ideologies of contemporary Islamist movements. In terms of Islamist politics, this applies in particular to Medinian times after the *hijra*, the move of the Prophet and his supporters from Mecca to Medina in 622. In Medina, according to Islamist interpretations, Muhammad represented in his person the unity of religion and politics in early Islam. Moreover, some Islamist intellectuals have turned the so-called community of Medina into their model of an Islamic polity that serves them as an ideal counter-model to the modern western national state (cf. Tezcan 2003, 157 – 65). In modern times, the life of the Prophet became exemplary in very new terms. In the modern search for fundamentals, early Islam and the Sunna of the Prophet offer an almost inexhaustible source to construct authenticity. This applies to all societal levels whether we look at states, social movements or individuals. In particular in the context of colonial domination, references to the example of the Prophet acquired the quality of indisputable authenticity in national and individual identity building processes.

Yet it is not only Islamists who relate the alleged unity of state and religion to the particular position of the Prophet in Medina. The German orientalist Fritz Steppat, for instance, asserted that, from the outset, the Islamic revelation also implied the foundation of an Islamic state. In assuming a political role in Medina, so runs his core argument, the Prophet combined religious and political functions. He was prophet and statesman at the same time, and set the example for future political developments in the Muslim world. In this way, the community of Medina came to represent the ideal of an Islamic polity (Steppat 1965, 319). In western scholarship, the topos of Muhammad as prophet and statesman goes back to the nineteenth century. Applying the then penetrating language of nationalism, nineteenth century historians often described the foundational phase of the Islamic revelation as a process of the national awakening of the Arabs. Paradigmatic for this assumption of the intrinsically political nature of Islam is Julius Wellhausen's article on Muhammad in the *Encyclopedia Britannica*. In this article, the German theologian and Arabist Wellhausen explains to a world audience that we should perceive the Koran as the Prophet's "weakest performance" whereas his actual historical importance lies in his political work at Medina (Wellhausen 1883). Apparently, orientalist scholars and Islamist ideologues interpret the history of early Islam in a similar way, constructing their understanding of the Prophet's life based on nationalist discourse and concepts of modern statehood. With respect to Islamist ideologies, this can be explained in the specific modern desire of Islamist thinkers to build up regimes of authenticity. Yet in the field of western scholarship, this image of the Prophet represents a mere anachronism.

From a scholarly perspective, defining the character of the Islamic religion by continually referring to the life of the Prophet is rather problematic. With regard to historical and material sources, we know only very little about Muhammad and the political, social and economic contexts in which he lived his life. Besides the scarce information given by the Koran, the standard written source of the life of the Prophet goes back to his biographer Ibn Ishaq (d. 767) and was transmitted in an edited version by Ibn Hisham (d. 833). The reconstruction of early Islam is therefore subject to interpretations based on relatively weak and scarce historical sources. Up to now, the scholarly questions on the historical reality which is reflected in the sources about the life of Muhammad are far from being settled. [1]

The mainstream of academic interpretations has related the refuge of the Prophet and his followers in Medina to a severe social crisis that had increasingly eroded the tribal order in the oasis of Yathrib (the area of Medina). When Muhammad arrived from Mecca in 622, so runs the argumentation, the tribes of Medina were caught up in permanent internecine strife, due to a scarcity of resources, in particular of arable land. The population of Medina was made up of heterogeneous and now sedentary factions of tribes whose conflicts had traditionally been mediated by customary tribal law. However, changing socioeconomic conditions meant that the traditional rules of revenge and reciprocity were giving way to a vicious circle of continuing blood feuds between the various tribal segments (Endres 1982, 65). In this situation, Muhammad, who allegedly had proved his steadfastness in Mecca, where he continued his proclamation in spite of large-scale rejection by the Meccan tribes, was considered the right person to mediate between the quarrelling tribes. He arrived in Medina in order to serve as an external mediator, a typical pattern in the tribal culture of Arab

---

[1] For a discussion of the limited sources and the consequently problematic standard of knowledge concerning the life of the prophet, see Chabbi (1996); Motzki (2000); Peters (1991).

societies in those days. In contrast to his precarious position in Mecca, where his revelation was seen as endangering the traditions of his own tribe, in Medina the Prophet was instrumental in re-establishing unity and shaping a new tradition (Watt 1956). [1]

The way in which the Prophet was able to combine Islamic revelation, charismatic leadership and the successful mediation of conflicts is documented in the Medinian suras of the Koran and in an "alliance contract," the so-called Constitution of Medina. [2] This document can be read as an attempt to establish a new confederation among conflicting tribes, which in some respects transcended the traditional rules of kinship-based reciprocity in customary law. In the language of socio-cultural evolution, the constitution exemplifies a transition from segmentation to stratification in the predominant mode of societal differentiation. Three stipulations in particular deviated from the segmented tribal order. First, the prosecution of crimes, which was previously perceived as being the exclusive responsibility of the family of the victim, was now laid down as an obligation of the whole community. Secondly, the contract demanded the prosecution of offenders even by their own family members, thus raising loyalty to the whole community above loyalty to one's immediate kin group. Finally, the document stipulated that "peace among believers" ranked above clan and family ties with regard to external kin groups. In this way the rulers of the

---

　① 　In his books about Muhammad in Mecca and Medina (1953 and 1956), W. Montgomery Watt basically relied on the validity of the traditions. Concerning the question of the invention of traditions with regard to legal and historical sources, Watt admitted a "tendential shaping" of the historical material. However, he was nevertheless convinced that a critical mind would be able to detect the historical reality from these sources (Motzki 2000: XII. XIII and Peters 1991: 302 – 303).

　② 　The document was most probably written shortly after Muhammad's arrival in Medina and according to my knowledge, its authenticity has not been questioned. However, the use of the modern concept of a constitution is certainly deceptive and does not reflect the tribal realities under which the document emerged. In this article I base my analysis on the versions of the document in Serjeant (1981) and Wellhausen (1889).

new alliance were evidently trying to prevent some segments of the confederation concluding separate peace agreements with its kinship-related enemies in cases of conflict, as had happened before.

The Constitution of Medina and Koranic sources render evidence of the Prophet's ability to re-establish social order in Medina through a combination of negotiation and coercion. In this gradual process of exclusion and inclusion, the revelation provided in functionalist terms a source of social cohesion that to a certain extent transcended the segmented character of tribal society. [1] Nevertheless, the new order largely consisted of traditional tribal regulations, such as the payment of blood money or the execution of convicts by the clans involved. Therefore, to call Muhammad's alliance contract with the tribes of Medina a constitution is a modern misnomer. In fact, the constitution represented a typical confederation of tribes, a relatively loose alliance of segmented kin groups, which maintained a high degree of autonomy for the individual tribe. The crucial innovation was that, by referring to God, Muhammad as his Prophet, and Islam in general, this confederation was based on an entirely new, religiously defined symbolic order (Noth 1987, 40). Only with regard to the sources of revelation, and not what in retrospect could be called his political functions did the Prophet hold some sort of monopoly. In the early years of the subsequent Arab conquests, however, this new religious order demonstrated its integrative capacity and provided a symbolic platform for the launching of subsequent Islamic empires. The reference to and the invention of Islamic traditions progressively contributed to the stratification of Muslim societies and the foundation of patrimonial forms of rule in which stratification replaces segmentation as

---

[1]　In terms of exclusion, it was the Jewish tribes of Medina who suffered most, as they did not accept the Prophet's revelation (cf. Wensinck 1975).

the dominant mode of social differentiation. Only in this sense was the community of Medina the point of departure for the formation of large systems of patrimonial rule that were based on extensive networks of trade, use of Arabic as a *lingua franca*, and an Islamic civilization with an urban and syncretistic yet relatively homogeneous culture (Lombard 1971).

In spite of these achievements, however, the early Islamic community was far from resembling anything close to a modern state. Differentiating between the political and religious functions of the Prophet is only possible in retrospect. In light of the segmented tribal reality of the Prophet's time, it is anachronistic to apply these modern functional concepts. Muhammad was not a statesman. Most probably he was a typical mediator among tribes whose special religious charisma contributed not only to the settlement of internal conflict in Medina, but also to the ideological stabilization of the Arab conquests that followed. Yet the historical process that began with the *hijra* or "flight" of the Prophet to Medina never came close to institutional patterns of statehood which include the legitimate monopoly of physical force and administrative control over people and territory. On the contrary, from the outset the blending of charismatic and tribal elements was insufficient to provide a structural basis for the establishment of larger Islamic polities. This general deficiency regarding the "example of the Prophet" in terms of political authority also becomes apparent when we now move to the revealed sources.

"The Koran is Our Constitution"

The slogan of contemporary Islamists, "The Koran is our constitution", points to revelation as the elementary basis on which an Islamic state ought to be built. ①There is no doubt that the Koran represents the most authoritative source for the religious justification of the political and social order in Islam. Unfortunately, the Medinian *suras* are relatively silent regarding useful prescriptions for the establishment of a modern political order. Only less than ten percent of the over six thousand verses of the Koran are concerned with legal or institutional matters (Laldin 2006, 57). The few authoritative rulings of the Koran are most precise in the field of the law of personal status, and they address some aspects of the criminal code and of modes of conflict resolution, as well as expressing in a very general way the necessity for consultation in public affairs. Looked at from an analytical perspective, these rulings merely reflect the social reality confronting the Prophet in the section before discussed tribal and segmented social environment of Medina. This applies in a similar way to the *sunna* of the Prophet, the traditions of his sayings and deeds that were compiled in more or less authoritative collections. The *sunna* ranks second in the sources of Islamic law and reemphasizes, reiterates, explains and specifies the general injunctions of the Koran and may serve as a source for rulings on which the Koran remains silent (Laldin 2006, 80). ②Given this character of the revealed sources of Islamic law, it is quite evident that an ideal political system for Islamic societies can hardly be derived from its primary religious sources. ③A brief analysis

---

① This slogan has its origin in the credo of the Muslim Brotherhood, combining the six short phrases: "God is our goal. The Prophet is our leader. The Qur-' an is our constitution. Struggle is our way. Death in the service of God is the loftiest of our wishes. God is great, God is great" (Mitchell 1969:193 – 94). With regard to the various Islamist movements, however, this slogan should not be understood in a literal sense. Most Islamist intellectuals are in general well aware of the fact that the Koran does not comprise constitutional rules for an Islamic state.

② In general, Islamic jurisprudence agrees on four sources of Islamic Law: the Koran, the Sunna, the consensus of the jurists (*ijma*) and reasoning by analogy (*qiyas*).

③ This is also documented by the growing legal body with which the regime in Saudi Arabia has extended its public laws, which are formally based on the Koran and the Wahhabi interpretation of the *sunna*.

of the political system of the Islamic Republic of Iran, the most firmly established "Islamic state," makes this lacuna of the revealed sources transparent.

Historically, the lack of an independent component of political authority in the religious sources already became apparent with the schism between Sunni and Shiite Islam (Noth 1987: 74). After the death of the Prophet in 632, the routinization, in Weberian terms, of his charismatic authority led to a fierce struggle over the legitimate succession. The point at issue was the conviction of a minority that the Prophet had appointed his son-in-law Ali as his successor. This "party of Ali" (*shiat Ali*), whose ideas on the succession were rejected by the majority of Muslims, formed the nucleus of Shiite Islam. While the Umayyad dynasty was able to establish a form of patrimonial rule based on a combination of pragmatism and genealogy, the Shia remained opposed to the emerging Sunni orthodoxy. Only in Iran did the founder of the Safavid dynasty, Shah Ismail, much later proclaim the Twelver Shia the state religion (1501). According to official Twelver Shiite doctrine, Ali was the first of twelve Imams in a line of succession from the Prophet. These successors of Ali did not hold real power, however, and in Shiite doctrine they are mainly perceived to have followed the Prophet in his moral and theological infallibility. In 874, this series of successions was interrupted by the disappearance of the twelfth Imam, Muhammad al-Mahdi al Muntazar, from which point the Shiite *ulama* took over spiritual authority in order to maintain the bonds between the hidden Imam and the believers (Ende 1989).

It was this spiritual authority of the Shiite *ulama* that served Ayatollah Khomeini as a religious building block for his political theory of the *velayet-e-faqih* or "guardianship of the religious jurisconsult" (Khomeini 1981). The political system of the Islamic Republic of Iran is theoretically grounded in the *velayet-e-faqih*, making the post-revolutionary constitution of Iran a good example of the difficulties in basing a modern state on religious sources. The formal structures of the Iranian state clearly follow the principles of modern legal authority, a form of political authority in the Weberian sense. In principle the Islamic Republic derives its legitimacy from formal procedures that have been established by the decision-making through political institutions themselves. This legal claim to power is documented in the republican constitution of Iran, whose structural make-up resembles to a large extent the constitution of the Fifth Republic of France. At least formally, the Islamic state apparatus recognizes a division of powers between the legislative, judicial and executive branches, a modern division of power which is entirely absent from the classical conceptions of Islamic law. Furthermore, political positions are temporarily assigned through electoral procedures, and between 1982 and 1983 it was state agencies that undertook the formalization and codification of the *sharia* in order to transform sacred law into a positive and applicable body of positive legal rules (Tellenbach 1996).

While these legal, procedural and institutional provisions reflect the republican idea of popular sovereignty, the religious elements of the Iranian constitution justify the exclusive right to power of the Shiite clerics in the name of the sovereignty of God. In Article Two, for example, the political order is grounded in belief in God, the Twelver Shiite Imamate and the "continuous *jihad* of the qualified jurisconsults." Article Five of the constitution reserves leadership to the most just, pious and able religious jurisconsult during the period of occultation of the last Imam. Moreover, Article Four stipulates that all legislation in finance, the economy, administration, culture, the military and politics, as well as in civil and criminal law, must conform to Islamic morality. ①It is the Guardian Council, consisting of six religious jurisconsults and six lawyers appointed by the Supreme Religious Leader,②which is in charge of supervising adherence to Islamic standards and has the right of veto over all legislation. The legal and religious legitimacy of the Islamic republic thus rests not on revealed sources, but on notions of both popular and divine sovereignty simultaneously, underpinning the clergy's claim to power in legal terms, as well as providing the constitutional means for the state elite to take decisions concerning officially acknowledged interpretations of the religious traditions (Tellenbach 1985, 267).

In establishing an Islamic order, Ayatollah Khomeini largely relied on the typical institutional features of modern statehood. The Islamic republic of Iran displays a specific version of modern state formation in which the symbolic order of Islam serves as a source to justify the power position of a certain religious-political elite and as a technology of domination, as a governmental way of integrating individuals into society by disciplinary means (cf. Foucault 1988, 153). This invocation of Islamic traditions in the name of the state was apparent in the rising number of Shiite *ulama* whom the regime placed in detention and banned from religious teaching while consolidating the post-revolutionary structures of the republic. Khomeini's *velayet-e-faqih* never went undisputed among Shiite clerics, and the state authorities made the acceptance of his political theory a precondition for the right to undertake religious teaching (cf. Mavani 2011). In the course of the Islamization of the state, political interests gradually superseded

---

① For an English translation of the Iranian constitution, see: http://www. iranologyfo. com/low-e01. htm.

② While the six religious members are directly appointed by the Supreme Religious Leader, the six lawyers are proposed by the Supreme Judge with the consent of the Supreme Leader and finally appointed by parliament.

the authority of traditional Shiite scholarship and subordinated the discursive structures of theological reasoning to the logic of political power.

The regime has subjugated the traditional intellectual and economic independence of the Shiite *ulama* to *raison d' État*. In the person of Khomeini's successor, Ali Khamenei, the political expediency of the regime even went so far as to appoint a Supreme Religious Leader who, at the time of his nomination, was lacking the necessary religious qualifications (Roy 1999, 207 – 209; Zubaida 1997). Nominating a candidate who did not have the status of an Ayatollah was a clear violation of the principles of the *velayet-e-faqih*. Previously staunch supporters of the Islamic revolution, such as the intellectuals Abdolkarim Soroush and the late Ayatollah Montazeri, later called for the full implementation of popular instead of divine sovereignty. Underpinned with religious arguments they demanded an independent judiciary, the right of freedom of expression and the restriction of the religious establishment to matters of religious and moral guidance (Abdo 2001; Soroush 2000). The political system in Iran does not at all resemble the ideal community of Medina, nor is it derived from the religious prescripts of the Koran and the *sunna* of the Prophet. Relating the Islamic Republic to the "golden age of Islam" and its holy scriptures is first and foremost a means in granting authenticity to Iran's post-revolutionary leadership. References to the Islamic traditions guaranteed the necessary authoritative inviolability for the new state elite to pursue their modern state building project based on an alternative "authentic" narrative to the regime of the Shah. Religious politics in Iran are just another way of establishing the modern state monopoly over the symbolic representation of society. This new regime of authenticity was particularly important in the consolidation of state power after the revolutionary breakdown of the old social order. Since then, however, it gradually has been used to justify the conduct of a mere kind of Machiavellian politics in religious garb. The Islamic Republic of Iran is just one form of an Islamic modernity of the organized society type which is based on historically specific interpretations of the traditions of Shiite Islam.

Islam and State Formation

Looking at the relationship between religion and politics in Islamic history in more general terms, we easily can find developments that resemble the rise of the modern state in Europe. This already applies to processes of pre-modern state formation often traced back to the death of Prophet Muhammad. The territorial expansion of the Islamic community and the internal strife over legitimate succession raised a series of crucial questions that could not be answered by the authoritative example of the Prophet alone. Consequently, different opinions about legitimate leadership in Islam have accompanied Islamic history right from its beginnings. In sharp contrast to the presumed unity of Islam and politics, a certain differentiation between the political and religious realms was already visible in the political and social developments during the *grandeur* (800 – 1100) of the classical Islamic empires (Lapidus 1975). This period, which was characterized by the formation of pre-modern political institutions, also saw the formulation of classical theories of legitimate rule. With this body of political theories, the classical scholars of Islam reacted to the political lacunae of the Koran and the traditions and tried to justify historical political practices in retrospect in a flexible and pragmatic way (Krämer 1999, 34). The so-called theories of the Caliphate, drawn up between the eighth and ninth centuries, are good examples of these exercises in political philosophy. They reflect the routinization of the Prophets charismatic authority and therewith the transformation of the charisma into traditional forms of legitimacy. In succession to the Prophet, the caliph shares in the charismatic authority of Muhammad and is able to guarantee the continuity of an Islamic polity that is in harmony with the divine will (Nagel 1981, 277).

Yet the decline of the early Islamic empires brought with it the evident failure of these classical theories of the caliphate. Their ideal theological and political constructions were replaced by a political philosophy that Hamid Enayat with respect to western political theory called "Sunni Realism." According to this new political theory, political authority only formally rested on the dispensation of justice and the maintenance of the divine order. In political practice, legitimate rule was defined merely by the coercive maintenance of internal and external security. In this way, Sunni Realism reflects the emergence of the relative autonomy of the state, a process that in Europe was conceptualized under the category of *raison d'État*. In its more extreme variants, Sunni Realism justified authoritarian rule through the sheer preservation of the ruling elite's claim to power. The ideal of this new conceptualization of political authority was the unconditional obedience to the rulers by the ruled, a political quietism that gradually found religious justification in the doctrines of Sunni orthodoxy (Enayat 1982).

This Islamic form of *raison d'État*, however, was not the only parallel to the history of European state formation. As in the pre-modern state in Europe, political authority was, in theory, not legislative authority, but a system of rule for the maintenance and protection of a divine order as revealed in the *sharia* (Johansen 1999: 281). Yet the example of the *zakat* clearly shows the discrepancies between the religious ideal and the social practice of rule. Originally, the *zakat* were one of the five pillars of Islamic faith and therewith an integral part of the *sharia*. Yet right from the beginning, the religiously motivated obligation to give alms collided with the rulers claim for "taxation." In this sphere of tension between the interest of political authority and the normative claims of religion, the *zakat* did not survive in their original form. Already the First Caliph, the *sahabi* (companion of the Prophet) and first caliph Abu Bakr (632 – 634), politicized the *zakat* in elevating them to an official form of "taxation." In this move, we can detect a very early and indigenous tendency of Muslim political authorities to monopolize the means of taxation, which later should become a central feature of modern statehood. Maintaining their original spirit of being a religious duty, the *zakat* first remained the only form of taxation for Muslims. However, in the thirteenth century at the latest, a more general right to taxation by the rulers was established (Haarmann 1975, 100 – 110). Later this politicization of taxation by the modern state allowed the Islamic institution of *zakat* in some places to regain its relative independence as a religious institution from the state.

Sociologically speaking, the relationship between religion and politics has been conditioned by the fact that the emergent modern state monopolies of physical force and taxation had to be based on a symbolic order that was able to transcend the narrow dimensions of patriarchal communities. The histories of both Islam and Christianity offer good examples for this close interaction between the rise of patrimonial empires and the spread of universal religions. Thereby, the stability of patrimonial rule was continuously contested by power struggles between political and religious authorities. This was, for instance, apparent in the two-fold role which the religious establishment played in the Ottoman Empire. On the one hand, the *ulama* legitimized Ottoman rule and religious institutions mediated between the distinct spheres of state power and everyday life. On the other hand, religious structures also built a buffer against central state administration and the *ulama* had an essential function in the justification of popular unrest. Thus, Islam took on the ambivalent roles of being a source of both political legitimacy and resistance against state authority (Inalcik 1964; Mardin 1971). In European history, this ambivalent political function of religion in patrimonial settings was eventually resolved in the "Peace of Westphalia" (1648). After a process of "confessionalization," i. e. the imposition of state power over religion, the early modern state in Europe was finally able to claim a third key monopoly: the monopoly of symbolic reproduction, which found its historical expression in the dominance of the territorial state over the church and religious life more general (Schilling 1992, 216 and 230; Gorski 2000).

Analyzing these historical developments, the subordination of religious institutions to state power was a first step toward the later functional separation of religion and politics in Europe. Historically, secularization did not directly appear as the separation of religion and politics, but first as-in Christian terminology-the identification of state and church. During the nineteenth century, the modern state in Europe was able to nationalize the symbolic reproduction of society through its secular educational system and thereby to generate its own sources of political legitimacy beyond religious symbolism. In the twentieth century, the Kemalist revolution in Turkey and the Islamic revolution in Iran mark historical events in which Muslim state authorities assumed control over religion, in identifying the modern state with a rigid secularist or an Islamist ideology respectively. From different directions, both states brought the means of symbolic reproduction under their control. In the Turkish case, more recent developments suggest that we can observe the gradual detachment of state authority from the religious realm similar to what in European history eventually brought about the constitution of the "twin tolerations": the "minimal boundaries of freedom of action ⋯ for political institutions vis-à-vis religious authorities, and for religious individuals and groups vis-à-vis political institutions" (Stepan 2000, 37). This centuries-long transition from state-dominated religion to the principle of religious freedom has been reflected in the expansion and increasing density of written formal law, a legal process that political and juridical theorists have described as the differentiation between religion and politics. In this context, modern state power was both consolidated and tamed through the distinction between the public and private spheres of civil law. Under the rule of law, the internal sovereignty of the state became subordinated to its self-imposed rules and transformed into the procedural sovereignty of democratic self-government. Relatively self-referential functional systems of religion and politics have emerged.

While we can observe similar patterns in the formation of pre-modern Muslim and European states, most national states in the Muslim world acquired modern statehood in a historically different way. They are postcolonial states achieving independence through processes of negotiations between regional actors and the great powers through the application of the already established "Westphalian" international norms of the modern "society of states." In this respect, the modern state-building processes in the Muslim world basically reflect the asymmetric power relations of the international system. Like a host of other postcolonial states, many Muslim states have been characterized by structural patterns of "negative sovereignty." According to this concept, modern statehood is guaranteed by international norms from the outside rather than being grounded in a domestic social process that has established internal and external sovereignty through legitimate political institutions (Jackson 1990). This structural context has severely obstructed social processes that, in a number of cases of European state formation, led to close identification between the state and society (cf. Tilly 1990). The prevalence of authoritarian rule in the Muslim world is therefore hardly the expression of a specific political culture of Islam. Rather, the resilience of authoritarianism founds its explanation in the particular historical and social contexts in which modern statehood has emerged in Muslim societies and has caused an almost chronic lack of political legitimacy with regard to modern political institutions.

In this context indigenous processes of modernization were combined with elements of modern imposition through colonial rule. The history of modern Egyptian state formation is a good example for this interplay of local and international forces in the formation of modern national states in the Middle East. In 1811, the Ottoman governor of Egypt, Muhammad Ali, massacred the leadership of the Mamluks, the traditional military establishment that for centuries controlled power in the Ottoman province of Egypt. It is convenient to perceive this event as foundational for the formation of the modern Egyptian national state. In Muhammad Ali's attempt to free Egypt from Ottoman control, we can observe the monopolization of physical force with regard to a certain territory and population, as well as the gradual evolution of a modern state administration. Moreover, the Egyptian ruler initiated economic reforms in the context of the expansion of the capitalist world market and launched a long-lasting reform project under which he sent several study groups to Paris and ordered the translation of French literature on science, law and the military into Arabic. In selectively borrowing from European models, Egypt's nineteenth-century state elite engaged into a conscious reformation of public institutions with a particular focus on the military and on education. There is no doubt that these top-down reforms in large parts of society were experienced as rather repressive acts by the state and did not have beneficial effects on all parts of society. However, in this respect Muhammad Ali's reforms were not so much different from other processes of modern state formation. Also in Europe state building was rarely a bottom-up process, but often an attempt of "defensive modernization" through which political and economic elites tried to safeguard their power position by implementing modern institutional reforms (Wehler 1998).

As a consequence of his authoritarian rule, from the mid nineteenth century onward, the still traditionally legitimized authority of the Egyptian khedive came under severe societal pressure. The country saw the rise of a modern constitutional movement which comprised a number of crucial intermediary groups between state and society such as younger bureaucratic and cleric state employees, intellectuals based on modern education, as well as professionally trained military personal. Demanding the transformation of the absolute monarchy toward a form of legal authority based on representative institutions, these constitutionalists initiated a social transformation that has been encompassed by the narrative of modernization as democratization. However, these clearly observable processes of indigenous modern state-formation were derailed in the context of the colonial penetration of the region. In 1876, the European Powers began to seriously interfere with Egypt's administration. At the appeal of the Khedive Ismail, European controllers headed the "Caisse de la Dette Publique", supervising the strained public finances of Egypt. The establishment of this foreign control over Egypt's state finances, disrupting the crucial linkage between state making and capital accumulation, was only a prelude to the eventual occupation of the country by Great Britain in 1882 (cf. Lutfi Al-Sayyid 1968, 1 – 37). The immediate cause to impose direct British rule on Egypt was the nationalist uprising of the officer group around Ahmet Urabi which formed a parliamentary government in 1881. The nationalist movement turned against foreign domination, epitomized in the foreign fiscal control of Egypt, and against the autocratic nature of the khedive's domestic rule. Together with British troops, the Egyptian aristocracy suppressed the revolt in summer 1882 and leading figures of the national movement went into exile.

The events of 1882 established a pattern of interaction between Egyptian leaders and international great powers which is exemplary for the more general model that Carl Brown developed for the understanding of modern Middle Eastern state formation. According to Brown, the "Eastern Question System" resulted from a center-periphery struggle in which domestic and international politics became thoroughly blended and confused (Brown 1984, 72). On the one hand, the Middle East provided European powers a convenient arena in which to fight out their rivalries with little risk, while on the other hand, regional and local forces were able to instrumentalize great-power politics to their own ends. Taken his device of systemic interaction together with core features of modern state formation, the boundaries of Middle Eastern states and the emergence of modern monopolies of physical force reflect compromises of both the interests of international great powers and the assertions of regional actors. The establishment of state monopolies in the region has not taken place in an environment of relatively free military competition, but in a regulated and restricted relationship among existing states and regional state-makers. In this international setting, however, state-society relations have been rather under-prioritized and the aspirations of constitutional and democratic movements fundamentally undermined. The successful formation of Middle Eastern states strongly relied on the relationship between international powers and regional state makers, as well as among the emerging regimes in the region. Politics in the region have developed a particularly state-centered character imagining modernity as an organized form of society through the ordering power of state authorities. This specific pattern of Middle Eastern politics has been reflected in a prevalent concept of security in the region that until today has privileged regime security at the expense of political representation and individual freedoms.

It is important to keep this structural background in mind when analyzing the relationship between religion and politics in Muslim states. A large number of post-colonial state-makers in the Middle East referred to different forms of an Islamic modern as a means of anti-colonial politics and in order to foster their political legitimacy by religious means. Declarations of Islam to the state religion are cases in point. Beyond the formal privileging of Islam, such declarations are reflected in the fact that in many Arab states only Muslims can serve in high-ranking state positions. The monarchies in Jordan and Morocco relate their right to rule to religion in a genealogical way, in tracing their ancestral lines back to the Prophet. In Lebanon, the religiously most segmented society in the Middle East, public offices and services have been distributed in accordance with sectarian schemes of proportional representation, closely associating political power and the distribution of societal resources with the citizens' religious affiliation. In Saudi Arabia, finally, the monarchy is based on an identification of dynastic rule with the dogmatic teachings of Wahhabi Islam, which can be traced back historically to the power compromise between the al-Saud family and the religious reform movement surrounding Muhammad ibn Abd al-Wahhab (1703 – 1792). [1]

In analyzing political processes in the Muslim world, religion has

---

[1]   For constitutional developments in the Arab world, see Sfeir (1998); the history of Saudi Arabian state formation is described in the "classical" book by Bayly Winder (1965), for a more recent account on Saudi politics, see Ménoret (2005).

in post-colonial politics continued to play a double role. On the one hand, many authoritarian regimes have tried to bolster their political legitimacy by reverting to the symbolic sources of Islam, declaring Islam as the state religion, allying themselves with the religious establishment, or elevating the sharia as a constitutionally defined source of law. They frequently resorted to religion as a technology of domination in claiming the sovereign right to organize society according to a self-designed model of an Islamic modernity. On the other hand, in the absence of constitutionally granted liberties, only the religious sphere has been able to offer some legal and territorial space free from state intervention. This applies in particular to the religious administration of the law of personal status and to the private administration of local mosques, two classic Islamic institutions that have found their way into the modern framework of Muslim states (Johansen 1999, 275). It is the religious sphere in which it has been possible to articulate political issues such as state sovereignty, legitimate authority and democratic reforms. Given these particular political opportunity structures, turning religious discourse into a means of establishing a public sphere, many social movements in the Muslim world appear to be religious movements. References to an Islamic modern also facilitated various forms of social activism in the context of authoritarian rule. Under the given historical conditions, religion and politics have, indeed, been intertwined in a particular way, and religion has evolved as both a source of political legitimacy for the ruling elites and a symbolic and organizational means for civil society. However, this relationship of religion and states clearly carries the signature of modern times.

From a historical perspective, this specific interlacement of Islam with politics is inseparably linked to the emergence and global spread of the modern state and the associated configurations of international power. It is not predicated by Islamic traditions as such but a result of the historically contingent ways in which Islamic traditions have served utterly modern purposes related to discourses about authenticity, political legitimacy and social order, as well as for the moral justification of public resistance to national and colonial forms of domination. The emergence of Islam as a modern religion therefore is inseparrately linked to modern state formation and its functionalist imperatives. First, references to Islamic traditions underpinned the "Westphalian right" of self-determination against colonial domination. The rise of Pan-Islamism formed the historical background against which Muslim countries began to establish forms of sovereign political authority in a world of national states. Second, the Islamization of political discourse was directed against post-colonial political elites in Muslim states themselves. Militant Islamist movements, in particular those whose ideologies are based on the thinking of more radical figures such as the Indo-Pakistani Ala al-Mawdudi or the Egyptian Sayyid Qutb, targeted Muslim political elites, accusing them of having corrupted Islam (Brown 2000). In this struggle between Islamist movements and authoritarian Muslim regimes, both sides have reverted to the *sharia*, elevating this field of normative deliberation to a central symbolic resource in their claims for political legitimacy. In the twentieth century, the *sharia* became therefore central place in Islamist regimes of modern authenticity.

Building an Islamic State on Sacred Law

In contemporary debates, the *sharia* is usually presented as an all-encompassing body of ritual, liturgical, ethical and legal rules. [1]

---

[1] A good overview of Islamic law and the relationship between the corpus of revealed "law" (*sharia*) and the subsequent evolution of Islamic jurisprudence (*fiqh*) is given in the article by Kamali (2000).

In western thought, this holistic image of the *sharia* largely has been transmitted by the academic discipline of Islamic studies. In the nineteenth century, the focus on philological methods put the interpretation of classical texts into the center of western studies of Islamic history. In the second part of the century, the literatures of the *fiqh* assumed importance as a source for both the reconstruction of Islamic pasts and the colonial administration of the imperialist present. Gradually the field of Islamic law moved into the centre of the new discipline of Islamic studies whose mainstream presented Islam as a "legal religion". [1] Due to a lack of sources about legal practices, western scholars of Islamic law tended to focused on classical texts which expressed the normative ideal of early Islamic orthodoxy. Consequently, they strengthened traditionalist views to perceive in these ideal constructions of the *sharia* the "true nature" of Islam. A real correspondence between normative ideal and social practices, however, only existed in parts of personal status law and religious endowments (Rohe 172 and 77). The ideal image of a corpus of Islamic law has been defective from the very beginning. A revealed Islamic legal order simply did not exist at the time of Muhammad's death. The Koran is definitely not a book of law, only less than three percent of its content is concerned with "legal matters" (Kamali 2000, 119). On the contrary, the early caliphs administered justice largely according to the traditionally established rules of customary law. This factual gap between the normative ideal and the legal sources has been reflected in the Islamic legal tradition by the principle of *siyasa sharia*. This principle of "governing the *sharia*" assigns to the ruler relatively wide discretionary powers in all fields in which the revealed legal sources are in-

---

[1]　Two founding fathers of modern Islamic studies, the Hungarian Ignaz Goldziher and the Dutch Christiaan Snouck Hurgronje were pioneers in this field and contributed to give the discipline a certain "legal bias".

sufficient. Moreover, the principle of *istislah*, legislation according to public interests and welfare (*maslaha*), has provided jurists and legislators with a legal tool to expand and adapt Islamic law to changing social conditions (Coulson 1957, 51).

Historically, the development of a specifically Islamic jurisprudence (*fiqh*) was closely related to the territorial expansion and dynastic stabilization of Islamic empires. In this process, Islamic jurisprudence did not emerge as a legal discipline in the narrow modern sense, but as a discursive field of knowledge whose scholars claimed religious authority and perceived the revelation as the major source of their judicial and ethical deliberations. Interestingly, Islamic law largely evolved in a state of detachment from political authority. This nascent functional differentiation between religious and legal fields was epitomized in the institutions of the judge (*qadi*) and the religious legal expert (*mufti*). Contrary to the *qadi*, the *mufti* who could release a legal report (*fatwa*) regarding social, juridical or ethical questions was not appointed by the state. It was his professional reputation and not support by political institutions that bestowed a *mufti* with judicial authority (Schacht 1965, 74). [1]Apparently even classical Islamic civilization already knew a specific kind of functional differentiation between religion and politics, one which left its marks on the *sharia*, which is almost entirely deficient regarding questions of political procedures and institutions, public administration and schemes of taxation (Noth 1980, 426). Vis-à-vis the political authorities, the classical Islamic jurists were the trustees of the Prophet's

---

[1]   Unlike the *mufti*, the judge (*qadi*) was appointed by the political authorities and therefore often "entirely dependent upon the political authority for the execution of his judgment" (Coulson 1957: 57). Thus, the development of Islamic law as a discursive body of knowledge took place independently from that of the state, while the legal practice was predominantly dominated by political authority and therefore not independent of the state.

religious heritage; and it was within this distancing from political authority that Islamic law developed into what some western scholars perceived as the "most distinguished and refined expression of Islam" (Johansen 1999, 268).

In light of this "private" and discursive character of Islamic Law, it is hardly surprising that legal practices in the Muslim world have been varied and thus deviated remarkably from the ideal of unity proclaimed by the orthodox representation of the *sharia*. Parallel to the spread of Sunni realism, we can observe the establishment of a dual legal system in Islamic empires. The legal system of the Ottomans could be considered paradigmatic with respect to this dualism. There, the *kanun* formed a legal body separate from the *sharia*, whose rules in juridical fields such as crime, property, warfare and the status of minorities largely resulted from state legislation. The thrust of the *kanun*, a perfect example of *siyasa sharia*, was broadly divided in three fields: legislation with respect to public interest and the relationship between individuals and the state; criminal law; and legal controversies concerning the interpretation of the *sharia* (Repp 1988, 124 – 125). The *kanun* combined rulings with an origin in both state legislation and officially accepted local forms of customary law. In fact, the Ottoman legal system was characterized by the co-existence of Islamic law, state law, customary law, and even Catholic canonic law (Reinkowski 2005, 130). In the course of the Ottoman reform process in the nineteenth century, the legal order was further rationalized, formalized and codified in accordance with European examples. In this process, Ottoman rulers began to codify Islamic laws and to ensemble written collections of customary law. Moreover, the Ottoman reformers also imported European codes into the many areas where the *sharia* was deficient. [1]

In the course of the modernization of the Muslim world, colonial practices and indigenous reforms enhanced further this locally and regionally disparate application of Islamic law. Many of the Arab successor states of the Ottoman Empire took the Ottoman legal reforms as a model and modernized their national legal systems in combining it with elements from different western systems. The modern codes of law in Muslim states therefore show various combinations of Islamic norms with customary law and law codices of western origin. In this way, the legalization of political authority in the nineteenth and early twentieth centuries was accompanied by the marginalization of the *sharia*. In most Muslim countries the state acts as legislator, only in Iran and Saudi Arabia state legislation has been moved to a theoretically lower level of administrative rule in order to formally comply with the ideal of divine legislation. In Turkey and Albania any references to Islamic legal rules was abolished (Rohe 2009, 203 and 243). In contemporary processes of legal reform, it is in particular the position of women which has been subject to major revisions. In putting religious norms in historical context, jurists have tried to reconcile modern norms with religious prescriptions. Thus the new family laws in Tunisia and Morocco, for instance, clearly deviate from traditional Islamic principles (Rohe 2009, 207). This contextualization of religious legal sources also has been a means to avoid the draconic forms of corporal punishment stipulated by the Koran (*hadd*; *pl. hudud*). Their recent re-introduction in states such as Iran, Pakistan, Saudi Arabia or Sudan therefore must be understood as religiously justified means of disciplinary policies of authoritarian regimes, rather than an "authentic" application of traditional rules. This becomes apparent in the ap-

---

[1] For a more detailed analysis of the Ottoman reform process, see Jung 2001, Chapter Three.

plication of *hudud* law in post-revolutionary Iran. There, the high number of executions was ordered by revolutionary courts which neither in their procedural practices nor in their selection of judges followed the rigid rules that *sharia* and *fiqh* traditionally prescribe (Peters 1994, 267).

Conclusions

The perception that religious law has developed into "the core and kernel of Islam itself" might be one of the contingent aspects in which Islamic history differs from the European Christian experience (Schacht 1965, 1). At first glance, the normative claims of the *sharia* represent a challenge to the legislative authority of the modern state and the underlying dominance of functional differentiation in modern society. Being a central point of reference in modern Islamic regimes of authenticity, the debate about *sharia* also may remain important for the future organization of political orders in the Muslim world (Krämer 1999, 58).[1]This prominence of the *sharia* in contemporary debates, however, is not due to an inseparable connectedness between religion and politics in the political history of the Muslim world. As in other parts of the world, in the history of Islam the relationship between religion and politics has not been fixed, but subject to historical contingencies and continuing social negotiation. Against the holistic pretensions of both Islamist ideologues and orientalist scholars, this selective interpretative sketch of Islamic history has pointed to various forms of

---

① Yet it would be wrong to view the Sharia and forms of "worldly" legislation as mutually exclusive. In addition to the sacred sources of the Sharia, the consensus of the scholars, public interest and social customs have played an important role among the recognized sources of Sharia. In this way, legislation based on rationalist and utilitarian reasoning is not unknown to Islamic law and jurisprudence. On the contrary, it has been an established legal practice, making the Sharia flexible enough to accommodate social change (Kamali 2000; 144 – 45).

indigenous and colonially induced instances of the institutional separation between religious, legal and political realms in Muslim societies. It therefore argues to perceive the inseparable relationship of religion and politics as a "modern myth" and to analyze Islamic history within the general framework of a socio-cultural evolution toward functional differentiation.

In spite of its holistic claims, the debate over the *sharia* itself has been molded by the experiences with social relations increasingly characterized by functional separation. In stark contrast to the discursive traditions of classical Islamic jurisprudence, calls for an implementation of the *sharia* are based on completely new conceptual foundations. While Islamic law first developed as a total intellectual discourse (Messick 1993, 3), the current public debate over *sharia* is cognitively grounded in the historically specific conceptual relationship between positive law and modern statehood. In the course of history, the *sharia* has gradually lost its previous qualities, i. e. of representing a religious, scholarly and holistic field of social reflection and deliberation. During the twentieth century, the *sharia* acquired a new meaning, closely related to autonomous logic of the modern legal system. Accordingly, Islamists view it as a rather fixed set of rules that should be enforced by the coercive means of the state. In order to achieve this new quality, the *sharia* has been reinterpreted in light of the pervasive and effective means of societal control which emerged with the autonomization of the modern state. As an essential body of Islamic traditions, in contemporary debates the *sharia* is predominantly interpreted through the lenses of political and legal discourses, depriving it gradually of its religious qualities. Bearing in mind the relative differentiation between the religious and political spheres in the formative phases of Islamic law, it is almost an irony of history that political Islamists today perceive the implementation of the *sharia* by political authority as the perfect instrument for the creation of an authentic Islamic order. Moreover, the *sharia* debate is the expression of a boomerang effect regarding state policies to instrumentalize Islamic law as a source in the struggle for political legitimacy. By reverting to religious symbolism, modern state elites themselves have made it possible for the public to judge political affairs according to the moral and normative standards of religion. The social ethics of Islam have thus assumed a central role in voicing legitimate criticism of authoritarian regimes. In the modern Muslim world the *sharia* clearly has moved from a religious institution into the domain of politics. Most decisively, however, it has been re-interpreted according to the model of the modern legal sub-system.

References

Abdo, Geneive (2001): Re-Thinking the Islamic Republic: A 'Conversation' with Ayatollah Hossein Ali Montazeri, in *Middle East Journal* 55 (1): 9 - 24.

Arenhövel, Mark (2005) "Die Erfindung der Pancasila. Zur Konstruktion einer staatsreligi? sen Einheitsvision in Indonesien," in Matthias Hildebrandt and Manfred Brocker, eds., *Unfriedliche Religionen? Das politische Gewalt-und Konfliktpotenzial von Religionen*, Wiesbaden: VS Verlag.

Brown, Carl (1984): *International Politics and the Middle East: Old Rules, Dangerous Games*, Princeton: Princeton University Press.

—— (2000): *Religion and State: The Muslim Approach to Politics*, New York: Columbia University Press.

Chabbi, Jacqueline (1996): Histoire et tradition sacrée: la biographie impossible de Mahomet, *Arabica* 43 (1): 189 - 205.

Coulson, N. J. (1957): The State and the Individual in Islamic Law, *The International and Comparative Law Quarterly*, 6 (1): 49 - 60.

Enayat, Hamid (1982): *Modern Islamic Political Thought: The Response of the Shi' i and Sunni Muslims to the Twentieth Century*, London: Macmillan

Press.

Ende, Werner (1989): Der schiitische Islam, in Werner Ende and Udo Steinbach eds. , *Der Islam in der Gegenwart*, München: C. H. Beck.

Endress, Gerhard (1982): *Einführung in die islamische Geschichte*, München: Beck.

Foucault, Michel (1988): *Technologies of the Self*, in: *Martin H. Luther*, *Huck Gutman and Patrick H. Hutton (eds.): Technologies of the Self. A Seminar with Michel Foucault*, Amherst: The University of Massachusetts Press.

Gorski, Philip S. (2000): Historicizing the Secularization Debate: Church, State, and Society in Late Medieval and Early Modern Europe, ca. 1300 to 1700, *American Sociological Review*, 65 (1): 138 – 67.

Haarmann (1975): Die Pflichten des Muslim-Dogma und geschichtliche Wirklichkeit, *Saeculum* 26:95 – 110.

Inalcik, Halil (1964): Turkey: the Nature of the Traditional Society, in: Ward and Rustow (eds.): *Political Modernization in Japan and Turkey*, Princeton: Princeton University Press.

Jackson, Robert H. (1990) *Quasi-States: Sovereignty, International Relations, and the Third World*, Cambridge: Cambridge University Press.

Johansen, Barber (1999): *Contingency in a Sacred Law: Legal and Ethical Norms in the Muslim Fiqh* (Leiden: Brill).

Jung, Dietrich (2001a): *Turkey at the Crossroads: Ottoman Legacies and a Greater Middle East*, with Wolfango Piccoli, London: ZED.

——(2011): *Orientalists, Islamists and the Global Public Sphere: A Genealogy of the Modern Essentialist Image of Islam*, Sheffield: Equinox.

Jung, Dietrich, Klaus Schlichte and Jens Siegelberg (2003): *Kriege in der Weltgesellschaft. Strukturgeschichtliche Erklärung kriegerischer Gewalt* (1945 – 2002), Wiesbaden: Westdeutscher Verlag.

Kamali, Mohammad H. (2000) "Law and Society. The Interplay of Revelation and Reason in the Sharia," in John L. Esposito, ed. , *The Oxford History of Islam* (Oxford: Oxford University Press).

Kamrava, Mervan (2011): *The Modern Middle East*, second edition, Berkeley: University of California Press.

Khomeini, A. R. (1981): *Islam and Revolution. Writings and Ceclara-*

tions of Imam Khomeini, translated by Hamid Algar, Berkeley: Mizan Press.

Kinzer, Stephen (2001): *Crescent & Star. Turkey Between Two Worlds*, New York: Farrar, Straus and Giroux.

KrÄmer, Gudrun (1999): *Gottes Staat als Republik. Reflexionen zeitgen ssischer Muslime zu Islam, Menschenrechten und Demokratie*, Baden-Baden: Nomos.

Laldin, Mohamad Akram (2006): *Introduction to Shariah and Islamic Jurisprudence*, Kuala Lumpur: CERT Publications.

Lapidus, Ira M. (1975): The Separation of State and Religion in the Development of Early Islamic Society, in *International Journal of Middle Eastern Studies*. 6:363 – 385.

Lewis, Bernard (1988): *The Political Language of Islam*, Chicago: The University of Chicago Press.

Lombard, Maurice (1971): *L' Islam dans sa première grandeur*, Paris: Flammarion.

Luhmann (1981): Geschichte als Prozess und die Theorie sozio-kultureller Evolution, in: Niklas Luhmann: *Soziologische Aufklärung*, Band 3, Opladen: Westdeutscher Verlag.

——(1986): *Ökologische Kommunikation. Kann sich die moderne Gesellschaft auf ökologische Gefährdungen einstellen?* Opladen: Westdeutscher Verlag.

Lutfi al-Sayyid, Afaf (1968): Egypt and Cromer. A Study in Anglo-Egyptian Relations, London: John Murray.

Mardin, Sherif (1971): Ideology and Religion in the Turkish Revolution, *International Journal of Middle East Studies*, (2): 197 – 211.

Marty E. Martin and R. Scott Appleby (1994): *Introduction*, in Marty and Appleby (eds.): *Accounting for Fundamentalisms. The Dynamic Character of Movements*, Chicago and London: The University of Chicago Press.

Mavani, Hamid (2011): Ayatullah Khomeini's Concept of Governance (*wilayat al-faqih*) and the Classical Shi'i Doctrine of Imamate, *Middle Eastern Studies*, 47 (5): 807 – 824.

Ménoret, Pascal (2005): *The Saudi Enigma. A History*, London: ZED books

Messick, Brinkley (1993): *The Calligraphic State. Textual Domination and History in a Muslim Society*, Berkeley: University of California Press.

Mitchell, Richard P. (1969): *The Society of the Muslim Brothers*, London: Oxford University Press.

Motzki, Harald (ed.) (2000): *The Biography of Muhammad. The Issue of the Sources*, Leiden: Brill.

Nagel, Tilman (1981): Gab es in der islamischen Geschichte Ansätze einer Säkularisierung? in Hans Roemer and Albrecht Noth, eds. , *Studien zur Geschichte und Kultur des Vorderen Orients*, Leiden: Brill.

Noth, Albrecht (1987): Früher Islam, in Ulrich Haarmann (ed.): *Geschichte der arabischen Welt*, München: C. H. Beck.

Peters, F. E. (1991): The Quest of the Historical Muhammad, *International Journal of Middle East Studies*, 1991 (23): 291 – 315.

Peters, Rudolph (1994): The Islamization of Criminal Law: A Comparative Analysis, in *Die Welt des Islams* 34, pp. 246 – 273.

Piscatori, James P. (1986): *Islam in a World of Nation-States*, Cambridge: Cambridge University Press.

Reinkowski, Maurus (2005): Gewohnheitsrecht im multinationalen Staat: Die Osmanen und der albanische Kanun, in Michael Kemper and Maurus Reinkowski (eds): *Rechtspluralismus in der Islamischen Welt. Gewohnheitsrecht zwischen Staat und Gesellschaft*, Berlin and New York: Walter de Gruyter.

Repp, Richard C. (1988): Qanun and Shari'a in the Ottoman context, in Aziz al Zmeh (ed.): *Islamic law. Social and historical contexts*, London and New York: Routledge.

Rohe, Mathias (2009): *Das Islamiche Recht: Geschichte und Gegenwart*, München: C. H. Beck.

Roy, Olivier (1999): The Crisis of Religious Legitimacy in Iran, *Middle East Journal* 53 (2): 201 – 216.

Schacht, Joseph (1965): *Introduction into Islamic Law*, Oxford: Clarendon Press.

Schilling, Heinz (1992): *Religion, Political Culture and the Emergence of Early Modernity. Essays in German and Dutch History*, Leiden: Brill.

Serjeant, R. B. (1981): *Studies in Arabian History and Civilisation*, reprint, London: Variorum.

Sfeir, George N. (1998): *Modernization of the Law in Arab States: An Investigation into Current Civil, Criminal and Constitutional Law in the Arab World*, San Francisco: Austin & Winfield.

Soroush, Abdolkarim (2000): *Reason, Freedom, & Democracy in Islam: Essential Writings of Abdolkarim Soroush*, Oxford: Oxford University Press.

Stepan, Alfred (2000): Religion, Democracy, and the "Twin Tolerations", *Journal of Democracy*, 11 (4): 37 – 57.

Steppat, Fritz (1965): Der Muslim und die Obrigkeit, *Zeitschrift für Politik* 12 (4): 319 – 332.

Tellenbach, Silvia (1985): *Untersuchungen zur Verfassung der Islamischen Republik Iran vom 15. November 1979*, Berlin: Klaus Schwarz Verlag.

——(1996): *Strafgesetze der Islamischen Republik Iran*, Berlin and New York: Walter de Gruyter.

Tezcan, Levent (2003): *Religiöse Strategien der machbaren Gesellschaft. Verwaltete Religion und islamistische Utopie in der Türkei*, Bielefeld: transcript.

Tibi, Bassam (2009): *Islams Predicament with Modernity: Politics, Religious Reform and Cultural Change*, London and New York: Routledge.

Tilly, Charles (1990): *Coercion, Capital, and European States, AD 990 – 1990.* Oxford: Basic Blackwell.

Turner, Bryan (1994): *Orientalism, Postmodernism & Globalism*, London and New York: Routledge.

Watt, Montgomery W. (1953): *Muhammad at Mecca*, Oxford: Clarendon Press.

——(1956): *Muhammad at Medina*, Oxford: Clarendon Press.

Wedel, H. (1996): Binnenmigration und ethnische Identität-Kurdinnen in türkischen Metropolen, *Orient* 37 (3): 437 – 452.

Wehler, Hans-Ulrich (1975): *Modernisiserungstheorie und Geschichte*, Göttingen: Vandenhoeck & Ruprecht.

Wellhausen, Julius (1883): Mohammedanism, *Encyclopaedia Britannica* 16 (9): 545 – 565.

——(1889): *Skizzen und Vorarbeiten: Viertes Heft, Muhammads Gemeindeordnung von Medina* Berlin and New York (reprint 1985).

Wensinck, Arent Jan (1975): *Muhammad and the Jews of Medina: With an Excursus on Muhammad's Constitution of Medina by Julius Wellhausen*, Freiburg: Schwarz.

Winder Bayly (1965): *Saudi Arabia in the Nineteenth Century*, London: Macmillan.

Zubaida, Sami (1997): Is Iran an Islamic State?, in J. Beinin and J. Stork (eds): *Political Islam*, London: I. B. Tauris.

教派主义与中东政治

王宇洁

　　教派主义是伴随着宗教在人类生活中的产生和发展而出现的。它是指人们对某一宗教或是宗教派别的强烈信仰和忠诚,以及由此对其他宗教或是教派及其信仰者产生的过高优越感、偏见、歧视甚至仇恨。这不仅存在于宗教与宗教之间,也存在于同一宗教传统的内部。在某些时候,产生于宗教内部的教派主义由于强烈的共同情感和自我认同感,更强调本教派信仰的唯一正确性,因而更具有排他性。在伊斯兰教内部,教派主义长期以来主要表现为逊尼派与什叶派的正统性之争,以及对与之相伴的有关差异和分歧的强调。

　　与世界上任何宗教一样,伊斯兰教产生后不久,内部即因为种种原因出现了意见的分歧,在此基础上进而产生了教派的区分。教派的产生与不同人群在早期穆斯林社会政治发展中的不同权力主张有着密切的关系,其本身也对政治的发展产生着重要的影响。在此后 1000 多年的历史中,逊尼派和什叶派两个教派的区分一直是伊斯兰宗教和政治思想争论的一个主要问题,同时也时常对伊斯兰世界的现实政治发展产生重要的作用。不论是在四大正统哈里发统治的结束时期,还是在伍麦叶王朝后期的社会动荡中,抑或蒙古人西征后留下的大片政治真空中,教派主义的旗号都曾被不同的政治力量所使用。

一、伊朗伊斯兰革命与教派主义因素的凸现

20 世纪的前半期是中东地区各伊斯兰国家政治格局变迁最为剧烈的一个时期。在奥斯曼土耳其帝国和伊朗的恺加王朝解体之后,现代民族国家纷纷建立起来。整个中东地区在 20 世纪中期出现了一种世俗化的趋势,在政治领域,带有世俗化色彩的思想超过了宗教背景的思想,一度成为各国主流的意识形态。同时,带有普世主义色彩的宗教观也在思想界扩散。这些一定程度上淡化了教派主义在该地区的影响,一些逊尼派知识分子也开始号召弥合不同教法学派之间的差异,包括逊尼派和什叶派教法学派间的差异。在这一大环境下,1959 年逊尼派世界最为知名的宗教学术中心爱资哈尔大学,宣布承认什叶派所属的加法里教法学派为伊斯兰教的第五大教法学派,与逊尼派当中盛行的四大教法学派享有同等的地位。而爱资哈尔大学的谢赫马哈茂德·沙尔图特也发布法特瓦,允许逊尼派和什叶派一起礼拜。此后,伊朗的知名什叶派宗教人士开始在开罗设立机构,致力于弥合不同教法学派之间的差异。在 1979 年伊朗伊斯兰革命之前,一些什叶派宗教组织非常活跃,在埃及出版了不少什叶派的书籍。逊尼派和什叶派两派宗教学者也在杂志上共同发表了多篇文章,以调和两个教派间的关系,促进相互理解。

但是,1979 年伊朗伊斯兰革命的爆发让这一趋势迅速中止了。在近代历史上,伊斯兰世界的绝大部分沦为西方的殖民地或是势力范围。虽然 20 世纪中期以来的民族解放和民族独立运动,让伊斯兰世界部分地摆脱了殖民主义的困扰,但是普遍来说,社会发展状况不尽如人意。在与受西方支持的犹太复国主义的斗争中,阿拉伯一方屡战屡败,受压迫、被西方主宰的第三世界情绪在伊斯兰世界蔓延。而在伊朗伊斯兰革命中,伊朗民众主宰了自己的命运。新政府对待美国、对待以色列的坚决态度,让有着深刻挫折感的伊斯兰世界感到振奋。霍梅尼的教法学家统治理论中虽有一定的什叶派因素,但是他号召伊斯兰世界大团结和统一的革命主张却是泛伊斯兰主义的。不同地区、不同背景的穆斯林从不同的角度对革命作出了解

读,有些认为这是对美帝国主义的沉重打击,有些则视其为对顺从美国的本国专制政府的挑战,有些认为这是摒弃西方式道路、以自己本土的方式来求发展的有益尝试,有些则视之为伊斯兰教的胜利,或是整个非西方世界的一次胜利。从总体上来说,这场革命极大地鼓舞了自近代以来屡屡受挫的伊斯兰世界,其影响不仅仅局限在什叶派社团,而是整个伊斯兰世界。

伊斯兰共和国建立之后,伊朗开始以伊斯兰世界团结的捍卫者自居,意识形态宣传具有非常明显的泛伊斯兰特点,并采取了一系列举措淡化自身的什叶派色彩,以证明这一诉求的正当性。在革命后不久,伊斯兰文化和指导部宣布禁止在讲道、出版、广播和电视节目中出现一切反逊尼派的言论;此后阿亚图拉霍梅尼向所有前往麦加和麦地那朝觐的什叶派穆斯林发布法特瓦,要求他们和逊尼派穆斯林一起,进行公开的集体礼拜;1982年,阿亚图拉阿里·蒙塔泽里启动了每年伊斯兰教历 3 月 12—17 日的伊斯兰"团结周"活动,以纪念先知穆罕默德的诞辰,等等。[①] 伊朗强化自身泛伊斯兰特性,并借此扩展其地区影响的做法,对沙特阿拉伯在伊斯兰世界的宗教地位和地区政治影响是一个巨大的挑战。

自 20 世纪初麦加和麦地那两圣地被纳入现代沙特阿拉伯国家的疆域以来,沙特就以两圣地的监护者和正统伊斯兰信仰的代言人自居,积极扮演着伊斯兰世界盟主和世界穆斯林精神领袖的角色。不错,什叶派的一些宗教信仰和宗教实践与作为沙特官方信仰的瓦哈比主义相悖,因此时常被认为违背了认主独一的根本信条。生活在沙特国内的什叶派因而遭遇严峻的挑战。但是沙特把建国的历程定义为反对异族统治、重振伊斯兰信仰的过程,此后其经济实力的增长和作为两圣地监护者的身份更强化了其在阿拉伯伊斯兰世界中的地位。它倡导建立了世界穆斯林大会和伊斯兰世界联盟两大泛伊斯兰国际组织,凭借掌握的巨额石油财富,在全球范围内开展活动。它领导伊斯兰世界联盟,并开办学校、资助从尼日利亚一直到马来西亚的穆斯林学生在沙特学习,其宗教与政治影响随之扩散到世界各

① Wilfried Buchta, "Tehran's Ecumenical Sociaty: A Veritable Ecumenical Revival or Trojan Horse of Iran?" in Rainer Brunner, Werner Ende, *The Twelver Shia in Modern Times: Religious Culture & Political Culture*, p. 333 – 334, Brill, 2001.

地的穆斯林社团。可以说瓦哈比主义激发其雄心,而石油财富资助其事业不断发展。沙特在伊斯兰世界的领导者地位由此奠定。

霍梅尼号召的伊斯兰世界大团结,是以伊朗为首、以伊斯兰革命为榜样的。他公开对沙特苦心经营的作为伊斯兰世界领袖、两圣地监护者的身份提出了质疑。他认为沙特奉行的君主制腐败、堕落,背离了真正的伊斯兰道路,它缺乏人民的支持,也不配担任麦加、麦地那两圣地监护者。由于沙特在美苏两极对抗的世界格局中一向属于亲美一派,霍梅尼指责沙特不过是美国在阿拉伯世界的走卒。伊朗对沙特泛伊斯兰主义运动领导地位的挑战,极大地影响了沙特地区战略的实施,伊朗和沙特之间的关系日益紧张。

自此之后,教派主义以一种更为明显的方式表现了出来,并成为地区政治中的一个重要标杆。虽然霍梅尼一直宣扬伊斯兰世界的大团结,但与西方认知的伊斯兰革命连锁反应相反的是,很多伊斯兰国家的政权并不认为伊朗革命是真正的伊斯兰运动的胜利。它是一场挑战各国现存政治秩序的政治动荡,更是什叶派对逊尼派的宗教挑战。代表逊尼派的沙特与代表什叶派的伊朗,在中东以及其他地区的穆斯林社团当中展开了以宗教为旗帜的意识形态宣传战,并将其与自身争取地区霸权和伊斯兰世界领袖的战略目标结合起来。

教派主义的影响涉及到地区格局和国际政治层面。什叶派和逊尼派在历史上就存在的差异和冲突被放置在伊朗和沙特两个地区大国扩展自己地区影响、谋求各自政治目标的斗争的背景下,显得格外引人瞩目。两国带有政治目的的教派主义宣传,使得教派主义成为当代中东地区政治中的重要因素。

二、作为宗教少数派的逊尼派和什叶派

中东各国不同程度地存在教派问题,其中伊拉克和黎巴嫩等国教派成分比较多样,教派冲突也比较明显。伊朗和沙特阿拉伯虽然都是以某一教派为绝对多数,但教派的区分依然对国家的发展具有重要的影响。具体来

说,什叶派在沙特国内是毋庸置疑的宗教少数派,而逊尼派在伊朗则屈居于什叶派之后。在教派主义的影响日益浓厚的背景下,作为宗教少数派的身份,让他们在所在国的地位和境遇都非常微妙。

近年来,无论是伊朗的逊尼派信徒,还是沙特的什叶派信徒,都受到了不断质疑。这种质疑一方面来自于其与主体信仰不同的宗教信仰,但更多的时候是对其国家忠诚的怀疑。沙特的什叶派被指责为"第五纵队"和"特洛伊木马",而伊朗的逊尼派则被视为分裂国家的重要威胁。

沙特阿拉伯的什叶派人口比例据估计大约在 10—15%①,其分布以东部省为主,占该省居民总数的三分之一左右。其中 90% 以上的什叶派穆斯林又集中居住在沙特油气资源最为丰富的哈萨、卡提夫和加瓦尔附近。近几十年来,石油资源的开发使得大部分什叶派的经济状况有所改善,但是他们在宗教、文化方面的处境并无多大变化。对于沙特这样一个以瓦哈比主义为立国之本的国家来说,承认什叶派的合法宗教身份就等于否定自己的宗教合法性。即使在 1959 年爱资哈尔大学权威学者发布法特瓦,认可什叶派乃是与逊尼派的四大教法学派并立的第五大教法学派之后,沙特依然拒绝承认什叶派的穆斯林身份。

在这种环境下,什叶派信徒的人身安全虽然有保障,但他们的宗教习俗和活动依然受到种种限制。政府一直竭力让什叶派在公共生活和私人生活领域之间划分出一个明确的界限。也就是说,什叶派信徒可以保持自己的传统,但不能在公开场合表露,更不应过分强调自己信仰的特殊性。什叶派作为穆斯林的身份不被认可,但又不是受到传统伊斯兰教法保护的"有经人",其地位要比沙特境内为数甚少的犹太人和基督徒更低。可以说,在海湾各国中,沙特国内的什叶派人数仅次于伊拉克,但是其融入现代国家的程度却是最低的。被占据主流的瓦哈比派意识形态排斥在外之后,什叶派的二等公民地位让其一直对外来的新鲜政治思想和政治环境的变动非常敏感。

伊朗伊斯兰革命之后,沙特国内的什叶派随即开展了一系列社会抗议

---

① Joshua Teitelbaum, "The Shiites of Saudi Arabia", in *Current Trends in Islamist Ideology*, Vol. 10, 2010.

运动,这促使政府对有关什叶派地区和社团的政策进行调整。但是,在社会经济条件有所改善的同时,沙特政府并没有采取积极的措施来融合什叶派国民。对什叶派的不信任感和文化方面的压力持续存在。伊朗革命后的10年,被沙特什叶派视为自身境遇最差的10年,沙特与伊朗之间的紧张关系使沙特什叶派时常被视为潜伏的"第五纵队"。

"911"事件之后,沙特连续几次遭受恐怖主义活动的威胁。出于对带有宗教色彩的极端主义组织迅速发展的忧虑,一些开明的逊尼派改革主义者意识到,相较于宗教极端主义者,什叶派对国家安全的危害更小。他们逐渐不再排斥与什叶派联合,进而共同倡导社会政治方面的变革,反对腐败,促进少数派权益。一场要求全面改革的社会政治运动席卷整个沙特。有研究者将这场运动称之为"伊斯兰—自由主义运动",因为它改变了此前沙特伊斯兰主义运动和自由主义运动各行其是的状况,表现出某种合流的迹象。① 在这种趋势下,沙特的什叶派反对派开始走上与政府的和解之路。在清楚地表达对沙特国家忠诚的前提下,他们提出了平等权利的要求,即要求国家正式承认什叶派是与逊尼派平等的国民,并尊重其权利。②

但是,伊拉克局势的变化把什叶派推上了国家权力舞台的中央,黎巴嫩真主党因其对以色列的不妥协态度在阿拉伯世界广受欢迎。在一个什叶派似乎要占据优势的时期,沙特作为逊尼派国家的代表似乎不会在此刻纵容什叶派力量的增长。国王阿卜杜拉一度准备公开与什叶派领导人会晤,但最终放弃了这一计划。除去外来影响,国王本人也很难说已经完全摒弃了对什叶派的提防之心。2007年一家科威特报纸的记者曾问及目前有什叶派在致力于转化逊尼派,沙特作为逊尼派穆斯林的宗教权威和真主法度的维护者,应该如何应对? 国王显然承认了问题中关于什叶派在力促逊尼派改宗的预设,回答说沙特的领导者在密切关注这一问题,但是什叶派的行动会失败,因为逊尼派坚信自己的信仰。③

---

① 吴彦:《沙特阿拉伯"伊斯兰—自由主义"运动初探》,《西亚非洲》2011年第4期。

② Joshua Teitelbaum, "The Shiites of Saudi Arabia", in *Current Trends in Islamist Ideology*, Vol. 10, 2010.

③ Joshua Teitelbaum, "The Shiites of Saudi Arabia", in *Current Trends in Islamist Ideology*, Vol. 10, 2010.

被视为什叶派世界精神祖国的伊朗,是全球什叶派人口最多、所占比例也最高的国家,但根据不同的估计,其境内也有 8% 的逊尼派人口。① 这些人口分布在伊朗全境各地,但主要居住在俾路支斯坦、库尔德斯坦和呼罗珊地区。革命后至今的 30 多年中,伊朗一直以泛伊斯兰主义和伊斯兰团结为号召,宣传伊朗经验的普适性,强调伊斯兰世界团结的重要性。但对于本国之内的教派主义问题,伊朗政府显然还未能完全解决。

确实,在伊朗伊斯兰革命爆发至今的 30 多年中,伊朗政府和官方宗教人士很少强调自身的什叶派特殊性。从法律上来看,逊尼派的合法宗教地位得到了法律的充分认可。但是,在政治参与方面,逊尼派实际上处于劣势;在宗教生活方面也一定程度上被忽视。自 1979 年以来,文化部就禁止在讲道、出版、广播和电视节目中出现一切反逊尼派的言论,近年来,最高领袖哈梅内伊也发布教令,明确禁止自己的追随者谴责前三大哈里发和他们的家人。但是事实上,有上百万逊尼派人口的德黑兰至今没有官方认可的逊尼派清真寺。据说哈塔米在竞选总统之时曾承诺当选后会修建一座,但是因为没有得到哈梅内伊的同意,这一承诺无果而终。

因为与民族问题相联系,教派主义对伊朗国家的挑战似乎更为严重。虽然伊朗各地都有逊尼派穆斯林,但是俾路支斯坦和库尔德斯坦地区的大多数居民都是逊尼派。他们不仅在宗教信仰上与主流的什叶派不同,还分属于不同的民族。其中库尔德人居住在伊朗西部,与伊拉克、土耳其的库尔德人地区接壤。俾路支人则居住在伊朗东南的锡斯坦—俾路支省,与巴基斯坦的俾路支省接壤。两者都属于跨境民族,并且不同程度上都有分离主义的倾向。伊朗地区库尔德人的自治运动在 1979 年后曾一度非常活跃。由于近年来局势的恶化,巴基斯坦俾路支分离主义运动也影响到了伊朗的俾路支地区。2003 年以来,俾路支地区曾发生多起反政府的暴力活动,主力是自称"真主旅"(Jundollah)的恐怖组织。就目前的情况看,这一地区暴力活动的组织和宣传方式越来越像邻国巴基斯坦和阿富汗的吉哈德组织,对外宣传中频频动用教派主义的观点来说明自身的正当性。

① Alex Vatanka, "Baluchistan gives Iran policy headache", *Jane's Islamic Affairs Analyst*, February 2011.

在这种局势下,伊朗政府一直强调与当地部落和宗教领袖合作的重要性。但是随着核问题的不断紧张化,伊朗面临的国际环境日趋严峻。伊朗政府宣称俾路支地区的反政府活动得到了美国的军事支持,一些逊尼派武装组织的首领也承认从美国方面获得了武器。目前紧迫的形势使得伊朗不得不在国内逊尼派问题上步步设防,这些防范措施带来的紧张气氛反过来又强化了普通逊尼派民众对政府的不满,也坐实了美国等国对伊朗宗教自由状况不佳的谴责,并进而成为遏制其扩大地区影响的道义借口。

可以说,"伊斯兰团结"是伊朗自伊斯兰革命以来的理想,也是推进其现实政治目标的有力手段。但是过去30年中,伊朗一直在宣传中致力于促进团结,却未能成功地在国内教派区分所产生的隔阂上搭建坚实的桥梁。实际上,由于与"伊斯兰团结"这一口号伴随的是伊朗影响力的向外扩展,其固有的政治诉求反而妨碍了其目标的达成,有些时候反而拉大了两派之间的距离。

确实,不论是伊斯兰团结还是教派主义带来的问题中,政治因素与宗教因素难分彼此。比如伊朗与沙特的紧张关系和互相攻讦,可以说是两者作为什叶派和瓦哈比派在宗教教义方面的根本差异所致,但也是两个地区大国之间的政治博弈。伊朗对哈马斯和巴勒斯坦解放事业的支持,可以说是为了配合自己反美的战略目标、争取在地区事务中的发言权,也可以看做是对穆斯林兄弟的一种支持。而伊朗国内逊尼派多数地区的民族分离主义与宗教因素相互纠葛,更加难以处置。

三、什叶派新月与地区政治

"911"事件之后,伊斯兰世界与西方关系日益紧张。但正是在这一大背景下,阿拉伯国家的什叶派却赢得了新的发展契机。伊朗伊斯兰革命之后的暴力斗争道路逐步被摒弃,什叶派社团走向与其他派别和解并对话的道路。他们借助政治手段,逐步摆脱了此前的弱势地位,在黎巴嫩和伊拉克等国政治进程中发挥着越来越重要的作用。

在伊拉克,萨达姆政权被推翻之后,政治上长期受到压制的什叶派影响力开始扩大。战争之初,美国的军事存在遭到了逊尼派的激烈抵抗。什叶派作为伊拉克国民,同样对美国在伊拉克的长期目标怀有戒心,但是占领毕竟为一直处于弱势的什叶派提供了难得的政治活动空间。这促使什叶派重新自我定位,改变逊尼派主宰近一个世纪以来形成的那种少数派心理,也让什叶派政治反对派重新充满活力,以便把人口优势转化为政治权力。事实上,自美国入侵伊拉克至今的 9 年时间里,什叶派已经从萨达姆时期人口统计学上的多数派,变成了事实上的多数派,在伊拉克政治舞台上的作用日益重要。

而在黎巴嫩这个中东教派最为繁多的国家里,以真主党为代表的什叶派也在政治上迅速崛起。从 20 世纪 90 年代中期以来,真主党的宗旨和策略已经逐渐发生变化,开始从一个什叶派政治军事组织向全国性政党组织过渡,并成为黎巴嫩民主进程的积极参与者。自 1992 年真主党首次参加议会选举以来,一直在议会中占据着大约 10% 的席位。而且在 90 年代中期,真主党成功地在黎巴嫩领导了一场重建地方民主管理的运动。在 1998 年一人一票的地方选举中,真主党在 15% 左右的市镇取得了绝对优势。2004 年,真主党控制的市镇增加到 21% 。

同时,真主党以"服务于民"为口号,积极从事社会服务。真主党及其附属组织在贝鲁特郊区、黎巴嫩南部等政府公共服务缺失的地区,提供垃圾清运、电力和饮水供应的服务。此外还在政府不愿和无力企及的地方修建学校、医院、公共卫生设施、低收入人群住房,并为小商业者提供贷款和资助。这些服务并不仅针对什叶派,而是面向所有低收入阶层。特别是在黎巴嫩南部地区,一些低收入的基督徒也把自己的子女送进真主党开办的学校学习。

与此同时,伊拉克和黎巴嫩的什叶派社团和组织与伊朗一样,一直坚持反美反以的立场。特别是在阿拉伯世界已普遍放弃了与以色列的正面对抗之时,真主党还在坚持同以色列开展武装斗争。什叶派坚定的反以立场使其在中东各国都有不少拥护者,一些逊尼派因为对其政治态度的认同转而受到什叶派信仰的吸引。美国著名的智库胡德逊研究所的一份报告指出,近年在埃及、叙利亚和约旦等国都有相当数量的逊尼派转而改宗什叶派。① 这一情况引发了逊尼派对什叶派复兴、什叶派主宰中东地区的猜疑和警惕。而什叶派在阿以关系问题上的统一立场,更使得他们被认为隶属于同一个阵营。

实际上,早在海湾战争之后,沙特的一些学者就认为以什叶派为核心的中东新秩序正在出现。最典型的两个例子是沙特著名的宗教学者麦加乌姆·库拉大学伊斯兰学院的院长萨法尔·哈瓦里和利雅得伊玛目穆罕默德·伊本·沙特大学古兰经研究的教授、纳斯尔·伊本·苏莱曼、欧麦尔向沙特高级乌勒玛协会提交的备忘录。哈瓦里警告说,一个由伊朗、(阿拉维派领导的)叙利亚、伊拉克,以及沙特和海湾其他君主国的什叶派组成的什叶派阵营将要形成。

此后,这一概念逐渐清晰。2004 年 1 月,约旦国王在接受《华盛顿邮报》访问时表达了对什叶派在伊拉克政局中影响力的关切,并提出了"什叶派新月地带"的说法②。这一概念迅速成为地区新秩序辩论中的核心词汇。一些人认为,在伊朗的支持下,从黎巴嫩到海湾国家会出现一个什叶派掌握政治主导权的"新月地带",由此改变中东地区的政治地图。为此,沙特在 2006 年开展了题为《什叶派新月地带与什叶派复兴:神话和现实》的国家安全评估项目,专门对伊朗的经济实力、油气资源、军备等情况进行了比较分析。

可以说,由于伊拉克和黎巴嫩什叶派新近的赋权,他们在地区政治中力量有所上升。结合此前一直特立独行的伊朗,在中东地区其他一些国家看来,似乎确实存在一个什叶派力量的复兴趋势。对这一趋势及其可能带来的威胁,更成为地区政治中的重要考量因素。

在伊拉克战争之后,叙利亚成为中东地区反美阵营中的主要力量,它面临的国际环境更为严峻。巴沙尔政权不断受到西方"纵容恐怖主义"、"殖民黎巴嫩"、"邪恶轴心成员"、"破坏和平进程"的指责。自 2012 年初以来,叙利亚问题不断恶化。而中东地区政治中以教派主义为标准,进行

① Isaac Hasson, "Contemporary Polemics Between Neo-Wahhabis and Post-Khomeinist Shiites", *Research Monographs on the Muslim World*, October, 2009, Hudson Institute.

② Robin Wright and Peter Baker, "Iraq, Jordan See Threat to Elections from Iran", *Washington Post*, December 8, 2004.

划线站队的局面再次出现。

叙利亚周围的阿拉伯诸国多对目前的巴沙尔政权持反对态度,急于促使其政权更迭的心情非常明显。在这种局面下,阿盟反对制裁巴沙尔政权的只有伊拉克和黎巴嫩,而阿盟之外的支持者只有人种上与叙利亚人有异的伊朗。阿拉伯国家多指责阿萨德家族的统治是作为少数的阿拉维派对多数逊尼派的暴政。在一些较为极端的逊尼派人士看来,叙利亚和伊朗的联合,已经成为逊尼派世界的最大威胁,其危害远远超过以色列人。在这种情况下,一些分析者就把这场国际政治的博弈归因于逊尼派和什叶派的差异,认为伊朗之支持叙利亚是因为宗教上的同源性,目前的动荡主要源自于逊尼派和什叶派长期以来的不和。

那么,目前凝聚所谓"什叶派集团"的力量到底是什么?从宗教上说,叙利亚的执政者是阿拉维派(又称努赛里派),隶属于什叶派当中的一个支派伊斯玛仪派。该派在发展过程中吸收了地中海沿岸各种宗教混杂的因素,长期被正统的什叶派宗教人士视为异端,与伊朗和伊拉克什叶派穆斯林奉行的十二伊玛目派有着非常重要的差异。可以说伊朗对叙利亚的支持,并不是单纯出自宗教上的亲近感。而且,在目前的局势中,叙利亚国内的逊尼派有很大一部分是支持现政权的。同时,伊朗自 20 世纪 90 年代起,就一直在阿拉伯世界各地精心培育逊尼派背景的政治力量。比如支持突尼斯的伊斯兰复兴运动,秘密支持埃及和利比亚的穆斯林兄弟会,约旦的伊斯兰行动阵线等,都不同程度地受到了伊朗的支持。这反证了在目前政局中,教派并不是唯一的决定因素。

可以说,使所谓什叶派集团在目前的政治变局中结盟的,最终是国家利益问题。在叙利亚目前的政治动荡中,阿盟和西方国家的共识是变更大马士革政权,进而削弱伊朗,并最终把伊朗的影响力压缩到波斯湾一带甚至封杀在伊朗本土。作为地区大国的伊朗,尽管一直受到西方的制裁和围堵,但它从来没有放弃成为地区强国的梦想。支持叙利亚、黎巴嫩、伊拉克等国的什叶派也一直是伊朗扩大其地区影响力的重要手段。为了避免战略上的孤立,伊朗必然也必须和叙利亚现政权站在同一立场上。这一点,远比宗教上的共性或是内部的差异性重要。

* * * * *

自第二次世界大战结束之后,现代民族国家成为中东地区主要的国家形式。在过去几十年的发展过程中,多数国家未能成功地寻找到一个作为全体国民共识并分享的认同体系,或是虽然宣扬伊斯兰教的主导地位,但是对其认识却分歧重重。在这种局面下,教派主义的因素非但没有削弱,相反,民族国家的出现和不同群体在国家体制内的政治利益之争,更加强化了教派身份认同,使之成为国内政治博弈中的主要因素。在缺乏稳固的国家认同的局面下,外界凡有风吹草动,各国的宗教少数派必然闻风而起。

在地区政治中,教派主义则是宗教在国际政治中惯常会发挥的作用的缩微反映。自苏联解体,特别是"911"事件之后,文明冲突的理论范式受到广泛的关注。对宗教在政治领域的作用和影响进行的研究越来越多。具体到中东地区的地区政治问题中时,就是关注伊斯兰教内部不同派别在地区政治中的影响和作用。实际上,这同在更大的国际政治范围内强调伊斯兰教、基督教或者犹太教的区分,以及由此产生的影响和作用是类似的。

但是,正如冷战范式从来未能完全决定国际关系的本质,也未能解释其复杂性一样,宗教对国际政治的影响也是既不能忽视,但也无需高估。国家行为是多种因素和动机共同发挥作用的结果,不是任何单一因素就可以完全予以解释的。宗教既不是目前中东地区安全问题的主要源泉,也不是治愈这一问题的灵丹妙药。如果把教派差异视为目前中东政治变动产生的主要原因,不仅不利于问题的解决,反而会使得所谓"逊尼派和什叶派的千年之争"成为真正的自我实现的预言。

The Secular Conflicts and the Future of Democracy in the Middle East

Adel Sabry

Introduction

"Bread, Freedom, Social justice" was a slogans echoed by the youth protesters in the countries of Arab spring during the last 2 years, which altered the regimes in many middle eastern countries. The slogans vocabularies varied from country to another, yet they were coincided after witnessing consensus by the diversified political powers (including the Islamic, liberal and national political forces) which participated in the recent events in Tunisia, Egypt, Yemen, Libya, Syria, Bahrain and Jordon. The slogans were reflecting the winds of changes which experienced in several Arab countries and revealed the consequences of the ruling regimes' failure in dealing with the genuine crisis of the fundamental deformations in the structures of the political and social forces during the last 2 decades.

The contemporary Arab events and the evolution of the governance crisis had a close association with the crumbling international systems, since the end of the Cold war between the two superpowers,

United States of America and Russia, in parallel to the growth of the role of the political Islamic forces through gaining great popularity by the communities which participates in the Arab revolutions although the political Islamic forces is still lagged compared to the leftist and liberal forces.

1.1. Preliminaries of the Arab spring revolutions

The Arab region has witnessed wide political changes that crossed borders of countries to others. Such changes were rapid and a surprise to many political analysts and political sociologists. However, there were signs of changes reflected by writings of youth and intellectuals. The Arab world suffers from a clash between two visions; one of the two is over-realism which sees change as something that should take place step by step and believes that the region will witness changes but won't add to democracy in all its cases. As dominant in the past period, freedom in Arab Islamic cultures wasn't of Arab value priorities. The maximum ceiling of freedom and justice in the history of Arab research was about "fair tyranny". [1]

On the contrary, reasons of rapid change had been grown in the Arab world, as the number of youth who had been long suffered from exclusion and discrimination by ruling power, directors in work and even within the family increased and made them discontent with current conditions. In its seeking for change, this discontented group made use of the large imbalance in distribution and monopoly of wealth by a small group of elites associated with ruling parties and the ruling family, despite the abundant human and natural wealth the Arab region enjoys, the decline of the State's economical and social role, the absence of freedom and violations of human rights. Family and religious

---

[1]   Dr. Haider Ibrahim Ali, *Journal of International Politics*, volume 184, Al Ahram publishing and Media house of Egypt.

sub-identities replaced the national identity, especially in countries with ethnic and religious diversity. The world powers' intervention in internal policies of countries of the region increased in the past period. All these situations were led to by colonial forces supported by authoritarian regimes loyal to the West.

Problems that were facing the Arab peoples were similar in content, even if they were from different sources. Therefore, chants echoed by angry protesters against authorities were largely similar; seeking for freedom, social justice and fair distribution of wealth.

In a historical moment, the Arab spring formed a real blow to regimes that took over power in Arab countries after its independence from colonial rule. The ability of these regimes to resist from the fifties of the last century till the first decade of the twentieth century was a subject of discussion in academic community; the so-called Arab exception. Such ability made Arab countries outside the scope of vulnerability to successive waves of democracy which swept the world.

A report issued by London School of Economics and Political Science including a group of studies on Arab spring and its repercussions written by Toby Dodge said, "The recent absence of democracy in Arab countries is due to the authoritarian structure that has been formed during the last long period, as military and religious leaders shared the great part of authority and influence while no civil force was able to hold or play a role in political landscape. Businessmen class which was intimate to play such a role was divided and heavily reliant on the State." According to the studies, these regimes have sought to modernize society and economy without leading to neither the politicization of society nor the emergence of political movements or forces that can compete regimes. After these regimes removed the forces which had the power and wealth during the colonial period, such as the class of large landowners, a local or Arab bourgeoisie class wasn't formed with influence or economic power to stand in front of the State power. When these regimes were exposed to severe pressures in the eighties of the last century where they failed to achieve development and good standard of living to their citizens especially after the collapse of oil prices in the mid eighties, regimes of Egypt, Algeria, Syria and Tunisia made partial transition to liberalism and privatization, so that the new bourgeoisie depends on the State.

1.2. Aim of the paper

The report summarizes those long-term repercussions for this defining moment in the history of the Middle East is unpredictable because such change is a product of internal social movement; with no role to foreign pressures. There are a lot of obstacles before a complete change; as ousting a tyrant president didn't lead to the downfall of governmental bodies, security institutes, ruling classes and capitalists beneficiary of past regimes. The revolutionary forces have no clear vision to alternative ideologies in order to gather various ideas of these forces. This vision is influenced by political division in Arab countries which their revolutions have been relatively settled as in Egypt, where Egyptian politicians disagree over a method of dialogue between them. So there are liberal coalitions formed both national and popular currents to face the political extension of religious parties represented by Freedom and Justice Party of the Muslim Brotherhood, and Al-Nour Party which expresses groups belong to the Salafi current. While we see a split between the Islamic current in the visions about the future of the State, we notice the liberal current has brought its tributaries from the far-left communist currents through the Nasserist, socialist and secular currents to the centrist and the far-right conservative currents. These differences reflect the state of division between political forces and imply the absence of harmony in the Arab street, with no strong leaders able to control the State or unite these political forces to save the country from its economic, security and social crises that impede the course of daily life of citizens.

1.3. Transformations accompanied by the revolution

The changes in the Arab street removed the traditional view of an Arab as a person who tends to silence and submission, and doesn't want change, whereas in fact an Arab is of the quality that may get sick but doesn't die. The strength of youth stirred change through their peaceful will and patience in dealing with hardships and adversities. At the same time, this strength of youth didn't find well-formed power working for directing their enthusiasm to re-build the State and to maintain its entities from internal decay or fragmentation. "What the Arab countries witnessed of rapid change in its political system was unpredictable and unexpected by most analysts and those interested in the fate of the Arab World."[1]

2. Internal Diversities Orientations

2.1. The international relations with the new diversified faiths

When the Arab spring was launched, it ignited the enthusiasm of other peoples looking for justice and freedom. It aroused the scary issue which big countries used to avoid with the help of ruling regimes in the Arab region. The success of the revolution means the ruling of new Arab elites with new trends whether from Islamists or nationalist populism. Even if such elites didn't take over power, the rise of political role for peoples and the rise of their level of participation in politics would lead to the rise of those peoples' influence over the Arab foreign policy. In both cases, there is a fear that the success of the revolution would push the Arab states into more conflicting politics

---

①   Mahmoud Mahfouz, a study on the Arab spring and mechanisms of reconciliation and equity, *Al-kalima magazine*, volume 75, Beirut.

with the world, and could be translated into threats to the interests of major powers regionally and internationally. It also may evolve into confrontations won't lead to Arab victory, but to deep Arab anger and additional failure to achieving goals through following these policies, as the analysis of the major powers said. Subsequently Arab peoples will increase its pressure on governments to show more assertiveness in dealing with the unfair foreign world, as they see it. It's a matter which deepens instability within the Arab states and strengthens religious and national extreme currents, giving a negative impact on regional arrangements and interests protected by those arrangements, as narrowing the gap between Arabs and Muslims on the one hand and between Arabs and the rest of the world on the other hand; causing conflict and tension to the entire international system.

2.2. Imbalance between Islamic and liberal orientation

The Arab events reflect imbalance between political forces in various communities. It's a case which led to the control of religious current over parliaments and states' administrations while liberal forces is being marginalized due to their inability to unite with citizens in facing the rising religious political currents. In order to understand the current political changes in the Arab World very well and to study reasons of Islamic dominance on political situations and its concept of a State, we need a historical analysis on the phenomenon of Islamism or Islamic University which emerged in the mid-nineteenth century. Trying to understand ideologies of these currents without the consideration of historical timeline context may lead us to mazes of endless contexts. Because Islamic thoughts had been changed over the last decades and Islamic movements have become disagree with each other on the concept of Islamic State with regard to matters such as application of the Sharia Law, public freedoms, participation of women and minorities and other religious terminologies that each party uses. [①]

"What made Islamic currents to take control over power through free elections after the eruption of the Arab spring wasn't spontaneous, but as a logical result of the recklessness practiced by secular forces through dictatorships whether by intimidation or persuasion." [②]

Some analysts assure that Arab revolutions, with some of them are still under conflict, will finally express the rising of organized Political Islam in the struggle for democracy, after the oust of regimes; in Tunisia at January 14, in Egypt at February 11, 2011, and in Yemen at February 1, 2012." [③]

"All revolutionary demands have become priorities, as people expect now to see the steps of executing them and turning them into facts." [④]

2.3. Diversified beneficiary

Some encourage a constructive dialogue between internal political forces to save community from the state of political disintegration, which will inevitably widen the rift among citizens. There were calls from political currents and some were from leaders of the Muslim Brotherhood and Salafi groups, urge to build bridges of friendship between Egypt and foreign countries. The recent visit of the Egyptian President Mohamed Morsi to China was a good example of the change in religious current in guiding relations between the homeland and abroad, as a delegation of Salafi leaders were keen on meeting Morsi at

---

① Dr. Amr Riad, the appendix to the Journal of International Politics, July 2012, Al Ahram publishing house, Cairo.

② Dr. Mahmoud Ismail, the appendix to the Journal of International Politics, July 2012, Al Ahram publishing house, Cairo.

③ Hani Nasira, *Journal of International Politics*, July 2012, Al Ahram publishing house, Cairo.

④ Dr, Ezzedine Choukri Fishere, Fi Ain Al-Asifa-in the Eye of the Storm-Qatar Foundation Publishing, 2012.

Cairo airport when arriving to the country from Beijing, just because they heard news on Chinese investments in Egypt estimated with $ 6 billion. The traditional view of the religious current about China was negative. There have always been comparisons between China's stances on the events in Syria and the dissatisfaction of the Muslim Brotherhood and Salafi currents with the vision by which China addresses the issue in Syria. This visit had taught leaders of the religious current a dimension in international affairs, raising the slogan of national interest is above any other issues. It's a matter that could limit the ability of this current to serve citizens and work to ensure the primary rights of a decent life without the loss of a friendly country.

In his research listening to unfamiliar voices, the Portuguese researcher Alvaro de Vasconcelos describes the new voices of the Arab revolutions as voices came out to tell the whole world that democracy and human rights are not exclusive Western values, but international ones. The voices also affirm the increasing world satisfaction that democracy means freedom and securing the basic human right. He asks the Europeans to listen to such new unfamiliar voices. Till now Europe deals conservatively with the Arab spring because of the previous European problems with Islam. They fear the power escalation of the Islamic movements in the Arab world instead of the European interests. The writer thinks that Samuel Huntington's clash of civilizations is wrong, illustrating that Muslims have many identities and strong hopes to achieve democracy, and there are many Arabs want democracy, even they are ready to die to achieve it. The writer warns that if Europe failed to develop cooperative relations with the new regimes in the area, this would be interpreted as hostility to Islam and a desire to prevent the Arabs to select their leaders. So they have to support the democratic transition in the Arab world.

3. Islamic Coexistence models

Islamists have other models of revolutions rather than the Arabs, which are the Iranian, Turkish, Malaysian, Pakistani and Indonesian models. Each of them has its own historical, social and cultural specialty. Some think that the Iranian model couldn't be repeated in Egypt as for the religious differences between both. The Shiite doctrine considers the Guardianship of the Islamic Jurists unlike the Sunni doctrine in Egypt which doesn't grant holiness to theocrats as Iran does. The great failure to achieve the Islamic model in Sudan divided the country between Muslims in the north and Christians in the south. Also the Pakistani model didn't keep the political stability in the country because of the military interference in authority and the politician's reliance on military people to support their powers. In Afghanistan, it gave prominence to tribes rather than state. The Turkish model remains the closest one to be applied in Egypt and Tunisia to maintain the civil state, limit the military powers, to control national security and to provide constitutional regulations to prevent the Islamist president to have full domination.

4. Towards a harmony of civilizations

Thomas Friedman, the famed American journalist, wrote in the New York Times, "The thing that was unleashed in Tahrir square is a tiger which is now at large, there is no way it can go back to its cage. A tiger will never allow others to use it for personal aims; it shall never feed on such lies once again." Those lines have become popular among Arab youth and those who are influenced by the American point of view; especially the young people who work in journalistic field. They indicate how pressing the need is for countries to try to achieve a political harmony between different parties and to start dialogue with foreign countries in order to keep a lid on that angry tiger. Otherwise, it will be a threat to all human beings. It's become clear that the rebel uprising in the Arab world, and especially in Egypt, is non-stoppable. Which takes us to the globally pressing question, how to support the Egyptian and Arab peoples' aspiration for freedom without disturbing the regional arrangements and the global system?[1]

The question has aroused controversy in the intellectual milieus. Some say that full freedom shall be maintained, so the restrains on freedom of discussion are not abused-again-as an excuse for oppression and dictatorship, while others called for a moral covenant to prioritize the National Interest, to avoid defaming people or their reputation and respect their privacy.

It's common to come across an Arab national dispute over a certain issue, especially if it's concerning the current situation of a country still suffering from revolutionary aftershocks. "The reformation calls are met with an opposition, which is natural. It's worth mentioning that this opposition prefers to be hidden, maybe because this opposition's real motive; or the strongest frontier's, is to take over power."[2]

We cannot allege that details of the future of the next Arab generation are complete, but they are totally unknown either. The Arab nation will continue to maintain diversity of religions, dialects, species, ideas and trends.

"We have no choice but to raise our children on an equation that may seem difficult; that is, to be strong enough to be able to denounce and end violence. The only path to power nowadays is to ac-

---

[1]　Dr. Ezzedine Choukri Fishere-Journal of International Politics, volume 184, Al Ahram publishing and Media house of Egypt.

[2]　Dr. Qadri Hefny, violence between the State's authority and society, General book organization, Egypt.

quire knowledge to build a more developed and modern world. ”①

The Arab world has finally taken a step forward, and is looking for a new formation of relations within its geographical borders and with the whole world. The effect of this change will not be confined to the regional level; it will extend to affect the whole human society. A new power is starting to exist, in the light of the newly found political and media liberty, restructuring political systems, fresh political fronts are taking part in public participation who own a strong desire for change. The Arab youth, who has been always deemed as reckless and indifferent to events, has led the battle for change, proved that they are capable of re-directing society to the right path and that they are ready for reformation and democracy.

The way to change and reform is not exactly paved. Nevertheless, an opposing force is working within the Arab societies to fuel sectarianism, religious and political fanaticism; and becoming a hindrance to the change and reformation. ②

4.1. Expectations

The power in favor of change is struggling to come over obstacles and opposition, leading the Arab nation to battles with this opposition. The thing which leaves the Arab people with two choices: either to surrender to suppression, tyranny and corruption or to go on a civil war where all contradictions will be justified. Hence, the movement for change will turn from a healthy one into a local clash of interests. The determination of these powers will hinder the change process in Arab societies. They, if won't fully stop change, will at least succeed in gaining the profit which was rightfully owned to people who

---

① Dr. Qadri Hefny, violence between the State's authority and society, General book organization, Egypt.

② The last resource.

led that movement.

There are challenges meeting the "Islamic-political current" that took over power concerning their capability of running a democracy. They often opposed tyrant, semi-liberal and semi-national regimes; describing these regimes as anti-Islam. How, then, will they run the Arab-spring countries, especially the ancient Arab society; Egypt.

Will they be able to build a political system capable of assimilating 90 million people who now want to be self-controlled and choosing their own destiny, those people no longer believe in the idea of a just tyrant or absolute obedience? How will they reconstruct an economic system capable of not only fulfilling the needs of those millions, but also to meet their hopes of gaining decent jobs, good salaries that will enable them to buy goods they fantasize about and of education that will teach them to use their potential to its maximum?

How will they handle a merciless global economy, which overlooks our nation almost all the time, whether deliberately or not? How these Islamic powers, which rule a shuttered and scattered society and institutions? How will they deal with a society calling for freedom while fighting each other and have no reference that everyone acknowledges? How will they meet the challenge of modernity from the position of a ruler rather than that of opposition or preaching?[1]

"The political future of the Arab spring countries will somehow subject to the relationship between the military generals and the Islamists. If it is a harmonic one, the Arab spring countries will tend to the Pakistani model. " [2]

"If Islamists want to establish a real democratic and civil state and take initial steps to build a political democratic block against the

---

①   Dr. Ezzedine Choukri Fishere, Fi Ain Al-Asifa, Qatar Foundation Publishing, 2012.

②   The last source.

military domination, even if there are real difficulties emerging from the competition and conflict, the Arab spring countries will get closer to the Turkish model. "①

Countries have cut a long way towards the civil state, which is able to build solid and stable agencies. Such countries need to support the democratic exercises, prevent the anti-authority and start establishing its democratic project step by step to lay-down the democratic exercises in the society. Democracy cannot be found without vital and effective people to participate in the public works and manage the country's civil affairs.

"People have the right to be happy after the downfall of the dictator but the sense of happiness and freedom will not be a full before destroying the totalitarian regime, building a legal, constitutional and judicial new life and establishing a new political regime to prevent the coming back of the dictator and the corrupted regime even in a new form. We should plan and work continuously to own the future, control the fate elements, establish and build a modern civil state reconsider everything and deal according to law and justice, away from monopoly trends. We not only need to eliminate the individual dictator but also all the reasons and roots of dictatorship.

We warn not to rely on the foreign support for the Arab regime's stability. The foreign support cannot achieve security or stability. It only works on the basis of the internal conciliation between the different components of the Arab society. Conciliation between authority and society, between the political, cultural and economic elites and between the religious and national components and orientations, to provide a new atmosphere increases the conciliation and consensus options and decreases open conflict between the available options on the

---

① The last source.

arena. ①

We have to conciliate with ourselves and rebuild new political and social contract on the patriotic and national levels to solve the problems that threaten both our existence and future. ②

There are many great defects in the Arab world and many hazards around us. We have no choice but to rearrange our conditions and terms of living on new basis that regards all the internal updates and aspirations and give prominence to our alliance and unity. So the Arab political elites should take practical and tangible steps to stop collapse and start building a new political life and to establish a new Arab project that achieves our renaissance to face the mega challenges of the domination forces in the Arab field.

The first step of collapse stoppage and rebalancing project of the Arab world is the reform and the development of authority and society inter-relation within the patriotic and Arab framework. This is the way to stop retreating and overcome the economic and political difficulties facing the Arab world for different reasons and factors.

Finally, we need to rebuild the relation between the authority and society in the Arab field on the basis of participation, equality and maintenance of human rights, to get engaged in a political reform project, eliminate tension points in all Arab countries and to paraphrase the role and job of the Arab agencies.

Democracy doesn't put an end to conflicts or divisions but regulates it politically considering legal and constitutional rules. There are variable political and social forces dealing with the Arab spring revolutions, and determining its main trend towards future. There are forces with interests contradict with the interests of the world's major

---

① The last source.
② The last source.

powers. Such forces only work with no real bias to topple the ruler, not its loyal regime in the Arabian Gulf. [1]

Conclusion

The events are changing rapidly in Egypt and the Arab region , while converting the stability into tension and more violence . The unsettled situation refers to the loss of the sprit of pacific dialogue between the political forces and the community groups . The loss of the dialogue language is reflecting the unsettled situations in the regions and leads to more disturbance in the international relations. The situations requires more effort done by the political parties and all the political forces to develop a formula for the dialogue among the national level , which will lead definitely to cooperative vision with different culture and countries.

The Arab region and the Middle East have always been considered a point of civilization clashes. On the other hand, when the Arab region succeed in unify the dialogue language, it convert into the point of culture conflicts melting point.

---

① The last source.

Religious Believers and the Secular State

T. Jeremy Gunn

During the past thirty years, much of the world appears to have become more religiously active and religion increasingly appears to be entangled in political matters. Religious majorities in many countries are pressing states to adopt and promote religious symbols, religious language, and religious activities. This can be seen most easily throughout the Muslim world, but in many other countries as well, including the United States, India, Poland, Russia, and Israel. Proponents of religion in politics frequently imagine that state-promotion of religion is good for religion and good for the state. The evidence, however, suggests that the involvement of religion in politics is often not good for the proper functioning of the state, but perhaps more interestingly, it is not good for religion.

I. Secularization Theory in the 1960s and Beyond

In the 1960s, the so-called Secularization Theory was the reigning theory in the field of the sociology of religion. Despite some disagreements among scholars, the proponents of the theory generally argued that the world was becoming more secular due to developments in science and medicine, the increase of rationality, and the continuation of aspects of modernity such as materialism, urbanization, industrialization, mass communications, globalism, and pluralism. As the influence of these new trends increased, it was argued, religion would have less of a hold on the popular imagination and that society would become increasingly more secular. Although the leading advocates of the theory did not predict a steady decline in religion nor its inevitable disappearance, they were impressed by signs that religion had already been losing its influence in modern industrialized countries, particularly in Europe, Japan, Australia, and New Zealand. Based upon the experiences of these and other countries, it was imagined that as countries modernized, industrialized, and became wealthier, the influence of religion would decline. Sociologists offered evidence of secularization by citing factors such as decreasing rates of church attendance as well as public opinion surveys that revealed a decreasing belief in the existence of God and a weakening of trust in religious institutions. Among the names most famously associated with the secularization theory in the 1960s were professors David Martin, Bryan Wilson, Thomas Luckmann, and Peter Berger. During the 1960s and 1970s, acceptance of the secularization theory was so broad that it became part of the prevailing wisdom in the academic world.

Sociologists at the time nevertheless recognized that there seemed to be one significant exception to the general trend of secularization: the United States. Although the United States was one of the leading industrialized countries in the world and operated the world's largest economy, the role of religion in the country had not diminished to the extent it had in European countries. Indeed, during the 1950s, there was something of a religious revival in the United States as shown by the increasing prominence of public symbols of religion and an increasing public recognition of the importance of religion. Attempts were made to explain why the United States did not fit the larger pattern of secularization.

II. 1979 as a Symbolic Year Signifying the Resurgence of Religion

There never was a time that religion was separated from politics. Rulers and states have long used religion to enlist popular support for political goals. Religious groups have used religion as a vehicle to obtain political power. Some states have sought to control religious activity as a means to control the population. Religious officials have long served in roles of religious advisers. Political leaders, from Constantine to Ataturk, have long attempted to influence religious doctrines.

Although religion has always been entangled with politics, during most of the 1970s the role of religion in state politics and in international affairs was not particularly strong. No state claimed to be a theocracy. Most Muslim-majority countries were under authoritarian political leaders and typically suppressed Islamist movements. The Israeli-Palestinian conflict was portrayed as a political struggle based on political and security claims and not on religious ideology. "Terrorist groups" in the Middle East were not associated with "Islam," but with Arab nationalism and the Palestinian cause. Prior to Jimmy Carter's presidential campaign in1976, no major candidate for the U.S. presidency had presented his personal religious beliefs as an important part of his persona since William Jennings Bryan at the beginning of the century. Regardless of the ultimate merits of the Secularization Theory, the salient images of most of the 1970s seemed to support rather than undermine it.

The year 1979 witnessed a salient change in the role of religion in politics. It was in 1979 that the government of the Shah of Iran collapsed and was replaced by the theocratic rule of the Ayatollah Khomeini. The Iranian example of the seizure of power by an Islamist force not only encouraged pre-existing Islamist movements, such as the Muslim Brotherhood, but also stimulated the creation of many new movements, including Hamas and Hezbollah. Later in 1979, Muslim militants seized the Grand Mosque at Mecca, revealing that even in Saudi Arabia the state could lose control over Islamist movements. In December of 1979 the Soviet Union invaded Afghanistan, leading to a 10 – year war that gave rise to a new generation of Mujahedeen, including the most famous of them all: Osama bin Laden. In the United States, 1979 was the year that the group "Moral Majority" was created that helped elect Ronald Reagan as President of the United States in 1980 and that brought to the fore 30 years of religion playing an often decisive role in American electoral politics.

The world has not been the same since. Particularly in the United States and the Muslim world, religion has played a powerful role in politics since 1979. India's second largest political party, the quasi-religious Hindu nationalist party (BJP), was founded in 1980 and came to power in 1998. For many years, the single best predictor of how an American would vote in elections was the number of times he or she attended church each week. (The higher number of times, the higher the likelihood of voting for the Republican candidate.) Governments of Muslim-majority countries, regardless of the actual piety of political leaders, increasingly couched policy decisions in religious terms. States increasingly moved toward at least quasi-theocratic rule, most prominently symbolized in the Taliban's Afghanistan and Sudan. On obtaining independence of the collapsing Soviet Union, the erstwhile atheist political leaders of the five newly independent Central Asian states all immediately began to prove their Islamic bona fides. Islamist movements arose throughout the Muslim world to challenge in the voting booth ostensibly secular leaders, perhaps most famously in Turkey (where Islamists succeeded in 2002) and Algeria (which suffered more than 10 years of civil war after the elections of 1991 were cancelled). The so-called "Arab Spring," beginning in 2011, is another recent development. Islamist movements helped overthrow governments in the Arab world (including Egypt, Tunisia, and Libya), and have since won elections in Egypt and Tunisia.

III. Attempts By Religion to Influence Politics

It is easily understandable why religious believers might wish to influence political decision-making. Though many religious believers consciously avoid what they see as the corrupt world of politics, others may reasonably believe that society could be improved were it to adopt sound religious teachings, including honesty (and transparency), suppressing vices (such as gambling, pornography, drugs, and alcoholism), or introducing laws that demand compliance with religious rituals. There are, of course, many powerful examples of religious believers intervening in the political process to promote good causes, whether ending the practice of slavery, promoting health and education for the poor, or resisting colonial powers. It similarly should be recognized that other religious believers and religious groups have also promoted the dehumanizing practices that other religious believers oppose, whether Apartheid in South Africa, the Inquisition, or the Taiping Rebellion. Religion's record in politics is mixed-with proponents and opponents each being able to cite compelling examples to support the conclusions they have reached.

Discussions about the relationship between religion and politics typically focus on the immediately preceding issue—the question about *which side of a political issue the religious believer promotes*—as well as the related question of *how successful religious actors are in influencing the political system.* This second question is obviously important for understanding the actual, concrete effects of religious actions on public life. I would, however, like to conclude my remarks by posing a somewhat different question; one that is perhaps too-often ignored by both the "secularists" and the "religious activists."

IV. To What Extent Does Religious Engagement in Politics Change Religion?

In 2003, I was asked to write a book that explained the influence of religion on American foreign policy. The book has since been published as *Spiritual Weapons: The Cold War and the Founding of an American National Religion* (Praeger, 2009). At the time I was asked to undertake the research, George W. Bush was the President of the United States and many people assumed that his personal religious beliefs had a significant influence on his decisions, and perhaps most importantly the decision to invade Iraq in 2003. My original goal was to assess the extent to which religious beliefs of Americans (including the President) and religious organizations in the United States influenced American foreign policy. When I began my research, I expected to find evidence of a very modest influence, and to find evidence that the supposed influence of religion had been exaggerated. I subsequently concluded that the influence was more significant than I had originally thought, but far less than many-particularly non-Americans imagined.

The startling discovery for me in my research, however, was to see not how religion influenced politics, but how politics influenced religion. I came to understand that *political conflicts shape peoples' understanding about religious doctrines.* To put this in social-scientific language (and to overstate it somewhat) : politics was not the dependent variable shaped by religion; rather, religion was the dependent variable shaped by politics. We might have expected that religion would have played something of a prophetic role, shaped by scriptures, teachings, and traditions that would then try to affect the political outcome. The salient message that I discovered was exactly the opposite : peoples' understanding of the meaning of their religion was shaped by political events. The interpreted the meaning of their religion through the lens of political events.

Let me offer three brief, but illustrative examples to illustrate this point. Prior to the Cold War (beginning approximately 1947), religious communities in the United States for the most part had not approved or adopted the term "capitalism" with regard to their religious attitudes. (There were some important exceptions, but they were a minority.) After the Cold War began, and after the United States sought to differentiate its ideology from that of the Soviet Union, the term "capitalism" was increasingly used as a counter-ideology from "communism." During the 1950s, religious communities in the United States increasingly used the term "capitalism" as a positive term to describe the American system as opposed to the "enemy" atheistic "communist" system. Whereas the merits of capitalism and socialism were broadly debated in the United States during the 1920s and 1930s, by the 1950s that was no longer the case. Any candidate for political office needed to accept "capitalism." While religious communities were not necessarily in the forefront of this baptism of the term "capitalism," they did accept it and religious leaders were able to "find" many examples of "capitalism" in Christian scriptures. Billy Graham pointedly said in the late 1940s, "Jesus taught the value of private property." In reality, Jesus had taught no such thing. Rather, Billy Graham, in the context of Cold War politics, inserted the economic doctrine of private property into his understanding of his own religion.

A second example. I teach a course entitled "Religion and Politics" in Morocco, where most of my students are Muslims. During a discussion one day in class, a student deeply trained in Islamic law offered an interpretation of the meaning of the term "jihad." Although the interpretation of "jihad" that he proposed was not new to Islam (indeed it could be traced back to the fourteenth-century scholar Ibn Taymiyyah), it was a minority interpretation throughout most of Islamic history. It has gained increasing acceptance as a response to the Palestinian conflict and the rise of modern Islamist movements. Although I do not wish to make any judgment about the particular motivations of the student, it was—in my understanding—an interpretation of Islam that has gained increasing acceptance less because of its roots in Islamic law and more because of modern political developments.

A third example. The Hindu nationalist party—the BJP—was created in 1980 in order to promote the traditions, culture, and Hinduism in India in response to the perceived influence of Muslims in the Congress Party. Although the BJP is not strictly a religious party like the Muslim Brotherhood or Hamas, it appeals to India's majority Hindus in order to gain political power for itself. Nevertheless, at core, it does not promote the core teachings of the *Bhagavad Gita* of Hinduism, but the *symbols* of Hinduism to gain popular support. It does not reach deeply into Hindu scripture, but uses symbols as a means of gaining support against Muslims. It is politics that shapes the "religious" response.

V. Conclusion

The role of religion in politics—both domestically and internationally—has increased in importance in the world since the 1970s. There are some who see this as a serious threat, and others who see it as a positive development. Although the debate continues about the actual affect of religion on politics, it is important to raise the question about the extent to which the involvement of religion in politics in fact undermines the value that religion brings to society.

Islam and the Battle for Pluralism in the Arab World

Alberto Tonini

Introduction

The historic changes that have taken place in North Africa since the beginning of 2011 call for a reassessment of the socio-political realities in the region. The fall of the Zine El Abidine Ben Ali, Hosni Mubarak, and Muammar Gaddafi regimes and the outbursts of discontent in Algeria and Morocco are the product of a deep transformation of these realities. The United States and Europe cannot fail to understand this and address it in their policies.

While different in many respects, Morocco, Algeria, Tunisia, Libya, and Egypt share a number of similarities with regard to the socio-economic and political causes of the revolts as well as the current phase of transition. The changes taking place in the region have exposed the fragility of the previous status quo and the lack of resonance and capacity for mobilization of traditional structures, such as the old political parties. They have also highlighted the unexpected vitality of societies, which were formerly deemed apathetic. At the same time, these changes have shown the tremendous resilience of old power structures that have not been completely dislodged by the revolts in Tunisia, Egypt, and Libya, and are trying, in Morocco, to steer the wave of change in their favour. While it is too early to grasp the full meaning of these transformations, it is critical to assess the prospects of these countries' development through the lenses of the new socio-political conditions and actors that are emerging and are likely to play an increasingly prominent role in the future of the region.

This paper highlights these different aspects of the on-going situation in the Arab World. The first part depicts the theoretical framework, in terms of possible interactions between religion and politics. The second part is devoted to the analysis of the recent events in some Arab countries, and the last section tries to draw the possible future scenarios.

Theoretical Framework

Can democracy be religious and, if so, how can it be religious? How can we bring religion into modern democratic politics, and how can modern democracy be reconciled with religion? In the famous formulation of Max Weber, modernity means basically a process of "disenchantment". So how can modernity be "re-enchanted" or at least permit a measure of re-enchantment?

Like Christianity, Islam has been sorely tempted by the lure of power and public dominion; this at least is the impression given by a large number of its adherents, especially by many so-called Islamic governments and Islamist movements (often labelled as "fundamentalist" in western media). As in the case of Christianity, this lure of collusion is baffling and disconcerting-given the strong commitment of Islam to human equality and its opposition to any kind of idolatry.

To speak in general terms, religion and politics are neither synonyms nor necessarily antithetical. On a theoretical level, one can distinguish a limited number of "ideal-typical" constellations involving the two terms. On the one hand, there is the paradigm of complete separation or isolation. In this paradigm, religious faith withdraws, or is forced to withdraw, into inner privacy while politics maintains a radical indifference or agnosticism. As can readily be seen, both sides pay a heavy price for this mutual segregation: faith by forfeiting any relevance or influence in worldly affairs, and politics by gradually shrivelling into an empty power game. In the historical development of religion and politics, this segregationist paradigm has been relatively infrequent. Much more common has been another paradigm or constellation: that of fusion or amalgamation-which may be accomplished in two ways or along two roads: either religion strives to colonize and subjugate worldly politics, thereby erecting itself into a public power (which may result in "theocracy"), or else politics colonizes religious faith by expanding itself into a totalizing, quasi-religious panacea or ideology. As history shows, both strategies have seriously tempted most religions in the past. [1]

From the angle of political theory or philosophy, one of the crucial demands today is the shift of attention from the "state" or central governmental structures to the domain of 'civil society' seen as an arena of free human initiatives. This shift of focus is a prominent ingredient in recent western political thought which, in this respect, has derived significant lessons from eastern European experiences (particularly the atrophy of society under totalitarian state bureaucracies). The shift brings into view a possible coexistence or symbiosis of reli-

---

[1]　Tony Evans, "The Limits of Tolerance: Islam as a Counter-hegemony?", *Review of International Studies*, vol. 37, n° 4, October 2011, p. 1757.

gion and democracy without fusion or identification. Such a symbiosis would be able both to re-energize democracy by elevating its moral and spiritual fibre (its commitment to the public good) and to enliven and purify religion by rescuing it from conformism and the embroilment in public power. In Ricoeur's words, by renouncing domination or 'religious despotism', religion would be capable of regaining its basic spiritual quality and thereby to serve as the 'salt of the earth' or the salt of democracy. [1]

In order to perform this role, religious discourse has to broaden its range and accommodate a more general humanistic vocabulary: especially the vocabulary of human rights, individual freedoms and social justice. In our time, engagement or confrontation with these issues is indeed a requisite for the relevance and viability of religion (Islamic or otherwise). Although not directly or not always nurtured by religious motives (at least in the modern era) , human rights discourse is today religiously unavoidable, and a religious faith oblivious to human rights-as well as to human freedom and justice-is no longer tenable in the modern world. In a religiously inspired democracy-no less so than in a secular regime-rulers (including religious rulers) cannot be self-appointed but need to be approved through democratic and transparent methods. [2]

In a remarkable recent study titled Islam and the Secular State, legal theorist Abdullah Ahmed An-Na'im has elaborated on these issues in a lucid and exemplary manner. In the opening chapter of the study, An-Na'im reflects on the relation between Islamic faith and the modern 'secular state', especially in a democratic context. As he

---

[1]   Fred Dallmayr, *The Promise of Democracy: Political Agency and Transformation*, N. Y. University Press, Albany, 2010, p. 161.

[2]   Abdolkarim Soroush, *Reason, Freedom, & Democracy in Islam*, Oxford University Press, 2002, p. 87.

asserts forcefully: "In order to be a Muslim by conviction and free choice, which is the only way one can be a Muslim, I need a secular state". By 'secular state' he means a political regime which both prohibits the public 'establishment' of religion and encourages the 'free exercise' of faith. A secular state, he notes, is "one that is neutral (though not indifferent or hostile) regarding religion, one that does not claim or pretend to enforce Shari'a-the religious law of Islam-simply because compliance with Shari'a cannot be coerced by fear of state institutions or faked to appease their officials". [1]

The Islamist groups facing the test of ruling power

The new challenge for the Islamist groups does not lie so much in their emergence on the political scene in North Africa as in the new conditions in which they are now operating, i. e. , their participation in the political process as a result of the removal of old regimes. In this sense, political Islam has long represented one of the defining features of the socio-political framework in the region.

With the birth of the Muslim Brotherhood in Egypt in 1928, Hassan El-Banna laid the foundations of religious, social, and political engagement with the state and society in Egypt. Since then, more than 85 branches have been created across the Islamic world, from Morocco to Indonesia. Political Islam has continued to diversify and develop depending on the different national and regional contexts. The Middle East's mainstream Islamist movements, most of which are branches of the Egyptian Muslim Brotherhood, began as single-issue parties, preoccupied with proselytizing and instituting sharia law. Be-

---

① Quoted in Fred Dallmayr, "Whither democracy? Religion, politics and Islam" in *Philosophy Social Criticism*, 2011, n° 37, p.437.

ginning in the 1990s, however, they increasingly focused on democratic reform, publicly committing themselves to the alternation of power, popular sovereignty, and judicial independence.

As a matter of fact, in the first decade of the XXI century, the role and acceptance of the Islamists in the political and social arenas have been framed within the more general debate about the role of Islam in society. The main cleavage thus ran between the secular regimes and the Islamist understanding of political discourse and practice, and little space was available for other forms of opposition. At the same time, the importance and power of mobilization of the Islamist movements, as well as the threat stemming from their radical nature were sometimes overblown by the incumbent regimes and the western public alike.

The case of Egypt is illustrative of this situation. On the one hand, the Muslim Brotherhood was not able to put forth a clear-cut political alternative to Mubarak's regime. Despite its growing interest in participating in the political process since 2003 and in particular since its prominent gain of around 20 percent of the seats of the People's Assembly in the 2005 elections, the Egyptian Muslim Brotherhood has always been on the defensive and has mainly been a reactive, rather than proactive component of Egyptian society, thus establishing its role as a conservative force. On the other hand, centripetal trends had started to materialize even before the opening of the transition phase after Mubarak's fall. It is since than that the multifaceted and complex nature of the Islamist movement started to materialize in a growing gap between the old and new generations and between the conservatives and the reformists. The cycles of repression and opening toward the Islamists, and the highly restrictive domestic political scene had contributed to keeping the movement united until February 2011.

For decades, Islamists postponed the difficult question of what they would do in power for a simple reason: the prospect of power seemed so remote. But the democratic wave sweeping the region has brought Islamists to the fore. The trend toward growing diversification and pluralism has undergone an acceleration with the Arab popular protests of 2011. The strengthening of the Islamist movements and the birth of new parties in North Africa has been accompanied by a growing fragmentation, or pluralism, both within the concrete manifestations of political Islam itself, which today encompass an increasingly wide spectrum of groups and claims, and at the level of interaction between the Islamist movements and parties and the other actors in the political arena in each country.

In Egypt, the split between the old generation of the Muslim Brothers and the new one has deepened. While the former group has only timidly lent support to the dispute of Mubarak, the latter has joined the revolts along with the tech-savvy youth of Tahrir Square. The multifaceted identity of what was sometimes defined as a homogeneous group has thus come into the limelight. Multiple identities characterize the members of the Islamist movements from the generational, social, and economic standpoints, and this in turn has influenced the participation of the Islamist movements in the Arab revolts.

Now they can be studied in a new light, both for the stronger fragmentation and pluralism within the Islamist camp across countries and within them-and in view of these parties' important victories in the first truly democratic elections in the region. What comes next may be the Arab world's first sustained experiment in Islamist integration.

Fortunately, for all their anti-imperialism, mainstream Islamists have a strong pragmatic streak.

That said, Islamists are not, and will not become, liberals. They remain staunch social conservatives and invariably hold distasteful views, including that women's rights should be limited and the sexes segregated. Given the chance, they will certainly try to pursue socially conservative legislation.

Yet to the consternation of their own conservative bases, the region's mainstream Islamist groups have also shown considerable flexibility on core ideological concerns. Despite popular support in the Arab world for the implementation of Shari'a, for example, many Islamist groups, including the Egyptian Muslim Brotherhood, have gradually stripped their political platforms of explicitly Islamist content. In the past few years, instead of calling for an "Islamic state", for example, the Muslim Brotherhood began calling for a "civil, democratic state with an Islamic reference". ①

Although most Islamist groups share a broadly similar ideology, their expression of it has differed depending on their unique domestic constraints and whether the group happens to be included in government. When a group is not included in government, and the ruling elite is unpopular and generally pro-Western, Islamists are more likely to define themselves in opposition to the government's policies to gain support.

As political systems across the Middle East open up, Islamist groups such as the Egyptian Muslim Brotherhood and Ennahda moved from the opposition into coalition or unity governments. During the euphoria of the democratic transition, new political parties-perhaps including Salafi groups that are more hard-line than the older Islamist organizations-will proliferate. As the parties compete for votes, the incentives for Islamists to indulge in anti-Western posturing to win more votes may be greater.

---

① Ashraf El Sherif, "Islamism After the Arab Spring", *Current History*, Dec. 2011, p. 360.

If we look to Egypt, the newly created Freedom and Justice Party has had to compete in the elections with other parties created out of the previous Islamist movement. The Muslim Brotherhood itself has split into two other parties, in addition to the Freedom and Justice Party, i. e. , *Al-Wasat* and the Egyptian Current Party (*Al-Tayyar al-Masry*). In addition, the Salafis, conservative radicals inspired by Saudi Arabia's puritan *Wahhabi* Islam, have also created a number of parties and have run in the elections with some success, after decades of disengagement from the Egyptian political scene. The existence of more political than ideological or doctrinal differences among these groups seems to indicate that over the next decade, the most dynamic debate will be among the diverse Islamists, not between Islamist and secular parties. [1]

Once actually in government, however, a new set of constraints and incentives usually prevail. Rather than ruling, Islamists will likely be partners in coalition or national unity governments. The experience of Ennahda in Tunisia is one of the most prominent cases. By creating a political party that, in Tunisia, largely builds its consensus on the fact that is was not compromised with the former regime, Islamist movements agree to abide by the (democratic) rules of the game that are being defined, to compete in elections, and to bargain with other political forces. The fact that Ennahda succeeded in securing only a relative majority, and thus has to strike a deal with other secular forces to govern, should be interpreted not as a weakness but as a positive outcome for the Islamist party itself, which has made it clear on different occasions that it is uninterested in ruling the country alone.

---

[1]　John Voll et al. , "Political Islam in the Arab Awakening: Who Are the Major Players?" *Middle East Policy*, vol. XIX, n° 2, Summer 2012, p. 14.

While it is still too early to fully assess the future role of these actors, a preliminary analysis suggests that they are more the product of the previous system and only mildly responsive to its change than completely new, independent, and proactive factors of change. This does not diminish the novelty and transformative role played by these actors, due to the changing political systems in the region and the complex interplay with other political forces. Nevertheless, the Islamists' capacity to reconcile them with existing structures and policies and to enshrine them in the constitutions that will be written over the next year should not be taken for granted. Despite their proven record of efficient organization with widespread religious and proselytizing networks, particularly in Egypt, political Islam is not as popular as the West makes it out to be. The many different voices that have expressed the desire for a different kind of polity, the end of corruption, and the promotion of pluralism from Casablanca to Cairo do not necessarily recognize themselves in the Islamist alternatives. The political scene has certainly become more pluralistic and although some of the new secular movements and parties are still embryonic, they are likely to become more and more competitive over the next few years, thus subtracting votes from the Islamists. [1]

The long heard slogan "*Al-Islam hua al-Hall*" (Islam is the solution) has not resonated much in Tahrir Square or elsewhere. What people want is jobs and better living conditions. This is why the Freedom and Justice Party in Egypt and the Justice and Development Party in Morocco have emphasized their socio-economic commitments and anti-corruption programs. Similarly, from the very beginning *Ennahda* in Tunisia has claimed to be willing to respect the separation of pow-

---

① Asef Bayat, "Arab Revolts: Islamists aren't Coming!" *Insight Turkey*, vol. 13, n° 2, 2011, p. 11.

ers, citizenship-based rights, and women's rights. At the same time, the party has disavowed the label of "Islamist party," preferring to describe itself as a political party with an Islamic frame of reference.

Moreover, mainstream Islamist groups are surprisingly sensitive to international opinion. They remember the outcry that followed Islamist electoral victories in Algeria in 1991 and the Palestinian territories in 2006 and know that a great deal is at stake-hundreds of millions of dollars of foreign assistance, loans from international financial institutions, and trade and investment. Islamists are well aware that getting tied up in controversial foreign policy efforts would cause the international community to withdraw support from the new democracies, thus undermining the prospects for a successful transition.

So, when it comes to foreign policy, mainstream Islamists have rhetorically retained much of the Muslim Brotherhood's original Arab nationalism and anti-Israel politics. Still, Islamist groups did not create the anti-Israel sentiment that exists in Arab societies; they simply reflect and amplify it. The Middle East provides such fertile ground for public posturing against Israel that many groups-not only Islamists but also leftists and nationalists-seek to outdo one another in demonstrating their dislike for Israel.

What should we do?

For decades, our policy toward the Middle East has been paralyzed by "the Islamist dilemma"-how can we promote democracy in the region without risking bringing Islamists to power? Now, it seems, we no longer have a choice. Popular revolutions have swept backed authoritarian regimes from power in Tunisia, Libya and Egypt. The new democratic governments formed in their wake include significant representation of mainstream Islamist groups. Like it or not, we will have to learn to live with political Islam. At any rate, the revolutions have made the short-sightedness of previous Western policy- avoiding formal contacts with the Muslim Brotherhood. The West knows much less about Egypt's most powerful social force than it should, and could. [1]

We tend to question whether Islamists' religious commitments can coexist with respect for democracy, pluralism, and women's rights. But what we really fear are the kinds of foreign policies such groups might pursue. Unlike the Middle East's pro-Western autocracies, Islamists have a distinctive, albeit vague, conception of an Arab world that is confident, independent, and willing to project influence beyond its borders. Democratic governments reflect popular sentiment, and in the Middle East, this sentiment is firmly against any foreign interference in the region.

There is no question that democracy will make the region more unpredictable. At their core, however, mainstream Islamist organizations, such as the Muslim Brotherhood in Egypt and Jordan and Ennahda in Tunisia, have strong pragmatic tendencies. When their survival has required it, they have proved willing to compromise their ideology and make difficult choices.

This should encourage our governments to enter into a strategic dialogue with the region's Islamist groups and parties. It will be better to develop such dialogue with the Islamist groups now, while we still have some leverage, rather than later, after they will have consolidated their power. [2]

---

[1]   Hamid, Shadi, "The Rise of the Islamists: How Islamists Will Change Politics, and Vice Versa", *Foreign Affairs*, vol. 90, n° 3, May/June 2011, p. 42.

[2]   Stephens, Philip, "The Highs and Lows of Democracy", *FT. com*, Dec. 15, 2011.

Future scenarios

So what does all of this mean for Tunisia, Egypt, and other countries facing popular upheaval? Like many others, Muslim Brotherhood activists in Egypt's Tahrir Square broke into applause when, on February 1, 2001, U. S. President Barack Obama called for a meaningful and immediate transition to genuine democracy in Egypt. Numerous Muslim Brotherhood members even said they wished the Obama administration would more forcefully push for Hosni Mubarak's ouster. Meanwhile, Sobhi Saleh, the only Brotherhood member in the Egyptian newly established constitutional committee, told *The Wall Street Journal* that his organization was "much closer to the Turkish example", suggesting that the Brotherhood would evolve in a more pragmatic, moderate direction. For their part, the Western media have tended to idealize the revolutions sweeping the Middle East. Tahrir Square was portrayed as a post-ideological utopia and Egyptians as pro-Western liberals in the making.

True, Egyptians (and Tunisians and Libyans) have wanted democracy for decades and showed during their revolution a knack for protest, peaceful expression, and self-governance. But the Arabs across the region have been protesting against authoritarian orders that the United States and Europe were, in their view, central in propagating. At their core, the revolutions sweeping the Middle East are about dignity and self-determination. For the protesters, dignity will mean playing a more active and independent role in the region. During the uprisings, the protesters have sensed that Western pressure on the autocratic regimes would prove critical to their success. Like any political group, Islamists are more cautious when they are vulnerable. But once Islamist groups solidify their position, they will have less patience for U. S. hectoring on Israel or the peace process. Already, they have started speaking more openly about their regional ambitions. On February 17, 2011, Mohammed Badie, the Egyptian Muslim Brotherhood's "general guide", stated that the revolution "must be a starting point for Egypt to take up its place in the world again, through recognizing the importance of our responsibilities toward our nations and defending them and their legitimate demands". Meanwhile, Hammam Said, the hard-line leader of the Jordanian Muslim Brotherhood put it more bluntly: "America must think seriously about changing its policy in the region, for people will no longer remain submissive to its dictates". [1]

In the transition phase, the introduction of constitutional and institutional reforms to devolve power will be critical. Proportional electoral systems that encourage the formation of coalition governments may be better than majority systems because they would make foreign policy formulation a process of negotiation among many parties, necessarily moderating the result. Already, most mainstream Islamists have significant overlapping interests with the rest of the world, such as seeing al Qaeda dismantled, policing terrorism, improving living standards and economic conditions across the Arab world, and consolidating democratic governance.

This is not a clash between Islam and the rest-this is a battle for pluralism. It pits the believers in pluralism from both secular and Islamist camps against those who cling to outdated notions of exclusion or superiority and insist on disenfranchising others. This means that all must work together to defend basic rights and transition to true democracies. Policies of exclusion must give way to inclusion. Only a

---

① Shadi Hamid, "The Rise of Islamists: How Islamists Will Change Politics, and Vice Versa", *Foreign Affairs*, vol. 90, n° 3, May/June 2011, p. 46.

coalition of pluralists can succeed in building a democratic society where the majority rules, where minority rights are respected, and where individual rights are safe and the rule of law applies to all, without favoritism.

The Development Trend of The Contemporary Islamists in the Aftermath of Arab Spring

——Case Study in Egypt and Tunisia

Wang Feng

The Middle East region has being experienced a historical change following the massive democratic movement taken place in Tunisia and other countries in the end of 2010 and in the beginning of 2011. Up to the present, the autocratic regimes in Tunisia and Egypt have been o-verthrown; the strong man in Libya has also been toppled, in particular with the powerful military support of the West and the gulf Arab countries. Most important, the contemporary Islamists have made a striking progress in politics by the means of political participation as a result of the historical change in the region. Especially, both of the Islamic Revival Party (Ḥizb al-Nahdah) in Tunisia and the Freedom and Justice Party (FJP) set up by the Muslim Brotherhood (MB) in Egypt have stepped into power and dominated the government in their countries. Therefore, the development trend of the contemporary Is-lamists is deserved to pay more attention in the future.

I. The definition of the Islamist

The term "Islamism/Islamist" denotes the views of those Muslims who claim that Islam, or the Islamic Shari'ah, provides guidance for all areas of human life, and who therefore call for the establishment of an "Islamic State" or an "Islamic Order".[1] In English, the use of term has gradually increased since 1990s. And it is one of the recognized alternatives to the "fundamentalism" along with the "political Islam".

The Islamists have primarily focused on political matters and had strong characteristic of politics or activism, although they are also concerned with economic, social and moral issues. Throughout most of its history, they have been the illegal political oppositions in many Middle East counties. However, the Islamists with evident characteristic of politics are differentiated from one another according to the way they act, and can be divided into three categories: "the moderate Islamist", "the radical Islamist" and "the extreme Islamist". A moderate Islamist is "one who does not use violence but works within the existing political system"[2]. The extreme Islamists are those who engage in terrorism or other forms of violence. The position of the radical Islamist lies between the two.

Many Islamists are moderate, for example, the Muslim Brotherhood in Egypt. The movement was initially announced as a purely religious and philanthropic society that seeking to spread Islamic morals and good works. For over 80 years, the goal of the movement never wavered, concentrating on the social and political areas, namely, re-

---

[1] John L. Exposito et al, *The Oxford Encyclopedia of the Islamic World*, Volume3, Oxford: Oxford University Press, 2009, p.191.

[2] Ibid, p.191.

solving the political and social issues by the implementation of the Shariʻah and the establishment of an Islamic state. For example, Ḥasan al-Bannā (1906 – 1949), the founder of the MB, argued that the full decline of the Islamic world had originated from the secularity and the materialism of the West. Therefore he advocated "a return to Islam" and the establishment of an Islamic government based on Qurʼān and sunnah. [1] Sayyid Qutb (d. 1966), the most famous theoretician of the MB and his colleagues led to an overall revision of the ideology of the movement. The key concept in Qutbʼs ideas is Jāhilīyah (total pagan ignorance). Sayyid Qutb abstracted this concept from any historical or geographical content, giving it a validity for all contemporary societies, including Muslim ones. The way out of Jāhilīyah is: a declaration of the total sovereignty of God. Thus Qutbʼs political concern was with the use of Jihad against Jāhilī societies including both the Western and so-called Islamic ones, and the establishment of an Islamic order-Islamic Ummah. [2]

The Ḥizb al-Nahdah in Tunisia is also one of the moderate Islamists. It traces its routs to the Qurʼānic Preservation Society (QPS), a cultural association founded in 1970. Out of this group, those who sought the political actions-coalesced around Rashid Ghannaoushi, announced the formation of the Movement de la Tendance Islamigue (MTI) in 1981. The MTI officially "called for the reconstruction of economic life on a more equitable basis, the end of single-party politics, and a return to the ʻfundamental principles of Islamʼ through a purging of ʻsocial decadenceʼ" [3]. And in order to take part in the

---

① John Esposito, *Islam and Politics*, Fourth Edition, New York; Syracuse University Press, 1998, p137 ~ 138.

② Conglin, the Re-orientation of the Fundamentalists, *Arab World Study*, Vol. 6, 2007.

③ John L. Exposito et al, *the Oxford Encyclopedia of the Islamic World*, Volume2, Oxford; Oxford University Press, 2009, p. 422.

political system in Tunisia, the MTI changed its name into Ḥizb al-Nahdah in 1989.

Apart from al-Nahdah and the Muslim Brotherhood, the contemporary Salafi groups in many Middle East countries are Islamists, too. These groups can be differentiated from each other through the form of political engagement they advocate. Some call for the violent action against the existing political order and for the establishment of a unitary state in the form of caliphate; Others argue for the non-violent political action; The third group is manifested by a quietist and more traditional posture, defying all forms of overt political action and calling for the obedience to Muslim rulers. [1]The Salafi Call Umbrella Movement belongs to the third group. It was founded in 1970s by the college students in Alexander, Egypt. It remained apolitical throughout most of its history, with its preachers "focusing on the importance of the strict religious observance and spurning democracy for prioritizing man's law over God's". [2] It also provided free medical social services to the orphans and the poor. However, the movement had been illegal under the rule of the Mubarak regime.

Though the Salafi groups are different from each other, a commitment to the following particular doctrines unites them. [3]

1. "a return to the authentic beliefs and practices of the first three generations of Muslims", which starting with the revelation of the Prophet Muḥammad(ca 610 C. E.) and ending around the time of Aḥmad ibn Ḥanbal's death (855 C. E.), and including the Companions of the Prophet, their followers, and the followers of their follow-

---

① John L. Exposito et al, *the Oxford Encyclopedia of the Islamic World*, Volume5, Oxford:Oxford University Press, 2009, p.26.

② AP, Cairo, December 6, 2011.

③ John L. Exposito et al, *the Oxford Encyclopedia of the Islamic World*, Volume5, Oxford:Oxford University Press, 2009, p.27.

ers;

2. " an emphasis on a particular understand of tawhid (God' s oneness) " , which the Salafi groups dividing into at least three categories: " the universal recognition of God' s absolute oneness and Lordship; the believers' acceptance of Allah as the one God; the unity of God' s names and attribute";

3. " Claiming that the only valid sources of authority are the Qur' ān and sunnah of the Prophet Muḥammad and the consensus (ijmā') of the first three pious ancestors" , which accepting the canonical Sunnī hadīth collections, yet restricting the use of the qiyās (analogical reasoning) as the valid source unlike the Sunnī muslims;

4. Arguing that a strict interpretation of the Qur' ān and sunnah " is sufficient to guide Muslims for all time and all over the world".

Hence, the Salafi groups are more conservative and rigid in light of their doctrines as compared with other Islamists.

II. Islamists Making Unprecedented Progress in Politics

After the autocratic regimes were overthrown, the Islamists have made significant progress in politics in Tunisia and Egypt. Except for the initial hesitation, many Islamists including al-Nahdah, the Muslim Brotherhood as well as the Salafi Call Umbrella Movement has begun to take positively part in the democratic movement in their countries. They have created their own parties, participated in the election of the parliament or the constituent assembly and the succeeding presidential elections. Up to the present, they have won all these elections and come to power successfully.

So is al-Nahdah. The first real and free democratic constituent assembly was held in October 23, 2011 in Tunisia after Ben Ali' s regime was overthrown. Al-Nahdah has secured 41 percent, or 89 seats in the 217 - seat constituent assembly, becoming the dominated party in the assembly. Then, al-Nahdah, as well as other two secular parties in the assembly, namely the Congress for the Republic and the Ettakatol formed the coalition government dominated by al-Nahdah. Hamadi Jbeli, the secretary general of al-Nahdah, has become the prime minister of Tunisia. The largely ceremonial presidency has been held by Moncef Marzouki, the head of the Congress for the Republic. And Mustafa Ben Jaafar, the head of the Ettakatol, has been elected as the speaker of the assembly which will draft a new constitution within one year. Soon, the coalition government took office in December 24, 2011.

So is the Muslim Brotherhood and Salafi Call Umbrella Movement. The MB has created their own party, the Freedom and Justice Party in April, 2011; the Salafi Call Umbrella Movement has set up several parties, including al-Nour Party in June, 2011. And then the Freedom and Justice Party and al-Nour Party have respectively won 47.18 percent and 24.29 percent of total 508 seats in the election of the lower house of the parliament held in November, 20119. Besides, they have also secured over 1/3 and 1/4 of total seats respectively in the elections of the upper house of the parliament held in January-February, 2012. Up to the present, Saad al-Katatni, the secretary general of the Muslim Brotherhood, has been elected as the speaker of the lower house of the parliament. Ashraf Thabet, from the al-Nour Party, has been elected as one of the deputy speakers. Moreover, Mohammad Morsi, the president of the Freedom and Justice Party, has officially won the presidential election held in May-June, 2012, and become the new president since the Mubarak regime was overthrown. The new coalition government dominated by the Muslim Brotherhood and the army has taken office in August 2, 2012.

The reason why the Islamists have made historical progress in politics lies in the following aspects.

Firstly, the great adaptability of the Islamist with the current democratic movement is vital for them to win significant victory in politics. Most important, in the aftermath of Arab Spring, whether al-Nahdah, or the Muslim Brotherhood, or the Salafi groups, has begun to reconcile their Islamist tenets with the current need for democracy, equality and secularity (the detailed information will be discussed in next part). The reconciliation is beneficial for the Islamists to reduce the concerns from the secular forces, including the army about the possibility of the implementation of Shari'ah by the Islamists, and to avoid of any likely further repressions. Meanwhile, it has facilitated the Islamists to legalize their parties or organizations the aim which they have pursued for decades of years and further to participate steadily in the current democratic process.

Unlike the above three, there are other Islamist groups, for example, Ḥizb al-Taḥrir in Tunisia which has refused to change their traditional principles at all, still calling for installing a regime based on Shari'ah as before. As a result, it hasn't been legalized in Tunisia and cannot take part in the current democratic process.

Generally speaking, it is the adaptability and timely reconciliation with the democracy that has ensured the Islamists to obtain a good opportunity for survival under new historical conditions and to make further progress in politics.

Secondly, compared with the secular parties in Tunisia or Egypt, many Islamists have been well-organized and influential in their countries. Thus once entering politics, the Islamists can convert their loyal following into political support within short time. For example, after the previous ruling party, Democratic Constitutional Rally (RCD), was dissolved in March,①2011, al-Nahdah has become the most influential organization with nation wide network in Tunisia. It has won more public support of the poor in the southern region in Tunisia. Other numerous parties are mostly secular with small scale and can not win necessary support within short term.

As for the Muslim Brotherhood, it has had an extensive and well-organized network of committed organizers, and has had public support through the charitable work of its professional members throughout most of its history. It is also influential in professional organizations such as the doctors' or lawyers' syndicates, and has built its own companies, factories, schools and hospitals long before the Arab Spring.

The noticeable success of the Salafi Call Umbrella Movement has also reflected its years of organizing throughout the country, which giving them a ready-made network of support when they entered politics. There are two million followers claimed by the movement. The movement has spread in Egypt through nationwide network of Mosques and preachers, religious organizations and a growing number of satellite TV stations. These traditional or modern means have allowed the Salafi message to reach a larger audience in a country of 85 million where one-third of the population is illiterate.②Like the Muslim Brotherhood, the movement has also offered social and medical services to the poor.

The last reason is that, it is not particular in Egypt or Tunisia that the Islamists are influential and could win more public support. It is the common phenomenon in the Middle East region, which to larger extent is decided by the un-thoroughness of the modernization lasting

---

① FAP,Cairo,January 23,2011.
② FAP, Cairo, December 7, 2011.

at least for about one century in this region. The modernization is characteristic with secularity and westernization, which resulting in the establishment of the political system with the separation of politics from region, and of the capitalist economic system in most of the countries. However, in the cultural and social aspects, there is only a minority of the elite class who has accepted to the bottom the western and secular world views, ideologies and values. The majority of the Muslim population has not truly accepted the secular and western outlook.

For example in Egypt, the traditional Islamic beliefs or values reign supreme among village population and the majority of its urban masses[1]. In particular, the village population and the poor are most likely to be influenced by the Islamic culture. They could as well get necessary aids from the Islamists. They therefore constitute the decisive support base of the Islamists. The middle class in this region anyhow hasn't thoroughly supported the ideology of Islamists. Yet, they don't refuse preserving the Islamic culture in the society and politics to some extent and therefore wish to offer an opportunity to the Islamists for ruling after latter's long-term repressions by the autocratic regime.

III. Re-orientation of the Islamist Principles

Following the Arab Spring, the Islamists in the Middle East region have re-oriented their guidelines and principles and exhibited diversified dimensions.

Al-Nahdah has tried to transform itself to be a non-theocratic

---

[1]　John Esposito, *Islam and Politics*, Fourth Edition, New York：Syracuse University Press, 1998, p.311.

'civil party' from an Islamist party. After returning to Tunisia in January, 2011, Rachid Ghannouchi, the previous leader of the party, has repeatedly said that Shari'ah, the Islamic law, 'has no place in Tunisia'; the party opposes the imposition of the Islamic law in Tunisia.[1] He has emphasized that "we have agreed … freedom of conscience, political pluralism, and 'gender equality'". As for the political system, Ghannouchi has said that Tunisia will take the model of Turkey instead of that of the theocratic Iran. From his perspective, the basic principle of Turkish model is the separation of religion from politics, although the state is ruled by an Islamic Party.[2] Other senior leaders of al-Nahdah have expressed similar points of view. They have said that the party will promote Tunisia to be a secular, democratic and modern state. They have agreed that "we are not an Islamist party; we are an Islamic party with the characteristic of Islam"[3].

Actually, al-Nahdah has already accepted the idea of modernity and democracy since the end of 1980s'. In particular from then on, in the thought of Ghannouchi, there has been gradually a deep understanding of Western and Islamic philosophies and a genuine concern for reconciling the basic tenets of Islam with modernity and progress. In his opinion, the West is neither superior nor inferior to Islam. "Ghannouchi sees coexistence and cooperation as the basis for the relationship between the two"[4].

As for the Muslim Brotherhood, in light of the program of the Freedom and Justice Party and the speeches of its senior leaders, this organization has also tried to reconcile its previous political and reli-

---

① 　www. nytimes. com/2011/02/11/world/africa/21tunisia/html/

② 　http://news. hexun. com/2011 – 10 – 27/13459909. html (2011 – 11 – 08).

③ 　http://en. wikipedia. org/wiki(renaissance Party (2011 – 7 – 14).

④ 　John L. Exposito et al, *the Oxford Encyclopedia of the Islamic World*, Volume2, Oxford, Oxford University Press, 2009, p310.

gious goals with modernity, secularity and democracy. Following the Arab Spring, the MB has called for the establishment of a non-theocratic democratic 'civil state' based on the Islamic law. Besides, in its program the FJP has stated that: the state is the source of the authority; the people have the inherent right to select its ruler; freedom, justice and equality are the inherent right of the people; pursuing justice and equality is the supreme goal of the democratic political system, etc. [1] Evidently, the nature of the program is that of the modern western politics instead of the Islamists. Because what the Islamists have argued for most of its history is that: the Qur'ān and the sunnah is all; all rights are derived from or entrusted by Allah, etc. In addition, the FJP also supports the free-market capitalism but "without manipulation or monopoly". Its program would include tourism as a main source of national income. [2] Essam al-Arian, the leading MB member has said, the Freedom and Justice Party will be based on Islamic law, "but will be acceptable to a wide segment of the population" [3]. Namely, the party's membership will open to all Egyptians who accept the term of its program. The spokesman for the party has also said that "the slogans of the revolution-freedom, social justice, equality-all of these are in the Shari'ah ". [4] Morsi, the president of the FJP has said that the party is a non-theocratic 'civil party' instead of the traditional Islamist party. [5]

Moreover, Mohammad Morsi has expressed similar opinions after he won the presidential election. During his 30 – minute speech, Morsi took a symbolic oath as the new president before the General

---

[1] http://en. wikipedia. org/wiki/Freedom_and_Justice_Party_(Egypt) (2011 – 07 – 29).

[2] Http: //en. wikipedia. org/wiki/Freedom and Justice Party (Egypt) (2012 – 09 – 16).

[3] Ibid.

[4] Ibid.

[5] http: //ngzb. gxnews. com. cn/html/2011 – 05/02/content – 536912. htm(2011 – 09 – 13)

Assembly of the Supreme Constitutional Court in June 30, 2012. He promised to lead "a modern, constitutional, national and civil country". He said Egyptians "have established their new life with freedom", and "there will be a great push for the freedom of thinking, change and innovation". Besides, in his inaugural speech as the new president delivered at Cairo University, Morsi said the future constitution will reflect national reconciliation, based on rights, justice and law. And in another speech delivered in Cairo's Tahrir Square, Morsi emphasized that people is the source of power and legitimacy. In addition, he promised to comply Egyptians obligation in regional and international affairs. He said "Egypt respects all the conventions and agreements she signed"[1].

Besides, according to the initial measures the new government led by the MB has taken, its foreign policies have shown the characteristic of the balanced, pragmatism and openness. Morsi or other leading members of the new government has visited Europe, the U. S., other Middle East countries, Africa and some emerging countries like China, Brazil, etc.

As compared with al-Nahdah and the Muslim Brotherhood, al-Nour Party founded by the Salafi Call Umbrella Movement is more conservative although it is undergoing some changes in religious and political aspects. In the past, the Salafi Call Umbrella Movement was apolitical, but now al-Nour Party has positively taken part in the political process. Al-Nour Party has also shown some flexibility in the fulfillment of Shari'ah in Egypt. However, al-Nour Party has insisted that the principles of Shari'ah should be the main source of legislation, although the Christians in Egypt will be allowed to have their

---

① Http://www. chinadaily. com. cn/xinhua/2012 - 06 - 30/content_6320906. html(2012 - 09 - 17).

own separate laws for their internal matters. [1]As for the Israeli-Palestinian conflict, al-Nour party has stated it would be committed to the 1979 Egypt-Israel Peace Treaty as a binding international agreement and willing to hold negotiations with Israel. However, it has said it would seek amendments to the agreement and oppose the normalization with Israel. [2]

Conclusion

Based on the above case study in Egypt and Tunisia, the contemporary Islamists have made unprecedented development in politics, even come to power successfully, and meanwhile have undergone significant changes in their guidelines following the great changes taken place in the beginning of 2011 in Middle East region. Combined with their traditional powerful influence on the grassroots, most of Islamists have also shown their great adaptability with democracy, progress and secularity, both of which are vital for them to survive and make further progress in politics. Most interesting, similar with what the Islamists actually have been within the previous decades of years, the contemporary Islamists have also manifested a diversified development trend in the aftermath of the Arab Spring. As we have mentioned before, the Islamist movement hasn't been a united one from the beginning, with their different focuses ranging from social aspects to political affairs, and also with different political categories from the moderate kind to the extreme one. So is the development trend of the contemporary Islamists in the aftermath of Arab Spring. Since then, most of them have actively tried to reconcile their Islamist tenets with the

---

[1] http://en. wikepedia. org/wiki/al-Nour_party/(2012 – 09 – 16)

[2] Ibid.

current need of democracy, equality and secularity. However, the transformation is to different extent and with diversified orientations. Some, for example, al-Nahdah in Tunisia has inclined to go beyond the attribute of an Islamist party, even the nature of an Islamic organization, with the evident characteristic of secularity. Other Islamists, like the Muslim Brotherhood, has tried to further soften its Islamist principles by calling for the establishment of a non-theocratic "civil state" yet based on the Islamic law, Shari'ah, thus with some characteristic of pragmatism and moderatism. As for al-Nour Party and other Islamists, they have manifested some flexibility in religion and politics, yet are more conservative and rigid than the above two. In addition, there is a minority of the Islamists who has refused to adjust themselves to the changeable political and historical conditions. Now that the Islamists have stepped into power, or taken part in the politics to some extent, their ideologies or guidelines would have great yet different influences on domestic or foreign policies in the future. And it is still too earlier to judge if the Islamists would be successful in ruling, which partly depending on the different ruling tactic of the Islamists, partly on the changeable domestic and outside political conditions as well.

Can Salafis Be Political Actors Like All Others? The Transformations of the Salafi Movement in Post – revolution Egypt

Stéphane Lacroix

My paper will focus on a movement that did not participate in the events of the Egyptian revolution, but which eventually came to be seen as one of the main beneficiaries of the post – revolution period: the Salafi movement. Becoming an influential force in the post – revolution period entailed a cost, however, because this meant that the movement had to abandon its attitude of rupture and retreat and start engaging with others at the social and political level. As a result of this, I argue, Salafis have faced entirely new challenges, and the diversity of responses they provided led to a division of Salafism into three different strains that represent three different social and political attitudes: what I call religious salafism, political – institutional salafism and revolutionary salafism. I will especially focus on the difficulties encountered by the political – institutional Salafi variant to impose itself as a legitimate actor in the eyes of both other actors and its own constituency. I will thus discuss the difficulties of transforming Salafism into a political movement as any other, that is, a movement ready to play by the rules of the political – institutional game.

I'll start with a bit of history, which will also be useful to clarify the concepts I will be using. Although it only started making headlines in the wake of the revolution, the existence of a Salafi movement is nothing new in Egypt. The first association explicitly claiming to be "Salafi" was called "Ansar al – Sunna al – Muhammadiyya" and was created in 1926, two years before the Muslim Brotherhood. But although the two organizations championed the idea of a revival of Islam, they did so in very different ways. For the Muslim Brotherhood, this revival was essentially expressed in political terms – the project of the Brothers was to create an "Islamic State". For Ansar al – Sunna Salafis, in contrast, what was needed was a religious revival, implying both a "purification" of the Muslim creed in order to put it in line with what they deemed to be "original – or Salafi – Islam", and a reform of individual social and religious practices, against Sufism in particular. Ansar al – Sunna, however, stopped short of developing any political vision. Another difference with the Brotherhood was that, far from being a mass movement, Ansar al – Sunna merely constituted a network of religious scholars whose main activity was to edit and publish books from the Salafi tradition.

In the 1970s, Egypt experienced what can be referred to as a second wave of Salafism. Those were the years of Anwar al – Sadat's presidency, and Sadate had allowed for Islamic movements to operate relatively freely in the country. At the forefront of those movements were the university groups called the Gama'at Islamiyya, whose ideology reflected a wide range of influences: they borrowed from the Muslim Brotherhood and they read Sayyid Qutb's books, but they were also very influenced by the Salafi literature made available through Ansar al – Sunna networks. The regional influence of Saudi Arabia, which now possessed the money to export its brand of Islam through a range of government funded institutions, added to the spread of Salafism.

The ambiguity that was present in the Gama' at Islamiyya's ideological fabric soon sparked lively debates among the groups' members. This led to a split around 1977 – 1978. The majority of Gama' at Islamiyya members joined the Muslim Brotherhood, where they were instrumental in reviving the organization which had been greatly weakened under Nasser. This is when Gama' at Islamiyya members Isam al – Aryan and Abd al – Mun' im Abu al – Futuh, among others, joined the Muslim Brotherhood. Others disagreed and advocated a radical and violent approach understood in the terms of Sayyid Qutb: those founded the group called al – Gama' a al – Islamiyya (in the singular form), later co – responsible for Sadat's assassination.

Finally, a third group decided to distance itself from the ideas of the Muslim Brotherhood altogether, and adopt a pure "Salafi" approach. The leading figures of that group were students at the faculty of Medicine of Alexandria University: among them were Yasir Burhami and Muhammad Isma' il al – Muqaddim. They decided to establish an organization which they called "al – da' wa al – salafiyya", the Salafi call or the Salafi da'wa. Just like Ansar al – Sunna, the Salafi da'wa's proclaimed that its aim was to purify the Muslim creed along Salafi lines, and to "correct" what was wrong in the Egyptian Muslims' social and religious practices. Their action was therefore limited to preaching, and had no explicit political dimension. And for the next three decades, they would make sure to avoid the political issue altogether.

The difference with Ansar al – Sunna, however, was that the Salafi da' wa's founders, despite being apolitical, *were harakiyyin* (activists). What they wanted the Salafi da' wa to be was a mass movement with a cohesive and well – organized structure, along lines somewhat similar to the Muslim Brotherhood. One of the founders of the organization was appointed as " *al - qayyim* " - the Salafi da'wa's equivalent of Muslim Brotherhood's guide, *al - murshid* . In the wake of Sadat's assassination in 1981, the Salafi da'wa, unlike most other Islamic groups, escaped persecution because of its quietist stance. In the subsequent years, the Salafi da'wa did even sometimes benefit from the covert support of the Egyptian security apparatus, which saw the Salafis as a useful counterforce to the more politicized Islamist groups. To be sure, the Salafis were also closely monitored and sometimes repressed, but they were in a much more favourable position than their competitors. In this context, the Salafi da'wa was able to expand its influence, beyond Alexandria, to most Egyptian governorates[1].

In the 2000s, the government decided to step up its anti - Brotherhood strategy by allowing Salafis to open satellite TV channels, many of them broadcasted through Nile Sat. Within a few years, about ten Salafi channels were created. Soon, they became extremely popular with Egyptian viewers, turning certain preachers such as Muhammad Hassan into nationwide "stars". This allowed Salafism to gain hundreds of thousands of sympathizers, and to extend its influence far beyond the organized networks of the Salafi da'wa.

When the revolution started on the 25th of January 2011, most Salafi cheikhs called for their followers not to join the protests. For a group which advocated individual religious reform, and did not believe that political activism was useful at all, that was hardly surprising. But the on the 8th of February, a few days before the fall of Mubarak, the Salafi leaders revised their position. The protests were no longer described as *fitna* ("chaos") but as *thawra* ("revolution"). Most

---

① See Stéphane Lacroix, *Sheikhs and Politicians: Inside the New Egyptian Salafism* , Brookings Doha Center Publications n°16, June 2012

observers at the time saw this as mere opportunism; this would however retrospectively mark the beginning of a deep evolution inside Egyptian Salafism.

In the wake of the revolution, a few figures in the Salafi da'wa argued that, because the context had changed, the da'wa's position towards politics should change as well. For them, this meant that, just as Muslim Brotherhood was about to establish its political party, the Freedom and Justice Party, the da'wa should establish its own party as well. The rationale was that, now that the political sphere was open, the Salafis needed a political representation to defend their interests and expand their influence.

Spearheading those calls was a man whose profile was relatively peculiar within the Salafi da'wa: Imad Abd al – Ghaffur, a doctor who had spent the last ten years living in Turkey where he had been working. As Abd al – Ghaffur explained to me in an interview, the Turkish experience of Islamic politics opened his mind, and he was waiting for the opportunity to "make the Salafi da'wa benefit from this experience"[1]. At the same time, Abd al – Ghaffur carried a lot of weight within the da'wa: he had been one of the founders of the organization in the late 1970s, and although he had moved away from it, he continued to enjoy great respect within it. After numerous debates, Abd al – Ghaffur managed to convince the da'wa's leadership to support his project. The role of Imad Abd al – Ghaffur was crucial here, because I don't think what happened was a natural evolution at all; Salafis could well have decided to remain out of politics, as happened with the Tunisian Salafis, most of whom have until now refused to enter the political sphere and even refuse any contact with the media.

---

[1] Interview with Imad Abd al – Ghaffur, Cairo, January 2012

The creation of Hizb al – Nur ("the party of light") was announced on the 15th of June 2011, and Abd al – Ghaffur was appointed as its president. Officially, Hizb al – Nur was to be the political arm of the Salafi da'wa, and the da'wa's help was instrumental in setting up the party. Within a couple of weeks, it already claimed 100000 members across Egypt. One of the early goals of Hizb al – Nur was to impose its existence as a political entity entirely independent in its agenda from the Muslim Brotherhood. This was needed because many Egyptians saw the Salafis as nothing more than a "reservoir of support" for the Brotherhood. This explains why Hizb al – Nur chose to compete against the Brotherhood in the legislative elections starting in November 2011. The competition was extremely fierce, but the Salafis were able to score a number of points.

First, the Salafis denounced the Brothers as "candidates of the old system", blaming them for being apparatchiks and opportunists who had happily participated in the fa? ade democracy of the Mubarak years. In turn, the Salafis turned their quietism during the Mubarak years into an advantage: because they had not been involved in politics, they argued, they had not been compromised. As opposed to the Brothers, they were entirely new political actors, and therefore the most capable of representing real change. To reinforce this impression, Hizb al – Nur strategically appointed spokesmen of a relatively young age, with no past in politics. One of them, the 28 – year old Nadir Bakkar, an elegant young man with a degree in management, generated a tremendous media hype. All the Brothers had to offer in return were spokesmen in their 50s, who had been in politics for decades and could not represent any form of renewal. In addition, Hizb al – Nur was quick to denounce the allegedly bourgeois nature of the Muslim Brotherhood and its leadership, described as disconnected from Egyptian society. Hizb al – Nur portrayed itself, in turn, as a true representative of the lowest classes of society.

This rhetoric was extremely effective. This, in addition to the fact that the party was able to rely on the extensive networks of the Salafi da'wa, mainly explains the success of Hizb al – Nur's campaign for the legislative elections. Against all odds, Salafis received about 29% of the votes, and 24% of the seats in the parliament. This success gave Hizb al – Nur an increasing assertiveness, not only in Egyptian politics, but also vis – à – vis the Salafi da'wa whose political arm it was initially supposed to represent.

From the beginning, Hizb al – Nur had been an entirely new experiment for Salafis. Because the Salafi da'wa had for the last thirty years systematically avoided political issues, Hizb al – Nur had had to elaborate its political discourse from scratch. It did so in a rather surprising way, by forming a committee of academics, many of them non – Salafis, to write the party's platform. The Hizb al – Nur leadership discussed the platform with them to make sure a number of religious red lines were not crossed, yet the result was a platform that was hardly distinguishable from that of any other party, except maybe for a slightly stronger insistence on the "Islamic reference". At the same time, the party's platform advocated "democracy" and "equal rights between Muslims and Christians". To be accepted by the commission of parties, the party had to include a certain percentage of Christians among its founding members – which it did. And finally, to be allowed to participate in the elections, it had to include a woman on each of its lists – which, again, it did, although the party did not publish the pictures of those women.

All of this represented a clear break from the positions of the Salafi da'wa: da'wa sheikhs had in the past denounced democracy as *kufr* ("impiety"), and insisted that Copts were not equal to Muslims. The involvement of women in the public sphere is also something the da'wa had always rejected. Despite this, it seems that the Salafi da'wa first accepted those concessions, convinced that they were the price to pay to enter the political sphere, and that they did not reflect a genuine commitment. Soon, however, conflicts between Hizb al – Nur and the Salafi da'wa started to occur. Those were the result of the autonomous dynamic to which the creation of Hizb al – Nur had given birth. With the foundation of Hizb al – Nur, a new social category had emerged, the Salafi politician, who increasingly identified with the political sphere and its rules, and developed what Bourdieu would call a political habitus. The result, I argue, was the birth of a new social phenomenon which I describe as political – institutional Salafism, clearly distinct from the religious Salafism of the Salafi da'wa's sheikhs.

Some of the examples mentioned previously illustrate this phenomenon: as explained earlier, Hizb al – Nur framed its competition with the Brotherhood in political terms, not in religious ones. That is, instead of trying to outbid the Muslim Brotherhood on religious ground as many had expected, what they did – by calling the Brotherhood "candidates of the system" and bourgeois – was playing on the political weaknesses of the Brothers.

Let us look at a few issues on which an open conflict between Hizb al – Nur and the Salafi da'wa took place. One was the question of political alliances. Imad Abd al – Ghaffur and Nadir Bakkar both declared on numerous occasions that Hizb al – Nur would have no problem forging political alliances with non – Islamist parties – even leftist or liberal ones – as long as they agreed on a number of shared political goals. This owed them an extraordinarily virulent response by Yaser Burhami, the leading figure of the Salafi da'wa, arguing that an Islamic party can only ally itself with other Islamic parties who share the common goal of implementing sharia. Here, the distinction between the political and the religious logic was clear.

Another clash happened when Muhammad Nur, one of Hizb al – Nur's spokesmen, attended a celebration for the Iranian revolution organized by the Iranian diplomatic bureau in Cairo. As a leading Egyptian political party, Muhammad Nur argued, it is normal for Hizb al – Nur to have relations with all states. But the sheikhs of the Salafi da'wa did not see it that way, and they were quick to denounce Muhammad Nur, using the Salafi theological argument that Shiites were heretics and that true Muslims should have no relation to them. Again, this reveals the distinction between the political logic of Hizb al – Nur and the religious, or even theological, logic of the Salafi da'wa[1].

The next major controversial stance of Hizb al – Nur was taken in April 2012. This is when Hizb al – Nur officially announced that, after an internal vote, it decided to back Abd al – Mun'im Abu al – Futuh for the presidential elections. Abu al – Futuh, an ex – Muslim Brotherhood leader, was known to be a liberal Islamist, and had previously received the support of leftists and liberals. The justifications provided by Hizb al – Nur Salafis were strikingly political: "the party didn't request from Abul Futuh that he commit to implementing the rulings of the sharia, and he didn't even offer that. We decided to support him because of his national project which permits the consensus of all national forces to rebuild Egypt and get it out of the dark tunnel". After which, he added: "We are not electing a Caliph or Amir al – mu'minin, just a president"[2].

---

[1] See Stéphane Lacroix, *Sheikhs and Politicians: Inside the New Egyptian Salafism*, Brookings Doha Center Publications n°16, June 2012

[2] "*Al – Nur wa – l – jama'a al – islamiyya: qana'atuna bi – l – mashru' al – watani li – Abu al – Futuh wara' ta'yidina lahu* (Al – Nour and al – Gama'a al – Islamiyya: we are supporting Abul Futuh because of our belief in his national project)," Al – Masriyyun, May 15, 2012

The comparison with the rhetoric used by the Brotherhood to support Morsi is striking: on the one hand, the Brotherhood were saying that there was only one Islamic candidate, Mohammed Morsi, and that Muslims had to vote for Morsi. On the other hand, Salafis were supporting Abu al – Futuh with purely political arguments, arguing that his policies were the best for the country. In a way, Hizb al – Nur had pushed so far its identification with the political sphere that it was now using an almost secular rhetoric.

Support for Abu al – Futuh wasn't however very popular within the Salafi da'wa. A number of leading sheikhs from the da'wa, including Muhammad Ismail al – Muqaddim and Sa'id Abd al – Azim, first publicly rejected the calls to support Abu al – Futuh. The difference between this controversy and the previous ones was however that this time, because of Hizb al – Nur's success in the legislative elections, the balance of power was much more favourable to Hizb al – Nur than to the Salafi da'wa. And so Hizb al – Nur's leadership was able to convince the Salafi da'wa to eventually join in and announce its support for Abu al – Futuh.

Hizb al – Nur and the Salafi da'wa organized meetings in support of Abu al – Futuh, and got involved in his campaign. In spite of this, Abu al – Futuh only came fourth in the first round of the presidential elections with 17% of the votes. This was a blow to Hizb al – Nur politicians and the whole strategy of political – institutional salafism. The Salafi base, it seems, was never able to understand the leadership's choice to back Abu al – Futuh. According to interviews made by the author, it seems that the majority of Salafis did not vote for Abu al – Futuh: some voted Morsi, some invalidated their votes, some stayed at home, and it seems even a few voted for the Nasserian Hamdin Sabbahi in order to make sure Abu al – Futuh wouldn't make it to the second round. [1]

This had three major consequences. First, the rivalry between religious salafism and political – institutional salafism, or in other terms between the Salafi da'wa and Hizb al – Nur, was revived, this time with the Hizb al – Nur leadership in a weaker position than ever. This led to an open confrontation between the two factions in September 2012, with the question of Hizb al – Nur's independence from the da'wa at the center of all debates[2]. After members of the conservative faction first tried to oust Imad Abd al – Ghaffur, they agreed to keep him in his current position until the next parliamentary elections are held. Then, a new president should be elected, and the pro – da'wa faction plans to present one of its representatives with the clear intention of regaining control of the party.

A second consequence is that growing calls are now being heard among Salafi sheikhs to declare the experiment of political – institutional Salafism a failure and to abandon politics altogether and revert to da'wa.

Finally, the apparent failure of political – institutional salafism could also benefit another group, which represents a third strain of Salafism that emerged in the second half of 2011: those I call "revolutionary Salafis". Just as Imad Abd al – Ghaffur is the godfather of political – institutional salafism, the main figure of revolutionary salafism is Hazem Salah Abu Isma'il. Abu Isma'il is a preacher and a lawyer, who is the son of a prominent figure of the Muslim Brotherhood, but who embraced Salafi ideas. Though he was not very well known before the revolution, Abu Isma'il has become a star in Egyptian politics since the Summer 2011. While religious Salafis remained in the

---

[1]   Interviews in Cairo and Alexandria, May 2012

[2]   Interview with Muhammad Nur, Amman, October 2012

mosques, and while political – institutional Salafis joined formal politics with the aim of entering parliament, Abu Isma'il built his legitimacy in a place in which Salafis had earlier been mostly absent: the
street, especially Tahrir square. There, breaking with the more moderate leanings of Hizb al – Nur, Abu Isma'il and his followers attended every demonstration they could to vocally express their opposition
to military rule in Egypt. In parallel, Abu Isma'il called for the establishment of a true Islamic State in the country, and for the immediate implementation of Sharia.

　　While his radical opposition to the SCAF earned him some respect among the broader revolutionary constituency, Abu Isma'il's
political program, in all its simplicity, attracted a growing number of
Salafis, especially from the youth. During the street battles of Muhammad Mahmud in November 2011, his appearances in front of his
followers were almost mystical moments: to them, he was nearly a
messiah, a saviour – figure who was seen as "having come to rescue
Egypt"[1]. A development worrying to some was that Abu Isma'il's
discourse had clear jihadi undertones: nothing surprising there, since
the language of revolution in Salafi Islam is precisely the language of
jihad. Consequently, a growing number of jihadis – many of them
former members of the group al – Jihad released after the revolution –
also started gathering around Abu Isma'il.

　　What complicated things was that Abu Isma'il had also declared
his candidacy to the Egyptian presidency. The momentum around him
was so strong that by March 2012, he had at least 20% in most of the
polls – some even ranked him first. The possibility of him winning
the election was taken seriously in Egypt and abroad. This was a
headache not just for most external and domestic actors, but also for

---

①　Interviews with proponents of Abu Isma'il, Cairo, November 2011 the major Salafi groups, including the leaderships of the Salafi da'wa and Hizb al – Nur. The reasons were that, first, Abu Isma'il's revolutionary rhetoric represented a complete departure from their traditional stances, and they rejected it; and second, they feared the rise to power of this proclaimed Salafi over which they had no control whatsoever. They made it clear that they would not support him, but they knew he was deeply appealing to their bases. What was even more embarrassing is that tens of Hizb al – Nur MPs, along with some of the major Salafi sheikhs, openly expressed support for Abu Isma' il. Early April 2012, their relief came from the Egyptian electoral commission which allegedly discovered that Abu Isma'il's mother, who spent the last part of her life in the United States, had obtained American citizenship. This represented a breach to Egyptian electoral law, and Abu Isma'il was disqualified. Although Abu Isma'il denied the fact, he was now out of the race.

Despite this, Abu Isma'il's star has continued to shine. And it is rumoured that a lot of Salafis, when told by the Salafi leadership to vote for Abu al – Futuh, actually put hand – written papers with Abu Isma'il's name in the ballot boxes. Since June 2012, Abu Isma'il has become active again, and he is currently founding a political party representative of his revolutionary Salafi line called Hizb al – Umma. Given the crisis it is going through, Hizb al – Nur may lose a significant part of its membership to Hizb al – Umma. And if this is doesn't happen, it is likely that Hizb al – Nur will have to radicalize its political line to compete with the maximalism of Hizb al – Umma. This may already be happening: Hizb al – Nur had previously insisted that it wouldn't call for strengthening the current Egyptian constitution's article 2 which states that "The principles (*mabadi*) of the shari'a are the main source of legislation". Now, Hizb al – Nur is pushing for it to be rephrased as "the rulings (*ahkam*) of the shari'a are the main source of legislation" – a much more explicit, and constraining, formulation.

All in all, the experiment of political – institutional Salafism is currently going through a real crisis. A possible explanation would be that, given the position already occupied by the Muslim Brotherhood in the political sphere, there was simply no durable political space available for a party such as Hizb al – Nur. If this is the case, one could say that political – institutional Salafism simply benefited from a favourable opportunity structure in the late 2011, but its success was purely contextual. The failure of political – institutional Salafism – if it is confirmed, and this still remains to be seen – would see Egyptian Salafism revert to the same tension that existed before the revolution between a religious Salafism generally weary of the political logic, and a revolutionary Salafism increasingly reminiscent of Jihadi Salafism. However, a lot will still depend on the performance of president Mursi, which may open new opportunities for Salafis. Hence, Salafi politicians may not have said their last word.

埃及伊斯兰主义者向爱资哈尔
宗教权威的挑战

王锁劳

2011 年 2 月 11 日,在位将近 30 年的埃及老总统穆巴拉克被迫将总统职权移交给武装部队最高委员会。不久,由穆巴拉克担任主席的埃及执政党——"民族民主党"被司法部门强行解散。埃及"一·二五革命"由此取得了第一个胜利,打破了"一个政党、一个领袖、一个总统"的僵化政治格局。此后由军人组成的"武装部队最高委员会"(Supreme Council of the Armed Forces,简称最高委员会)对埃及实行军管,直至 2012 年 6 月 30 日新总统宣誓就职为止。在军管期间,最高委员会批准了一系列法律,为埃及的政治过渡奠定了必要基础。其中最高委员会于 2011 年 3 月 28 日发布的第 12 号法令,对 1977 年第 40 号法律《政党法》进行了较为全面的修正,以适应革命后建立多党选举制的要求。修正案简化了成立新党的条件,明确规定:党的原则、纲领和行动方式不能建立在宗教、阶级、性别、语言等基础上,并且必须拥有至少 5000 签名的创始成员,而且签名名单必须上报政党事务委员会核实。[①] 但在实际操作过程中,一些明确追求宗教目的的政党,如下面介绍的四个政党,最终也获得了政党事务委员会的批准,拥有了在

---

① "The Main Features of the Amended Law on Political Parties 2011", Decree No. 12 Issued by the Supreme Council of the Armed Forces, March 28, 2011, 见埃及国家信息网:http://www. sis. gov. eg/En/LastPage. aspx? Category_ID = 1162

埃及合法从政的身份。

最大的伊斯兰政党是穆斯林兄弟会（Muslim Brotherhood，简称穆兄会）下属的"自由与正义党"（Freedom and Justice Party，缩写 FJP），它于 2011 年 4 月 30 日宣布成立，选举穆兄会高级成员穆罕默德·穆尔西（Mohamed Morsi）担任党的主席。第二大伊斯兰政党是赛莱菲达瓦集团（Al-Dawa Al-Salafiya）于 5 月 12 日宣布成立的"光明党"（Al-Nour Party），选举伊迈德丁·阿卜杜·加福尔（Emad al-Din Abdul Ghafoor）担任党的主席。第三大伊斯兰政党是伊斯兰集团（Islamic Group）于 6 月 20 日宣布成立的"建设与发展党"（Construction & Development Party），塔利格·祖马尔（Tareq Al-Zomor）出任党的领导人。第四大伊斯兰政党是 8 月 30 日被批准成立的"真道党"（Al-Asalah Party），它是由另一些赛莱菲人士创建的，阿迪勒·阿卜杜·马格苏德·阿菲菲（Adel Abdel-Maksoud Afifi）是该党的主要领导人。这四个伊斯兰政党在埃及革命后的过渡阶段发挥了重要作用，本文关注的重点是这些伊斯兰政党与爱资哈尔系统错综复杂的关系。

所谓爱资哈尔系统，是指在爱资哈尔清真寺基础上形成的一个庞大宗教体系，其职责和使命主要包括阿拉伯语学习、伊斯兰教知识传授、《古兰经》与"圣训"研究、教法解释与教法令发布、教职人员培养、宗教书籍发行与出版，等等。爱资哈尔体系的组织机构主要包括爱资哈尔清真寺、爱资哈尔长老府、埃及穆夫提总院、爱资哈尔大学、伊斯兰研究院等。爱资哈尔清真寺（Al-Azhar Mosque）建成于公元 972 年，由当时统治埃及的法蒂玛王朝哈里发下令而建，字面意思为"最辉煌华丽的清真寺"，据说源于对先知穆罕默德女儿法蒂玛·扎赫拉（Fatimah Al-Zahrah）的纪念。① 爱资哈尔清真寺的教长就是"爱资哈尔长老"（Sheikh Al-Azhar），这一称号同时拥有"爱资哈尔大伊玛目"（Grand Imam of Al-Azhar）头衔，他是埃及逊尼派穆斯林的最高宗教领袖。爱资哈尔长老府（Mashyakhdom of Al-Azhar）是爱资哈尔长老的日常行政办事机构，是爱资哈尔最高宗教权力施展之地。埃及穆夫提总院（Dar Al-Ifta Al-Misriyyah）是埃及大穆夫提（Grand Mufti）的日常行

---

① 祁学义：《爱资哈尔大学教育和学术功能探析》，《阿拉伯世界研究》，2009 年第 2 期，第 76 页。

政办事机构,是埃及官方最高的教法解释和教法令发布之地。爱资哈尔大学(Al-Azhar University)是埃及伊斯兰最高宗教学府,专门培养伊斯兰高级宗教人才,也被视为全世界逊尼派穆斯林的最高宗教学府。爱资哈尔大学日常事务由爱资哈尔大学校长(President of Al-Azhar University)负责,接受爱资哈尔长老的领导。伊斯兰研究院(Academy of Islamic Research)是爱资哈尔系统的研究单位,其成员都是学富五车的宗教学者。

　　虽然爱资哈尔在埃及享有至高无上的宗教地位,但爱资哈尔的宗教权威并非没有遭遇过质疑和挑战。历史上爱资哈尔曾经长期享有相对独立的宗教地位,能够自主开展教学与研究,甚至能够就一些影响穆斯林生活的重大政治与社会问题发表独立见解,与当时的政治领袖并不总是保持一致。然而,埃及前总统纳赛尔(Gamal Abdel Nasser, 1956 – 1970)于1960年代对爱资哈尔进行现代化改革,在爱资哈尔大学新增商业、医学和工程等非宗教学科,同时将爱资哈尔长老、大穆夫提和爱资哈尔大学校长的任免权力掌握在政府手上。爱资哈尔系统成为埃及政府用以达到政治目的的"宗教工具或盾牌",逐渐丧失了相对独立的宗教地位。[①] 2011年埃及革命推翻了穆巴拉克政权,一方面使长期受到压制的伊斯兰主义者(Islamist)获得解放,为伊斯兰政党登上政治舞台扫清了道路;另一方面使长期受到穆巴拉克支持的爱资哈尔系统遭受打击,为伊斯兰政党大胆向爱资哈尔发起挑战和索取宗教特权创造了条件。

伊斯兰政党威逼爱资哈尔长老辞职

　　爱资哈尔现任长老是艾哈迈德·塔伊布博士(Ahmed Al-Tayeb),他是前总统穆巴拉克于2010年3月18日通过第62号总统令任命的,接替于3月10日突然在沙特访问时去世的前爱资哈尔长老穆罕默德·赛义德·坦塔维博士(Muhammad Sayyid Tantawy),穆巴拉克当时因病在德国接受治

---

① Hossam Tamam, "A revival of Al-Azhar", *Al-Ahram Weekly*, 19 – 25 August 2010, Issue No. 1012. http://weekly. ahram. org. eg/2010/1012/focus. htm

疗。① 穆巴拉克任命塔伊布为埃及伊斯兰教领袖,是有充分理由的:其一,塔伊布曾任执政党——民族民主党政策计划委员会的成员,而穆巴拉克为该党的主席,穆巴拉克的次子贾拉勒为该委员会书记;其二,塔伊布曾于2002 – 2003 年任埃及大穆夫提,其后又长期担任爱资哈尔大学校长(2003 – 2010),他可说是爱资哈尔系统中最负声望的宗教领袖;第三,塔伊布根红苗正,从小接受爱资哈尔传统教育,1969 年毕业于爱资哈尔大学宗教基础学院,他不仅精通伊斯兰历史文化,而且通晓西方历史文化,在法国索邦大学获得博士学位,能够熟练运用法语和英语;第四,塔伊布素以博学、开明、温和著称,他深谙爱资哈尔的古老传统,反对激进和极端宗教思潮,坚持中间主义和温和理性的思想路线。②

正因为塔伊布长老与前执政党和穆巴拉克父子关系密切,在埃及18天革命中塔伊布长老总体上保持低调,既不明确表态支持革命,也不明确表态反对革命。这种模棱两可的态度引起部分爱资哈尔师生的强烈不满,一些师生自发前往解放广场,高举“爱资哈尔支持革命”的标语。甚至爱资哈尔官方发言人穆罕默德·拉法阿·塔赫塔维(Muhammad Rifaa Al-Tahtawi),也于2011 年2 月4 日辞职,宣布支持解放广场的示威者,要求穆巴拉克立即辞去总统职务。③ 穆巴拉克政权垮台后,塔伊布长老一度饱受攻击,攻击既来自社会各界,也来自爱资哈尔系统内部,包括同情穆兄会和赛莱菲的人士。爱资哈尔长老府的工作人员曾于3 月下旬把大门锁上,阻止塔伊布长老进入他的办公室。塔伊布长老被迫向掌权的军方最高领导人坦塔维元帅(Mohamed Hussein Tantawi)提出辞职,但是没有被后者接受。④ 这是塔伊布长老在革命后第2 次提出辞职,此前在3 月上旬他第1 次提出辞职,引发爱资哈尔师生举行大规模游行,要求他收回辞呈,继续留

---

① 《穆巴拉克恢复活动、任命爱资哈尔长老》,埃及《金字塔报》,2010 年3 月19 日。

② 爱迈尼·马吉德:《塔伊布:我将坚持爱资哈尔的中间主义》,埃及《金字塔报》,2010 年3 月19 日。

③ "Al-Azhar spokesman resigns and joins Tahrir protesters", *Egypt Independent*, February 4, 2011.

④ 瓦利德·阿卜杜·拉赫曼:《埃及:爱资哈尔长老第2 次提交辞呈 武装部队拒绝接受》,伦敦《中东报》,2011 年3 月23 日。

任爱资哈尔长老之位。①

　　进入革命后的第二年,塔伊布长老再次遭遇强大的辞职压力,不过这次并非来自爱资哈尔系统,而是来自掌握了议会和政府实权的伊斯兰政党,尤其是穆兄会下属的自由与正义党以及赛莱菲阵营的光明党。2012 年 6 月 30 日,革命后的首位民选总统穆罕默德·穆尔西宣誓任职。当天下午穆尔西总统前往母校开罗大学发表就任总统后的首次公开演讲,根据礼仪规定,在演讲前总统应该单独接见前来祝贺的达官贵人。爱资哈尔长老相当于副总理级别,应该属于被接见的尊贵客人。可是塔伊布长老一直在大厅等候,眼见其他贵宾都被领到单独场所与总统会见,却无人过来理睬他。为了捍卫爱资哈尔的尊严,塔伊布长老一怒拂袖而去。穆兄会与爱资哈尔的冲突就这样公开爆发了。显然穆尔西总统或他的手下故意怠慢了爱资哈尔长老,而爱资哈尔长老也在内心深处反感这位一张口便拿伊斯兰教说事的非专业宗教人士。但在舆论压力下,穆尔西总统于 7 月 3 日打电话给塔伊布长老,主动表达歉意并示好,而塔伊布长老则表示感谢。② 表面看来,这场危机好像结束了,实则不然,双方的芥蒂反而更加深了。

　　穆尔西身为总统,按照穆巴拉克时代的惯例,他拥有任免爱资哈尔长老的权力。但是在革命以后,为了显示与穆巴拉克时代的决裂,他不能简单照搬和沿袭穆巴拉克时代的做法,他在考虑使用其他办法撤免爱资哈尔长老。他在全国大学生联合会第一次总会开幕式上说"要求对爱资哈尔进行根本性的变革,正在通过稳步的实际步骤进行当中"③。他表示支持在最近通过选举原则对爱资哈尔长老和爱资哈尔大学校长进行更换。以塔伊布长老为首的爱资哈尔高层,明显感受到了来自总统府的敌意,不得不采取措施以求自保。他们根据《调整爱资哈尔法》的规定,于 2012 年 7 月 9 日组成了"大乌里玛(Ulema)协会"(Grand Ulema Association),其成员共有

---

　　① 瓦利德·阿卜杜·拉赫曼:《爱资哈尔集会 卢克索省要求爱资哈尔长老保留其职》,伦敦《中东报》,2011 年 3 月 8 日。

　　② 穆罕默德·阿布杜·哈桑宁:《埃及:爱资哈尔长老在接到共和国总统的电话后危机结束》,伦敦《中东报》,2012 年 7 月 4 日。

　　③ 瓦利德·阿卜杜·拉赫曼:《埃及:大乌里玛协会宣布支持塔伊布 穆尔西总统支持选举爱资哈尔长老》,伦敦《中东报》,2012 年 9 月 18 日。

26 名,以爱资哈尔长老为会长。大乌里玛协会成员都是非常著名的宗教学者,该机构可说是埃及伊斯兰教权威的最高代表。①9 月 17 日,大乌里玛协会召开会议,一致通过决议,支持塔伊布继续留任爱资哈尔长老。这就等于否定了穆尔西总统关于撤换爱资哈尔长老的决心,剥夺了穆尔西总统以及总统背后的穆兄会干涉爱资哈尔宗教事务的合法性。②

进入革命后的第三年,爱资哈尔长老又一次面对辞职压力,这一次直接来自爱资哈尔大学生,间接来自伊斯兰政党。2013 年 4 月 1 日中午,爱资哈尔大学学生城食堂发生食物中毒事件,大约 500 多名学生入院治疗。事件发生后,情绪激动的爱资哈尔学生举行抗议示威,要求爱资哈尔长老和爱资哈尔大学校长立即辞职。为了平息事态,爱资哈尔最高委员会只好将爱资哈尔大学校长乌萨玛·阿卜杜(Osama El-Abd)革职。③无独有偶,4 月 29 日晚,大约 161 名爱资哈尔大学生在晚饭后再次出现中毒症状。事件发生后,又有不少学生上街游行,甚至阻断城市道路,要求爱资哈尔长老辞职。连续在同一所大学发生两起同类事件,看来像是有人蓄意破坏,不像是食物变质或污染。根据检察官的调查,爱资哈尔大学城饮食科科长阿提夫·法鲁克·穆罕默德作证说,在第二次中毒事件发生的当天下午 2 点左右,100 多名男女学生在爱资哈尔学生会主席的率领下,强行闯入食堂厨房,随后当天晚上 8 点就出现了中毒事件。鉴于爱资哈尔学生会与穆兄会关系密切,一些阿拉伯媒体作家猜测,食物中毒事件的主谋可能是穆兄会,目的是威逼爱资哈尔长老辞职。④

---

① 瓦利德·阿卜杜·拉赫曼:《组成埃及大乌里玛协会 消息人士否认爱资哈尔长老干预了成员名单》,伦敦《中东报》,2012 年 7 月 10 日。

② 瓦利德·阿卜杜·拉赫曼:《埃及:大乌里玛协会宣布支持塔伊布 穆尔西总统支持选举爱资哈尔长老》,伦敦《中东报》,2012 年 9 月 18 日。

③ "Al-Azhar sacks university president over food poisoning scandal", *Ahram Online*, 3 April 2013, http://english. ahram. org. eg/NewsContent/1/64/68365/Egypt/Politics-/AlAzhar-sacks-university-president-over-food-poiso. aspx

④ 穆罕默德·阿里·易卜拉欣:《杀害爱资哈尔长老》,伦敦《阿拉伯人报》,2013 年 5 月 3 日。另见穆罕默德·哈马西:《针对爱资哈尔长老的阴谋》,伦敦《阿拉伯人报》,2013 年 4 月 4 日。

爱资哈尔反对伊斯兰政党挑起宗教矛盾

为什么爱资哈尔长老遭到伊斯兰政党的排斥？笔者认为,主要源于爱资哈尔长老和他所代表的爱资哈尔系统,与伊斯兰政党在以下几个重大问题上的尖锐对立。

第一,反对取消或修改1971年宪法第二条。埃及18天革命后,要求修改宪法的社会呼声持续高涨。现行埃及宪法是1971年通过的,第二条规定:"伊斯兰教是埃及国教,阿拉伯语是埃及官方语言,伊斯兰教法原则是立法的主要源泉。"这一条当初在1971年制定和在1980年修订时就存在着极大争议,如今在革命后的新形势下争议再现。主要表现为三种观点:一是自由派和世俗派知识分子的观点,认为应该回归1923年宪法,突出埃及的"世俗性",强调穆斯林和基督徒完全平等,取消宪法中关于伊斯兰教是埃及国教的规定。二是科普特基督徒的观点,正如埃及科普特教会官方发言人拉菲克·杰里什(Rafiq Jarish)所表达的,他形容第二条是"国家机构内所有狂热分子的肥沃土壤",要求宪法不应包含任何宗教色彩,即便保留第二条,也应把伊斯兰教法定为立法源泉之一,而不是主要源泉。①三是伊斯兰政党的观点,赛莱菲真道党副主席马穆杜哈·伊斯梅尔(Mamduh Is-mail)称:真道党坚持修改现在的宪法第二条,建议取消"原则"一词,使这一条变为"伊斯兰教法是立法的主要源泉"。他说:"取消仅仅针对'原则'一词,该条其他部分保持不变。"②

以上三种观点虽然内容不同,但都属于修改派,只是修改的目的和方向大相径庭。爱资哈尔系统提出了另一种观点,既反对取消第二条,也反对修改第二条。早在2011年2月15日革命刚过,针对要求取消宪法第二

---

① 沙阿班·阿卜杜·希塔尔:《宪法第2条惹争议 尽管反对将其纳入修订范围》,伦敦《中东报》,2011年2月17日。

② 瓦利德·阿卜杜·拉赫曼、玛丽·瓦只底:《关于宪法第2条出现分歧 爱资哈尔否认达成中间建议》,伦敦《中东报》,2012年7月7日。

条的呼声,塔伊布长老就批评道:"这些呼声是在挑动灾难,为动乱打开大门。"①后来在修宪过程中,他又多次强调:"宪法第 2 条是红线,危害它就是在危害民族属性。"②爱资哈尔的立场遭到赛莱菲人士的强烈攻击。不少赛莱菲组织将实施伊斯兰教法视为伊斯兰国家的法定义务,作为其建党或集会的主要政策目标。因此,他们坚持主张修改宪法第二条,取消"原则"一词,体现"伊斯兰教法"在新宪法中的神圣地位。2012 年 11 月 9 日,多个赛莱菲组织在解放广场联合举行示威集会,大约有 2 万名支持者参加,一些赛莱菲头面人物纷纷到场,如马格迪·赛义德长老(Magdi Al-Sayed)、阿卜杜拉·沙克尔(Abdallah Shaker),以及赛莱菲总统候选人哈姆宰·艾布·伊斯梅尔(Hazem Abu Ismail)等。③

在爱资哈尔长老与赛莱菲人士的斗争中,越来越多的埃及人担心修改宪法第二条将开启教派冲突之门,导致穆斯林与科普特基督徒的严重对立和埃及社会的分裂,故此爱资哈尔长老的立场最后被广泛接受。在立宪会议提交的供全民公投的新宪法草案中,第二条的内容维持不变。可是为了照顾赛莱菲人士急于实施伊斯兰教法的关切,新宪法草案专门增加第 219 条,对第二条提到的"伊斯兰教法原则"进行补充说明:"伊斯兰教法原则包括总体证明,其基础和教法规则,和其来源,被逊尼派教法学派所尊重。"④据权威专家分析,新宪法增加这一条,并不意味着伊斯兰教法可以在埃及顺利全面实施,最终决定是否实施伊斯兰教法的权力在很大程度上掌握在爱资哈尔手上。⑤新宪法第 4 条规定:"爱资哈尔大乌里玛协会有关伊斯兰

---

① 《爱资哈尔警告不要破坏宪法第 2 条》,埃及《金字塔报》,2011 年 2 月 16 日。

② 瓦利德·阿卜杜·拉赫曼、玛丽·瓦只底:《关于宪法第 2 条出现分歧 爱资哈尔否认达成中间建议》,伦敦《中东报》,2012 年 7 月 7 日。

③ Amani Maged, "No compromise", *Al-Ahram Weekly*, 14 November 2012. http://weekly. ahram. org. eg/News/259/17/No-compromise. aspx

④ 《〈埃及宪法草案〉最后全文》,《今日埃及人报》2012 年 12 月 2 日发布,http://www. almasryalyoum. com/node/1283056

⑤ Clark Lombardi and Nathan J. Brown, "Islam in Egypt's new constitution", *Foreign Policy*, December 13, 2012, http://mideast. foreignpolicy. com/posts/2012/12/13/islam_in_egypts_new_constitution? wp_login_redirect = 0

教法相关事务的意见将被听取"。①

　　第二,反对旨在为政党利益服务而滥发教法令(fatwa)。发布教法令是伊斯兰世界日常宗教行为之一,有关发布者的资格和条件向来存在争议。在埃及,隶属于爱资哈尔系统的大穆夫提是官方认定的权威教法令发布者。但是在后穆巴拉克时代的政治转型中,伊斯兰政党为了赢得更多选票和支持者,唆使同情本党的宗教人士滥发教法令,造成了恶劣的社会影响,激化了教派之间的矛盾,遭到了爱资哈尔的强烈反对。

　　2012 年 5 月 23 - 24 日,埃及举行革命后首次总统选举。由于热门候选人多达 6 位,民调显示第一轮投票难以一锤定音。为了支持穆兄会自由与正义党前主席穆尔西当选,部分宗教人士使用教法令这一宗教工具为穆尔西拉票。亚历山大易卜拉欣统帅清真寺教长艾哈迈德·马哈罗(Ahmed Al-Mahalaw),于 5 月 11 日在周五聚礼演讲中呼吁听众投票给穆兄会候选人穆尔西,并且说投票给他是"教法义务"。②第一轮投票结果,穆尔西与穆巴拉克政权最后一任总理沙菲克分别胜出,两人定于 6 月 16 - 17 日举行第二轮对决。由于这两人都不是理想的总统候选人,前者隶属于宗教党派,后者隶属于前政权阵营,故此一些党派呼吁抵制或放弃投票。6 月 1 日,著名宗教人士优素福·卡尔达维(Yusuf Al-Qardawi)在周五聚礼演讲中,要求在第一轮投票中落败的哈穆丹·苏巴希(Hamdain Subahiy)和艾布·法图哈(Abu Fatuha)转而支持穆尔西。③6 月 2 日,埃及伊斯兰最高理事会成员、前人民议会议员、著名宗教人士优素福·巴德利(Yusuf Al-Qardawi)长老发布教法令,他说:"谁抵制总统对决投票,谁就是罪人,谁呼吁抵制,谁就是傻瓜。"④在宗教人士的鼎力支持下,穆兄会候选人穆尔西成功当选革命后首位民选总统。

---

　　① 《〈埃及宪法草案〉最后全文》,《今日埃及人报》2012 年 12 月 2 日发布,http://www.almas-ryalyoum.com/node/1283056

　　② 穆罕默德·阿吉姆:《教法令和宗教召唤点燃总统选举的马拉松》,伦敦《中东报》,2012 年 6 月 2 日。

　　③ 《卡尔达维要求苏巴希和艾布·法图哈支持穆尔西和革命》,2012 年 6 月 1 日,http://www.ikhwanonline.com/new/Article.aspx

　　④ 瓦利德·阿卜杜·拉赫曼:《优素福·巴德利长老对〈中东报〉说:穆尔西竞选总统成功有赖于悔改和悔恨》,伦敦《中东报》,2012 年 6 月 2 日。

2012年8月14日,达格哈利亚省传教士希沙姆·伊斯兰(Hashim Islam),在埃及外交官俱乐部以爱资哈尔教法令委员会成员和爱资哈尔世界乌里玛协会秘书长的身份发表讲话,形容将于8月24日举行的抗议穆尔西总统和穆兄会的百万人集会是"背叛者的革命"。他说:"那些人起来要杀害你们,你们就杀害他们,你们中的某些人被杀了,就在天国里;而你们杀死他们,他们得不到赔偿金,他们的血算是白流。"①这份充满暴力和血腥的教法令发布后,不仅遭到苏巴希、巴拉迪、艾布·法图哈等几位前总统候选人的抨击,也遭到伊斯兰政党如光明党发言人纳迪尔·巴卡尔(Nadir Bakar)、伊斯兰集团舒拉会议主席阿萨姆·达尔巴赖博士(Aisam Darbalah)的谴责。甚至穆兄会达瓦宣教部负责人阿卜杜·赫利格·谢里夫(Abd Al-Khaliq Sharif)也批判这份教法令的荒谬。②8月16日,爱资哈尔伊斯兰研究院秘书处发表声明,指责希沙姆·伊斯兰冒充爱资哈尔身份,抨击这份教法令违背了伊斯兰教不得滥杀无辜的宗教精神,因为《古兰经》明确规定:"你们不要违背真主的禁令而杀人,除非因为正义。他将这些事嘱咐你们,以便你们了解。"(第6章第151节)③

2012年12月8日,穆尔西总统公布新的《宪法声明》,下令于12月15日就埃及新宪法草案举行第一轮公投。第一轮公投顺利结束后,埃及又于12月22日举行第二轮公投。由于宪法公投是穆尔西总统与其背后的穆兄会大力推动的,埃及一些反对党呼吁抵制投票。为了诱使更多选民走出家门前往投票站,一些支持穆尔西总统和穆兄会的宗教人士站出来拉票。如赛莱菲达瓦行政委员会副主任雅西尔·布尔哈米(Yasir Burhami)长老于12月20日发布教法令,针对一位已婚女子询问在丈夫反对公投的情况下是否可以出家投票的问题,他回答说:"你可以找另外的理由,不要提公投

---

① 瓦利德·阿卜杜·拉赫曼:《下令杀死穆尔西总统反对者的教法令在埃及引发极大愤怒》,伦敦《中东报》,2012年8月16日。

② 乌萨玛·白什比什:《阿卜杜·赫利格·哈桑·谢里夫长老谴责杀害8月24日出席者的教法令》,2012年8月16日,穆兄会网站:http://www.ikhwanonline.com/new/Article.aspx

③ 乌萨玛·白什比什:《爱资哈尔谴责伊斯兰长老的教法令、呼吁团结和高举祖国利益》,2012年8月16日,穆兄会网站:http://www.ikhwanonline.com/new/Article.aspx

之事,告别丈夫出家门,然后自己去投票。"①这一公然鼓励欺骗和撒谎的教法令,遭到了爱资哈尔宗教专家的批评。爱资哈尔大学伊斯兰教法学院教授阿里·纳扎尔博士(Ali Al-Najar)说:"所有形式的欺骗和编造的理由都应被拒绝,无论欺骗导致什么利益和好处,比如丈夫与妻子之间关系的改善……"②

2012 年 12 月 25 日,赛莱菲真道党主席阿迪勒·阿卜杜·马格苏德·阿菲菲发布教法令,称不允许向基督徒祝贺生日。他说:"真道党不会向任何基督徒发贺电,不参加他们的圣诞节或生日。"③对于这个教法令,爱资哈尔伊斯兰研究所秘书长阿里·阿卜杜·巴基(Ali Abd Al-Baqi)长老批评说:"这个教法令有其僵硬的一面,伊斯兰教并不答应。如果我们看伊斯兰历史,先知穆罕默德如何给基督徒让路,尽管他们在路上对先知造成了伤害"。④在实际行动中,爱资哈尔长老不仅在每年圣诞节到来之际向科普特大主教发去贺电,而且还亲自出席相关纪念活动。

爱资哈尔的独立地位与爱资哈尔的穆兄会化

回顾革命两年来爱资哈尔系统与伊斯兰政党在埃及政治转型中的互动关系,笔者得出以下两点看法:

第一,爱资哈尔系统通过自身的不懈努力,已经在后穆巴拉克时代的多党民主体系中找到了自身的位置,强化和巩固了爱资哈尔至高无上的宗教地位与宗教权威。埃及 2012 年宪法草案经过 12 月 15 日和 22 日两轮全民公决后,赢得了 63.8% 的支持率。穆尔西总统于 12 月 26 日签署并立即生效实施。2012 年宪法与 1971 年宪法相比,拥有不少新的亮点,最大的亮

---

① 瓦利德·阿卜杜·拉赫曼:《埃及:允许妻子欺骗丈夫前去参加公投的教法令引起争议》,伦敦《中东报》,2012 年 12 月 21 日。

② 瓦利德·阿卜杜·拉赫曼:《埃及:允许妻子欺骗丈夫前去参加公投的教法令引起争议》,伦敦《中东报》,2012 年 12 月 21 日。

③ 瓦利德·阿卜杜·拉赫曼:《赛莱菲禁止向基督徒祝贺生日的教法令在埃及引起争议》,伦敦《中东报》,2012 年 12 月 28 日。

④ 同上。

点在笔者看来,就是新增的第 4 条:"爱资哈尔是一个包容性的独立的伊斯兰机构,有权不受干扰地处理其全部事务,承担在埃及和世界传播伊斯兰教、宗教知识和阿拉伯语的责任,爱资哈尔大乌里玛协会有关伊斯兰教法相关事务的意见将被听取。爱资哈尔长老是独立的,不能被解职,有专门法律规定爱资哈尔长老从大乌里玛协会成员中挑选。国家确保提供足够的资金以便爱资哈尔实现其目标"。① 通过仔细解读宪法第 4 条条文,我们不难发现,这一条是专门给爱资哈尔量身定制的,它包含三层意思:一是在总体上规定了爱资哈尔的法律地位、职责与权限,核心要点是爱资哈尔的"独立性",政府不能干涉爱资哈尔事务;二是规定了爱资哈尔长老的地位和任免办法,核心要点是爱资哈尔长老的"独立性",他与国家领导人没有隶属关系,国家领导人也不能任免他,只能从大乌里玛中遴选;三是规定了国家与爱资哈尔的关系,国家必须保证爱资哈尔拥有足够的经费开支,为爱资哈尔的宗教活动提供后勤保障。

2012 年宪法给予爱资哈尔如此优厚待遇,表明爱资哈尔才是这场埃及革命最大的受益者之一。爱资哈尔之所以赢得如此高的礼遇,除了历史和文化传统方面的因素之外,另有两个现实因素不可不谈。其一,爱资哈尔在过去两年来的埃及政治动荡中不负众望,努力稳定社会,避免教派冲突和民族分裂,堪称埃及社会的中流砥柱。爱资哈尔于 2011 年 6 月 20 日推出了一部《爱资哈尔文件》(Al-Azhar Document),这是爱资哈尔召集各党派负责人和社会贤达人士反复讨论和磋商之后形式的,其中包含 11 条各方均可接受的基本原则。目的是在动荡和混乱的政治转型期,凝聚全民共识,明确行为准则,促进埃及的团结和统一,避免穆斯林与基督徒的冲突,维护埃及的长治久安。② 爱资哈尔在乱世中方显英雄本色,赢得了埃及民众的高度信赖。其二,在穆兄会和赛莱菲等政治伊斯兰(Political Islam)组织全面掌握国家政权的情况下,为防止这些刚刚登上权力宝座的伊斯兰主义者,打着"伊斯兰教"的名义"轻举妄动"和"胡作非为",客观上需要一支

---

① 《埃及共和国宪法 2012》,2012 年 12 月,见埃及国家信息网:http://www. sis. gov. eg/Ne-wvr/con1. pdf

② 《爱资哈尔文件:为了埃及的明天》,2011 年 6 月 20 日,见埃及国家信息网:http://www. sis. gov. eg/Ar/Story. aspx? sid = 52847

能够在宗教地位和宗教权威上足以抗衡政治伊斯兰的力量,而爱资哈尔恰恰能够满足这一社会要求。新宪法赋予爱资哈尔"独立"的宗教权威,在很大程度上反映了埃及社会各界对政治伊斯兰势力掌权的普遍担忧。

　　第二,以穆兄会和赛莱菲为代表的政治伊斯兰力量在掌握国家政权之后,也在利用国家权力资源抢占爱资哈尔的宗教地盘,蚕食爱资哈尔的宗教影响力,争夺爱资哈尔的宗教话语权,努力在宗教上与爱资哈尔分庭抗礼。有两个突出现象值得关注:其一,政治伊斯兰组织在革命后成立了自己的"教法协会",全称为"独立中间伊斯兰学者协会",就一些重大问题发布有利于自己的教法令,完全不受爱资哈尔大穆夫提的管辖。该协会包括隶属于赛莱菲、穆兄会和伊斯兰集团的宗教学者及政治家,著名人物有赛莱菲长老穆罕默德·哈桑尼(Muhammad Hasan)、穆兄会副总训导师海依拉特·沙特尔(Khairat Al-Shatir)、赛莱菲著名律师哈姆宰·艾布·伊斯梅尔(Hazem Abu Ismail)、赛莱菲达瓦集团的雅西尔·布尔哈米(Yasir Burhami)等人。①其二,爱资哈尔系统内部同情和支持伊斯兰政党的师生越来越多,尤其是在穆兄会和赛莱菲掌握政权之后,其相对激进的思想路线和较为极端的行动纲领获得了不少爱资哈尔师生的认同。甚至一些爱资哈尔高级宗教人士也在自觉为穆兄会和赛莱菲说话。例如前文提到的以发布杀戮教法令闻名的传教士希沙姆·伊斯兰,他拥有十足的爱资哈尔血统,而且确实是爱资哈尔教法令委员会成员。该委员会秘书长赛义德·阿米尔博士(Said Amir)不仅没有否认希沙姆·伊斯兰的成员身份,而且替他辩解,称"这个教法令是伊斯兰长老的个人意见,不是爱资哈尔教法令委员会的意见",又说"表达意见是教法和法律保证的每个人的自由"。②

　　由于爱资哈尔是埃及官方法定的伊斯兰教育机构,绝大多数穆兄会和赛莱菲专职宗教人士其实都是从爱资哈尔大学毕业的。也就是说,爱资哈尔既培养了一大批温和、理性和宽容的宗教神职人员,也培养了一小撮偏激、狂热和极端的宗教从业者。目前阿拉伯和埃及媒体热议的一个话题是

---

　　① 瓦利德·阿卜杜·拉赫曼:《赛莱菲禁止向基督徒祝贺生日的教法令在埃及引起争议》,伦敦《中东报》,2012 年 12 月 28 日。

　　② 瓦利德·阿卜杜·拉赫曼:《下令杀死穆尔西总统反对者的教法令在埃及引发极大愤怒》,伦敦《中东报》,2012 年 8 月 16 日。

"爱资哈尔的穆兄会化"。①如果这是一个真实而不是杜撰的新现象,对于埃及的未来恐怕将是凶多吉少。试想一下,埃及新宪法已经授予了爱资哈尔不受国家政治约束的"独立"地位,如果将来连爱资哈尔本身都已经"穆兄会化"了,那么谁来秉持广受赞扬的爱资哈尔中间主义路线?当然在未来埃及也可能出现另一种情况,那就是穆兄会和赛莱菲等政治伊斯兰组织的"爱资哈尔化"。如果是这样,你中有我,我中有你,相互渗透,相互影响,可能更有利于消弭极端主义思潮。

　　(该文曾以"政治伊斯兰激进抑或温和:埃及伊斯兰政党同爱资哈尔的斗争"为题,发表于《西亚非洲》2013 年第 3 期)

---

① 见哈利德·哈鲁布博士:《爱资哈尔穆兄会化的危险》,阿联酋《联合报》2013 年 4 月 8 日。又见巴德尔·穆罕默德·巴德尔:《关于穆兄会化的担忧》,埃及《金字塔报》,2013 年 5 月 11 日。

第二部分

◎ 多元信仰与社会治理

宗教、民族主义与暴力

——一种整合性进路[*]

[美]菲利普·高斯基 居拉伊·蒂尔克曼-德尔维什奥卢

导 论

充分地理解宗教、民族主义与暴力(religious-nationalist violence),对社会科学家和政策制定者来说,是一项极为紧迫的任务。在过去的 20 年里,各类族群、民族主义或宗教性质的内战,空前高涨。[②] 并且,"20 世纪 80 年代以来,宗教的民族主义族群,相比于非宗教的民族主义群体,更需要为日益增多的暴力冲突负责"(Fox 2004,p. 715)。

然而,相关领域的研究文献却仍然高度分裂,呈现出理论上的片面性。例如,关于宗教民族主义的文献虽然不多,却高速扩张。但就其对暴力的关注程度而言,这些文献主要试图从单纯的宏观文化的角度,来解释宗教

---

* 感谢 Gorski 教授在联系版权过程中提供的帮助和 Annual Reviews 的慷慨授权。文章原题为 "Religion,Nationalism and Violence:An Integrated Approach"。Translated and reprinted with permission from the *Annual Review of Sociology*,Volume© 2013 by Annual Reviews,http://www. annualreviews. org.

② 在 1946 年至 2001 年的 225 次武装冲突中,有 115 次发生于从 1989 年到 2001 年的 12 年间(Gleditsch et al. 2002);冲突的绝对数字,在紧随冷战结束的 90 年代早期,达到了顶峰(Blattman& Miguel 2010)。先后关系是否就是因果关系呢? 这仍然值得讨论(Fearon&Laitin 2003,Kalyvas&Balcells 2010)。

民族主义的暴力。但暴力修辞与暴力行动之间的关联性,常常是微乎其微的。尽管宏观文化主义的进路(macro-culturalist approach)在社会学和人类学中占有支配性地位,但在政治科学和经济学中,却盛行着一种微观理性主义的进路(micro-rationalist approach)。这种进路用贪婪、牢骚和枪支,来阐述族群宗教的暴力(ethno-religious violence)。但这种进路难以解释族群宗教的分裂和暴力的符号维度。同时,两种研究进路也都没有充分考虑中层的精英内部冲突和共同体划界。

因此,我们认为,这里需要一种统贯性综合(coherent synthesis),它包含了宏观文化主义的进路和微观理性主义的进路,并以中间层次加以补充。在这一方向上,尽管也有一些富有前景的成果,但这些研究并未真正公平地对待宗教场域。他们或者忽视了宗教,或者把它与文化场域搅拌在一起,特别是将它纳入族群特质(ethnicity)之中。换句话说,他们倾向于把宗教、文化与族群特质之间的关系,看作既成的事实,而不是一种可变之物。

本文接下来的内容,将作如下安排。第一部分通过评论近来有关宗教民族主义的著作,构建了我们的分析对象。第二和第三部分,就宗教、民族主义及暴力的主题,比较和对照了各种文化主义进路和理性主义进路的优势和弱点。第四部分考察了两项重要的综合成果,并确认了它们的主要缺陷。在结束这篇评论的时候,我们将关注,为什么需要关注族群宗教的冲突(ethno-religious conflicts),为什么需要把宗教带回族群民族主义冲突的理论(theories of ethno-nationalist conflict)。

宗教与民族主义:文化主义的进路

出于本文的目的,我们将宗教民族主义(religious nationalism)定义为一种社会运动,它用民族之名主张权利,并以宗教来界定民族。当人们断言"他们的民族建立在宗教之上"(Rieffer 2003)的时候,当宗教在"意味着归属于某个特定民族的诸观念之中占据核心"(Barker 2009,p.13)的时候,宗教民族主义就出现了。

直到非常晚近的时期,宗教民族主义仍然看似一个自相矛盾的术语。

多数社会科学家和历史学家,将民族主义的兴起视为现代化的一部分,从而也就是世俗化的一部分(Anderson 1991,Gellner 1983,Greenfeld 1996)。民族主义可以取代宗教:它可以成为政治性宗教(Smith 2000)、替代性宗教(Seton-Watson 1977),或者单纯就是一个宗教(Hayes 1960)。但民族主义无法与宗教共存,就像传统不能与现代性结合在一起。

这种状况在20世纪90年代早期得到了改变,这归功于宗教运动在世界范围内的复兴,以及共产主义在东欧和俄国的崩溃。宗教民族主义研究著作的涓涓细流(Asad 1999,Tambiah 1992,Van der Veer 1994,Van der Veer & Lehmann 1999),在过去十年间,被一场名副其实的滔滔洪水所取代,这不仅发生在社会学,也发生在其他相邻的领域,如人类学、历史学、政治科学和国际关系(Eastwood 2010,Friedland 2011,Juergensmeyer 2006)。

这些学者都同意,存在着一种独特形式的宗教民族主义。但在有关这种民族主义兴起的时间点和原因上,他们有意见分歧。一些学者把它描绘为一种晚近的现象,以不同的方式将它上溯为世俗主义的失败(Juergensmeyer 1993),对殖民主义的反动(Jaffrelot 2007),民众对西方世俗民主制的失望情绪(Lee 1990),以及在动荡世界中对本体论安全的追寻(Giddens 1991,Kinnvall 2004)。另一些学者认为,自从民族国家形成以来,宗教就对它产生了从未间断的影响(Grosby 1991,Roshwald 2006)。这类作品大多关注犹太－基督教的选民(chosen peoples and elect nations)话语,把它作为西方民族主义的文化模板(Gorski 2000,Grosby 2002,O'Brien 1994,Smith 2003)。一些学者将宗教改革视为重要的转折点,因为拉丁基督教王国的分裂、宗教战争以及国家教会的创立,为民族认同的发展设置了舞台(Kohn 1944,Marx 2003)。另一些学者则将英国稍后以新教为基础的民族认同的起源,放置在18世纪英法敌对的背景之中(Colley 1992,Hutchison & Lehmann 1994,Newman 1987,Straughn& Feld 2010)。但也有一些学者将民族主义的起源追溯到了古代。譬如,格罗斯比(Grosby 1991)认为古代以色列是现代民族主义的实例,而不仅仅是一个模板(同样参见 Gat &Yakobson 2013)。

尽管在《新约》中,"基督教回避了任何尘世中的应许之地的观念"(O'Brien 1988,p.3),但它依然为民族认同提供了一种叙事模板。在这一脉络下,近来讨论东欧宗教民族主义的著作指出,殉难与弥赛亚主义的主题,或许要比拣选(chosen-ness and election)的观念重要得多(Jakelic 2004, Merdjanova 2000)。例如,现代波兰民族主义将波兰描绘为"诸民族的基督",波兰的分裂之"死"是在为其他民族赎罪,波兰在共产主义之后的"复活",则为其他民族的重生铺平了道路(Zubrzycki 2006)。东正教的民族主义运动,尤其在俄国,广泛利用了治权转换(translatioimperii)的亲缘话语,亦即认为莫斯科是"第三罗马",其使命不仅是拯救斯拉夫人,更是拯救一切人性(McLeod 2006)。当代塞尔维亚民族主义者将自己描绘为"十字架上的受难民族",她于1389年被突厥人击败于科索沃战役(Ivekovic 2002),最终经由这一苦难拯救了余下的斯拉夫人(Perica 2002, Sells 2006)。与此相似,在西班牙,巴斯克人和加泰罗尼亚人的民族主义,严重地依赖于各类宗教符号,诸如玛利亚崇拜(Zuleika 1988)和殉难(Dowling 2012, Dunstan 2008)。

宗教在非西方民族主义运动的形成中,同样扮演了重要的、乃至于更为重大的角色(Jaffrelot 2007, Little & Swearer 2006, Von der Mehden 1968)。弗里德兰(Friedland 2001, p. 129)指出,伊朗、斯里兰卡、印度、巴基斯坦、沙特阿拉伯、以色列以及巴勒斯坦的民族认同,全都"弥漫着宗教的叙事与神话,符号主义与仪式"。范德维尔(Van der Veer 1994)认为,印度始于19世纪的国族建设(nation-building),依赖于印度教徒、锡克教徒和佛教徒之间的宗教对立情绪。与基督教《新约》不同,[犹太教的]《托拉》和[伊斯兰教的]《古兰经》不仅涉及个体与神的关系,也涉及在政治上组织起来的信徒共同体。因此,相比于西方民族主义,某些非西方民族主义的宗教根源要更深。

但正如维尔弗里德·施波恩(WillfriedSpohn 2003)近来指出的,非西方民族主义之著述,经常以两种颇为精微的方式,受到世俗化叙事的影响。一些学者将西方的民族国家模式,描绘为西方世俗价值的传送带,这些世俗价值有助于驯服宗教冲突(Breuilly 1993, Hefner 1998, Tibi 1990)。民族主义的传播,点燃了"激烈的宗教民族斗争,这些斗争遍布全球,包括卷入其中的伊斯兰主义者、印度教民族主义者、拉美五旬节派信徒和弥赛亚的犹太民族主义者"(Shenhav 2007, p.7)。为了说明这一独特的持久性,另一批西方学者将之归咎于全球化。在这种进路中,宗教民族主义被塑造为一种防御性回应,旨在反对由世俗文化的世界体系挥动的全球化力量(Arnason 1987,Meyer 1999)。

多元现代性进路的倡导者,提出了另一种宗教民族主义解释(Eisenstadt 1987,Spohn 2009)。他们把近来族群宗教运动的高涨,看作"不同文明之多元架构的组分,这些架构不仅体现在民族国家的形成和民主化方面,也体现在宗教的变迁和世俗化方面"(Spohn 2003,p. 281)。然而,通过把各个地区和国家划归给某些宗教文明或政治文明(如伊斯兰文明、犹太文明、印度文明和儒家文化圈),这种路径有时夸大了文化差异从上至下的影响,同时也低估了地方史和地方语境的影响。例如,尽管讨论伊朗(Aburaiya 2009)、土耳其(Haynes 2010)、巴勒斯坦(Lybarger 2007)和达吉斯坦(Gammer 2002)的著作,全都聚焦于伊斯兰民族主义,但他们的分析表明,这些不同国家的宗教民族主义,具有截然不同的结构:在伊朗和土耳其,伊斯兰民族主义运动发展成了旨在针对从上至下的、外在强加的西方化和世俗化尝试的一种反动;在巴勒斯坦,民族主义运动形成了反对以色列犹太民族主义的一个堡垒;在达吉斯坦,民族主义运动的实现方式,是在国家精英与苏非派宗教领袖(Sufi sheikh)之间达成结盟,共同对抗更为保守的瓦哈比派(Wahhabi)势力。但在黎巴嫩,民族主义运动则是转向基要主义的伊斯兰民族主义组织,亦即真主党(Hizbu' llah)的产物(Saad-Ghorayeb 2002)。

此外,虽然属于同一文明的不同个案之间可以存在差异,但属于不同文明的个案却也可以——并确实——分享了共同的方面。譬如,南亚的宗教民族主义,可以在内部区分为佛教、印度教、伊斯兰教以及锡克教的民族主义,并且大多反对殖民主义——就此而言,这些民族主义同日本的神道教运动存在着极大的差异(Skya 2009)。然而,所有这些运动共享了反西方的立场,即使日本从未被殖民过。与此类似,虽然以色列是一个非西方国家,但由于它与西方国家共享了希伯来圣经的教海,同样的圣经意象也就出现在了以色列犹太民族主义当中。值得讨论的是,美国和以色列的宗教民族主义都制造了各式各样的暴力片段。

但不变之物是不适宜用来说明可变之物的。那么,在什么条件下,宗教民族主义的动员会导向暴力？现在我们就要转向这个问题。

暴力的文化主义理论

在当代社会科学内部，人们可以区分两种关于冲突和暴力的基本研究进路：文化主义和理性主义。文化主义的各种进路，不仅主宰了社会学的著作，也盛行于人类学、历史学、文学和宗教研究。但这些进路可以进一步细分为 3 条主要的谱系：休谟主义、涂尔干主义和施米特主义。

休谟主义谱系中具有开创性的文本是《宗教的自然史》(*Natural History of Religion*, Hume 1757［2009］)。该书的中心论点是多神论先于一神论——这个论点如今广被接受，却在那个时代充满争议。但至少对今天的人来说，这本书最具挑衅性的论点是：多神论天然导致宽容，而一神论一般引致迫害。之所以如此，休谟写道，是因为多神论"允许其他教派和民族的诸神参与共享神性"，而不像在一神论中，"对其他神的崇拜会被视为荒唐和不虔敬"，从而"为别有用心的人提供了一种伪装，即把他们的敌手描绘为渎神者(profane)"(Hume 1757［2009］, p. 161)。①

近年来，休谟的论点已经开始在大量著作中复兴，其中既包括学术作品，也包括大众读物。例如，乔纳森·基尔希(Jonathan Kirsch)提出，"一神论的结果是激发残暴乃至狂热，而多神论大多不会有这些东西"(Kirsch 1998, p. 2)。他还认为，今日恐怖主义的神学根源，不在古兰经，而在希伯来圣经。文学研究者雷吉娜·施瓦茨(Regina Schwartz)将休谟命题与施米特命题——我们将在下文详细讨论——联系在一起，同时指出，希伯来圣经中的叙事，引入了一种至今尚不为人所熟知的认同形式，即"暴力的认同形成"(Schwartz 1997)。她意味深长地指出，旧约在上帝的选民与其他诸民族(God's people and nations)之间，划出了一道尖锐而互斥的边界，从而为宗教暴力创造了文化的前提(Schwartz 1997, p. x)。著名的埃及学家扬

---

① 中译引自休谟：《宗教的自然史》，徐晓宏译，上海：上海人民出版社，2003，第 62－63 页，略有改动。

·阿斯曼(Jan Assmann)的一系列专著和论文,在德国引发了一场激烈的论战,他有感于弗洛伊德关于一神论的摩西世系的思考,提出了一个与休谟稍有不同的论点(Assmann 1997)。"对我来说,重要的不是区分唯一真神和众神,而是辨别宗教里的真理与虚妄",他称之为"摩西区分"。在犹太教中,暴力迫害仍然是"犹太人的内部事务",指向"'居住在我们中间'的埃及人和迦南人"(Assmann 2009, p. 17)。另一方面,在基督教和伊斯兰教中,这种迫害在十字军的暴力东征和穆斯林的圣战(jihads)中被外部化了。

如果休谟命题是正确的,那么,我们现在可以期待(a)一神论的兴起伴随着宗教暴力的急剧增长,(b)多神社会(如亚洲和非洲的大部分地区)的历史,相对而言,应当与暴力无涉。尽管历史资料尚不足以允许我们给论点(a)下一个明确的结论,但我们却有足够的理由怀疑论点(b)的正确性。当然,这背后时常隐藏着的陈旧而固定的模式,也是我们必须拒斥的,即认为西方宗教是暴力的,东方宗教是和平的。伟大的印度教史诗充斥着暴力的场景,印度的历史也遍布着武装的冲突(事实上,《薄伽梵歌》中那些最著名的段落,都发生于战场)。东亚的佛教史,到处都是武装僧侣。南亚也有它自己的武士苦行派。佛教,尽管传统上严厉谴责暴力,但也拥有其自身的正义战争理论和神圣暴力形式(Jerryson&Juergensmeyer 2010)。

那么,总体而言,宗教可能助长暴力吗?这是新无神论四骑士(the four horsemen of the new atheism)——道金斯(Dawkins2008)、丹尼特(Dennett2007)、哈里斯(Harris2005)和希钦斯(Hitchens2009)——提出的诸多论点之一。每一位作者都提供了一种世界史叙事,一方面将暴力与宗教,另一方面将宽容与理性,紧密地联结在一起。但这种道德计算,需要一些创造性解释。比如,20世纪的极权主义暴行(即法西斯主义和共产主义),在某种程度上,必须从无神论者的资产负债表中清除出去。反之,有信仰的和平代言人(如甘地和马丁·路德·金),必须被重塑为隐秘的人文主义者。毫不奇怪,四骑士这种挑起争端的过火做法,引发了大量嘲讽式的抗辩(Eagleton 2009, Hart 2009)。我们无法在这里详细概括他们的批判,但这些争论的主题是很清楚的:宗教与暴力的关系,要比休谟及其今日的追随者认识到的,远为复杂和偶然;在一神论与多神论或宗教与理性之间作出过于笼统的区分,并无助于我们解决问题。

涂尔干主义传统的根源,超出了《宗教生活的基本形式》(Durkheim 1912 [2001])的范围,它从于贝尔和莫斯讨论"献祭"的文章(Hubert &Mauss 1898 [1964]),一直延伸到涂尔干自己的《社会分工论》(1893 [1984])。当然,在《社会分工论》中,涂尔干曾提出,原始社会靠机械团结凝聚在一起,这种团结以社会的相似性和强加的一致性为前提;而现代社会则通过有机团结联合在一起,这种团结建立在社会的差异和功能的互赖之上。从这个观点可以得出一个颇为反直觉——从而也是吸引人的——的论点:刑罚,乃至更为简单的社会冲突,事实上增强了社会的团结。齐美尔(Simmel 1903)曾经提出过相同的论点,科塞(Coser 1964)则对之进行了详细的讨论。根据于贝尔和莫斯的解释,献祭仪式服务于类似的目的:修复和净化共同体。在《宗教生活的基本形式》中,涂尔干(1912 [2001])对这个基本论点作了一般化处理,延伸到了宗教的仪式本身。他认为,通过仪式引入的"集体欢腾"状态,是宗教共同体的经验基础,实际上也是社会生活的经验基础。然而,在涂尔干的阐释中,献祭仪式仅仅扮演了边缘的角色,暴力则被彻底忽视。

但对吉拉尔(Girard 1995)来说,正好相反,献祭仪式的首要功能,与其说制造了团结,不如说分散了侵犯(aggression)。欲望——这里不单单指意图占有别人之物,而是成为他人之所是——在一切人类群体中制造了密集的、零和的竞争。吉拉尔将这种欲望称之为"模仿欲"(mimetic desire)。通过将忌妒和敌意转移给第三方,也就是替罪羊,共同体回复到了和谐的状态。吉拉尔指出,古代宗教特有的献祭仪式,是起源于真实事件的原型仪式,标志着从动物到人类的过渡。在其后期作品中,吉拉尔提出,替罪羊必须拥有某些特征(Girard 1986,2011)。首先,她或他必须近似于——或被认为近似于——竞争者。其次,替罪羊必须是一个边缘人物,以致其献祭不会引发复仇。

吉拉尔的研究方法,让我们了解原始社会仪式暴力中的"如何"(the how)与"是谁"(the who)。埃里克松(Erikson 1966)的《倔强的清教徒》(Wayward Puritans)则表明,涂尔干的框架可以延伸至献祭暴力的现代情节,如新英格兰地区的女巫大流行。有关现代道德恐慌的开创性著作则显示,涂尔干的框架同样可以富有成果地应用于世俗的边界危机(Cohen

2002）。戴维斯（Davis 1973）讨论新教圣像破坏运动（iconoclasm）的杰出论文证明，指向物质对象的暴力同样司空见惯。最近，佩普（Pape 2005）用涂尔干（1897［1951］）的"利他主义自杀"理论，阐述了自杀式爆炸的社会逻辑；克雷默（Kramer 1991）认为黎巴嫩发生的自我殉节行动，是由伊斯兰运动之间的模仿性竞争驱动的。沿着这一脉络，马文和英格尔（Marvin & Ingle 1999）提出，美国的民族认同包含着流血牺牲的仪式。

20 世纪 90 年代，耕耘于宗教暴力领域的社会学家，采纳了一种叙事学转向。他们在这么做的时候，也就是在追随许多有影响力的"第三波"（Adams et al. 2005）历史社会学家，后者对叙事表现出了浓厚的兴趣，认为叙事不只是表征的模式，同时也是行动的模板（Sewell 1992，Somers 1994，Steinmetz 1992）。这些历史社会学家的灵感，按照顺序，有一部分来自那些卓越的哲学家和批评家关于叙事性和认同之关联的讨论作品（Ricoeur 1990，Taylor 1989）。文学研究者完成了一批有关叙事性和民族认同的前沿著作（Bhabha 1990），社会科学家则迅速跟进（Calhoun 1994）。宗教暴力的文化主义研究，大多关注启示录叙事（apocalyptic narratives）。

中世纪史学家和早期现代史学家，已经充分地研究过各类千禧年运动和意识形态（Cohn 1957）。但社会学内部对于启示论（apocalypticism）的兴趣，源起于 20 世纪 80 年代对暴力膜拜团体的研究，诸如发生于詹姆斯镇①和韦科②的事件（Bromley & Melton 2002，Hall et al. 2000）。学者发现，这类群体的一个共同特征是关于宇宙之战的异象（a vision of cosmic war），一场发生于善、恶力量之间的终极决战，膜拜团体的成员试图借暴力对抗催生这场决战，或以交托生命的方式实现逃离。启示录叙事同样被证明是宗教民族主义和恐怖组织的诸多暴力形式的共同特征（Jewett & Lawrence 2003，Juergensmeyer 1993）。

---

① 原文为"Jamestown"，疑为"Jonestown"之误。琼斯镇（Jonestown）是臭名昭著的"人民圣殿农业计划"的实施地。1978 年 11 月 18 日，在人民圣殿教教主吉姆·琼斯的带领下，该"计划"导致 900 多人的集体非正常死亡。——译者注

② "韦科惨案"始于 1993 年 2 月 28 日，终于 4 月 19 日，历时 50 天。该年，美国执法人员围困大卫教派的一个支派位于德克萨斯州韦科（Waco）附近的总部，造成双方共 86 人在事件中死亡。——译者注

但我们应当给予启示录叙事以何种权重？文化社会学中强纲领的提倡者认为，叙事框架拥有强大的力量，可以驾驭乃至决定个体或集体行动的进程；在这个意义上，这些叙事类似于剧本或策略书（Smith 2005）。然而，对特定运动的仔细研究，一般会得出更为适切的结论。基本的问题是，暴力修辞比暴力行动更为常见（Melton & Bromley 2002）。就千禧年主义的膜拜团体而言，暴力的结果通常包含了介入因素。其中，有些是外生的，如怀有敌意的媒体关注，或用法律强制延长的均衡。还有一些是内生的，如运用强有力的献身机制或严厉的社会边界，从而使人更加难以从群体或运动中平静脱身。这些结论表明，在研究宗教民族主义暴力的时候，我们更需要关注中层的过程。

宗教暴力研究的施米特主义进路是更为晚近的经典。卡尔·施米特（Carl Schmitt）是纳粹政权直言不讳的支持者，甚至在二战后依旧倔强地不愿表示悔改。这一点比之马丁·海德格尔，有过之而无不及。施米特思想的复兴，大约始于他在 1985 年的逝世。这种复兴不是指他支持极权主义的右翼思想，而是他批评自由主义的左派思想（Agamben 1998，Mouffe 1999）。随着一系列事件的到来，如美国针对恐怖活动的战争、阿布格莱布监狱的美军虐囚事件，以及围绕关塔那摩拘留"敌方战斗人员"的冲突，施米特有关自由民主制的真实基础的论点，突然之间又开始切中题意（Agamben 1998，2005；Kahn 2008；Scheuerman 2006）。譬如，乔治·布什在 2001 年的声明"你（们）要不是和我们一道，就是和恐怖主义同处一室"，让我们想起了施米特的主张："真实的政治"以划分敌/友为前提（Schmitt 2007）。阿布格莱布监狱令人毛骨悚然的囚犯裸照，以及关塔那摩湾监狱加强审讯的报告，使人想起阿甘本（Agamben 1998）的"赤裸生命"及"神圣的人"等概念，这些政治弃儿的存在，确认了政治的边界（Schmitt 2005）。布什政府主张关塔那摩具有治外法权的地位，从而把敌方战斗人员置于美国法律之外，这正回应了施米特的著名格言：主权者就是那个可以宣布紧急状态或例外状态（Ausnahmezustand）的人。

然而，很少有人注意到施密特主义进路和涂尔干主义进路之间的高度相似性，特别是阿甘本和吉拉尔（但请参见 Hussain&Ptacek 2000，Palaver 1992）在神圣的人与献祭牺牲之间，在奠立或重铸（re/found）国家的主权行为与组成或重组群体的暴力行为之间建立的关联。透过这一棱镜，人们大概可以看到，施米特主义进路是对涂尔干主义进路的一种延伸，从原始的图腾群体，到现代的自由主义国家（Datta 2006）。这两种研究进路都指向了符号和情感的逻辑，为原本看似无意义和非理性的宗教与政治暴力的仪式化行为奠定了基础。他们使这些仪式的目标和过程清晰可见，这是纯粹的理性主义阐释完全做不到的。然而，为何这种暴力行为极为罕见，为何触发它们的物质和关系构型如此稀少，这是施密特主义进路和涂尔干主义进路仍然没能解释的空白。而这一点，恰恰是理性主义进路的优势。

暴力的理性主义理论

在经济学、政治科学和国际关系中，理性主义的研究进路占有支配性地位。这种进路的形成，受惠于两股独立作品潮流的交汇。第一股潮流是比较－历史政治经济学的理性选择版本，它最初产生于20世纪70年代，成员主要是一小群以华盛顿大学为中心的跨学科学者，且大多以欧洲为研究对象。他们最初的抱负，旨在说明集体行为（如族群和民族主义的动员）与社会秩序（如市场和国家的形成）。我们称他们为"西雅图学派"（the Seattle School）。

第二股较晚汇入的潮流，是政治经济学中更偏博弈论的版本。它于20世纪80年代晚期被首次详细阐述，其倡导者是一个发展经济学的国际小团队。他们的主要目标，是旨在说明集体暴力和社会失序（如内战和国家的失败）。他们大多研究非洲。第一个群体在政治社会学内略有影响，但第二个群体从根本上形塑了比较政治学。我们称后者为非洲学派（the African School）。

西雅图学派本身是另一种理论交汇的产物，即两种不同的经济史研究进路：奥尔森式的（Olsonian）和诺斯式的（Northian）。奥尔森（1965）曾经指出，由于搭便车和相关动力学的存在，个体的自利为群体动员设置了难以克服的障碍，这意味着，成功的集体行动一般需要提供选择性激励。在科斯（Coase 1990）讨论"企业"的开创性著作基础之上，道格拉斯·诺斯和其他学者(Alchian& Benjamin 2006,North 1990,Williamson et al. 1991)精心阐述了一种交易成本理论,如信息收集和产权保护的成本。科斯曾经指出,企业存在的理由是降低成本。诺斯及其同僚只是把这个论点延伸到了国家。

随后,西雅图学派的其他成员将奥尔森和诺斯的模型,应用到了群体动员和国家形成的问题上(Kiser & Schneider 1994,Levi 1989)。比如,赫克特及其同事(1982,Hechter& Levi 1979)将族群－民族主义的动员解释成了一个集体行动的问题。赫克特反对传统的理论,他认为成功的动员在个体层面都是理性的(即,这些动员为个体行动者带来了净收益)。在他看来,这甚至可以应用于集体暴力:如果(if and when)参与集体暴力符合他们的自我利益(即,只要这是获取金钱和权力的最有效手段),个体就会这么做。

但事实真是如此简单? 最近,柯林斯(Collins 2009)有关集体暴力的微观动力学的著作,就对此提出了疑义。其中一个原因——当然不是唯一的——是,人身暴力(physical violence)与特定的技巧和技术有关。换成经济学的语言来说,人身暴力需要人力和生理资本。非洲学派的一项核心成果已经将这些资本要求,纳入了集体暴力的生产函数(production function)之中。

非洲学派源于两股思想运动的交叉:芝加哥学派(the Chicago School)和博弈论。早在20世纪50年代,加里·贝克尔和其他人便开始将经济学理论应用到非经济学的问题之中,诸如种族关系和家庭生活——这些问题曾经专属于社会学(Becker 1976)。截至80年代早期,芝加哥大学的乔恩·埃尔斯特(Jon Elster)和(之后的)其他人将经济学理论包括博弈论,应用到了原本属于政治科学的问题之中。博弈论的有关形式——非合作博弈的均衡理论——在二战期间被首次提出(Von Neumann & Morgenstern 1944)。在冷战年代,它对兰德公司(RAND Corporation)和美国国防部的军事计划制定者及策略专家,拥有巨大的影响力(Boulding 1962,Schelling 1960)。90年代,一些发展经济学家开始将博弈论应用到了内战问题上。

非洲学派的主要缔造者是经济学家杰克·赫舒拉发(Jack Hirshleifer)。众所周知,赫舒拉发在去加州大学洛杉矶分校(UCLA)之前,曾在兰德公司(1949–1955)和芝加哥大学(1955–1960)工作过。他的基本预设是:"除了生产和交换技术,个体和群体还可以运用冲突技术参与竞争。"(Collier et al. 2009;Grossman 1991;Hirshleifer 1991;p. 133)。实际上,这包含了两个预设:统治者在征税和掠夺之间做出选择,技术则影响这两种策略的相对价格。赫舒拉发阐述的基本模型接下来还纳入了计算,即暴力收益的增长依赖于(a)人力资本的可及性(即,训练有素的士兵与熟练工人的市场价格对比),以及(b)可掠夺资源的存在(如石油或钻石)。与西雅图学派不同,非洲学派承认,暴力冲突的经济学模型必须包含生理和人力资本。

赫舒拉发的模型并没有提到西雅图学派的核心论点,即,那些最初参与集体行动的理性个体,为何很少参与集体暴力。对于该问题的一个(诺斯式)回答,是将族群当成民族国家的功能等价物——族群通过实行产权保护、提供人身安全和分配财富等措施(Wintrobe 1995),有能力降低交易成本。在非洲学派的语境下,这并非一个毫无道理的假设。

但如果这样,新的问题也产生了:族群及其领袖,何时选择与国家及其统治者合作? 在一些列有影响的论文中,法国发展经济学家让-皮埃尔·阿藏(Jean-Pierre Azam)指出,对于这个问题的回答,依赖于各项条件,包括(a)国家履行其基本职能(即保护财产和人身安全)的能力;(b)国家为在族群间公平分配资源而作出郑重承诺的能力(Azam 1995,Azam&Mesnard 2003)。

理性主义进路有益地纠正了民族主义文献中的两个共同倾向:(a)民族集体的实体化(hypostasization),(b)将非理性动机归咎于民族主义分子。非洲学派同时还让我们注意到另一种倾向:(c)人身暴力的自然化。然而,难道理性主义者没有矫枉过正吗? 难道社会群体在某种意义上和在某些情况下不是"真的存在"(really real)吗? 难道非物质动机(如情感)和符号目的(如荣誉)没有经常在群际冲突中扮演核心角色吗? 集体暴力真的只是手段和动机的函数吗?

理性主义进路也有一些根本缺陷。首先,对方法论个体主义的教条式信奉,迫使他们将社会范畴当作外生性因素(exogenize the social)(Arrow 1994)。就此而言,这意味着将族群、民族和宗教的认同,视作外在于模型的既有之物或主观之物(Cramer 2002)。其次,个体理性的先验预设,使理性主义的守旧派无法看到人类认知天生具有的启发能力(heuristics)

（Brubaker et al. 2004）。事实上，人们的归类与忠诚，与其说是非理性的，不如说是前理性的。最后，有充足的理由相信，大多数人对于人类内部的自相残杀深恶痛绝（Grossman 1995）。让人杀戮可不仅仅是动用资本那么简单；这其中包括对他们的性情倾向的去自然化和对其被害人的妖魔化。

这些困境也不仅仅是元理论上的；相反，它们造成了理性主义进路在经验应用上的持久困惑。这种经验性应用的典型做法，就是借助于族群语言分块的客观指标，尝试将族群性自然化，从而也就是去社会化。毫不奇怪，这场理论运动在经验上失败了（Cederman&Girardin 2007）。此外，还有人试图保留理性的假设，这种不屈不挠的努力坚持认为，民族主义领袖在行为上是理性的（即犬儒式和目的性的），即使其追随者并非如此（Hechter 2000）。但个案研究的证据通常表明，无论是领导者还是追随者，其物质性动机和符号性动机全都混杂在一起。

对于这些矫枉过正，文化主义进路提供了一些修正。比如，他们坚持集体范畴（涂尔干）和符号范畴（格尔茨）的现实性，从而有助于我们对族群、民族和宗教的认同的内容，从理论上作出阐述。类似地，他们坚持意义和叙事在社会生活中的重要性，从而有助于我们理解荣誉和价值在人类行动中的作用。总之，他们更加强调了民族主义暴力的某些特征。例如，他们说明，为何暴力可能指向符号性目标，即使摧毁这个目标并无助于从物质上削弱敌人（Hassner 2009）。与此相似，他们还说明，为何仪式性亵渎的某些形式可能触发暴力，即使其中并没有涉及物质利益的得失（Kaplan 2007）。

虽然文化主义进路和理性主义进路确实可以某种方式相互补充，但简单的综合仍然无法得出一种充分的理论（adequate theory）。这样的理论，首先在本体论上就是前后不一的，因为两种进路在对待社会范畴和符号范畴的现实性上，存在着根本的冲突。进一步说，即便是一种统贯的综合，也依然可能在本体论上缺乏完整性，因为这两种进路都没有对中层的社会现实作出充分的理论阐述。一方面，文化主义进路大多关注宏观层次的文化，是如何经由仪式和认同，形塑与指导微观层次的意义的，但它几乎闭口不谈正式制度和权力等级。另一方面，理性主义进路关注微观层次的互动，是如何经由集体行动与正式等级，巩固和约束宏观层次的制度的，但它对于仪式和认同依然三缄其口。因此,这里需要的正是这样一种统贯的综合,它同时在物质要素与符号要素的维度上,容纳社会现实的三种独立分析层次。

综合性进路

目前,我们看到了两种致力于综合的富有前景的成果。[①] 第一种成果从布迪厄的"实践政治经济学"(political economy of practice)那里受到了启发,其主要的缔造者是罗杰斯·布鲁贝克(Rogers Brubaker)、安德烈亚斯·威默(Andreas Wimmer)和他们在 UCLA 的学生。我们把他们称之为洛杉矶学派(the Los Angeles School)。第二种成果结合了理性选择的政治经济学和李普塞特/罗坎式(Lipset/Rokkan-style)的政治社会学,其主要构筑者是耶鲁大学"秩序、冲突与暴力"项目的斯塔西斯·卡里瓦斯(StathisKalyvas)及其学生和同事。我们把他们称之为耶鲁学派(the Yale School)。这两个学派都发展和完善了中层机制理论,只不过都没有充分地纳入宗教。

布迪厄的理论,建立在三个主导概念和两种要素之上:场域、资本和惯习,以及客观要素与主观要素(Gorski 2013,Swartz 1997)。因此,社会场域既是客观的位置空间,也是为了位置的主观竞争,类似于磁场和运动场。各种形式的资本(如经济资本、文化资本和社会资本),全都既有客观的存在(如有形资本、学术证书或网络结构),也有主观的存在(如动产[personal property]、具身性技巧或情感贯注)。惯习同样如此。就其是一套存储于人体的性情倾向而言,惯习是客观的,但就其是一套人类心智使用的认知图式而言,它又是主观的。简言之,布迪厄的理论蕴含着三个层面的社会本体论和两个维度的社会现象学。有一种运用这些概念的方式,是将民族和国家概念化为权力场域,将公民社会的群体和制度概念化为场域及其专属

---

① 第三种是由查尔斯·蒂利(Charles Tilly)、西德尼·塔罗(Sidney Tarrow)和杰克·古德斯通(Jack Goldstone)提出的抗争政治进路,但其倡导者并未花大力气关注族群、民族主义或宗教。

资本,将个体行动者和互动概念化为身体惯习与认知图式。① 这当然不是唯一的方法,却是对当下目标最有益的。

　　洛杉矶学派最大的贡献,是更为统贯和完整地阐述了族群与民族主义的认同及动员,既避免了文化主义者的整体论和观念论,也绕开了理性主义者的还原论和物质论(Brubaker 1996,2004;Wimmer 2002,2008)。他们认为,集体认同并不是简单地来自于一种(号称的)共享文化,但也绝不是由(假定的)客观自然赋予的。相反,它们随着持续进行的、无休无止的社会斗争,时而兴起,时而消解,或更恰当地说,时而加强,时而减弱。这些社会斗争,关乎竞争中的认同范畴的相对显著性,或换用布迪厄的术语来说,是针对支配性的"关照(vision)和划分(di-vision)原则"的"分类斗争"。至于是族群性胜于阶级(族群范畴居于中心),还是相反(族群范畴处于边缘),这都不是固定或给定的,而是任何一方皆可不断争取的。就此而言,族群性和民族主义不是结构而是过程,不是实体而是关系,不是事物而是事件。再者,集体行动也不单单是一些前社会形式的理性或利益的函数,更不是自由浮动的脚本或叙事之单纯展演。利益同样可以是位置性的和符号性的,在这个意义上,利益具有不可化约的社会性。但文化的约束也为创造性和即兴发挥,留下了足够的空间。因此,族群的动员和冲突,与符号性排斥联系在一起的程度,通常不会弱于物质性剥夺。集体仪式,尽管可能再生产团结,却也标示了族群的边界和等级,并对之加以正当化。就此而言,族群和民族主义的动员及冲突的关键机制,既不存在于文化的自主结构,也不存在于个体行动者的自我利益,而是处于宏观和微观的层次之间。

　　耶鲁学派的主要贡献,在于阐明了族群民族主义暴力冲突的关键机制和常规动力(Kalyvas 2003,2006;Wilkinson 2004)。这一成果的产生,得益于他们同内战现象的持续交锋,以及集体暴力的理性主义进路的不断祛魅。理性主义或霍布斯主义的进路提出,内战可以理解为局部冲突的单纯聚合。一旦中央当局瓦解,自然状态中一切人对一切人的战争就会出现。

① 这些类别既可以扩大,如将国际体系概念化为权力场域,也可以缩小,如将某特定群体或制度概念化为权力场域。

就此而言,内战仅仅只是局部宿怨的汇聚。一种施密特主义进路的文化主义版本提出,内战可以从一种主导性裂痕(master cleavage)的角度得到理解,这种裂痕源自主权的中心。就此而言,局部层次的暴力仅仅展现了国内的敌/友之分。这两种理论都只有部分正确。一方面,普通人中间的暴力(on-the-ground violence),的确较为典型地表现出一种局部的逻辑。内战可以为清算私人恩怨提供政治上的借口。然而,霍布斯主义的解释暗示,暴力常常含有选择性,不会不加鉴别。再者,暴力经常需要借助主导性裂痕来实现正当化;动机可以是私人的,辩护却必须是公共的。另一方面,围绕某种主导性裂痕——意识形态的、族群的或宗教的,等等——的政治两极化,经常发生在内战爆发之前;而且,在此之后的内战解释,一般都诉诸于这一主导性裂痕,从而赋予它一种持续的显著性。因此,对政治暴力逻辑的充分阐释,必须清楚地建立有关中层机制的理论,这些机制存在于局部或地方共同体的内部冲突当中,它们在中心与边缘、精英与大众之间作出调节。

结　语

20 年前,有一个共识还在广泛流传:现代民族主义是一种内生性的世俗现象(Anderson 1991,Gellner 1983,Hobsbawm 1992)。事实早已不是如此。如今,该科目的一流学者承认,(a)现代民族主义或许拥有宗教的谱系(如有关拣选的叙事);(b)民族认同常常沿着宗教裂痕(如新教和天主教,印度教和穆斯林)而形成;(c)民族主义的修辞和仪式,经常取材于宗教;(d)宗教民族主义可能是一种现代独有的民族主义(Brubaker 2012)。即便如此,将宗教因素纳入学术文献[的事业],还远未完成。这至少有 4 个原因:(a)有关宗教民族主义的最初的著作,大多采纳了文化主义的视角,这种视角经常(错误地)将启示录叙事当做宗教暴力的充分理由;(b)新兴宗教(膜拜团体)和宗教民族主义运动[经常]引发暴力,对于这类暴力的细致个案研究一再显示,共同体内部的动力学、政治语境和历史偶然性具有的重要意义,尽管如此,这些发现却并没有被社会学的民族主义文献很好地吸收;(c)社会学和政治科学中的主流民族主义文献,就算没有完全忽视宗教,也是不断地把宗教同族群性混淆在一起;(d)在经济学中,族群冲突的理性主义进路以十分狭隘的工具论和物质论理解暴力,忽视了神圣范畴和符号范畴作为暴力的触发器和靶子的作用。

以上讨论的族群冲突的综合性进路,通常也会忽视宗教,尽管如此,他们却比之前的诸种进路更有可能将宗教纳入考虑范围,这要归功于其三个层次和两种维度的建筑式样。在洛杉矶学派的布迪厄主义模型中,宗教被认为是(a)权力的民族或跨民族场域之内的一个自主场域;(b)社会行动者可以积累和交换的专属于某一场域的资本(即宗教资本);(c)个体惯习的组成成分,这种惯习形塑于家庭和学校的社会化,激活于特定的语境和脉络。于是,宗教民族主义可以理解为"关照和划分原则"跨越宗教和非宗教场域的同步,由此,宗教的原则和民族的原则变得更加显著,两者也更为紧密地联系在了一起。这种结合源自精英在几个相关场域分组之后的策略性结盟。这种进路的主要优势在于,它使得对宗教民族主义动员的分析,表现出解释上的富足性和历史上的偶然性。

另一方面,在耶鲁学派的新古典政治社会学中,宗教被认为是(a)国家或国际局势(national and international landscape)内的主导性裂痕,(b)地方和地区精英及制度,(c)个体的认同和荣誉之来源。从这一视角来看,宗教民族主义常常包含有一种结盟,即,通过共同体内部的对抗,在宗教方面的主导性裂痕(即宗教与宗教之间,或宗教与世俗之间)与个体的认同之间建立联系。之所以导致这一结果,是因为个体在社会生活不同层面上的利益和动机,均沿着宗教断层线的进行了(部分)同步。这种进路的一个优势在于,它为策略性诡计留下了巨大的空间,不仅是精英欺骗大众,也可以是大众欺骗精英。

尽管这两个框架可以通过更充分地纳入宗教——其制度、精英和认同——而变得更加强大,但当前的宗教民族主义著作,同样可以从一个更加全面广泛的理论框架中汲取力量。必须承认,如今有大量新近著作,关注到了中层机制在触发宗教民族主义暴力过程中的作用。该领域的学者已经开始致力于分析精英和意识形态(Fukase-Indergaard&Indergaard 2008,Hassner 2011),政治精英和宗教精英的结盟(De Juan 2008,Dowling 2012,

Fleming 2010，Gammer 2002，Hasenclever&Rittberger 2000，Miner 2003，Perica 2002，Verkhovsky 2002），以及针对神圣空间的对抗（Bacchetta 2010；Friedland& Hecht 1998；Gorenberg 2000；Hansen 1999；Hassner 2003，2009）。但惟有借助理论，这些研究成果才能实现概念上的整合与经验上的概括。

（张文杰译）

参考文献

Aburaiya I. 2009. Islamism, nationalism, and Western modernity：the case of Iran and Palestine. *Int. J. Polit. Cult. Soc.* 22:57 – 68

Adams J, Clemens ES, Orloff AS, eds. 2005. *Remaking Modernity：Politics, History, and Sociology.* Durham, NC：Duke Univ. Press

Agamben G. 1998. *Homo Sacer：Sovereign Power and Bare Life.* Stanford, CA：Stanford Univ. Press

Agamben G. 2005. *State of Exception.* Chicago：Univ. Chicago Press

Akturk S. 2009. Persistence of the Islamic Millet as an Ottoman legacy：mono-religious and anti-ethnic definition of Turkish nationhood. *Middle East. Stud.* 45:893 – 909

Alchian AA, Benjamin DK. 2006. *Property Rights and Economic Behavior.* Indianapolis, IN：Liberty Fund. 760 pp.

Anderson B. 1991. *Imagined Communities.* London：Verso

Arnason J. 1987. Nationalism, globalization and modernity. In *Global Culture*, ed. M Featherstone, pp.4 – 40. London：Sage

Arrow KJ. 1994. Methodological individualism and social knowledge. *Am. Econ. Rev.* 84:1 – 9

Asad T. 1999. Religion, nation-state, secularism. In *Nation and Religion：Perspectives on Europe and Asia*, ed. P. van der Veer, H Lehmann, pp. 178 – 97. Princeton, NJ：Princeton Univ. Press

Assmann J. 1997. *Moses the Egyptian：The Memory of Egypt in Western*

Monotheism. Cambridge, MA: Harvard Univ. Press. 276 pp.

Assmann J. 2009. *The Price of Monotheism*. Stanford, CA: Stanford Univ. Press. 140 pp.

Azam Jp. 1995. How to pay for the peace? A theoretical framework with references to African countries. *Public Choice* 83:173 – 84

Azam JP, Mesnard A. 2003. Civil war and the social contract. *Public Choice* 115:455 – 75

Azegami N. 2012. Local shrines and the creation of 'State Shinto.' *Religion* 42:63 – 85

Bacchetta p. 2010. The (failed) production of Hindu nationalized space in Ahmedabad, Gujarat. *Gender Place Cult.* 17:551 – 72

Barker PW. 2009. *Religious Nationalism in Modern Europe: If God Be for Us*. New York: Routledge

Becker GS. 1976. *The Economic Approach to Human Behavior*. Chicago: Univ. Chicago Press

Bhabha HK. 1990. *Nation and Narration*. London/New York: Routledge. 333 pp.

Blattman C, Miguel E. 2010. Civil war. *J. Econ. Lit.* 48:3 – 57

Boulding KE. 1962. *Conflict and Defense: A General Theory*. San Francisco: Harper

Breuilly J. 1993. *Nationalism and the State*. Chicago: Univ. Chicago Press

Bromley DG, Melton JG. 2002. *Cults, Religion, and Violence*. Cambridge, UK: Cambridge Univ. Press

Brubaker R. 1996. *Nationalism Reframed: Nationhood and the National Question in the New Europe*. New York: Cambridge Univ. Press. 202 pp.

Brubaker R. 2004. *Ethnicity Without Groups*. Cambridge, MA: Harvard Univ. Press. 283 pp.

Brubaker R. 2012. Religion and nationalism: four approaches. *Nations Natl.* 18:2 – 20

Brubaker R, Loveman M, Stamatov p. 2004. Ethnicity as cognition. *Theory Soc.* 33:31 – 64

Bush GW. 2001. *Address to a joint session of Congress and the American people*. Speech, Sept. 20, Washington, DC. http://georgewbush-whitehouse. archives. gov/news/releases/2001/09/20010920 – 8. html

Calhoun CJ. 1994. *Social Theory and the Politics of Identity*. Oxford, UK/ Cambridge, MA: Blackwell. 350 pp.

Cederman LE, Girardin L. 2007. Beyond fractionalization: mapping ethnicity onto nationalist insurgencies. *Am. Polit. Sci. Rev.* 101:173

Coase RH. 1990. *The Firm, the Market, and the Law*. Chicago: Univ. Chicago Press. 217 pp.

Cohen S. 2002. *Folk Devils and Moral Panics: The Creation of the Mods and Rockers*. New York: Routledge. 201 pp.

Cohn N. 1957. *The Pursuit of the Millennium*. Fair Lawn, NJ: Essential Books. 476 pp.

Colley L. 1992. *Britons: Forging the Nation*, 1707 – 1837. New Haven, CT: Yale Univ. Press. 432 pp.

Collier P, Hoeffler A, Rohner D. 2009. Beyond greed and grievance: feasibility and civil war. *Oxf. Econ. Pap.* 61:1 – 27

Collins R. 2009. *Violence: A Micro-Sociological Theory*. Princeton, NJ: Princeton Univ Press

Coser L. 1964. *The Functions of Social Conflict*. New York: Free Press. 192 pp.

Cramer C. 2002. *Homo economicusgoes* to war: methodological individualism, rational choice and the political economy of war. *World Dev.* 30:1845 – 64

Datta Rp. 2006. From political emergencies and states of exception to exceptional states and emergent politics: a neo-Durkheimian alternative to Agamben. *Int. Soc. Sci. J.* 58:169 – 82

Davis NZ. 1973. The rites of violence: religious riot in sixteenth-century France. *Past Present* 59:51 – 91

Dawkins R. 2008. *The God Delusion*. Boston, MA: Houghton Mifflin. 464 pp.

De Juan A. 2008. A pact with the devil? Elite alliances as bases of violent religious conflicts. *Stud. Confl. Terror*. 31:1120－35

Dennett D. 2007. *Breaking the Spell: Religion as a Natural Phenomenon*. New York: Penguin. 464 pp.

Dowling A. 2012. For Christ and Catalonia: Catholic Catalanism and nationalist revival in late Francoism. *J. Contemp. Hist*. 47:594－610

Dunstan I. 2008. The martyr wars: past and present polemics between Basque and Spanish nationalists over Christian victimhood during the Spanish Civil War. *J. Iberian Latin Am. Res*. 14:77－106

Durkheim É. 1893 (1984). *The Division of Labor in Society*. Transl. WD Halls. New York: Free Press. 352 pp.

Durkheim É. 1897 (1951). *Suicide: A Study in Sociology*. Transl. JA Spaulding, G Simpson. New York: Free Press

Durkheim É. 1912 (2001). *The Elementary Forms of Religious Life*. Transl. C Cosman, ed. MS Cladis. Oxford, UK/New York: Oxford Univ. Press. 358 pp.

Eagleton T. 2009. *Reason, Faith, and Revolution: Reflections on the God Debate*. New Haven, CT: Yale Univ. Press. 185 pp.

Eastwood J. 2010. Nationalism, religion and secularization: an opportune moment for research. *Rev. Relig. Res*. 52:90－111

Eisenstadt SN. 1987. *European Civilization in a Comparative Perspective: A Study in the Relations Between Culture and Social Structure*. Oslo/Oxford, UK/New York: Nor. Univ. Press. 162 pp.

Erikson K. 1966. *Wayward Puritans: A Study in the Sociology of Deviance*. New York: Wiley. 228 pp.

Fearon JD, Laitin DD. 2003. Ethnicity, insurgency, and civil war. *Am. Polit. Sci. Rev*. 97:75－90

Fleming M. 2010. The ethnoreligious ambitions of the Catholic Church and the ascendancy of communism in post-war Poland (1945 – 50). *Nations Natl.* 16:637 – 56

Fox J. 2004 The rise of religious nationalism and conflict: ethnic conflict and revolutionary wars, 1945 – 2001. *J. Peace Res.* 41:715 – 31

Friedland R. 2001. Religious nationalism and the problem of collective representation. *Annu. Rev. Sociol.* 27:125 – 52

Friedland R. 2011. The institutional logic of religious nationalism: sex, violence and the ends of history. *Polit. Relig. Ideol.* 12:1 – 24

FriedlandR, Hecht R. 1998. The bodies of nations: a comparative study of religious violence in Jerusalem and Ayodhya. *Hist. Relig.* 38:101 – 49

Fukase-Indergaard F, Indergaard M. 2008. Religious nationalism and the making of the modern Japanese state. *Theory Soc.* 37:343 – 74

Gammer M. 2002. Walking the tightrope between nationalism(s) and Islam(s): the case of Daghestan. *Cent. Asian Surv.* 21:133 – 42

Gat A, Yakobson A. 2013. *Nations: The Long History and Deep Roots of Political Ethnicity and Nationalism.* New York: Cambridge Univ. Press. 447 pp.

Gellner E. 1983. *Nations and Nationalism.* Ithaca, NY: Cornell Univ. Press. 150 pp.

Giddens A. 1991. *Modernity and Self-Identity: Self and Society in Late Modernity.* Stanford, CA: Stanford Univ. Press. 264 pp.

Girard R. 1986. *The Scapegoat.* Baltimore, MD: Johns Hopkins Univ. Press. 216 pp.

Girard R. 1995. *Violence and the Sacred.* New York: Contin. Int.

Girard R. 2011. *Sacrifice.* East Lansing: Mich. State Univ. Press. 103 pp.

Gleditsch NP, Wallensteen P, Eriksson M, Sollenberg M, Strand H. 2002. Armed conflict 1946 – 2001: a new dataset. *J. Peace Res.* 39:615 – 37

Gorenberg G. 2000. *The End of Days: Fundamentalism and the Struggle for the Temple Mount.* New York: Free Press. 275 pp.

Gorski PS. 2000. The Mosaic moment: an early modernist critique of modernist theories of nationalism. *Am. J. Sociol.* 105:1428 – 68

Gorski PS. 2013. Bourdieusian theory and historical analysis: maps, mechanisms, and methods. In *Bourdieu and Historical Analysis*, ed. PS Gorski, pp. 327 – 66. Durham, NC: Duke Univ. Press

Greenfeld L. 1996. Nationalism and modernity. *Soc. Res. Int. Q.* 63:3 – 40

Grosby S. 1991. Religion and nationality in antiquity: the worship of Yahweh and ancient Israel. *Eur. J. Sociol.* 32:229 – 65

Grosby S. 2002. *Biblical Ideas of Nationality, Ancient and Modern*. Winona Lake, IN: Eisenbraums

Grossman D. 1995. *On Killing: The Psychological Cost of Learning to Kill in War and Society*. Boston, MA: Little, Brown. 367 pp.

Grossman HI. 1991. A general equilibrium model of insurrections. *Am. Econ. Rev.* 81:912 – 21

Hall JR, Schuyler PD, Trinh S. 2000. *Apocalypse Observed: Religious Movements and Violence in North America, Europe, and Japan*. London/New York: Routledge. 228 pp.

Hansen TB. 1999. *The Saffron Wave: Democracy and Hindu Nationalism in Modern India*. Princeton, NJ: Princeton Univ. Press

Harris S. 2005. *The End of Faith: Religion, Terror and the Future of Reason*. New York: Norton. 352 pp.

Hart DB. 2009. *Atheist Delusions the Christian Revolution and Its Fashionable Enemies*. New Haven, CT: Yale Univ. Press. 253 pp.

Hasenclever A, Rittberger V. 2000. Does religion make a difference? Theoretical approaches to the impact of faith on political conflict. *Millenn. J. Int. Stud.* 29:641 – 74

Hassner RE. 2003. "To halve and to hold": conflicts over sacred space and the problem of indivisibility. *Secur. Stud.* 12:1 – 33

Hassner RE. 2009. *War on Sacred Grounds*. Ithaca, NY: Cornell Univ.

Press. 222 pp.

Hassner RE. 2011. Religion and international affairs: the state of the art. In *Religion*, *Identity and Global Governance*: *Ideas*, *Evidence and Practice*, ed. S Lamy, P James, pp. 37 – 56. Toronto: Univ. Toronto Press

Hayes C. 1960. *Nationalism*: *A Religion*. New York: Macmillan

Haynes J. 2010. Politics, identity and religious nationalism in Turkey: from Atat ̈ urk to the AKP. *Aust. J. Int. Aff.* 64:312 – 27

Hechter M. 2000. *Containing Nationalism*. Oxford, UK: Oxford Univ. Press

Hechter M, Friedman D, Appelbaum M. 1982. A theory of ethnic collective action. *Int. Migr. Rev.* 16:412 – 34

Hechter M, Levi M. 1979. The comparative analysis of ethnoregional movements. *Ethnic Rac. Stud.* 2:260 – 74

Hefner RW. 1998. Multiple modernities: Christianity, Islam, and Hinduism in a globalizing age. *Annu. Rev. Anthropol.* 27:83 – 104

Hirshleifer J. 1991. The technology of conflict as an economic activity. *Am. Econ. Rev.* 81:130 – 34

Hitchens C. 2009. *God Is Not Great*: *How Religion Poisons Everything*. New York: Hachette. 336 pp.

Hobsbawm EJ. 1992. *Nations and Nationalism Since* 1780: *Programme*, *Myth*, *Reality*. Cambridge, UK/New York: Cambridge Univ. Press. 206 pp.

Hubert H, Mauss M. 1898 (1964). *Sacrifice*, *Its Nature and Function*. Transl. WDHalls, ed. EE Evans-Pritchard. Chicago: Univ. Chicago Press. 165 pp.

Hume D. 1757 (2009). *Dialogues and Natural History of Religion*. Ed. JCA Gaskin. New York: Oxford Univ. Press. 256 pp.

Hussain N, Ptacek M. 2000. Thresholds: sovereignty and the sacred. *Law Soc.* Rev. 34:495 – 515

Hutchison WR, Lehmann H. 1994. *Many Are Chosen*: *Divine Election and Western Nationalism*. Minneapolis, MN: Fortress. 306 pp.

Ivekovic I. 2002. Nationalism and the political use and abuse of religion: the politicization of Orthodoxy, Catholicism and Islam in Yugoslav successor states. *Soc. Compass* 49:523 – 36

Jaffrelot C. 2007. *Hindu Nationalism: A Reader*. Princeton, NJ: Princeton Univ. Press. 391 pp.

Jakelic S. 2004. Considering the problem of religion and collective identity: Catholicism in Bosnia and Herzegovina, Croatia and Slovenia. In *On Religion and Politics*, ed. C Lovett, P Kernahan, 13:1 – 22. Vienna: IWM

Jerryson MK, Juergensmeyer M. 2010. *Buddhist Warfare*. Oxford, UK/ New York: Oxford Univ. Press. 257 pp.

Jewett R, Lawrence JS. 2003. *Captain America and the Crusade Against Evil: The Dilemma of Zealous Nationalism*. Grand Rapids, MI: W. B. Eerdmans. 392 pp.

Juergensmeyer M. 1993. *The New Cold War? Religious Nationalism Confronts the Secular State*. Berkeley: Univ. Calif. Press. 292 pp.

Juergensmeyer M. 2006. Nationalism and religion. In *The SAGE Handbook of Nations and Nationalism*, ed. G Delanty, K Kumar, pp. 182 – 91. London/ New Delhi: SAGE

Kahn PW. 2008. *Sacred Violence: Torture, Terror, and Sovereignty*. Ann Arbor: Univ. Mich. Press

Kalyvas SN. 2003. The ontology of "political violence": action and identity in civil wars. *Perspect. Polit.* 1:475 – 94

Kalyvas SN. 2006. *The Logic of Violence in Civil War*. Cambridge, UK: Cambridge Univ. Press

Kalyvas SN, Balcells L. 2010. International system and technologies of rebellion: how the end of the Cold War shaped internal conflict. *Am. Polit. Sci. Rev.* 104:415 – 29

Kaplan BJ. 2007. *Divided by Faith: Religious Conflict and the Practice of Toleration in Early Modern Europe*. Cambridge, MA: Belknap Press Harvard Univ. Press. 415 pp.

Kinnvall C. 2004. Globalization and religious nationalism: self, identity and ontological security. *Polit. Psychol.* 25:741 – 67

Kirsch J. 1998. *The Harlot by the Side of the Road: Forbidden Tales of the Bible*. New York: Ballantine Books. 395 pp.

Kiser E, Schneider J. 1994. Bureaucracy and efficiency—an analysis of taxation in early-modern Prussia. *Am. Sociol. Rev.* 59:187 – 204

Kohn H. 1944. *The Idea of Nationalism: A Study in Its Origins and Background*. New York: McMillan

Kramer M. 1991. Sacrifice and fratricide in Shiite Lebanon. *Terror. Polit. Violence* 3:30 – 47

Lee RLM. 1990. The state, religious nationalism, and ethnic rationalization in Malaysia. *Ethn. Racial Stud.* 13:482 – 502

Levi M. 1989. *Of Rule and Revenue*. Berkeley/Los Angeles: Univ. Calif. Press

Little D, Swearer D, eds. 2006. *Religion and Nationalism in Iraq: A Comparative Perspective*. Cambridge, MA: Harvard Univ. Press

Lybarger LD. 2007. *Identity and Religion in Palestine*. Princeton, NJ: Princeton Univ. Press

Marvin C, Ingle DW. 1999. *Blood Sacrifice and the Nation: Totem Rituals and the American Flag*. Cambridge, UK/New York: Cambridge Univ. Press. 398 pp.

Marx AW. 2003. *Faith in Nation: Exclusionary Origins of Nationalism*. New York/Oxford, UK: Oxford Univ. Press. 258 pp.

McLeod H. 2006. *World Christianities, c. 1914 – c. 2000*. Cambridge, UK/New York: Cambridge Univ. Press. 717 pp.

Melton JG, Bromley DG. 2002. Challenging misconceptions about the new religions—violence connection. In *Cults, Religion and Violence*, ed. DG Bromley, JG Melton, pp. 42 – 56. Cambridge, UK: Cambridge Univ. Press

Merdjanova I. 2000. In search of identity: nationalism and religion in Eastern Europe. *Relig. State Soc.* 28:233 – 62

Meyer J. 1999. The changing cultural content of the nation-state: a world society perspective. In *State/Culture: State Formation After the Cultural Turn*, ed. G Steinmetz, pp. 123 – 44. Ithaca, NY: Cornell Univ. Press

Miner SM. 2003. *Stalin's Holy War: Religion, Nationalism and Alliance Politics*, 1941 – 1945. Chapel Hill: Univ. N. C. Press

Mouffe C. 1999. *The Challenge of Carl Schmitt*. London/New York: Verso Books

Newman G. 1987. *The Rise of English Nationalism: A Cultural History*, 1740 – 1830. New York: St. Martin's. 294 pp.

North DC. 1990. *Institutions, Institutional Change, and Economic Performance*. Cambridge, UK/New York: Cambridge Univ. Press. 152 pp.

O'Brien CC. 1988. *God Land: Reflections on Religion and Nationalism*. Cambridge, MA: Harvard Univ. Press

O'Brien CC. 1994. *Ancestral Voices: Religion and Nationalism in Ireland*. Dublin: Poolbeg

Olson M. 1965. *The Logic of Collective Action; Public Goods and the Theory of Groups*. Cambridge, MA: Harvard Univ. Press. 176 pp.

Palaver W. 1992. A Girardian reading of Schmitt's political theology. *Telos*1992:43 – 68

Pape RA. 2005. *Dying to Win: The Strategic Logic of Suicide Terrorism*. New York: Random House. 335 pp.

Perica V. 2002. *Balkan Idols: Religion and Nationalism in Yugoslav States*. New York: Oxford Univ. Press

Ricoeur p. 1990. *Time and Narrative*, Vol. 1. Transl. K McLaughlin, D Pellauer. Chicago: Univ. Chicago Press

Rieffer B-AJ. 2003. Religion and nationalism: understanding the consequences of a complex relationship. *Ethnicities* 3:215 – 42

Roshwald A. 2006. *The Endurance of Nationalism: Ancient Roots and Modern Dilemmas*. Cambridge, UK/New York: Cambridge Univ. Press. 349 pp.

Saad-Ghorayeb A. 2002. *Hizbu'llah: Politics and Religion*. London: Pluto

Schelling TC. 1960. *The role of theory in the study of conflict*. RAND Res. Memo. RM-2515, RAND, Santa Monica, CA

Scheuerman WE. 2006. Carl Schmitt and the road to Abu Ghraib. *Constellations* 13:108 – 24

Schmitt C. 2005. *Political Theology: Four Chapters on the Concept of Sovereignty*. Transl. G Schwab. Chicago: Univ. Chicago Press. 70 pp.

Schmitt C. 2007. *The Concept of the Political.* Transl. G Schwab. Chicago: Univ. Chicago Press. 126 pp.

Schwartz RM. 1997. *The Curse of Cain: The Violent Legacy of Monotheism.* Chicago/London: Univ. Chicago Press. 211 pp.

Sells M. 2006. Pilgrimage and "ethnic cleansing" in Herzegovina. In *Religion and Nationalism in Iraq: A Comparative Perspective*, ed. D Little, D Swearer, pp. 145 – 56. Cambridge, MA: Harvard Univ. Press

Seton-Watson H. 1977. *Nations and States: An Enquiry into the Origins of Nations and the Politics of Nationalism.* London: Methuen

Sewell WH. 1992. Introduction: narratives and social identities. *Soc. Sci. Hist.* 16:479 – 88

Shenhav Y. 2007. Modernity and the hybridization of nationalism and religion: Zionism and the Jews of the Middle East as a heuristic case. *Theory Soc.* 36:1 – 30

Simmel G. 1903. The sociology of conflict. *Am. J. Sociol.* 9:490 – 525

Skya WA. 2009. *Japan's Holy War: The Ideology of Radical Shinto Ultranationalism.* Durham, NC/London: Duke Univ. Press

Smith AD. 2000. The 'sacred' dimension of nationalism. *Millenn. J. Int. Stud.* 29:791 – 814

Smith AD. 2003. *Chosen Peoples: Sacred Sources of National Identity.* Oxford, UK: Oxford Univ. Press. 330 pp.

Smith p. 2005. *Why War? The Cultural Logic of Iraq, the Gulf War, and*

Suez. Chicago: Univ. Chicago Press. 254 pp.

Somers MR. 1994. The narrative constitution of identity: a relational and network approach. *Theory Soc*. 23:605 – 49

Spohn W. 2003. Multiple modernity, nationalism: a global perspective. *Curr. Sociol*. 51:265 – 86

Spohn W. 2009. Europeanization, religion and collective identities in an enlarging Europe: a multiple modernities perspective. *Eur. J. Soc. Theory* 12 :358 – 74

Steinmetz G. 1992. Reflections on the role of social narratives in working-class formation: narrative theory in the social sciences. *Soc. Sci. Hist*. 16:489 – 516

Straughn JB, Feld SL. 2010. America as a "Christian nation"? Understanding religious boundaries of national identity in the United States. *Sociol. Relig*. 71:280 – 306

Swartz D. 1997. *Culture and Power: The Sociology of Pierre Bourdieu*. Chicago: Univ. Chicago Press. 333 pp.

Tambiah SJ. 1992. *Buddhism Betrayed? Religion, Politics, and Violence in Sri Lanka*. Chicago: Univ. Chicago Press. 203 pp.

Taylor C. 1989. *Sources of the Self: The Making of the Modern Identity*. Cambridge, MA: Harvard Univ. Press. 601 pp.

Tibi B. 1990. *Islam and the Cultural Accommodation of Social Change*. Boulder, CO: Westview. 272 pp.

Van der Veer p. 1994. *Religious Nationalism: Hindus and Muslims in India*. Berkeley/Los Angeles: Univ. Calif. Press

Van der Veer P, Lehmann H, eds. 1999. *Nation and Religion: Perspectives on Europe and Asia*. Princeton, NJ: Princeton Univ. Press

Verkhovsky A. 2002. The role of the Russian Orthodox Church in nationalist, xenophobic and anti-Western tendencies in Russia today: not nationalism, but fundamentalism. *Relig. State Soc*. 30:333 – 45

Von der Mehden FR. 1968. *Religion and Nationalism in Southeast Asia*.

Madison/Milwaukee/London: Univ. Wis. Press

Von Neumann J, Morgenstern O. 1944. *Theory of Games and Economic Behavior*. Princeton, NJ: Princeton Univ. Press. 625 pp.

Wilkinson S. 2004. *Votes and Violence: Electoral Competition and Ethnic Riots in India*. Cambridge, UK/New York: Cambridge Univ. Press. 293 pp.

Williamson OE, Winter SG, Coase RH. 1991. *The Nature of the Firm: Origins, Evolution, and Development*. New York: Oxford Univ. Press. 235 pp.

Wimmer A. 2002. *Nationalist Exclusion and Ethnic Conflict: Shadows of Modernity*. Cambridge, UK/New York: Cambridge Univ. Press. 319 pp.

Wimmer A. 2008. The making and unmaking of ethnic boundaries: a multilevel process theory. *Am. J. Sociol.* 113:970 – 1022

Wintrobe R. 1995. Some economics of ethnic capital formation and conflict. In *Nationalism and Rationality*, ed. A Breton, G Galeotti, P Salmon, R Wintrobe, pp. 43 – 70. Cambridge, UK: Cambridge Univ. Press

Zubrzycki G. 2006. *The Crosses of Auschwitz: Nationalism and Religion in Post-Communist Poland*. Chicago: Univ. Chicago Press. 277 pp.

Zuleika J. 1988. *Basque Violence: Metaphor and Sacrament*. Reno: Univ. Nevada Press

政治体中的信徒－公民困境

——群体资格路径

方　文

导　论

一、政治体中的信徒－公民困境

政治共同体的典范形式,到目前为止,依然是国家,即占有一定领土并能合法垄断暴力的政治实体。尽管国家建立的路径、历史遗产和在世界体系中的相对位置存在差别,但"公意"(general will)即所有人民的一致同意,是也应该是政治共同体建立的规范基础和合法化来源,它以宪法作为共同而超然的政治语法。因此,政治共同体的规范原则和合法化来源,应该奠基于哈贝马斯所勾画的"宪政爱国主义"(constitutional patriotism)情操之上(Harbermas,1994;Michelman,2001),以超越和统合共同体内部的不同族群、宗教、语言等多元文化共同体的差异。在此意义上,政治共同体,也是以民族记忆和英雄传奇为基本素材的道德共同体和牺牲共同体(the sacrifice community)。

在政治体公民的多元群体资格和多元社会认同结构中,其政治共同体的群体资格和公民认同及国家认同,应该占据优先地位,以超越地域、族群、宗教和语言的分歧和差异。但对作为宗教徒的公民而言,他们对跨国家的宗教共同体的忠诚可能超越对政治体的忠诚,从而成为政治体的离心力量。而这就是信徒—公民困境。

中国社会转型及其和平崛起,已经拓展了中国人的活动舞台。在国际层面,它伴随地缘政治格局和利益关系的重大调整;而在国内,不同区域、不同民族、不同阶层和不同户籍人群之间的社会认知和利益分化甚至是冲突,也在不断加剧。所有这些,都对国家建设提出挑战。

中国社会转型中的国家建设目标,就是牢固确立宪法作为共同而超然的政治语法,培育和强化"宪政爱国主义",以超越和统合人民共和国内部的不同地域、族群、宗教和语言等多元文化共同体的差异。换言之,在共和国所有公民的多元群体资格和多元社会认同结构中,其政治共同体的群体资格和公民认同及国家认同,应该占据优先地位,以超越地域、族群、宗教和语言的分歧和差异。

中国国家建设的现实严峻挑战,是台独、藏独和疆独势力。它们不仅是国内问题,敌视中国的不同国际势力也都想乘机介入。台独、藏独和疆独的社会心理意涵,有两方面涵义。对这些分裂势力而言,他们企图用地域认同、民族认同、宗教认同来凌驾甚至替代公民认同和国家认同;而对国际敌对势力而言,他们企图用种种方式来丑化和打击中国人的公民认同和国家认同的认同信心(identity confidence)。其中,极端的宗教认同占据中心,是信徒—公民困境的典型代表。

二、宗教认同:叠合认同

无论是欧洲宗教经验、美国宗教经验还是中国宗教经验之间的差异,无论是宗教世俗化范式、宗教市场论范式及其替代范式之间的激烈论争,宗教制度和宗教生活,仍然是当代社会制度和精神生活的基本面向(如Yang, 2006)。但任何宗教都是活在具体的宗教徒群体追求神圣的行动中。它们本质性地体现在宗教徒群体在身、心、灵的活动中被践行的生命体悟和人生实践,对生命意义和生活目的的集体关切,对于超验价值的共同体验和群体承诺。

宗教认同的建构/重构,主要是以宗教叙事(religious narratives)作为建构因子。有 4 种基本的话语叙事：本体叙事(ontological narrative)或自传叙事、内在叙事(internal narrative)、公开叙事(public narrative)和元叙事(matanarrative)(Somers，1994)。

萨默丝的叙事论，成为阿默曼论辩宗教认同的理论基础。尽管阿默曼质疑萨默丝把社会行动还原为文本和言辞的合理性，但她明晰地主张在以肉身呈现的宗教行动中，宗教叙事具有核心地位。宗教叙事，是信徒以"神圣他者"(Sacred Other/s)为核心的多重叙事的生产和再生产过程(Ammerman,2003)。以肉身在场为出发点，信徒在宗教制度所勾画的框架下，在同伴之间，在和神圣他者的私人沟通中，不断叙述平安、喜悦和恩典，也不断言说焦虑、困扰和挣扎。

但对任何的宗教徒而言，他并不仅仅只是宗教徒，他还参与世俗的社会生活，是国家公民。逻辑上，宗教徒和公民有三种可能关系。第一种类型是宗教徒/公民合一，如在现代神权国家中；第二种是信徒的宗教认同促进其公民认同的建构(如 Lichterman，2008)。第三种就是本文关注的信徒—公民困境。

杨凤岗对美国华人基督徒的经验研究，洞悉了信徒—公民的复杂纠葛。这些华人基督徒，如何成为基督徒，如何成为美国公民，又如何保持其中国的文化共同体的资格，成为不停息的争夺中心。杨凤岗发现，华人基督徒的显著目标是解构华人认同，而重构叠合认同(adhesive identity)(Yang，1999)

本文目的是在叠合认同的基础上，以行动者的多元群体资格为视角(方文，2008a；2008b)，来分析和解释宗教徒的信徒—公民困境。

何为宗教徒——多元群体资格路径

一、行动者的多重群体资格

在任何社会语境之下，都存在既定的社会分类(social classification)或社会范畴化(social categorization)机制(方文，2008b)。有关社会范畴化机制的感悟,是人社会知识体系的一部分,也是共享实在的一部分。无论是基于先赋的品质还是后致的特征,甚至是特定制度化的标定,人在生命历程中被归属于不同的群体,拥有多元群体资格(multiple memberships)。先赋的品质,是和个体出身相关联的社会范畴属性,如年龄、性别、族群,甚至是户籍和出生地;后致的特征,则是个体在社会化过程中所主动寻求的社会范畴属性,如教育水平和个人职业,甚至是消费和品味;而由制度化的标定所赋予的特征,则是特定制度语境对人的社会范畴属性的限定,如城里人和乡下人,甚至是藏传佛教传统中对喇嘛、班禅和活佛的选择过程。人的社会存在的本质,实际上可具体化为人的多元群体资格在社会生活中的具体表征过程。而对宗教行动者而言,宗教群体资格只是其多重群体资格的一个面向。

就先赋的群体资格而言,接生的关口、"诞生的创伤"(birth-trauma)和出生后的庆典,就是其进入社会的入会条件和入会仪式(rites of initiation);就后致的群体资格而言,不同转折关口的考试和资格证书就是其入会条件,而典礼和迎新会则是新成员的入会仪式;就由制度化的标定所赋予的群体资格而言,程序性的安排、选择、认定和裁决是其入会条件,并伴随对应的入会仪式。无论是入会条件和入会仪式,还是对群体资格的评价,在一定程度上和在一定范围内,都是社会共识的(social consensual)。尽管秘密社团的入会条件和入会仪式不为外群体所知,但它们也是内群共享知识的一部分。

二、宗教皈依的内涵

皈依,是指非宗教信徒变为一种宗教信徒的过程,或者从一种宗教信徒变成另一种宗教信徒的过程。对已经禀赋多元群体资格的行动者而言,皈依的结果是他主动地获得一种新的群体资格,即宗教群体资格。而对没有自主判断和行为能力的个体如婴儿或昏迷病人而言,我们基于推定同意(inferred consent)原则。这有两层涵义。第一,我们推定他们的法定监护人的意愿是其意愿的合适代表;第二,如果他们有自主判断和行为能力,我们推定他们的行动意愿和其法定监护人的意愿一致。

宗教群体资格,对皈依者而言,具有积极的认知/情感/价值意蕴,即社会认同感。

　　对一神教而言,其宗教群体资格是单一而排他的;而对多神教而言,宗教群体资格可以是多重而叠加的。一神教和多神教的区分可得以引申。第一,宗教群体资格的权重有别。一神教的群体资格之于皈依者更为珍贵,更为凸显;第二,入会条件有别。因为一神教是高度排他的,其群体资格的获得要经受更严厉的考验。第三,去皈依的后果有别。如果皈依者对其特定宗教群体资格没有社会认同感,他就会忽视或放弃这种资格,或者寻求新的宗教群体资格。这个过程,可称之为去皈依(de-conversion)。皈依和去皈依,是宗教变迁的基本动力之一。对一神教而言,去皈依的社会心理后果更为严重,也更为持久。

　　在一神教和多神教之间,以及一神教的不同教派之间,入会条件和入会仪式有别。有的条件更为严厉而苛刻,仪式更为庄重而神圣。这些差别不是随意的安排,而是有深刻的社会心理意蕴。

　　宗教市场论学者艾纳孔也曾注意到这个基本问题。他主张,严厉性(strictness),使宗教组织更为强大,也更有吸引力,因为它降低"搭便车"(free-riding)(Innaccone, 1994:1180)。艾纳孔的解释差矣。严厉条件的入会仪式,依据认知失调论(the theory of cognitive dissonance)(Festinger, 1957;Aronson and Mills, 1959),会使皈依者产生对宗教群体资格的高承诺、依恋和认同,会使皈依者更为珍爱自身的宗教资格。

　　还有庄重而神圣的仪式。马歇尔构造了有关仪式活动的综合理论模型仪式实践论(the theory of ritual practice)。在马歇尔的模式里,仪式活动有两个基本元素:仪式给参与者所创造的共在情景(co-presence)和仪式实践(ritual practices)或仪轨,有种种社会心理过程和机制,渗透其中(Marshall, 2002:360 – 380)。首先是共在情景。共在,通过群体界定、人际比较和群体极化(group polarization),对信念有直接效果;共在又通过依恋(attachment)、相似性和最简范畴化(mere categorization)等社会心理机制,对隶属感(belonging)有直接效果;共在,同时还会激发其他重要的社会心理过程,如去个体化(deindividuation)、生理唤醒(arousal)和社会促进(social facilitation),以及从众(conformity)和心理感染(mental contagion),对仪式参与者的认知、情感和行为所有方面,都有显著影响(Marshall, 2002:361 –

363）。

其次是仪式实践。马歇尔明确主张,在共在情景中,参与者在面对反常（anomaly）、过渡（transitions）或更新（renewals）事件时,他们总得做点什么（Marshall, 2002:363 - 368）。在仪式实践的表演中,参与者对自身和同伴行为的不当归因（misattribution）,他们所体验的认知失调（cognitive dissonance）,以及对自身和同伴行为的自我觉知（self-perception）等,都极大地强化宗教信念和隶属感。共在情景和仪式实践,在庄重而神圣的仪式中,使参与者能超越俗世的羁绊,体验到超验的价值,并因此强化自身的信仰。

三、宗教群体资格的识别和觉知

物以类聚,人以群分。为了理解所生活的世界,行动者不得不对人和物等进行分类,并把他们纳入不同的范畴中,以削减环境的复杂性。分类过程,亦即社会范畴化过程（social categorization）。

范畴化,只能是行动者的范畴化,它们同时也是行动者的基本认知潜能和认知工具。即使是在原初状态下,行动者也能进行初始分类或范畴化。而4 - 5月大的幼儿也开始辨别家人和外人,开始有“认生”反应。泰费尔则发现,对6 - 7岁的儿童而言,即使他们对不同国家最多只有些许的经验知识,他们也能以自己的肤色为界限来明确地表现好恶。借助社会范畴化,行动者一方面能对社会环境进行切割、分类和秩序化,并因此而采取灵活权衡的社会行动,另一方面,也为自我参照提供了一个定向系统,它们创造和界定行动者在社会中的位置（Tajfel and Turner, 1986: 15 - 16）。

范畴化过程具有交互性。其一,行动者一出生,就生长在既定的社会范畴化语境中,被分类和标定。其二,行动者以自我为中心,对自身和在场的他人进行分类,把自身和他人纳入确定的群体之中,但同时行动者自身也被在场的他人所分类。其三,行动者的分类和他人的分类具有最低限度的重叠共识。也正因为如此,对群体资格的评价是社会共识性的,并且社会范畴化体制是共享实在的一部分。

作为范畴化主体,行动者并不是宗教市场论学者所鼓吹的“理性经济人”,他是“被驱动的策略家”（the motivated tactician）（方文,2005；Taylor, 1998）。在种种形式的理性人或经济人的人观假定（personhood）中,行动者被认为能完备地收集与问题情景相关的信息,进而进行完备的加工并作出最优决策。就宗教实践而言,潜在信徒,依照宗教市场论者的逻辑,他们为了满足其灵性生活的需要,在多元化的宗教商品市场上,能够理性的权衡并作出最优决断,从而购买最优的宗教商品。这是商品逻辑和功利逻辑在超验领域傲慢而狂妄地扩张。当代社会认知研究也已经雄辩地解构了此类假设(Kahneman, et al. , 1982/2001; Fiske, 1991)。而奠基于理性经济人假设的宗教市场论,因此也面临困境。

"被驱动的策略家",意味着行动者有可资利用的多元信息加工策略,而这些策略的选择,则基于行动者的目标、动机、需要以及社会环境中的力量。具体说,行动者,有时如"朴素科学家"(na? ve scientist),对相关任务的信息,进行系统而认知努力的加工,有时又如"认知吝啬者"(cognitive miser),在面临任务情景或问题情景时,进行启发式和认知节俭的加工。但无论如何,他们的社会认知加工过程,总是为了满足其目标和动机。因此,有关行动者的线形图像,正被一个复杂的能动者所替代。他能在复杂的社会过程和社会情景中,对范围广泛的信息如即时的社会语境、自身的内在状态和远期目标,保持高度的敏感,并能援引可资利用的社会和文化资源,主动地认知和建构社会实在。

行动者社会范畴化的基本策略是(多重)二元编码(the binary codings)(Beyer, 1998; Chaiken et al. , 1999)。在对人和物等进行分类的过程中,行动者的主宰偏好是采用对立概念来进行区分。二元编码的分类策略或二元编码机制,有两个直接后果。第一,在任何社会语境之下,基于特定显著的分类线索,在场的所有人以分类者为核心,被纳入内群体和外群体之中。尤其明显的是在宗教场域中,通过社会范畴化,宗教群体与外群体得以区分,并且这种区分是社会共识性的。第二,行动者在共时和历时的分类体制下,基于交互性的范畴化过程,被纳入多重的二元编码的逻辑之中,他因此会负荷多重的群体资格。

对宗教行动者而言,在其宗教群体资格之外,他还同时负荷其他多重的群体资格。只有在其宗教资格凸显时,他才是宗教徒。其宗教资格如何凸显以引导其心理活动和行为表现,就成为另一基础性难题。有关社会知识激活的社会认知研究,就专注于这一难题,并有典范性的研究成果。

把社会知识的激活机制和群体资格的凸显关联起来,需要进行辨析。行动者在其毕生社会化过程中,无论基于启发式加工还是系统加工,都会型塑其独特的社会知识体系,其基本单元就是社会范畴。行动者的社会知识体系,关乎特定的社会和文化语境,关乎自身和他人的态度、能力、情感和行为及其行为后果,也关乎特定群体资格的获得、条件及其行为准则。行动者的社会知识体系,并不是逻辑连贯的,而是"领域—特异的"(do-main-specific),分别对应于不同面向的语境。这些"领域—特异的"的社会知识,在特定语境下处在潜伏状态,等待被激活和调动。如果与特定群体资格相对应的"领域—特异的"的社会知识或社会范畴被激活和调动,就可以逻辑合理地推断他的群体资格被激活和调动,并相应地引导和主宰后续的心理和行为。因此,多重群体资格的行动者在具体情景下凸显其特定群体资格的问题,就可转换为行动者的社会知识体系中"领域—特异的"的社会范畴被激活和调动的问题。

在希金斯启动研究(priming)(Higgins, et al, 1977)的基础上,社会知识的激活机制被系统地揭示出来(Higgins, 1996)。第一是可接近性(ac-cessibility)。通过范畴启动或被频繁使用,社会知识体系中与特定范畴相对应的"领域—特异的"知识从潜伏和沉睡状态转变为准备状态或待命状态(readiness)。处在准备状态或待命状态的社会知识,类似于行动者手头的工具箱(tool-kit),时刻准备派上用场。第二是可用性(applicability)。待命状态的社会知识或工具箱,在面对问题情景或任务时,存在两种情况:吻合或者不吻合,匹配或者不匹配。只有吻合或匹配的待命知识,才能被应用,亦即具有可用性,或称之为"吻合优度"(goodness of fit)。而那些不匹配的知识,尽管被激活而处在待命状态,它们也不会被应用,就像工具箱中不合用的工具一样。可接近性和可用性主要关注行动者的因素。

在此之外,希金斯主张特定情景中刺激或线索的显著性(salience)也会激发特定范畴的激活。如在我们所研究的基督新教场域中,与基督新教有关的刺激无处不在,具有高度的显著性。它必然会从信徒——非信徒这个维度在信徒身上激活宗教范畴,并且同时在非信徒或慕道者身上激活"我不是信徒"的知识。宗教信徒和非宗教信徒之间可觉知的差异或符号边界(Lamont and Fournier, 1992;Lamont and Molnar, 2002),通过二元编码的范畴化逻辑,得以型塑。

宗教徒何为

一、宗教群体资格的强化逻辑

宗教徒对其宗教群体资格的积极评价,即是宗教认同。换言之,宗教群体资格对其具有积极的认知/情感/价值意蕴。而这种宗教认同,通过社会比较过程而得以强化。

费斯汀格最先系统构造了精美的社会比较论的假设—演绎体系,来解释和预测个体有关能力和观点的社会比较过程,并在逻辑上涵盖了社会学传统中的参照群体论和相对剥夺论这些中层理论模型(Festinger, 1954)。但费斯汀格的社会比较过程只是内群的人际比较,它仅基于个体的人格特征。泰费尔则把人际比较过程拓展至内群与外群之间的群际比较(Tajfel, 1981:254 - 67)。特定群体资格的显著意义,只有在和他群体的关系中,亦即在与他群体的比较和对比中,才呈现出来(Tajfel, 1981:256 - 259)。我属群体(one's own group)的评价,决定于对特定的他群体的参照。这种参照,依据价值——负荷的品质和特征通过社会比较而获得。内群和外群之间,积极的差异比较(discrepant comparison)产生高声望,而消极的差异比较则会导致低声望。通过内群/外群比较,积极评价我属群体的压力,导致社会群体力图把自身和其他群体区别开来。

概言之,社会比较过程有两类:内群的人际比较和内群与外群之间的群际比较。通过内群人际比较产生内群分化(in-group differentiation),而通过内群和外群之间的群际比较产生外群同质性(out-group homogeneity)。

二、宗教内群分化准则:灵性资本

世俗社会群体中的内群分化和精英生产逻辑,主要是基于权力资本、经济资本和文化资本,并形成特定的角色结构和地位结构。我们的实地研究发现,在宗教群体内部,这些世俗社会中的分化逻辑是不相干的。宗教群体有其独特的内群分化和精英生产逻辑,其准则或尺度是灵性资本 (spiritual capital)。

宗教市场论学者也注意到这类问题。艾纳孔在其宗教市场论的图式中,类比经济资本,构造了"宗教资本"(religious capital)的概念。宗教资本,是宗教信徒所拥有的"与特定宗教有关的技能和经验,它们包括宗教知识、对教会仪轨和教义的熟悉程度,以及与宗教同伴的友谊网络"(转引自 Verter, 2003:158)。艾纳孔对宗教资本的界定,涵盖了布尔迪厄多元资本论中的社会资本(同伴的友谊网络)和文化资本(教会仪轨和教义的熟悉程度和宗教知识)。但艾纳孔恰恰放弃了宗教的核心特征:信仰者的情感承诺。在艾纳孔的宗教资本基础上,斯达克和芬克把宗教资本理解为对特定宗教文化的掌握和依恋程度(斯达克和芬克,2004:150)。但这些宗教市场论学者,对宗教生活的理解,有致命的偏差。请比较一个不信仰基督宗教的基督宗教学者和一个不识字的乡村虔诚基督徒之间的宗教文化修养。前者可能对基督教义和《圣经》以及基督宗教的历史演化和现状,有系统而雄辩的修养,但他不信;而后者,可能连上帝或基督这些字都不会写,但上帝在他的心里。

在布尔迪厄符号资本的基础上,伏太尔构造了灵性资本的概念(Verter, 2003)。但伏太尔过分强调信徒功利性的灵性资本积累和传递的逻辑,以求在社会位置层级化的激烈竞争中,获得优势。就我们的实地研究而言,这些都是无关紧要的。

在伏太尔研究的基础上,灵性资本,可界定为宗教徒在其灵性活动中劳动的积累和所蒙受的恩典。宗教群体内部,不同信徒所蒙受的恩典和自身的灵性努力是不同的,其结果是灵性资本不同信徒身上的分布是不一样的。正是这种偏异的分布,内群分化和精英生产逻辑可以辨析出来。基于我们的实地研究,灵性资本可从三个方面进行度量:信仰的纯粹性程度、宗教行为的卷入性程度和宗教群体内部人际网络中的相对位置(方文,2005)。

三、宗教徒惯例性和典范性的行为模式

特定群体资格一旦获得,它就是动态的,而不是凝固的。换言之,群体

资格通过规则化的社会行为得以不断地彰显出来。它有两个基本功能。其一，规则化的社会行为，从外显的意义上不断地生产和再生产可觉知的群体标志。而这些群体标志是识别和评价群体资格的基本线索，同时也是群际符号边界的线索。这些标志，主要有话语行为模式，消费模式，容貌风度和品位。

其二，规则化的社会行为，是群体记忆和群体社会表征体系（Farr and Moscovici，1984；Moscovici，2000）的载体。其结果是群体资格的显著性被不断地激活，群体社会认同和群体符号边界在行动中不断地生产和再生产（Lamont and Fournier，1992；Lamont and Molnar，2002）。

而对宗教群体而言，其惯例性和典范性的行为模式，主要是读经、和教友定期的聚会和定期地参加宗教仪式。通过这些典范性的社会行为，宗教徒在行动中不断地强化自身的宗教资格，不断地体验和重构跨时空的神圣共同体的群体记忆和群体社会表征体系，不断生产和再生产群体社会认同以及和与他群体的符号边界。

宗教徒的圣／俗生活

一、宗教原教旨主义

当代宗教徒的群体资格的获得和宗教认同的建构过程，发生在理性化、市场化和世界除魅的语境下。世界的去神秘化过程（demystification），自身非预期地播撒了两粒种子，一粒是世界的再神秘化过程（remystifica-tion），另一粒是反抗去神秘化过程。强烈主张世界的再神秘化过程，并反抗去神秘化过程的民众、组织和运动，也就是宗教原教旨主义（religious fun-damentalism），它以激进的宗教参与和宗教认同为表征（Emerson and Hart-man，2006：128）。

必须再次强调，宗教资格只是宗教徒多元群体资格的一个面向，尽管是权重可能很重的一个面向。但对宗教原教旨主义者而言，在其多元的群体资格中，其宗教群体资格，几乎在所有语境下都被激活，而具有显著性。

可以把宗教徒在其宗教资格主导下的生活称之为宗教生活或神圣生活，而由其他多元群体资格所主导的生活称之为世俗生活。宗教徒的宗教生活是基于灵性资本，而世俗生活则是基于权力资本、经济资本和文化资本，或统称为世俗资本。宗教徒的灵性资本，在有些语境下，可能具有全能资本特性，可能转化为形式不同的世俗资本，如在神权国家中。尽管如此，因为灵性资本和世俗资本各自发挥作用的领域有别，宗教徒的宗教生活和世俗社会得以区分。

如果宗教徒的灵性资本蜕变为全能资本，宗教徒的宗教群体资格几乎在所有情景下都具有显著性。

多元资本之间的相互竞争和不可替代，是健全社会功能分化的基本特征，也是行动者潜能完备实现的可能条件。行动者身上是多种力量交互博弈的战场，但它动态而均衡。它从一个侧面表明功能分化的不同群体在社会生活中各自独具的尊严和合法性，以及行动者多元群体资格之间不可替代的独具尊严和合法性。如果一种资本形式具有全能特征，它能替代或转换为可欲求的其它所有资本形式，如中国社会中的权力资本，这种社会就是高度僵化而独断的社会。在其中，权力成为"赢者通吃"的手段，"仕而优则学"现象，也就不足为怪了。

如果灵性资本逾越其合法性的领域，替代或转换为可欲求的其它所有资本形式，宗教徒动态而多元的群体资格就已名存实亡，他所有的生活被宗教资格所主宰，他的宗教资格几乎在所有情景下具有显著性。如果宗教行动者的宗教资格几乎在所有情景下都具有显著性，他们的灵性资本就转变为生命资本。

二、极端宗教徒的灵性资本：生命资本

生命资本是指以生命为武器的意愿和能力。它与自杀和杀人不同。自杀者厌恶生命，而杀人者蔑视生命。他们都没有体会到生命的高贵、无价和尊严。但行动者在支付生命资本的时候，我们能感受到行动者对生命的眷念。

生命资本是所有人都拥有的潜在资本形式，它无价而唯一，无可替代也不可复生，它是也应该是终极目的而不是任何其它目的的手段。其价值

超越所有的资本形式,具有神圣而超验的品质。当生命资本替换为其它资本形式的时候,生命被贬低,被践踏。大多数人没有意愿、没有机会、也没有勇气用生命作为最终手段。生命成为生命资本,只有有限的几种可能。其一,绝望中的无助者。面对困境时,他们没有任何可以倚靠,唯有生命,只有一次机会的生命。其二,杀身成仁的义士。他们用生命来成就理想、信念和忠诚。其三,极端的宗教徒。当肉体生命被认为是灵性生命或永恒生命的手段时,肉体生命的尊严就会被贬低。他们随时准备为其宗教资格和极端认同支付生命资本。而宗教性的自杀袭击者,就是基于极端的宗教认同而支付生命资本。

基于灵性资本,有可能识别潜在的宗教性自杀袭击者和其他宗教极端分子。

恐怖主义是社会学新的研究领域。恐怖主义社会学已关注下列基本议题:恐怖主义的社会起源和社会建构;作为政治暴力和沟通手段的恐怖主义;恐怖主义的组织化、恐怖分子的社会化以及恐怖主义的社会控制(Turk,2004)。但如何识别和监控潜在的恐怖分子,仍然是研究上的挑战。基于灵性资本,有可能识别潜在的宗教性恐怖分子。因为对宗教性的自杀袭击者和其他宗教极端分子而言,宗教群体资格是其生命的唯一,在几乎所有情景下都具有显著性。他们时刻准备着用生命作为武器去实现自身对宗教资格的承诺和忠诚。他们的灵性资本必然和普通信徒有可觉知的差别。

在国家建设过程中,如何建构从容而恰当的认同技术以强化公民认同、消解极端的宗教认同,并且使宗教认同成为公民认同建构的资源? 所有这些基本难题,群体资格视角可能提供洞识和灵感。

参考文献

方文,2005,《群体符号边界如何形成? 以北京基督新教群体为例》,《社会学研究》第 1 期。

——2008a,《学科制度和社会认同》。北京:中国人民大学出版社。

——2008b,"转型心理学:以群体资格为中心",《中国社会科学》第 4

期。

斯达克和芬克,2004,《信仰的法则:解释宗教之人的方面》,杨凤岗译。北京:中国人民大学出版社。

Ammerman, N. T. 2003, "Religious Identities and Religious Institutions". Pp. 207 – 224 in M. Dillon ed. *Handbook of the Sociology of Religion*. Cambridge University Press.

Aronson, E., and Mills, J. 1959 "The Effect of Severity of Initiation on Liking for a Group". *Journal of Abnormal and Social Psychology*, Vol. 59:177 – 81.

Chaiken, S., and Trope, Y. (Eds.) 1999 *Dual-Process Theories in Social Psychology*. New York: Guilford.

Emerson, M. O. and Hartman, D. 2006, "The Rise of Religious Fundamentalism". *Annual Review of Sociology*, Vol. 32:127 – 44.

Farr, R. M., and Moscovici, S. (Eds.) 1984 *Social Representation*. Cambridge: Cambridge University Press.

Festinger, L. 1954 "A Theory of Social Comparison Processes". *Human Relations*, Vol. 7:117 – 140.

——1957 *A Theory of Cognitive Dissonance*. Stanford: Stanford University Press.

Fiske, S., and Taylor, S. E. 1991 *Social Cognition* (2nd ed.). New York: McGraw-Hill.

Habermas, J. 1994 "Struggles for Recognition in the Democratic Constitutional State." Pp. 107 – 148 in C. Taylor et al. *Multiculturalism: Examing the Politics of Recognition*. Edited and Introduced by A. Gutmann. Princeton, N. J.: Princeton University Press.

Higgins, E. T. et al 1977 "Category Accessibility and Impression Formation". *Journal of Experimental Social psychology*, Vol. 13:141 – 54.

Higgins, E. T. 1996 Knowledge Activation: Accessibility, Applicability and Salience. In E. T. Higgins and A. E. Kruglanski (Eds.) *Social Psychology: Handbook of Basic Principles* (Pp133 – 168). New York: Guilford Press.

Iannaccone, L. R. 1994, "Why Strict Churches Are Strong." *American Journal of Sociology*, Vol. 99:1180 – 1211.

Lamont, M., and Fournier, M. (Eds.) 1992, *Cultivating Differences: Symbolic Boundaries and the Making of Inequality*, The University of Chicago Press.

Lamont, M., and Molnar, V. 2002, "The Study of Boundaries in the Social Sciences." *Annual Review of Sociology*, Vol. 28:167 – 95.

Lichterman, p. 2008. "Religion and the Construction of Civic Identity". *American Sociological Review*, Vol. 73:83 – 104.

Marshall, D. A. 2002 "Behavior, Belonging, and Belief: A Theory of Ritual Practice". *Sociological Theory*, Vol. 20, No. 3:360 – 380.

Michelman, F. I., 2001, "Morality, Identity and 'Constitutional Patriotism'". *Ratio Juris*, Vol. 14, No. 3:253 – 71

Moscovici, S. 2000 *Social Representations: Explorations in Social Psychology*. Cambridge: Polity.

Somers, M. R. 1994, "The Narrative Constitution of Identity". *Theory and Society*, Vol. 23, No. 5:605 – 649.

Tajfel, H. 1981 *Human Groups and Social Categories: Studies in Social Psychology*. Cambridge: Cambridge University Press.

Tajfel, H., and Turner, J. C. 1986 The Social Identity Theory of Intergroup Behavior. In S. Worchel et al (Eds.) *Psychology of Intergroup Relations* (Pp7 – 24). Chicago: Nelson-Hall.

Taylor, S. E. 1998 The Social Being in Social Psychology. In D. T. Gilbert et al (Eds.) *The Handbook of Social Psychology* (4th ed. 2Vol. s) (Vol. 1: 58 – 95). New York: McGraw-Hill.

Turk, A. T. 2004 "Sociology of Terrorism". *Annual Review of Sociology*, Vol. 30:271 – 86.

Verter, B. 2003 "Spiritual Capital: Theorizing Religion with Bourdieu Against Bourdieu". *Sociological Theory*, Vol. 21, No. 2:150 – 174.

Yang, Fenggang(杨凤岗), 1999, *Chinese Christians in America: Conver-

sion, *Assimilation*, *and Adhesive Identities*. The Pennsylvania State University Press.

Yang, F. G. 2006, "The Red, Black, and Gray Markets of Religion in China." *The Sociological Quarterly*, Vol. 47:93 – 122

Religion, Science, and Governance

Graeme Lang

Introduction

Governance can be complicated by the allegiances of religious believers, who may devote much of their allegiance to the religion or the deity or in some cases to the religious leader, which may reduce or even replace primary allegiance to the state and its leaders. Whether or not this is a problem for governance depends on the agendas of the state or of particular leaders or regimes, and the extent to which those agendas may promote behavior or policies which conflict with religious doctrines or claims or with the agendas of religious leaders. In any case, the supernatural realm, and the prospect of eternal reward (or eternal punishment, or prolonged afterlife/next-life consequences) cannot be matched by any combination of state-allocated rewards and punishments if those supernatural consequences are extreme, and fervently believed.

Hence, there is always a possibility of conflict between policies of the state or regime, and what is prescribed within a religion. Religious allegiances, in any case, may be stronger than allegiances to the state or to any particular regime. ①

It is rare that such alternative allegiances lead to direct conflict with a state, if the state provides a neutral framework within which religions can be practiced without repression. However, religion-state interactions can become antagonistic, under conditions which can be specified,② and when that occurs, it can precipitate a spiral of action-reaction into increasingly conflictual relations which can substantially transform the focus, energies, and religious imaginations of the believers, and may also affect the character, actions, and image of state agencies.

By far the most common outcome among most contemporary societies is some mutual accommodation between the state and religions, in which each adapts to the aims and organizations of the other. But

① Allegiance within religious groups can be explained, and variations modeled, using a small number of variables. There is a large body of research on various mechanisms used to socialize members and bolster or maintain commitment. This kind of analysis has been incorporated into work on a variety of ideological communities (see, for example, Kanter, 1972). The 'religious economy' perspective (Stark and Bainbridge, 1987; Stark and Finke, 2000), also provides a framework for analyzing religious commitments in terms of rewards (otherworldly, and this-worldly) provided by particular groups. Where a religious group provides important material, social, or economic resources to members which cannot easily be gained outside the group, commitment is accordingly enhanced. Where other groups or agencies within the society provide such benefits without requiring the investments of time, energy, and belief required in a religious group, some of the motivations for religious allegiance are accordingly weakened, as long as individuals are free to seek those benefits according to their best assessment of costs and benefits.

② State-religion relations can become antagonistic when state repression selectively targets a religious group more than others; that is particularly likely when the state or regime favours or represents one of the religio-ethnic groups within the society, and thus creates a perception of injustice against the targeted religio-ethnic group or groups. The greater the resources of the targeted group, the greater the resistance. Of course, antagonism toward the state or toward other religions can also develop within a religious enclave led by a charismatic leader, especially if he/she embraces a messianic mission.

this requires substantial flexibility on both sides (of course, " the state" and "religion" are reifications, and there are many persons and groups, often with different and even conflicting goals, within what are loosely referred to as "states" and "religions").

In this paper, I explore the relation between religions, ideologies, and governance, with the goal of outlining ways in which religions, and more broadly, diverse worldviews, can be accommodated within a framework of common norms which can facilitate civilized, pluralistic discourse and constructive collaborations. The goal is also to take advantage of the contributions which religions can make to collective well-being while avoiding the risks of religion-related conflicts with followers of other religions or with the state.

The following is an outline of this analysis, with some references, elaborations, or qualifications in footnotes.

1. Diversity in religious or ideological belief is inevitable, and irrepressible:

* Human societies and the diversity of human motives, needs, and experiences, always produce religious or ideological diversity.[①] Therefore:

* All societies and states have some diversity in religions and worldviews. The larger and more complex the society, the greater the

---

① Diversity in religious belief and practice can occur through migration of some believers into new contexts where conditions are different, splitting of existing groups over differences of opinion (where splitting is possible), leadership competition when would-be leaders develop their own ideas which differ from those of current leaders, competition for adherents among rival groups leading to innovations by some of them tailored to under-serviced subgroups (as described, for example, in the ' religious economy' literature, eg. Finke and Stark, 2006), and differences among innovators in social class, gender, knowledge, exposure to ideas from other groups, etc.

inevitable diversity in religions and worldviews. ①

＊ Diversity cannot be eliminated because diverse opinions and practices can always be hidden from scrutiny. Thus,

2. Repression is costly, and cannot completely suppress diversity

＊ Repression never achieves complete religious or worldview orthodoxy.

＊Repression in the service of orthodoxy is costly: it requires continual monitoring, intensive socialization, sanctions, and punishment.

＊ Repression has other costly consequences, including inhibition of critical thinking and free inquiry, and partial suppression or disruption of processes which are important for the sciences; repression can also lead to defections of skilled people, internal resistance, and increased inter-group tensions, with the possibility of aggression or violent reactions under certain conditions.

＊ The more complicated and diverse the society, and the greater the informational, social, and economic resources available to individuals, the greater the difficulty, and the higher the cost, in attempts to repress diversity or enforce orthodoxy.

3. Constitutions provide legal and moral frameworks for harmonious diversity

＊ The constitution of a society can provide a framework for coexistence of competing religious ideas, ideologies, and worldviews, without any of those becoming dominant. For that to occur, none of

---

① Density of population, social-structural complexity of the society, and extent of exchanges with neighboring societies should increase diversity of religious belief in the longer-term. This could be modeled in a set of equations (see also Stark and Bainbridge, 1987:70 - 71).

those religions should be referenced in the constitution.

＊ Some state constitutions include references to religious ideas or themes, including favor for a particular religion or deity, etc. This can cause troubles within a society as adherents of those religious ideas use them against those who don't adhere to or accept those ideas; more moderate or generic references to religion and deities are less troublesome,[1] but continual work may be required to prevent attempts to strengthen those provisions in the service of a particular religion or religious worldview.

＊ Constitutions can provide for tolerance of civilized diversity, without favoring any particular religion or ideology except the ideology of civilized pluralism in the service of a good life for all citizens.

＊ Constitutions can incorporate social goals which are widely held within religions, such as social justice, compassion for the underprivileged, the right to education for all, and so on, and thus elicit approval and support from religious believers but with entirely secular goals and ideals and without explicit reference to any religious ideas.

4. Competition of ideas and worldviews leads to collective benefits

＊ Diversity of religions and worldviews can lead to competition among views and claims, which (if it is managed peacefully in an e-

---

① For example, the conceptions of *pancasila* in Indonesia required belief in 'God' but recognized 'God'-belief in several major religions, all of which must be tolerated. "Announced in 1945 by Sukarno, the President of the newly independent nation of Indonesia, *pancasila* (literally, the 'five principles') can be summarized as follows: (1) belief in god; (2) a just and civilized humanitarianism; (3) national unity; (4) Indonesian democracy through consultation and consensus; and (5) social justice···. The principles are weakly religious, since they include 'belief in god' but nothing more specific. The weakness of the religious principle is deliberate. In effect, *pancasila* institutionalizes tolerance among religions, since any theistic religion which advocates benevolence and national unity can claim adherence to the national ideology. However, this ideology is not entirely secular and pluralist, since it does specify 'belief in god'." (Lang and Wee, 2004).

galitarian milieu where all groups have equal rights) can stimulate improved formulation of ideas and more sophisticated analysis (including comparative analysis).

* Some of this competition may actually increase the sophistication and success of the production and 'marketing' of religious goods and services, and the tailoring of those goods and services to the needs of particular sections of the population, as argued by some sociologists of religion, using in particular the 'religious economy' paradigm for the study of competition among religions (see especially the work of Rodney Stark and others, eg. Stark and Bainbridge, 1987; Finke and Stark, 2004). The paradox is that competition can lead to innovation and greater success in finding ways to attract or hold adherents, and potentially, to greater religious participation than in a society where a religious monopoly is enforced by the state (i. e. , the 'lazy monopoly' idea).

* Political leaders in some historical multi-ethnic, multi-religious polities actually sponsored discussions and debates among representatives of competing or co-existing religions, without precipitating conflicts between those groups, using 'rules of debate' which allowed all to present their ideas and ruled out claims based solely on the sacred authority of religious texts. ①

---

① For example, Fraenkel (2012) recounts "the case of a theological debate in the multicultural world of medieval Islam, described by the historian al-Humaydi (d. 1095): 'At the [...] meeting there were present not only people of various [Islamic] sects but also unbelievers, Magians, materialists, atheists, Jews and Christians, in short unbelievers of all kinds. Each group had its own leader, whose task it was to defend its views [...]. One of the unbelievers rose and said to the assembly: we are meeting here for a debate; its conditions are known to all. You, Muslims, are not allowed to argue from your books and prophetic traditions since we deny both. Everybody, therefore, has to limit himself to rational arguments [hujaj al-'aql]. The whole assembly applauded these words'."

* Such debates and presentations, well-managed, can facilitate dialogue and at least, greater mutual understanding; it can also facilitate the search for common ground on some social and political issues.

* Pluralism, within a framework of rational and fair adjudication, facilitates competition among ideas, comparative analysis, bridging efforts between worldviews, and hence, intellectual vibrancy in a society. Pluralism, of course, includes both secular and religious worldviews.

* Scientific and secular worldviews may compete with some religious ideas and worldviews, and to the extent that the sciences and a scientific worldview are taught as the key to knowledge of the world and how it works, they help to ensure that religions do not monopolize truth claims about the world and perpetuate empirically unsound claims, and provide a common framework in the search for knowledge which can be accepted by all groups regardless of ethnicity, religion, or social structural position in the society. [1]

5. Religions can provide useful social services which contribute to social harmony

* Many religions advocate and practice humanitarian services and relief for disadvantaged people even if they are not believers. Some of the social services are motivated by religious rewards (eg. in the afterlife, or next life, or in favor bestowed by deities which brings rewards in this life). These social services can be valuable for a soci-

---

[1] Of course, science can also be used and exploited by powerful groups in society, and funding for scientific research can be affected by the priorities of elites. However, in complex modern societies, in which free inquiry is institutionalized in education and the media, such influences and impacts on science can also be studied and critiqued, as occurs in all open societies. The broad range of scientific enterprises and specialties greatly exceeds the capacity of elites to control scientific research and output.

ety, if they include helping people with special needs, organizing social or educational services for a population lacking some of these
services, comforting people in distress using this-worldly assistance or
counseling, and so on. Religions which include moral teaching directing believers to engage in such social-service activities can make valuable contributions to collective social well-being (Liu, 2011). Such
shared ideas about moral behavior can become themes in inter-religious dialogues and ecumenical outreach (although much of that dialogue and outreach is intended to facilitate peaceful co-existence a-
mong religions).

  * It is possible to incorporate some of these themes and ideals
into the basic secular framework of goals of the state, or of political
parties and agendas within the society. This should be useful in elici-
ting religious support for state activities and aims, to the extent that
these goals are serious addressed in state policies.

  6. The state can facilitate mutual tolerance and accommodation a-
mong religions by serving as an guarantor of pluralism and worldview
diversity

  * Peacefully managed diversity among religions, without repression or state favoritism for any particular religion, can facilitate inter-
ethnic harmony and collaboration. Another term for such diversity, as
a feature of society, is 'pluralism'.

  * The state should provide a legal framework and constitutional
justification for pluralism, that is, for tolerance of diversity and intol-
erance of repression (eg. by preventing censorship and favoritism of
any particular religion or ideology by state agencies, and ensuring that
religions cannot repress other religions or worldviews).

∗ However, this also requires that the state find ways to ensure that religious monopolies on socialization and inquiry do not occur within substantial sections of the population, particularly, through control of educational and media organizations. If that occurs, pluralism may be squeezed out of public life in some parts of a society, with baleful consequences for free inquiry and scientific progress.

7. Science is a good basis for governance, and governance processes

∗ The only creditable methods of verifying truth claims to the satisfaction of anyone are found in the sciences, where these sciences are self-governed, and provide open forums for testing, and supporting or rejecting, truth claims and theoretical explanations about the world.

∗ The sciences require not only critical thinking, and free inquiry, but the teaching of critical thinking and free inquiry. They require an openness to the possibility that any truth claims are flawed or wrong, and regular open forums in which truth claims are critically scrutinized, tested, and discarded or substantially modified according to the results of research. They also require that there is no authority which is above and protected from such critical analysis. They involve open and transparent contestation on the basis of research findings, and any researcher has an equal right to do such research, and make such challenges or innovations on the basis of research findings. In this sense, the sciences operate like liberal democracies in which all have the right to challenge and contest ideas and claims through research conducted according to the standards of scientific disciplines. ① Unlike value-positions within democracies, however, truth claims in the sciences can be evaluated according to generally agreed methods of investigation and demonstration.

＊ Science is experimental, and the results lead to further experiments. Experimentation and empirical studies in the pursuit of knowledge are essential for science, and important for resolving debates about public policy.

＊ Truth claims from religions which cannot be verified empirically are not creditable for non-believers. Since there is always a diversity of religions and worldviews, and no rational method of adjudication is possible between many of the claims embedded within religions, the state cannot credit religious truth claims, or base any decisions or policies on them, or support socialization which includes those truth-claims, unless they can be verified through scientific methods.

＊ So: all societies should make science (rather than religion, or philosophy, or ideology) the basis for contestation and testing of ideas which involve or are based on truth claims, or which are intended to guide public policy. Where knowledge is inadequate, research and experimentation is the only path to better knowledge.

———————————

① Robert K. Merton briefly discussed these themes in "The ethos of science" (Merton, 1994 [1942]) and "Science and the social order" (Merton, 1994[1938]). Ferris (2010) provides an extensive analysis of the paradigm-similarities between science and 'liberal democracy', and shows that founders and early leaders of some liberal-democracies such as the U. S. A. were strongly interested in and influenced by the sciences as a foundation for the pursuit of knowledge and of reality-based policies, including through experimentation to find out what works best. In China, scientists such as Xu Liangying, Fang Lizhi, and Li Xingmin also extensively discussed the importance of free inquiry and of democratic openness throughout a society for the culture and practice of scientific work (Miller, 1996:204 –217).

＊ But science requires that all authority in a society should be subject to such critical scrutiny, wherever truth claims are made as the basis for policies or decisions.

＊ Science requires a reasonable set of processes for disseminating research and critical inquiry. In the sciences, such purposes are served by conferences, journals, and publications accessible to all researchers, with some quality-control using peer review. Outside the sciences, such results must be disseminated by other means. These can include briefings by scientists for policy-makers and citizen groups. But it is more efficient and effective to add some coverage of important scientific results in channels of information open to people who wish to take advantage of such knowledge in order to participate in pubic affairs. This generally means, open, critical, and accessible mass media or at least, forms of dissemination to which ordinary people can have access.

＊ A society in which scientific worldviews are widespread and well-understood will provide much less space and credulousness for religious truth claims about the natural world and human affairs, or for proposals to bring religious authority into the authority of the state.

＊ Social, political, and cross-cultural origins of diverse religious beliefs can be studied, and subjected to reasoned analysis, with plausible accounts of the social sources of religious beliefs. This is a legitimate topic for sociological, cultural, and historical research, and such research is inevitable in a society of diverse beliefs which guarantees freedom of inquiry. It may be threatening to some believers (since such analysis seems to explain 'belief' using this-worldly analysis, thus making it unnecessary to rely on supernatural sources for belief such as revelation or instruction from deities), but no attempts to suppress such analysis can be accepted into the agendas of the state or the educational system, or the management of the mass media. Such research contributes, inevitably, to some "relativizing" of religious belief,[①] and to secularizing trends within a society. This is unavoidable.

＊ Top scientists have been found to be overwhelmingly non-religious, or religious only in a sense in which religion has no direct relevance for human decision-making (eg. vague deism in which there is held to be some kind of supernatural force, deemed "god", but with no relevance to daily life or human decision-making).[②] The scientific worldview leaves little space for deities and supernatural actions in the real world, although it has nothing directly to say about alleged supernatural realms which are outside of natural causation. Another way to put it is that science brings much more of the world into the realm of rational action based on scientific research, compared to societies which provide much less space for science in the public realm.

＊ Science is a natural ally of governance guided by reality, and a non-ally of governance guided by religious ideology or by fundamentalist claims (whether religious or political). Science is likely to flourish in, and contribute to, democratic governance, and to be in-

---

① In secularization theories, "relativization" is a process in which comparative analysis or experience of advocacy by diverse religions leads to reduced credibility for any particular religion. This occurs partly because it is clear that reasonable people can hold very different beliefs for mere "socialization" reasons (eg. family background), and partly because comparisons or comparative analysis of beliefs show that there is no objective way to decide between rival deities or rival religions, especially since they all base claims on unverifiable sources such as 'revelation', and unverifiable events such as miracles (and the claimed miracles, such as healings, are often identical, although allegedly caused by deities in different religions).

② See for example Larson and Witham (1998, 1999).

hibited by, and contribute less to, authoritarian governance where that governance is based on ideological, religious, or other dogmatic principles.

8. Fundamentalism produces fundamental conflicts with a pluralist framework

∗ Some religious groups can be characterized as 'fundamentalist'. [①] I define this (following Lang and Wee, 2004), as follows: (a) there is a small set of basic principles which are considered both necessary and sufficient for the overall guidance of human behavior; (b) these have been extracted by some authoritative process (i. e. , authoritative for members of the group) from a text or body of material which is claimed to have impeccable origins, and hence, 'sacred' status (i. e. , it is an unchallengeable source of truth); this may be a single text, or a collection of texts or writings or sayings.

∗ The implication of a fundamentalist position is that this collection of material, and the principles derived from it, and perhaps the methods by which those principles were derived from the collection, should be taught——even exclusively——as the guide for living and

---

① Following Lang and Wee (2004): The concept of "fundamentalism" was developed to describe certain movements within Protestant Christianity in the 20th century, but has been partially generalized in recent decades to refer to a variety of religious movements with some similar characteristics. However, "fundamentalism" has been under-theorized in sociology, even for the analysis of religious groups, and the process of abstracting a more general definition is on-going, and still incomplete. On reasons why "fundamentalism" has been under-theorized in sociology, see Reisebrodt (1993). Eisenstadt (1999) describes characteristics of what he calls "modern Jacobin movements", which share the goals of radical mobilization and transformation of society using some unchallengeable utopian model. He illustrates with both religious and political cases of this kind of 'Jacobinism'. Eisenstadt's conceptualization, however, still includes some features of particular types of movements. For example, he builds the ideas of "anti-modernism" and "anti-enlightenment ideology" into his definition of fundamentalism. These are not essential features of fundamentalism, as defined here.

for action in society. This, however, puts the fundamentalist position in direct conflict with the overall framework and collective commitments of a pluralist society with an educational system which teaches a scientific worldview. Pluralism and science are incompatible with a fundamentalist approach to belief, socialization, and social interaction.

* Fundamentalist organizations may be religious, or non-religious but ideological, as in some dogmatic political movements with fundamentalist features; as fundamentalist groups, they share a number of features with fundamentalist religious groups and can be analyzed using similar concepts. [1]

* Some fundamentalist groups and organizations have the aim to "capture" the state or other important social institutions, and implement the fundamentalist program in education and in some state policies. This occurs in various kinds of societies, including some which have key features of "liberal democracies", such as the U. S. [2]

* The paradox of pluralism is that it provides space for funda-

---

[1] Competing sectarian political groups have been analyzed in a similar way (see for example, O' Toole, 1977). With a formal definition of fundamentalism, devoid of any specific content for the beliefs, the concept can be further generalized to accommodate non-religious forms of ideological fundamentalism, which will allow useful comparisons (otherwise conceptually difficult) between a variety of ideologically dogmatic groups which share properties that have enormous sociological consequences. For example, in China a secular ideological fundamentalism shaped the lives of several hundred million people for a generation——Maoism before and during the Cultural Revolution. The Maoist state between 1966 and the mid-1970s produced intellectual and social phenomena which followed from a fundamentalist vision. Like some religious fundamentalist movements, Maoism attempted to replace an earlier, more complex and subtle system with a much simpler and more forceful vision of the world and of appropriate behavior within the world, and to base that vision on a small set of writings which were treated as virtually sacred, and about which critical analysis was prohibited, or extreme costly (Lang and Wee, 2004).

[2] On theocratic aims of some fundamentalists in the U. S., see Phillips (2006) and Hedges (2006).

mentalisms, and the emergence of fundamentalist sectors or subcultures within the society, which may aggressively "push back" against the pluralist model of tolerance, reliance on the sciences, and critical inquiry about religions. These subcultures, if their populations are large and they have the resources to produce their own media, publications, and "experts", can cultivate and reproduce substantial scientific ignorance and pseudo-science, putting sustained pressure on public institutions and on governance. [1]

  * Fundamentalisms have advantages over the sciences as a basis for allegiance, because they provide simple answers, strong group identity, assurance of rightness, and innumerable group processes at various scales, from micro-level group activity to meso-level organizational actions, which reinforce the sense of rightness and group-assurance, and also provide buffers against diffusion of scientific knowledge or exposure to ideas from other world-view groups. It is very important that such groups are not able to 'capture' important institutions in the education system and in the media. Strong state support is required for scientific work and scientific education throughout the educational system, and for at least some scientific education for journalists.

  * A number of societies have attempted to implement a kind of 'weak fundamentalism' as part of a national constitution or framework, in order to enshrine some ideas or values at a moderately sacred

---

[1] On fundamentalist pressure on political decision-making, and on widespread scientific ignorance or illiteracy in the U.S., see for example Gore (2007), Jacoby (2008), and Mooney and Kirshenbaum (2009); on the impact of so-called conservative or right-wing control of some media and "think-tanks", see Brock (2004), and Jacques et al. (2008). It is notable that belief in evolution and in human-caused global warming is lower in the U.S. than in almost all other open societies, at least substantially because large sectors of the population inhabit subcultures in which such views are promoted by media and religious organizations which comprise most of the flow of discourse within that subculture.

level beyond the reach of normal policy-discussion. This has occurred in Indonesia (as noted above in regard to *pancasila*), Singapore, Malaysia, and other countries (Lang and Wee, 2004). It is usually a compromise among religious and political groups whose ideologies cannot be reconciled in a strong version of a fundamentalist constitution. In pre-modern China, state commitment to Confucianism played a similar role in statecraft.[①] Pluralist forces within those societies have to struggle against the constraints and threats which result from the legal consequences of these arrangements and state commitments.

　　* War and other threat-conditions can lead to more authoritarian leadership, suppression of dissent, and severe constraints on intellectual pluralism. The more the society is militarized and infused with threat-messages promoting military vigilance, the greater the pressure and impact on critical inquiry, and on intellectual pluralism.[②]

　　9. Transitions from fundamentalist to more pluralist societies

　　* It is possible for repressive fundamentalist societies to develop pluralist modes of thinking, social organization, and governance. The causes of such changes included failure of fundamentalist ideologies to deal with complex realities; destructive consequences of trying to im-

---

　　① As we note in Lang and Wee (2004): Confucianism and various commentaries and adaptations of Confucian writings formed a kind of 'fundamental' corpus of philosophy, morality, and statecraft in China for much of the past two thousand years. The dominance of this corpus was maintained by the state through the examination system, in which candidates had to memorize selections from the canon and the commentaries in order to be successful in the exams and gain entrance to the imperial bureaucracy. Rival systems were carefully watched, and periodically suppressed. The Confucian corpus, suitably interpreted, served the interests of the state by contributing to social harmony and to acceptance of authoritarian and hierarchical relationships. However, the Confucian writings, including the approved commentaries, comprised a very complex corpus allowing much room for critical exploration and analysis.

　　② For some impacts of war and militarism in the U. S. , see Bacevich (2005) and Hedges (2010).

pose a fundamentalist ideology on an ideologically diverse population; and the delegitimization of a fundamentalist state through military defeat or economic decline.

　＊ Structural changes can also favour the evolution of pluralist principles and institutions. For example, immigration can lead to the growth of ethnic and religious diversity within a society, which can lead (after the inevitable struggles) to negotiation of a more pluralist framework for the society. Increasing differentiation within society through urbanization, the growth and diversification of a tertiary scientific, technical and professional sector, and the resulting expansion and diversification of higher education can also lead to more pluralist accommodations to the resulting diversity of ideas, institutions, and modes of career socialization.

　＊ Evolution from more fundamentalist toward more pluralist forms of thinking and organization has also occurred as a result of experience with the competitive advantages of a more pluralist and authority-challenging system of discussions and debates for the production of useful knowledge (Lang and Wee, 2004). For example, the institutionalized methods of producing, disseminating, and critically evaluating knowledge which we call 'modern science' developed out of the competitive multi-state system in Europe over the past 400 years, and that competitive system was one of the key factors in the development of modern science (Lang, 1997). The growth and institutionalization of these more critical methods of inquiry naturally led to conflicts with older and more "fundamentalist" institutions and ideologies, but the clear or anticipated benefits of a less fundamentalist approach to knowledge within that competitive multi-state system made it ultimately impossible for religious or political institutions to enforce a fundamentalist hegemony over knowledge and education. The evolution of secular pluralist educational institutions in Europe, since the 13th century, from what had originally been much more fundamentalist institutions, is one of the most remarkable of the transformations from fundamentalist to more pluralist institutions and discourses.

＊ The success of science as an enterprise has led some enthusiastic utopians to imagine that they could use scientific planning to re-engineer society and nature on a large scale, using general models. When applied on such a scale, however, these models are invariably too simple to work well in the real world. Before their flaws are exposed, their enthusiastic exponents can do enormous damage if these programs are implemented in authoritarian systems. James Scott has called such programs of forced change "authoritarian high modernism" (Scott, 1998). Their historical failures are a result of the fact that such models are always too simple to accommodate the complexity of local conditions, and thus they lead to sterility, inefficiency, and in some cases, to society-wide catastrophe (as in the "Great Leap Forward" in China between 1958 and 1961). [1] These failures are not the fault of science. Instead, they are the product of the fatal combination of authoritarian systems and leaders who misunderstand the problems of applying science to the real world (Lang and Wee, 2004). More commonly, an increasingly science-oriented society is also an increasingly open and intellectually pluralistic society, since the culture of science is critical, skeptical, egalitarian, tolerant of experimentation as a basis for action or progress, and indeed, insists on

---

[1] On the so-called "Great Leap Forward", see Dikötter, 2010, and Yang, 2008.

such experimentation wherever possible before decisions are made and resources committed.

Conclusions

Religions and religious diversity are an inevitable feature of any society, and attempts to repress religion or enforce religious or ideological orthodoxy have many costs and negative consequences, and will always tend to fail in the longer term. This is especially unavoidable in any complex society in which citizens have many resources for pursuing inquiries and cultivating ideas. Meanwhile, religions can contribute in many ways to public discourse about morality, to care for the disadvantaged, and to other constructive features of society. The most universally defensible way to achieve harmony in a society is to ensure that pluralism, science, free and critical inquiry, and tolerance for religious and ideological diversity and discourse are institutionalized in the basic framework of governance, education, and public communication.

Competition among ideas through free discourse and inquiry, and even through debates between representatives of rival beliefs and ideologies, can have many benefits, including greater mutual understanding, the normalization of peaceful inter-faith dialogue and debate as a feature of public life, and the cultivation of comparative analysis of belief, which in turn can enhance critical thinking.

Fundamentalism as a type of belief system (whether secular, as in some political ideologies, or religious) threatens this kind of governance framework, and is ultimately incompatible with it. Paradoxically, pluralist societies are relatively tolerant of fundamentalist minorities even where those minorities want to capture important institutions and implement a fundamentalist program of education, worldview, morality, or family life. If they are able to do so, they will inculcate beliefs which dispute the scientific worldview or specific scientific findings, despite consensus about these findings or conclusions among scientists. This is not a simple problem in pluralist societies, and one of the tasks of governance is to ensure that religions in general, and fundamentalist groups in particular, do not have exclusive control over key institutions of the society, even if they have some influence.

However, fundamentalist societies can evolve into more tolerant and pluralist societies due to structural differentiation, diffusion of ideas and experiences from other societies, and cultivation of research activity and inquiry within the society. Fundamentalist organizations can also develop more pluralist orientations when the basic framework of the society is pluralist, and is founded on equal rights of expression for all (including secular and scientific views). Social and structural changes can lead to this kind of evolution from more fundamentalist to more pluralist forms of social life.

Science as a method of learning about the world, especially through experimentation, is the best epistemological system for developing realistic and reality-grounded policies and activities. But science must get strong state support, because it is disadvantaged in some important respects compared to fundamentalism, and is more costly to learn, and to practice. The institutions and standards of science are egalitarian and critical, and the sciences flourish best in open societies which tolerate and support free inquiry, and wide-ranging critical analysis. Such societies are also the most likely to provide safe contexts for harmonious relations among religions and between religions and the state.

References

Bacevich, Andrew J,2005, *The New American Militarism: How Americans Are Seduced by War*, N. Y. : Oxford University Press.

Brock, David,2004, *The Republic Noise Machine: Right-Wing Media and How it Corrupts Democracy*, N. Y. : Crown Publishers.

Dikötter, Frank, 2010, *Mao's Great Famine: The History of China's Most Devvastating Catastrophe, 1958 – 1962*, London: Bloomsbury.

Eisenstadt, S. M, 1994, "Fundamentalism, phenomenology and comparative dimensions", in M. E. Marty and R. S. Appleby, eds. , *Fundamentalisms Comprehended*, Chicago: University of Chicago Press.

Ferris, Timothy,2010, *The Science of Liberty: Democracy, Reason, and the Laws of Nature*, N. Y. : Harper Perennial.

Finke, Roger, and Stark, Rodney,2006, *The Churching of America: 1776 – 2005*, New Brunswick, N. J. : Rutgers University Press.

Fraenkel, Carlos, 2012, 'In praise of the clash of cultures'. *New York Times*, 2 September.

Gore, Al,2007, *The Assault on Reason*, N. Y. : Penguin Press.

Hedges, Chris,2006, *American Fascists: The Christian Right and the War on America*, N. Y. : Free Press.

Hedges, Chris,2010, *Death of the Liberal Class*, N. Y. : Nation Books.

Jacoby, Susan, 2008, *The Age of American Unreason*, N. Y. : Pantheon Books.

Jacques, Peter, Dunlap, Riley E. , and Freeman, Mark, 2008. "The Organization of Denial: Conservative Think Tanks and Environmental Sceptic-ism," *Environmental Politics* 17:349 – 385.

Kanter, Rosabeth Moss, 1972, *Commitment and Community*: *Communes and Utopias in Sociological Perspective*, Cambridge: Harvard University Press.

Lang, Graeme. 1997. "Structural factors in the origins of modern science: a comparison of China and Europe", in Steven Totosy de Zepetnek and Jennifer Jay (eds.), *East Asian Cultural and Historical Perspectives*, Edmonton: University of Alberta, Research Institute for Comparative Literature and Cross-Cultural Studies, pp. 71 – 96.

Lang, Graeme, and Wee, Vivienne, 2004, "Fundamentalist ideology, institu-tions, and the state: a formal analysis", in Santosh Saha (ed.), *Religious Fun-damentalism in the Contemporary World*: *Critical Social and Political Issues*, Lan-ham, Md. : Lexington, pp. 47 – 70.

Larson, Edward J., and Witham, Larry, 1998, "Leading scientists still reject God", *Nature*, vol. 394, 23 July, p. 313.

Larson, Edward J., and Witham, Larry, 1999, "Scientists and religion in America", *Scientific American*, September, pp. 88 – 93.

Liu Peng. 2011. "On the problem of developing a mechanism for the par-ticipation of religion in the social services sector", In Fenggang Yang and Graeme Lang (eds.), *Social Scientific Studies of Religion in China*: *Methodolo-gy*, *Theories and Findings*, Leiden and Boston: Brill, pp. 227 – 243.

Merton, Robert K, 1996, *On Social Structure and Science*. Edited with an introduction by Piotr Sztompka, Chicago: University of Chicago Press.

Miller, H. Lyman, 1996. *Science and Dissent in Post-Mao China*, Seattle: University of Washington Press.

Mooney, Chris, 2012, *The Republican Brain*: *The Science of Why They Deny Science-and Reality*, Hoboken, N. J. : John Wiley & Sons.

Mooney, Chris, and Kirshenbaum, Sheril, 2009, *Unscientific America*: *How Scientific Illiteracy Threatens Our Future*, N. Y. : Basic Books.

O'Toole, Roger, 1977, *The Precipitous Path*: *Studies in Political Sects*, Toronto: Peter Martin Associates.

Phillips, Kevin,2006, *American Theocracy: The Peril and Politics of Radical Religion, Oil, and Borrowed Money in the 21st Century*, N. Y. : Viking.

Reisebrodt, Martin, 1993, *Pious Passion: The Emergence of Modern Fundamentalism in the United States and Iran*, Berkeley, Calif. : University of California Press.

Scott, James C,1998, *Seeing Like a State: How Certain Schemes to Improve the Human Condition have Failed*, New Haven: Yale University Press.

Stark, Rodney, and Bainbridge, William S. , 1987, *A Theory of Religion*, N. Y. : Peter Lang.

Stark, Rodney, and Finke, Roger, 2000, *Acts of Faith: Explaining the Human Side of Religion*, Berkeley: University of California Press.

Yang Jisheng,2008. *Tombstone: The Untold Story of Mao's Great Famine*, Translated by Stacy Mosher and Guo Jian (2012),London: Allen Lane (Penguin).

宗教事务管理法治化

——成就、挑战与展望

刘金光

不断提高法治化水平,是依法管理宗教事务的必由之路。改革开放以来,我国的宗教事务管理,按照 1982 年颁布实施的《中华人民共和国宪法》规定的大原则,①根据依法治国的大方略,不断推动对宗教事务的管理从依政策为主向依法管理转变。特别是经过最近 10 多年的努力,我国宗教法制建设已经取得了显著成就,宗教工作法治化水平不断提高,宗教界人士和信教群众的法律素质也逐步提高。但是,随着国际形势的不断变化,改革开放的不断深入,宗教方面不断出现新情况新问题,宗教事务管理的法治化进程也面临前所未有的挑战。随着依法治国战略的实施和建设法治政府的推进,必然要求政府管理部门不断提高宗教事务管理的法治化水平。本文拟从宗教事务管理法治化取得的成就、遇到的挑战以及今后时期的展望等三个方面,对推进宗教事务管理法治化问题进行探讨。

---

① 关于宗教的内容主要体现在《中华人民共和国宪法》的第 34 条和 36 条规定中。参阅:《中华人民共和国宪法典(宪法 30 周年纪念版)》,中国法制出版社,2012 年出版。

一、宗教事务管理法治化是中央实施
依法治国方略的必然要求

依法治国方略是中共十五大提出的,并于 1999 年写入经修改的宪法。它的核心要义就是依照宪法和法律的规定,通过各种途径和形式管理国家事务、管理经济文化事务、管理社会事务,保证国家各项工作都依法进行。这是中国共产党治国理政从观念到方式上的重大变革,具有划时代的重大意义。这其中当然包括对宗教事务也要依照法律去管理。

(一)宗教事务管理法治化是建设法治政府的必然要求

1999 年,国务院发布了《关于全面推进依法行政的决定》,这是国务院第一个系统阐释依法行政的文件。这个文件要求加大行政执法力度,确保政令畅通。要强化行政执法监督。2004 年 3 月,国务院发布的《全面推进依法行政实施纲要》①明确提出了建设法治政府的目标,对于规范政府行为提出了新的更高的要求。纲要要求,要理顺行政执法体制,加快行政程序建设,规范行政执法行为,严格按照法定程序行使权力、履行职责。建立健全行政执法主体资格制度。②2005 年,国务院办公厅发布了《关于推行行政执法责任制的若干意见》,规定要依法界定执法职责,建立健全行政执法评议考核机制,认真落实行政执法责任,加强推行行政执法责任制的组织领导。2008 年 6 月 18 日国务院公布了《国务院关于加强市县政府依法行政的决定》。这是落实 2004 年国务院发布的《全面推进依法行政实施纲要》的基础性部分。主要针对基层矛盾比较多,民众参政意识高涨的情况,政府如果不强调基层法治建设,势必影响到维护稳定和发展。因此,这个决定规定,要严格行政执法,改革行政执法体制,完善行政执法经费保障机

---

① 《国务院关于印发全面推进依法行政实施纲要的通知》(国发〔2004〕10 号),http://www.gov.cn/ztzl/yfxz/content_374160.htm
② 王宝明:《法治政府—中国政府法治化建设的战略选择》,外语教学与研究出版社,2010 年出版。

制,规范行政执法行为,加强行政执法队伍建设,强化行政执法责任追究。
2010年10月15日,国务院办公厅颁发《国务院关于加强法治政府建设的
意见》①,这是国务院关于依法行政最新的系统规定,并第一次提出"法治
政府建设"的概念。这个意见规定,要严格规范公正文明执法。要求严格
依法履行职责。完善行政执法体制和机制。规范行政执法行为。2011年3
月28日,中共中央政治局就推进依法行政和弘扬社会主义法治精神进行
第27次集体学习,时任中共中央总书记的胡锦涛同志在主持学习时强调:
"全面推进依法行政、弘扬社会主义法治精神,是坚持立党为公、执政为民
的必然要求,是推动科学发展、促进社会和谐的必然要求。是党的十七大
为适应全面建设小康社会新形势、推进依法治国进程而提出的一项战略任
务,对深化政治体制改革、发展社会主义民主政治,对全面实施依法治国基
本方略、加快建设社会主义法治国家,对建设富强、民主、文明、和谐的社会
主义现代化国家、实现党和国家长治久安具有十分重要的意义。"胡锦涛同
志的讲话还提出了明确的要求:"各级党委要按照科学执政、民主执政、依
法执政的要求,带头维护社会主义法制的统一、尊严、权威,坚持依法办事。
各级政府要认真履行宪法和法律赋予的职责。广大党员、干部特别是领导
干部要带头遵守和执行宪法和法律。要加强对全体人民的普法宣传教育,
深入开展社会主义法治理论教育,特别是要加强与人民群众生产生活密切
相关的法律法规宣传,加快在全社会形成学法遵法守法用法的良好法治环
境。"②

　　法治作为一个与人治相对应的概念,最核心的思想就是通过法律规范
国家权力、特别是行政权力,也就是说政府行为必须受到法律的控制,严格
依照法律规定的权限和程序行使权力。法治政府最基本的特征:就是把自
身的权力自觉地限制在法律的范围内,严格依法办事,以防止权力被滥用。
因此,法治政府不仅要求公民守法,更要求自己带头守法。

　　依法加强对宗教事务的管理,是贯彻依法治国基本方略的必然要求。

① 《国务院关于加强法治政府建设的意见》(国发〔2010〕33号),http://www.gov.cn/zwgk/2010-11/08/content_1740765.htm
② 胡锦涛强调:《推进依法行政,弘扬社会主义法治精神》,http://www.gov.cn/ldhd/2011-03/29/content_1833760.htm

依法对宗教事务的管理,主要包括三方面的内容:一是规范宗教活动主体从事宗教活动的行为,要求宗教团体、宗教活动场所、宗教教职人员和信教公民,在宗教活动中应当遵守宪法、法律、法规和规章,维护国家统一、民族团结和社会和谐。二是规范政府的行政行为,要求政府必须依法保护正常的宗教活动、维护宗教团体、宗教活动场所和信教公民的合法权益。三是依法惩处各种违法行为。

在依法加强对宗教事务的管理中,必须按照中央关于建设法治政府的要求,自觉做到合法行政、合理行政、程序正当、高效便民、诚实守信、权责统一。

(二)宗教事务管理法治化也是建设服务型政府的要求

2004 年,国务院发布《全面推进依法行政实施纲要》,提出了转变政府职能,建设服务型政府的任务。2010 年 3 月 5 日,温家宝总理在《政府工作报告》中指出,要"努力建设人民满意的服务型政府"。①

宗教工作与建设服务型政府的关系:一是要在宗教工作中始终着眼于维护信教群众的合法利益;二是要弘扬法治精神,培育对法的信仰,培植对法的忠诚,倡导对法的依赖;三是要在宗教工作中弘扬法治精神,改变以内部政策为依据处理宗教事务的做法,不断提高法治化水平。

二、宗教事务管理法治化取得的成就

改革开放以来,伴随社会主义民主与法制建设进程,宗教工作逐渐纳入制度化、法制化的轨道,走上了依法管理宗教事务之路。依法加强对宗教事务进行管理,既是实施依法治国方略的必然要求,更是党和政府在新的历史时期处理宗教问题的实践中总结出来的重要经验,丰富和发展了马克思主义宗教观。

---

① 温家宝:《努力建设人民满意的服务型政府》,http://news. xinhuanet. com/politics/2010 - 03/05/content_13102634. htm

（一）我国依法管理宗教事务的历程和启示

改革开放以来，依法管理宗教事务主要经历了以下三个阶段：

一是酝酿阶段（1978 年—1990 年）。十一届三中全会后，党在拨乱反正、落实宗教政策的同时，比较系统地总结了建国以来在宗教问题上正反两个方面的历史经验，于 1982 年发布了《关于我国社会主义时期宗教问题的基本观点和基本政策》（中发〔1982〕19 号）①，这是中国特色社会主义宗教理论和政策形成的重要里程碑，全面恢复和贯彻落实宗教信仰自由政策，政府宗教工作部门恢复正常工作，各级爱国宗教团体相继恢复建立，宗教工作走上了正轨。② 与此同时，我国在宗教法制建设方面开始了一些探索。社会主义时期的历部宪法都规定了我国公民宗教信仰自由的权利和义务，与此同时，《刑法》、《民族区域自治法》、《民法》、《教育法》等有关法律都明确了保护公民宗教信仰自由的条款。③ 1988 年 3 月，广东省政府率先出台了《宗教活动场所行政管理规定》，开辟了地方制定宗教法规的先河。但就全国范围而言，依法管理宗教事务还没有正式提出，也没有形成全国性专门的宗教方面的法律。这个阶段的突出特点是，依据政策管理宗教事务。

二是起步阶段（1991 年—2003 年）。随着社会主义市场经济的进一步发展，宗教领域在思想观念、管理方式、价值观念、法律观念也发生了深刻变化，宗教工作的深度和广度不断加大，宗教涉及到的社会公共事务大量增多。根据依法治国方略的要求，党和政府逐步将宗教工作作为社会公共事务的组成部分，由政府对宗教事务进行依法管理。1990 年全国宗教工作会议及会后下发的《中共中央、国务院关于进一步做好宗教工作若干问题的通知》，鲜明提出了要依法加强对宗教事务的管理，并明确要求要加快宗

---

① 中共中央文献研究室综合研究组、国务院宗教事务局政策法规司编：《新时期宗教工作文献选编》，宗教文化出版社，1995 年版，第 54 页至 73 页。
② 刘金光：《中国特色社会主义宗教理论与政策形成的重要里程碑——纪念中发〔1982〕19 文件发表 30 周年》，载《中国宗教》，2012 年第 3 期。
③ 国家宗教事务局政策法规司编：《宗教事务条例相关法律法规及政策手册》，宗教文化出版社，2010 年版。

教立法工作。① 1994 年国务院颁布了《中华人民共和国境内外国人宗教活动管理规定》和《宗教活动场所管理条例》两个单项宗教行政法规,据此,国家宗教局颁布了《宗教社会团体登记管理实施办法》、《宗教活动场所登记办法》和《宗教活动场所年度检查办法》三个配套部门规章。各省(区、市)也都根据国家的有关法律法规,结合各地实际,制定了地方性行政法规。这个时期,宗教工作实现了从过去单一依靠政策管理,向依法管理和政策指导并行并重的管理方式的转变。

三是形成阶段(2004 年—现在)。随着依法治国方略的实施,党和政府对宗教问题的认识逐步深化。作为社会管理和公共服务的一部分,宗教事务逐步纳入法治轨道,更加法律化和规范化。2004 年,按照中央"通过制定社会政策和法规,依法管理和规范社会组织、社会事务"的统一部署,国务院颁布了《宗教事务条例》,依法管理宗教事务迈上了新台阶。这部条例按照依法治国、依法行政的要求,把党对宗教的方针政策具体化为行政法规,为依法管理宗教事务提供了较为全面的法律依据。② 此后,国务院有关部门制定颁布了《宗教活动场所设立审批和登记办法》、《宗教教职人员备案办法》、《宗教活动场所主要教职任职备案办法》、《藏传佛教活佛转世管理办法》、《宗教活动场所财务监督管理办法(暂行)》等一系列部门规章,各地也都陆续修订本地已颁布的相关行政法规、规章 ③,有关宗教事务管理的法律框架体系已构建起来,各级政府宗教事务部门依法决策、依法管理和依法行政的能力不断增强,宗教事务行政公职人员的法制观念和执法水平逐步提高,依法管理宗教工作的局面基本形成。

回顾改革开放以来依法管理宗教事务的历程,与世界其它国家的宗教立法相比较,可以得出以下四点经验:一是始终坚持将党的宗教政策上升为法律法规;二是始终坚持立足我国国情完善法律法规;三是始终坚持与教规教义相结合管理宗教事务;四是始终坚持综合运用各领域法律法规共同管理。认真总结这些经验,科学把握依法管理宗教事务规律,对于做好

---

① 中共中央文献研究室综合研究组、国务院宗教事务局政策法规司编:《新时期宗教工作文献选编》,宗教文化出版社,1995 年版,第 217 页。

② 帅峰 李建主编:《宗教事务条例释义》,宗教文化出版社,2005 年出版。

③ 国家宗教事务局政策法规司编:《宗教法规规章制度汇编》,2010 年出版。

新世纪新阶段的宗教工作具有十分重要的意义。①

（二）当前我国的宗教法制建设成就

经过多年的努力,我国在宗教法制建设方面取得了显著成就,

初步形成了较为完备的宗教法律体系,确立了基本的宗教法律制度,实现了对宗教事务的依法管理有法可依。

1. 已经建成的宗教法律体系

目前,我国的宗教法律体系是由国务院的行政法规、国家宗教事务局的部门规章及规范性文件和地方性法规及政府规章等几个方面构建起来的。

由国务院颁布的宗教方面的国家行政法规有两个:一是于1994年颁布的《中华人民共和国境内外国人宗教活动管理规定》,二是2004年颁布的《宗教事务条例》。②1994年由国务院颁布的《宗教活动场所管理条例》,由于其主要内容已经列入《宗教事务条例》,因此这部新单项行政法规中止执行。

根据上述国务院颁布的两部上位行政法规,近些年来,国家宗教事务局加大了立法力度,陆续制定颁布了11个部门规章,它们是《中华人民共和国境内外国人宗教活动管理规定实施细则》;《宗教活动场所设立审批和登记办法》;《宗教活动场所财务监督管理办法》;《宗教教职人员备案办法》;《宗教活动场所主要教职任职备案办法》;《藏传佛教活佛转世管理办法》;《宗教院校设立办法》;《宗教院校聘用外籍专业人员办法》;《藏传佛教寺庙管理办法》;③《宗教院校教师资格认定和职称评审聘任办法(试行)》;《宗教院校学位授予办法(试行)》④等。同时,在《宗教事务条例》颁布后,各省、自治区、直辖市和少数较大城市、自治州制定或修订了地方性

---

① 刘金光:《世界各国对宗教的立法及实践》,载《宗教与世界》,2011年第10期。

② 国家宗教事务局政策法规司编:《宗教法规规章制度汇编》,宗教文化出版社,2010年出版,第2页至15页。

③ 国家宗教事务局政策法规编:《宗教政策法规文件选编》,宗教文化出版社,2012年5月出版,第 页。

④ 国家宗教局网站,http://www.sara.gov.cn/zcfg/bmgz/17897.htm

法规和政府规章 27 部。

上述这些行政法规和部门规章以及地方性的法规规章,涉及到了宗教事务管理的主要方面,对宗教事务的管理提供了法律依据,为宗教事务管理法治化提供了坚实的基础。

2. 法律确立的基本的宗教法律制度

现行的宗教方面的法律法规和部门规章,确立了以下几个宗教法律制度:

(1)关于宗教团体的法律制度

宗教团体从作为爱国宗教组织的性质来看,是我国各宗教各自组成的由宗教教职人员和信教群众参加的爱国爱教的联合组织或教务组织,是党和政府争取、团结和教育宗教界人士和信教群众的桥梁。①从现代社会管理的角度来看,是非营利性的社会组织。② 对宗教团体的管理,形成了以下法律制度:

第一,登记管理制度。目前,我国社会团体统一由民政部门登记,由登记管理机关和业务主管单位双重负责管理,并按照社会团体活动地域分级登记管理。③宗教团体也是如此,即"归口登记,双重负责,分级管理"。基本程序如下:一是要经业务主管部门审查同意;二是要向登记管理机关申请筹备成立;三是要向登记管理机关申请登记。④

第二,年度检查制度。按照《社会团体登记管理条例》规定,政府对社会团体实行年度检查制度,即业务主管单位和登记管理机关对已登记的社会团体执行法律、法规、政策的情况,按照法定的内容和程序进行监督检查,以确认社会团体是否具有进行开展活动的资格的行政执法行为。宗教团体也要接受同样的年度检查制度。

(2)关于宗教活动场所的法律制度

宗教活动场所,是指经依法登记、拥有崇拜设施、组织信教群众开展集

---

① 国家宗教事务局政策法规司编:《宗教政策法规文件选编》,宗教文化出版社,2012 年出版,第 21 页。

② 帅峰、李建主编:《宗教事务条例释义》,宗教文化出版社,2005 年出版,第 39 页。

③ 同上,第 65 页、第 248 页。

④ 同上,第 65 页。

体宗教活动、为信教群众信仰生活提供服务的寺院、宫观、清真寺、教堂及其他固定宗教活动处所,属于非营利性社会组织。① 对宗教活动场所管理的法律制度有如下两方面:

第一,设立审批和登记。需要两道程序,即必须先提出设立申请,经批准后方可进行筹备工作,筹备工作完成后,还须向所在地的县级人民政府宗教事务部门申请登记,经登记后即取得合法地位,可以开展宗教活动。②

第二,管理制度。一是宗教活动场所的自我管理:实行民主管理;建立健全规章制度。二是政府有关部门的监督检查:政府宗教事务部门依法履行管理职责;政府有关部门的监督检查。③

(3)关于宗教院校的法律制度

我国实行宗教与教育相分离的原则,但法律保护宗教界内部通过设立宗教院校来实施宗教教育。④宗教院校是指宗教团体举办的培养宗教教职人员和其他宗教专门人才的全日制院校。对宗教院校的管理主要依靠以下法律制度:

第一,举办主体。全国性宗教团体或省、自治区、直辖市宗教团体是宗教院校的举办主体,其他组织或个人不得设立宗教院校。⑤

第二,宗教院校的设立审批。宗教院校的设立审批权限在国家宗教事务局,省、自治区、直辖市人民政府宗教事务部门对本省省、自治区、直辖市宗教团体申请设立宗教院校有初审权。⑥

第三,管理体制。国家宗教事务局是宗教院校的行政主管部门,依据有关法律、法规、规章和政策对宗教院校进行监督、检查、指导。各全国性宗教团体建立教育委员会,科学规划宗教院校教育体系,审查、统编宗教专业课教材,指导教师资格认定和职称聘任、学生学位授予、课程设置等工作。

---

① 帅峰、李建主编:《宗教事务条例释义》,宗教文化出版社,2005 年出版,第 75 页。
② 同上,第 77 页至 79 页、第 83 页。
③ 同上,第 87 页至 92 页。
④ 同上,第 57 页。
⑤ 同上,第 59 页。
⑥ 帅峰、李建主编:《宗教事务条例释义》,宗教文化出版社,2005 年出版,第 59 页。

（4）关于宗教教职人员管理的法律制度

宗教教职人员是指各宗教专门从事教务活动的人员。宗教教职人员的范围，由各宗教全国性宗教团体依本宗教的教义教规并结合实际情况确定。①对教职人员的管理有如下法律制度：

第一，认定和备案。一是认定，宗教团体是认定的主体。各全国性宗教团体依照《宗教事务条例》等法规规章和本宗教的教义、教规及传统，制定了本宗教的教职人员认定办法，宗教团体根据本宗教的认定办法开展认定工作。②二是备案，政府宗教事务部门是备案的主体。宗教团体对宗教教职人员的认定完成后，必须报相应的人民政府宗教事务部门备案。③

第二，有下列情形之一的，不予备案：一是未按照本宗教的宗教教职人员认定办法认定的；二是提供的备案材料不属实的。

第三，监督管理。宗教教职人员认定备案后，受以下四方面的监督：宗教活动场所管理组织、有关宗教团体、宗教工作部门、当地信教群众。

（5）对宗教财产管理的法律制度

为了切实保障宗教团体、宗教活动场所的财产权益，《宗教事务条例》及相关宗教法规明确规定宗教财务受法律保护。同时还做了如下三方面的规定：

第一，宗教财产管理应当执行国家的财务、会计制度。按照《社会团体登记管理条例》规定，宗教团体作为社会团体，必须执行国家规定的财务管理制度。根据财政部的要求，社会团体执行事业单位财务管理制度。根据财政部制定，宗教活动场所属于民间非营利组织，必须执行《民间非营利组织会计制度》，同时，宗教活动场所的财务要按照《宗教活动场所财务监督管理办法（试行）》进行管理。

第二，财务收支情况接受监督。宗教团体、宗教活动场所的财务收支情况和接受、使用捐赠情况，既要向当地县级以上人民政府宗教事务部门报告，又要以适当方式向信教群众公开。

---

① 国家宗教事务局政策法规司编：《宗教团体教规制度汇编》，2012 年出版。
② 同上。
③ 国家宗教事务局政策法规司编：《宗教政策法规文件选编》，2012 年出版，第 83 页至 84 页。

第三，依法纳税和依法享受减免税优惠。宗教团体、宗教活动场所必须执行国家规定的税收管理制度，依法纳税。同时，按照我国税法规定，宗教活动场所用于举行宗教活动的房屋及其附属的宗教教职人员生活用房，免征房产税、城镇土地使用税，宗教活动场所举办文化、宗教活动销售门票的收入免征营业税，等等。

政府宗教事务部门要依法履行指导和监督管理职责。履行职责时要严格遵守有关法律、法规。同时明确要求政府宗教事务部门在依法管理的过程当中：一是不得侵占、哄抢、私分、损毁或者非法查封、扣押、冻结、没收、处分宗教活动场所的合法财产；二是不得以任何方式授意、指使、强令宗教活动场所会计人员伪造、变造、销毁会计凭证、会计账簿和其他会计资料，提供虚假财务会计报告。否则，要依法给予行政处罚，构成犯罪的，法追究刑事责任。①

（6）关于重大事项的许可制度

第一，大型宗教活动管理制度。大型宗教活动是指跨省、自治区、直辖市举行的超过宗教活动场所容纳规模，或者在宗教活动场所外举行的大型集体宗教活动。举办主体是宗教团体、寺观教堂，其他任何组织和个人不得举办大型宗教活动。举办大型宗教活动，需要事先向活动举办地的省、自治区、直辖市人民政府宗教事务部门提出申请，获得批准后方可举办，同时相关部门要落实责任，确保大型宗教活动安全有序进行。②

第二，大型露天宗教造像管理制度。有两方面的规范要求：一是明确修建主体，即除宗教团体和寺观教堂可以提出修建大型露天宗教造像的申请外，其他任何单位和个人都无权提出申请。二是确定审批权限，即修建大型露天宗教造像的申请由省级人民政府宗教事务部门审核同意后报国家宗教事务局审批。③

第三，宗教出版物管理制度。一是涉及宗教内容的公开出版物，属于

---

① 国家宗教事务局政策法规司编：《宗教法规规章制度汇编》，宗教文化出版社，2010 年出版，第 39 页至 45 页。

② 国家宗教事务局政策法规司编：《宗教政策法规读本》，宗教文化出版社，2012 年出版，第 82 页至 84 页。

③ 同上，第 85 页至 86 页。

重大选题,公开出版时应当经由所在地省、自治区、直辖市人民政府出版行政部门审核后,报国务院出版行政部门备案,未经备案不得出版。二是宗教团体、寺观教堂按照国家有关规定可以编印宗教内部资料性出版物。但在印刷或复制宗教内部资料性出版物时必须到省、自治区、直辖市人民政府出版行政部门办理准印证或复制委托书,在办理准印证前,事先要报省、自治区、直辖市人民政府宗教事务部门审批。①

（7）关于宗教涉外事务的法律制度

政府鼓励和支持宗教界在平等友好、相互尊重的原则上开展对外交流,但需要遵守相关的法律规定。

第一,宗教院校的涉外事务规定。一是宗教留学人员的选派和接收由全国性宗教团体负责。二是选派和接收宗教留学人员按国家有关规定办理。三是宗教院校聘用外籍专业人员资格需要报国家宗教局审批并得到国家外专局的认可。②

第二,邀请国外宗教团组来访及组织我国内宗教团组出访的有关规定。外国人在中国境内进行宗教活动需遵守中国的法律法规。③

第三,非宗教交往不得附加宗教条件。④

三、依法管理宗教事务的内涵和要求

宗教事务管理法治化,必须深刻认识和准确把握依法管理宗教事务的内涵和相关要求,否则就会出现管理界限不清、胡乱管理、越俎代庖、管理不到位等问题。

（一）依法管理宗教事务的内涵

宗教是由宗教意识、宗教制度、宗教礼仪、宗教活动、宗教设施等多种

---

① 国家宗教事务局政策法规司编:《宗教政策法规读本》,宗教文化出版社,2012 年出版,第 80 页至 81 页。
② 同上,第 97 页至 98 页。
③ 同上,第 103 页至 104 页。
④ 同上,第 96 页至 97 页。

要素组成的复杂体系。宗教不仅是一种思想意识、一种观念形态,还是一种社会现象,一种社会实体,是社会的组成部分,对社会产生着广泛的影响。宗教实体必然与其他社会实体或社会整体之间发生关系,宗教活动与社会公共利益和国家利益都有着密切关系。宗教活动是在现行社会秩序内开展的,就必须受现行社会秩序的约束和规范。宗教事务是社会事务的一个重要组成部分。因此,政府依法对宗教事务进行管理,是依法对社会事务进行管理的一个重要组成部分,是履行正常的职责。①

1. 依法管理宗教事务的基本概念。依法管理宗教事务,是指政府根据宪法和有关法律、法规及规范性文件,对宗教方面涉及国家利益、社会公共利益的关系和行为,以及社会公共活动涉及宗教界权益的关系和行为进行的行政管理。

2. 依法管理宗教事务的涵义解析。

第一,政府对宗教事务的管理必须依据宪法和有关法律、法规及规范性文件进行。②要求宗教必须在法律、法规和政策的范围内活动,也要求政府宗教事务部门必须依法行政和依法管理。政府宗教事务部门依法办事,是权责统一的,既有权也有责,既不能失责,又不能越权。政府部门依法行政的目的,是为了维护公民的合法权益,这其中也必然包括信教的和不信教公民的合法权益。

第二,依法对宗教事务进行管理是政府对有关宗教的法律、法规和政策的贯彻实施进行行政管理和监督。③ 不能把对宗教事务的管理同实行宗教信仰自由政策对立起来。政府对宗教事务的管理,首先是要依法保护宗教团体和宗教活动场所的合法权益,保护宗教教职人员履行正常的教务活动,保护信教群众正常的宗教活动。对正当的宗教信仰、正常的宗教活动和宗教界的合法权益进行干涉或侵犯的行为,是法律、法规和政策所不允许的,这些行为一旦发生应当予以及时纠正,触犯刑律的,要依法处理。同时,也要通过依法管理,实现宗教活动的规范化,妥善处理宗教方面的人民

---

① 王作安:《中国的宗教问题和宗教政策》,宗教文化出版社,2010 年 4 月第二版,第 132 页。
② 同上,第 133 页。
③ 中共中央文献研究室综合研究组、国务院宗教事务局政策法规司编:《新时期宗教工作文献选编》,1995 年出版,第 216 页。

内部矛盾,坚决制止敌对势力和不法分子打着宗教旗号进行违法犯罪活动,抵御境外势力利用宗教进行渗透。

第三,对宗教事务进行管理,是为了使宗教活动纳入法律、法规和政策的范围,不是去干预宗教团体的内部事务。实现宗教活动的正常化,符合国家和社会的利益,也符合各宗教的利益。要实现宗教活动正常化,除加强政府对宗教事务的依法管理,还要依靠各爱国宗教团体发挥积极作用,自主地处理好自己的事情,加强自我教育和自我管理。没有这两个方面的结合,依法管理就达不到预期的目的。因此,对宗教事务进行管理本身就要求支持和鼓励宗教团体办好自己的内部事务,而不是去包办或干预。[①]当然,宗教团体的自主管理,也不能超越国家法律法规,违反现行政策规定,政府对此负有依法监督责任。如果进行的宗教活动妨碍了正常的社会秩序,损害了其他公民权益,导致公民生命损害、财产损失,政府就要依据有关法律进行干涉和处理。

(二)政府部门要努力提高依法管理宗教事务的水平

1.要提高法律意识、增强法制观念。随着宗教工作逐步走上法治化轨道,法律意识就成为宗教工作干部一项不可缺少的素质。宗教工作干部要增强学习法律法规的自觉性,积极主动参加法律知识培训活动,在工作中学会并善于运用法律法规去分析、处理宗教问题。近期的重点就是要学习和贯彻落实好国家宗教事务局制定的《全国宗教工作系统法制宣传教育第六个五年规划》[②],着力提高宗教工作干部的法律意识和法律素质,切实增强宗教工作的法制观念。

2.要不断改变观念、切实改善管理。在依照法律加强管理的同时,宗教工作还需要增强群众观点和服务意识,做好信教群众的工作是宗教工作的根本任务。[③]宗教工作干部要乐于和善于做群众工作。要用公仆的赤

---

① 王作安:《中国的宗教问题和宗教政策》,宗教文化出版社,2010 年 4 月第二版,第 134 页。

② 《全国宗教工作系统法制宣传教育第六个五年规划》,载国家宗教事务局政策法规司编:《宗教政策法规文件选编》,宗教文化出版社,2012 年出版,第 394 页至 400 页。

③ 《胡锦涛在政治局第二次集体学习时强调:全面贯彻党的宗教工作基本方针》,2007 年 12 月 20 日 03:02, http://politics.people.com.cn/GB/1024/6675949.html

诚,满腔热情地为广大宗教界人士和信教群众服务,维护他们的合法权益。在实施依法管理的过程中,既要坚持原则、依法行政,又要注意方法策略、教育引导,并寓教育引导于依法管理之中。只有改善管理,才能切实加强管理。宗教界也会欢迎这种管理。①

3.要坚持依法行政、严守权限程序。②在依法管理宗教事务的过程中,各级政府宗教事务部门处于主导地位,扮演着重要角色。政府宗教事务部门在行使管理权力时,必须以法律为准绳,必须在法律授予的职权范围内行使职权,必须依据法律规定的要求和程序管理宗教事务,既不越权,也不失职。

(三)宗教界人士和广大信教群众要知法懂法守法

宗教团体负责人及工作人员、宗教教职人员、宗教活动场所管理组织成员、宗教院校教师和学生以及广大信教群众要树立法律至上、国法大于教法的观念,自觉地学习国家相关的法律知识,学习宗教事务方面的法律法规和部门规章,自觉做到知法、懂法、守法,提高维护法律尊严的自觉性,增强在宪法、法律、法规和规章范围内开展活动的意识,自觉接受政府宗教事务部门的依法管理和监督,抵制各种非法的宗教活动。同时也要学会依法表达自己的利益诉求,依法解决各种矛盾和纠纷,学会运用法律手段维护自身的合法权益。③

四、宗教事务管理法治化面临的挑战

随着国内外形势的不断变化,宗教方面出现许多新情况、新问题,使宗教事务管理法治化面临着许多挑战。

---

① 叶小文:《宗教七日谈》,宗教文化出版社、中共中央党校出版社,2007年出版,第88页至89页。
② 宋大涵主编:《依法行政辅导读本》,中国法制出版社,2011年出版,第69页至84页。
③ 国家宗教事务局政策法规司编:《宗教政策法规读本》,宗教文化出版社,2012年出版,第13页。

(一)国际因素造成的挑战

一是全球化,造成政治多极,文化多元。一方面国界虚化,国际交流频繁,另一方面各种思潮碰撞,矛盾冲突增多。整个世界显示出依存与分裂、统一与多样并存的局势。①

二是宗教极端主义,使宗教民族身份凸显,宗教的民族性、文化性和民族的宗教性、文化性增强,民族主义更高尚、更具道德感和感召力,宗教成为文化的核心标识,民族宗教身份认同冲击或替代传统的阶级、政党认同。②

三是互联网,导致社会碎片化与网络一体化,也造成一些无形与有形群体性事件的发生。言论自由与羊群效应,导致国家权威衰减与社会权威上升。③

这些形势的变化与发展,一方面改变了宗教和文化传播方式,另一方面加强了宗教的民族性和文化性,同时加强了宗教的国际性,对推进宗教事务管理法治化进程造成挑战。

(二)国内因素造成的挑战

一是随着改革开放的不断深化,社会急剧转型,结构持续开放,活力不断增强,造成一些制度断裂失效。

二是思想多元化趋势加快,道德失范人、信仰缺失的情况日益凸显。

三是利益格局调整,城乡差别与贫富差距拉大,造成社会矛盾增多。④

这些情况的变化与演化,一方面为宗教发展扩展了空间,另一方面导致社会控制力减弱,管理宗教事务难度加大,同时也使宗教方面的矛盾触点增多,复杂性加大。

---

① 卓新平:《"全球化"的宗教与当代中国》,社会科学文献出版社,2008 年出版。
② 金宜久:《当代宗教与极端主义》,中国社会科学出版社,2008 年出版。
③ 刘金光:"国际互联网与宗教渗透",载《中国宗教》,2003 年第 3 期,第 27 页至 29 页。
④ 卓新平:《"全球化"的宗教与当代中国》,社会科学文献出版社,2008 年出版,第 257 页至 278 页。

（三）宗教工作本身造成的挑战

一是宗教界自身还存在着宗教思想陈旧、制度建设不足、人员素质不高，导致爱国宗教团体发挥作用不够等问题，宗教界自身建设亟待加强。[①]

二是宗教自身情况的发展变化挑战我们的应对能力。比如：宗教发展呈较快趋势、信徒结构发生变化；境外势力利用宗教对我渗透呈加剧趋势；"三股势力"等境内外敌对势力利用宗教破坏民族团结、危害国家安全的事件时有发生；宗教方面的非法违法活动屡禁不止，等等。[②]

三是宗教工作力量薄弱，特别是在基层，党政领导重视不够、宗教工作执法主体削弱，宗教工作机构、编制、经费严重不足，无法应对日趋复杂、任务繁重的管理工作。[③]

五、展望：如何进一步提高宗教事务管理的法治化水平

在看到宗教事务管理法治化取得的成就的同时，必须面对存在的问题和挑战，思考对策，才能进一步提高宗教事务管理的法治化水平。

（一）必须坚持依法管理与积极引导并重

一是要加强宗教思想建设。宗教界要自觉主动开展宗教思想建设，比如基督教的神学思想建设、天主教的民主办教和本地化探索、伊斯兰的解经以及佛道教的讲经说法活动。政府部门对此给予要重视、推动和支持。

二是支持宗教界服务社会人群。通过开展公益慈善事业，是宗教融入社会、顺应时代呼唤的必由之路。政府部门要解放思想，真心实意地采取

---

① 张全录："对加强宗教团体自身建设的几点思考"，载《中国宗教》，2012年第10期。
② 王作安：《中国的宗教问题和宗教政策》，宗教文化出版社，2010年第二版，第434页至435页。
③ 同上，第422页至423页。

措施,鼓励和支持宗教界广泛开展公益慈善事业。①

三是引导和推动宗教界加强自身建设。要把和谐寺观教堂的创建活动打造成引导和推动宗教界加强自身建设的一个重要平台,通过开展创建活动,引导和推动宗教界进一步加强制度建设、组织建设和道风建设;通过开展创建活动,着力于人才培养,进一步提高宗教教职人员队伍的素质。②

四是继续加强和创新对宗教事务的管理。一方面要健全法制,加强宣传,深化培训,加大执法力度,树立法律权威,使所有涉及国家利益和社会公共利益的宗教事务都置于法律的规范下。另一方面要重视源头设计,要在制度设计的源头上,在体制机制的创新上下工夫,加强和创新对宗教事务的管理。

(二)必须坚持政府管理与宗教自治并重

一是要发挥政府行政功能与宗教自治功能并行并重。一方面要切实加强基层宗教工作行政执法主体建设,没有健全的基层行政执法主体,再好的法律法规也无法落到实处。二是要发挥宗教团体的自律与协同作用,推动落实宗教团体的规章制度。

二是挖掘和利用政府行政资源与社会资源共用。要推动对宗教事务的社会化管理,充分利用社会上各有关方面的资源,对宗教事务进行综合管理。要打开寺观教堂和宗教工作的围墙,让宗教在党政相关部门的监管和社会的监督下健康发展。

三是推动宗教事务管理方式多元化。管理的主体要从一元变多元,管理的方式要从线性变互动,同时要注意刚柔相济,疏堵结合。要善于寓管理于教育之中,通过做细致的思想工作解决管理中的难题。

(三)坚持社会管理与提供公共服务并重

宗教组织属于一类社会组织,宗教活动场所属于满足信教群众信仰需

---

① 国家宗教事务局、中共中央统战部、国家发展和改革委员会、民政部、财政部、国家税务总局:《关于鼓励和规范宗教界从事公益慈善活动的意见》(国宗发〔2012〕6号),载国家宗教事务局政策法规司编:《宗教政策法规文件选编》,宗教文化出版社,2012年出版,第355页至360页。

② 《中国宗教界关于建设"和谐宗教、和谐寺观教堂倡议书"》,载《中国宗教》,2007年第2期。

要的公共设施,政府相关部门应该改变以往重监管轻保护、重管理轻服务的做法,在通电、通水、通路、消防等方面提供必要的公共服务。宗教教职人员是社会的一个群体,应该纳入社会保障体系当中,为他们提供社会保障。要树立寓监管于保护、融管理于服务的意识。要通过这样的管理与服务,使宗教界与党和政府以及社会各个方面共担社会责任、共享发展成果。

中国改革及其信仰转型

李向平

　　改革开放30年来,信仰危机问题如影随形,经济发展成就备受关注,而与此紧密联系的信仰问题也一直是中国社会各方面舆论与道德焦虑的核心。特别是伴随着中国经济的巨大发展与社会变迁的深层表现,利益分化、共识断裂的现象格外严峻。因此,在这样一个利益分化、却又要求深化改革的时代,信仰概念呈现为一个非常多元的现象,政治信仰、民族信仰、宗教信仰、文化信仰、国家信仰……与此同时,面对当下以及未来十年中国发展道路的讨论,有关信仰的问题也得到格外关注。因此,中国改革开放事业的深度发展,必然推进中国信仰的重新建构;而中国信仰的重新建构,当然也是深入改革的重要动力。

　　理性而深入地研究、讨论当代中国信仰,对于中国社会形成价值共识,对于执政党合法性的建设与信仰转型、对于社会诚信的构成、对于中外文化观念的进一步汇通、对于中国社会文化的建设与繁荣,均非常重要。

　　在超越了固有宗教学领域基础上,我们从信仰社会学维度反思当代中国改革开放诸问题,认为当前中国涌现以民族民粹主义、国家主义、政党基要主义为特征的三大信仰思潮,均与经济发展而信仰结构未能转型密切相关,由此构成了当代中国的"瓶颈式"改革难题。究其问题根源,主要出自于"主义信仰"的革命党信仰模式尚未完成向执政党信仰转型,难以宪政民主践行信仰。为此,中国信仰之最彻底的问题,乃公共权力的信仰核心,应是基于公共权力祛魅之后的理性化,超越"信仰论政治"模式,建构政党国家对法律与宪政的信仰,进而使信仰转型成为社会文化建设与深入改革的深层动力。

本文拟从中国社会的三大信仰思潮、政治改革与信仰转型、民主法制建设的信仰动力、公民信仰与社会文化建设等层面的互动关系出发,研究与讨论当代中国的多元性公共信仰的构成及其特征,如何走出"信仰论政治"的固有模式,促使法律、宪政成为社会普遍信仰等等问题,借以梳理未来中国信仰的基本架构。

一、"信仰"作为中国问题

"信仰"概念,是目前中国社会被使用最广泛,同时也是最有歧义的词汇之一。因此,人们在批评社会现象、深入改革之时,常从信仰层面着眼,以至于把其他社会问题与信仰关联。于是,当代社会舆论出现了与此紧密相关的三种观念:第一种是始于1980年代的信仰危机论,其次是议论多年的信仰缺失论,再次是近年呈现的信仰无用论。

信仰危机论,肇始于对"文革"时期、信仰作为一种权力工具等信仰现象的反思,其主要原因是长期以来,中国虽有被称为"信仰"的政治教义,但并不存在真正的信仰,进而导致信仰现象的高度政治化。于是,当这种神圣教义与社会真实经验相互抵牾之时,信仰危机就不可避免。它以当时《中国青年》发表的《人生的路为什么越走越窄》的文章为起因,以人活着有什么意义的问题为基点,对改革开放、社会变迁以及经济发展提出了一个普遍性的价值要求,即一个开放公正的社会须以信仰为基础,社会经济的发展须以信仰的构建同步。

信仰缺失论,基于一种怀疑主义。它不仅是怀疑现实世界中的那些固有的价值观念,而且还根本怀疑人类是否真能拥有长久和普遍的价值,怀疑那些充满了功利主义的信仰形式,最后把这种怀疑归因于信仰的根本不存在,同时也要求去建构一种新的信仰。一般是基于具有终极性而神圣性特征的宗教信仰判断,认为那种具有稳定且制度化宗教信仰体系,方能给人以智慧、构成心灵上的抚慰，特别是能够基于宗教信仰进而构成一个社会普遍价值规范，基于信仰抽象建构为一个社会准则。至于信仰无用论，则是认为当代中国缺乏一个社会认同予以普遍支持的信仰体系。

信仰无用论，则是集中于对信仰之功利性或私人性的批评，认为那种以求神为依归的信仰方式，总是以"无事不登三宝殿"的信仰方式，局限于个己的现实利益欲求，在神人之间进行象征性的利益交换。就当前中国信仰的社会现状而言，这种功利性信仰诉求招致的批评最为严重。中国人目前不缺信仰，各种信仰形形色色、林林总总，不一而足。但这些信仰太缺乏社会认同，太私己、太个人化了，所以即便有信仰，却无法构成对社会人群普遍性的价值约束，为此，有信仰的，却局限于私人的神秘认同，实际上等同于没有信仰。

如此三类信仰评论，事关中国信仰现状与复杂多变的信仰关系。无论是危机论，还是缺失论或无用论，实际上是"信仰焦虑"综合征，表面上，学界与社会都在议论，中国虽有被称为"信仰"的政治教义，同时还有五类宗教信仰与形形色色的民间信仰，但并不存在真正的信仰。①

中国信仰之所以会呈现如此复杂混乱的现象，一方面，是因为中国语境之中的"信仰"概念很有歧义，各种定义甚至会构成冲突；一方面，也是由于经济发展超前、体制改革滞后所导致人们对信仰规范的强烈期待，进而使信仰成为改革开放以及未来十年中国深度改革所面临的一个重大问题。难以想象，一个经济发展、政治民主的社会，能够建立在一个没有信仰或信仰混乱的价值基础之上。以至于说，一个具有普遍认同的信仰结构，才能够与一个经济发展、政治民主的社会紧密联系。

"在处理信仰问题上，中国人不似西方人，一定要把信仰置于宗教的范畴，把信仰视为对神的信仰，或者是以对神的信仰为中心，反而是把信仰作为生活之方法与智慧；既有对神的信仰，亦有人本信仰。这是因为，中国人对待文化、信仰，本不出自本体论、神圣目的论的进路，而是一种方法论"②。

所以，"中国的宗教和信仰往往不是单纯的宗教和信仰，他们常常被镶

---

① 徐贲：《中国并不存在真正的信仰》，《中国新闻周刊》，2012 年 7 月 10 日。
② 唐逸：《理性与信仰》，广西师范大学出版社，2005 年，第 406 – 407 页。

嵌在权力与秩序之中而难以得到一种纯粹的呈现形式"①。依人依事,具体处理神人关系、神圣与世俗之间的关系,在这些关系之中,中国信仰构成了这样一种特点,它"并不确信或深究神圣意志的结构,以制度形式来表达人与神圣意志的交通,倾向于神人交往、日常实践、权力认同等形式来反复加强对某些权力神圣意志的确认和信仰"。②因此,处于社会变迁与结构转型中的中国信仰,如果要实现相应的变迁与重建,就不仅仅是单纯的信仰的,而具有更加复杂丰富的社会权力内涵,特别是在历经重大改革、变迁的中国政治秩序之后,中国信仰模式才会呈现变迁与转型的可能。诚然,也正是因为三十年来权力与社会秩序的变迁与改革,中国信仰问题才呈现出了当下的多重面向和多元视野。

中国社会具有一个信仰中心,类似于"帝国隐喻"③,甚至能够建构一种"象征权力"或"符号权力"④,使信仰对象能够神圣化,同时也囊括了所有中国人、中国宗教的信仰功能。无论是佛教、道教,还是后来的基督教等等,虽然具有不同的信仰体系,但在这些信仰现象背后,它们大多能够汇总到这样一个信仰中心的结构之中,并以此信仰中心为圆点,并与国家权力紧密整合,依赖权力制度而具有了国家、民族的意识形态信仰特征。因此,中国人的信仰实践方式,常常是以此信仰中心作为一个联结方式,通过象征或符号权力等中介,在国家治理、意识形态、社会交往关系、人际伦理之中,建构社会变迁、权力建构、甚至是利益交往、社会共识的多重关系。

在中国人的信仰实践与信仰认同过程中,参与建构的往往有权力、哲学、意识形态、道德伦理、身份利益等诸多因素,潜在地分离出不同层面的信仰及其认同方式。为此,中国人的信仰构成,还表现在中国信仰的多重结构:官方信仰、学者信仰、宗教信仰、民间信仰、家族信仰等等。这多重信

---

① 李向平:《信仰、革命与权力秩序——中国宗教社会学研究》,上海人民出版社,2006年,第1页。
② 李向平:《信仰是一种权力关系的建构》,《西北民族大学学报》,2012年,第5期。
③ Sangren, Steven, 2000, *Chinese Sociologics: An Anthropological Account of the Role of Alienation in Social Reproduction*, London: The Athlone Press. Feuchtwang. Stephan 1992, Boundary Maintenance: Territorial Altars and Areas in Rural China, *Cosmos*, Vol., pp. 93 – 109.
④ 符号权力是一种"神圣化"的权力,是使对象变得神圣的权力。斯沃茨:《文化与权力:布尔迪厄的社会学》,陶东风译,上海译文出版社,2006年,第55页。

仰关系,彼此贯通而又相对独立,甚至出现上下冲突,前后脱节,很难用一个简单的判断来概括中国人的信仰特征。①

正如梁漱溟所说,"宗教问题是中西文化的分水岭。"②强调的就是中国人的伦理关系本位与团体信仰实践方式为主的基督宗教的信仰方式不同。西方人一旦涉及信仰,大多归属于宗教;中国人却不一定。当然,即使在西方,宗教的概念也是一种"现代性构造"。③所以,在中国语境中讨论信仰问题,更应扬弃像"宗教"这样的词汇,代以"信仰"来研究中国相关问题,这样才能真正地以平等多元主义的立场看待中国信仰传统,更能抓住不同信仰及不同信仰传统之间比较与交流的真正问题。

二、权力信仰危机与改革瓶颈

不同的信仰,关键是在于不同建构过程;而在此建构过程之中,信仰建构中得以渗透进来的各种因素诸如权力、利益、身份、族群等,也同时会借助于信仰的建构而成为了信仰的内涵。由此观之,那种始于 80 年代的信仰危机现象,实际上就是一种以象征权力作为信仰对象的危机,是这种信仰面对经济发展而消解了自身的神圣性所带来的危机,甚至是以经济发展替代了信仰,以为经济发展就是信仰本身。正是因为这种象征权力导致的危机,才能成为普遍性中国问题及其整个社会的信仰危机。而这个象征权力的信仰,曾经就是改革开放前的总体社会的神圣化与合法性结构。

所以,信仰曾经是权力的象征建构,那么,信仰危机就是象征权力建构过程的中断,以及这种建构能力的危机。在中国语境中讨论信仰问题,唯有进入信仰的建构及其实践过程,更能抓住信仰问题的实质,以"信仰问

---

① 牟钟鉴、张践:《中国宗教通史》(下),北京:社会科学文献出版社,2000 年,第 1219 – 1221 页。但其限于官方信仰、学者信仰、民间信仰三类,还应有家族信仰、宗教信仰、民族信仰、国家信仰诸类型。参李向平:《信仰但不认同——当代中国信仰的社会学诠释》,北京:社会科学文献出版社,2010 年。

② 梁漱溟:《中国文化要义》,上海人民出版社,2005 年版,第 46 页。

③ 威尔弗雷德·坎特威尔·史密斯:《宗教的意义与终结》,董江阳译,北京:中国人民大学出版社,2005 年,第 353 – 375 页。

题"为核心展开对中国问题的研究以及中国改革之深化。

当代中国社会的改革开放,正当面临一个巨大的再转型、再变迁。国家权力、经济发展、社会运作等模式,均需一个更深入的改革与开放。在此背景之下,不同社会力量都在寻找各种思想资源,以论证自身的改革话语——有向中国传统寻找思想资源的,一些人诉诸于毛泽东时代的"新民主主义",另一些人诉诸于传统的"儒家宪政主义";向西方寻求思想资源的群体则更多,包括民主派、经济自由主义者、新左派、民族主义等等,不一而足。所有这些充满价值观的思想流派所强调的,都是中国的改革应当向哪个方向进行。① 这些话语的建构,表面上似乎都不在讨论信仰问题,但均与中国信仰紧密相关。因为,信仰重建能够为中国的改革开放提供神圣化的象征权力。

面对如此现状,信仰问题既关乎个人的精神关怀、社会运行的价值规范,同时也是政治改革、深度开放的基本内涵,不得不呈现如此复杂的格局。从此层面而言,信仰危机现象事关国家建设与中国认同,早已是中国未来体制改革的重大问题,不可一再忽视。

改革开放以前,中国被看作是一个依凭意识形态信仰整合起来的社会,主要依据主要领导人对一个社会应该是什么的政治认知即意识形态而组织起来,并通过如城乡二元体制、单位与户口制度、无数政治团体以及强大的行政权力来实现这一整合。一个高度行政化、政治化的社会,与计划经济一起,使意识形态及其信仰显得格外重要,并由此在中国社会中创造出新的象征权力与符号权力,方能完成如土地改革、集体化、工商业国有化等一系列政治任务。

然而,当代中国 30 年的经济发展,政府在很大的程度上成为了利益主体,这就使人们对政治的信念、对政府权力的信任也发生了相应的改变。特别是"随着意识形态首要性的销蚀,许多党政干部开始形成各种各样的思想,包括物质主义、旧左派和新左派、西方自由主义、民族主义甚至宗教信仰。更严重的是党员干部的腐败。以往党政干部政治忠诚是衡量他们

---

① 郑永年:《十八大与中国的改革问题》,共识网,2012 年 7 月 31 日。

政治业绩的最重要标准,现在金钱已经替代了政治忠诚".①这些现象都在提示这样一个重大问题:政府在成为经济利益主体的时候,是否还能够继续成为意识形态信仰的象征主体? 这就是当代中国信仰、或者是主导、制约中国信仰的根本性问题。它说明了,在继续强调政治意识形态主导性地位的同时,如何把社会制度的改革与完善,从以意识形态信仰为政治基础,转变为以宪法为权力合法性基础、以信仰为社会公共资源而非权力的合法性证明资源。这就是当前中国体制改革、民主、宪政建设的重大动力问题。

可以说,市场经济和全球化的快速发展一旦成为国家权力继续存在的主要方式之后,这就不可能再度回归到由意识形态信仰建构起来的社会秩序之中了。这就是构成了肇始于 1980 年代以来信仰危机的逐步发生,以及渐渐强烈的政治社会学内涵。从信仰与社会、权力的关系来说,如在一个封闭专制的社会中,信仰往往是传统权力施行意识形态独断的工具;即便有些信仰,也只能流失于信仰者个体的神秘认同。反之,如果在一个开放社会,无论一神信仰,还是多神信仰,甚至无神论信仰,皆能在信仰间的互动当中,构建并遵守一种信仰交往的公共规则,共同建构一个社会的公共信仰。

其中,既关乎个人的精神关怀、社会运行的价值规范,同时也是政治改革、深度开放的基本内涵。从此层面而言,信仰危机所导致的信仰焦虑,事关政党国家建设与中国认同,早已是中国未来体制改革的重大问题,不可一再忽视。

三、改革难题与三大信仰思潮

从某种程度上说,1949 年以来毛泽东的遗产,是建立了一个列宁式政党,让一个列宁式的政党国家能够运作、发展起来。与此同时,毛泽东在很大程度上,非常充分地利用儒家意识形态建构国家的方式,并使用一个信仰马克思主义的列宁主义政党建构国家机构,进而整合整个社会。1980 年

---

① 郑永年:《中国共产党意识形态的当代转型》,凤凰周刊,2011 年 7 月 11 日。

代之后,邓小平的政治遗产,是在保持强大政治权力体系的同时,建立了区别于传统的一个经济制度。在毛泽东时代,经济与政治制度大都出自苏联模式,尽管有圣人信仰的传统特征,但基本上来说是苏联模式,以继续革命、阶级斗争的方式在建构一个主义、一个领袖的革命党信仰方式。邓小平时代的政治制度虽然仍属苏联模式,但经济制度是朝向资本主义的市场经济。因此,邓小平最大的贡献是把政治上的苏联模式和经济上的西方自由模式结合一起。这是历史上的第一次,也是一种创造。① 他以经济发展的方式强化了革命党信仰方式。

因此,在毛泽东与邓小平所留下的最大的政治遗产之中,最有影响的,应当是政治制度的运作基于一种意识形态信仰 ②,以信仰方式建党治国。所以,与传统治国文化整合的马克思主义实践,一般具有两个基本前提:一是国家整合社会,二是意识形态信仰整合国家。但是,从 20 世纪 90 年代开始,中国领导人却非常成功地组织起一种以利益为基础的社会秩序,并从这样一种秩序中获益,使中国社会固有的整合体制不得不发生了极大的变化。"毛泽东强调把'道德'作为激励人民行为的方式,而邓小平似乎更赞成以'利益'来激励人民"。邓小平的南巡,开启了中国从在意识形态基础上建构社会秩序,向以利益为基础建构社会秩序的转变,从政治社会向经济社会的转变。这似乎在说明,中国共产党在施行改革开放 30 年以来,意识形态已经实现了逐步地成功转型。③

但是,在这个转型过程中,不得不承认,意识形态及其信仰转型是有所滞后的。特别是执政党以经济发展作为公共权力合法性基础之时,经济利益似乎就只成为了信仰重建的基础,直接以经济发展作为统治权力的神圣化建构路径。这样,经济发展进入信仰结构,而没能想到经济利益也会促使固有的理想主义变成空想空谈之后,人们陷进了拜金主义,失落了固有

---

① 《毛泽东与邓小平的政治遗产》,2011 年 10 月 19 日 – 20 日,辛亥百年论坛,美国哈佛大学。

② 马克斯·韦伯倾向于将意识形态视为论证权力统治合法性的信仰体系;R. 阿隆、D. 贝尔、M. 李普塞特等视之为一种"世俗宗教";T. 帕森斯定义为社会群体使世界易于理解的解释框架、认知系统,而吉尔兹则视之为文化符号系统如宗教、美学或科学的符号系统之一。John B, Thompson, Studies in the Theory of Ideology, Los Angeles; Berkeley, University of California Press, pp.42.

③ 参见郑永年:《中国共产党意识形态的当代转型》,凤凰周刊,2011 年 7 月 11 日。

的信仰。这个时候,重新强调理想主义,强调信仰,反而在"道德"与"利益"——其实是"信仰"与"权力"之间——一再凸显了一道难以弥补的鸿沟。殊不知,以利益为基础的权力秩序兴起,必然会导致意识形态信仰难以避免的淡化与衰落。

这个时候,经济越是发展,用于追求经济利益的公共权力越是强大,权力信仰之危机就越发变本加厉,信仰危机日益加剧,以至于不可收拾。所以,重建执政党信仰以及遏制权力信仰危机的根本是,政治权力的神圣化或合法性不能继续建立在经济发展基础上;而对那种建立于固有意识形态信仰基础上的政治秩序来说,重建信仰或赋予信仰的宪政基础,方才是民主政治及其秩序得以重构的基本动力。

政治经济权力与信仰关系的完备型整合关系,促成了一方独大的政治权力与经济实力,并且被建构为一种信仰象征结构,进而以象征权力的方式制约了其他信仰及其实践方式,使经济发展替代固有信仰,甚至是主导、主宰了其他社会信仰的自由实践。

在此背景下,人们已难以回归固有的理想主义。因为这种利益化的公共权力直接或间接地构成了当代中国信仰危机的主要原因。那种基于传统的天地君亲师的信仰方式,传统父母官、天子、圣人等,既是道德楷模,也是信仰对象。辛亥革命之后,"天地君亲师"被转成"天地国亲师",而列宁主义政党政治所建构起来的"主义信仰",实际上就把这种传统信仰方式,置换成为对领袖、意识形态政治的信仰[1]。延至三十年经济发展,当这些官员及其权力直接成为经济利益主体之时,它们就难以继续成为整合社会的信仰资源或直接的信任对象了。

虽然当代中国各界有识之士,大多在为这种"信仰焦虑",尽一切可能寻求有效药方。有人主张"读经",用民族传统文化意识来为病人"固本";有人主张"反对利用外来文化意识搞自由化",把病人关进隔离室,在病人身上"打防疫针";还有人要输入国外新兴的人文宗教,给中国文化"输入人造血浆",恢复新陈代谢的生命……一般而言,这些议论汇成了当代中国社会颇有影响力的三大信仰思潮。

---

① 李向平:《20世纪中国的"信仰"选择及其影响》,《学术月刊》,2012年,第5期。

　　其一,是那种基于民族、民粹主义的信仰主张,以信仰建构当代中国的夷夏大防,可以称之为"民族信仰主义"。其基本原则是,非我族类,其心必异。凡是中国的,就是正确的;凡是正确的,就应当信仰。表现为汉民族对炎黄信仰的崇拜,对儒教信仰的强化,以及对外来宗教及其相关价值理念的排斥。主张以民族共同体为信仰标准,重建一元化的民族、国族,乃至皇汉主义的信仰,以主导其他各种信仰,重新强调本土传统信仰与外来宗教信仰之华夷之辨,以此区分信仰之正统与非正统,主张强大起来的中国人不再应当具有外来信仰,维护中国文化的正统性与合法性。这种思潮,以所谓"儒教宪政"为代表。

　　民族信仰或以民族为信仰对象,本非坏事,但是一定要以民族信仰作为中国复兴之本,成为民主宪政之本,这就会成为问题。一个现代国家之中,各种民族共存,多元信仰并立,如何只能以一种信仰为其合法性与神圣性的基础呢? 依儒教宪政的逻辑推演下去,中国社会还可以出现佛教宪政、基督教宪政、道教宪政、伊斯兰教宪政等等。不过,严格地说,这些信仰现象却也说明了信仰问题与现代民族国家的正当性证明方式,具有深刻的内在关系。强化了信仰关系与现代民族国家合法性方式的互动,或者说,不同国家权力形态同时也能够制约或建构不同的信仰体系、乃至信仰模式的多种构成方式。

　　其次是"国家信仰主义",以国家权力作为信仰建设之主体。近年来,建立"国教"的(国家宗教)主张渐多。有主张以佛教建立国教,认为佛教传入中国已经两千多年,成为了中国宗教,中国如果要建立国家宗教,非佛教莫属。当然也有立儒教为国教者,构建儒教宪政主义,认定每个中国人都应当是儒教信徒,都是孔圣人的弟子;还有以道教为国教者,以为只有道教才是真正的宗教,并立国教惟道教正宗。

　　这些国教主张者,以传统宗教为信仰主体,但是其建构主体却依赖于国家公共权力,直接以传统信仰及其实践方式构成中国当代信仰的基础,再次强调华夷之辨,最后将以儒教或佛道教信仰及其主张,建构为公共权力神圣性与合法性的基础,抵制外来文化宗教,以其传统之正统性获得独尊。

　　很明显,这些国教主张者,进一步深化了信仰建构与民主宪政建设之

间的内在矛盾。面对中国改革的深入,仅仅是传统信仰的偏重或重建,应
无济于事。因为这种传统信仰方法,无法解决权力政治及其官员的信任危
机,无法淡化公权力对信仰的独断与左右,只能是继续依附于权力层面、继
续为权力独断发挥功能,最终构成一元论独尊型信仰结构。

其三是政党基要主义。这种信仰思潮忽视了当代中国从革命党到执
政党的转型趋势,忽视了这一转型过程中必然会呈现的信仰变迁要求,主
张回到革命党的信仰传统,一个党、一元信仰、一个领袖,行政权力整合社
会,象征权力整合意识形态,以象征系统施行信仰表达。这就遮蔽了革命
党和执政党信仰方式的异同与转型。

早在民国初年,孙中山就提出了"主义信仰"的概念,从议会政党过渡
到革命党,最后以领袖崇拜建立了高度一元、权力集中的革命党体制,最后
形成了二十世纪列宁式政党的信仰传统。尤其是这种"主义信仰",曾经与
"五四"以来的各种宗教替代思潮深度整合。其中,最著名者包括梁漱溟的
伦理替代宗教、陈独秀的科学替代宗教、蔡元培的美育替代宗教、冯友兰的
哲学替代宗教等。而这种"主义信仰"和宗教替代思潮的影响,一直持续到
1949 年以后。"文革"时期对毛泽东的个人崇拜也可以看到其中的影子。
其中的历史教训,遗留至今,汇合成为当今社会渐渐强烈的"信仰焦虑",很
值得执政党予以梳理与总结。

可以说,上述三种信仰思潮,彼此具有深度关联。但其问题根源,主要
源自于"主义信仰"的革命党信仰模式尚未完成向执政党信仰转型。特别
是当政府官员及其公权力业已成为经济主体,构成"权贵资本主义"之际,
那种有关民族信仰、国家信仰主义及其主张,实际上就很可能在它们之间
建构了一种深层关联。因为这种信仰传统的主要对象之一,就是以其个人
的、私己的关怀方式,充满了对固有大人物、圣人及其道德楷模的精神依
附,无助于政治改革以及民主宪政的建设。尤其是在有关信仰神圣资源依
旧为象征权力所掌控的时候,国家的民族的等传统信仰习惯常常是固有权
力自我为圣、内圣外王的证明工具。

借用约翰·罗尔斯的话来说:"这样的情形如何可能——那些信奉基
于诸如教会或圣经等等宗教权威之宗教学说的人,同时又如何能坚持合理
宪政民主体制的合理政治理念? ……这后面的问题,重新表明了合法性观

念的意义,以及公共理性在确定合法性法律时的作用。"①应当指出的是,一个现代"国家的内部功能不是去安排社会模式,而是去提供一种与不同的生活与思想类型相一致的基本秩序结构。"②这说明国家本身不是一种信仰模式,而人的信仰及其社会秩序的建构,在一个民主的国家里面,是基于可能被证明的信仰,以及能够保证信仰及其神圣的关怀不会被来自外面的权力所滥用。

四、政治改革与信仰转型

国内学术界在总结、研究前苏联解体的论著之中,大多都会提到一个重要的原因,那就是政治信仰淡化。但是,信仰的淡化如何导致了苏联的解体? 大多论著则语焉不详,大多是泛泛而谈,加强马克思主义宣传教育云云。

现代社会面临高度的利益分化,经济社会的发展恰好又赋予了多元利益存在的合法性。革命党合法性的基础在于打天下和高度的意识形态信仰整合,执政党是否仍然以这些特点作为合法性基础,亟待深入思考。革命党的合法性基础,一是打天下,强调意识形态信仰对整个社会的整合,即高度的政治正确与意识形态正确。毫无疑问,一个执政党必须要有自己的政治文化,而政党信仰则是其中的核心,这是执政党的灵魂和历史地位。执政党的合法性基础,是不是还是以意识形态,或者是以革命党的信仰方式作为合法性基础? 如果要回到革命党"主义信仰"乃至领袖崇拜的固有传统,然后以其作为已经多元化的社会利益及其价值观念的整合工具,这是执政党在未来一个时期内领导地位如何奠定的问题,跟政治信任、政治文化建设、政治认同和国家认同的分别和强化皆紧密相关。其中与信仰重建紧密相关的问题是,如何从信仰层面实现从革命党到执政党的转变。

与信仰问题紧密相关,是社会主义核心价值体系的建立,但是不够。

---

① 约翰·罗尔斯:《万民法》,吉林人民出版社,2001 年,第 160、161 页。
② 伊安·哈里斯:《伯林及其批评者》,载以赛亚·伯林《自由论》,胡传胜译,南京译林出版社,2003 年,第 399－400 页。

目前的社会主义核心价值体系的共识性不够。国家哲学要解决的问题,是国家的基本理念是不是有最大多数的公民乐意认同、理性认同。这样就会使得国家的精神基础得以整合,而不是在精神上一盘散沙。其次,国家哲学在秩序上提供贴近日常生活的准则,这就是"兜底的价值观念"。① 从政治学的层面言之,国家哲学是以中立、中性的特点,寻求能够整合中国公民,或至少是绝大多数公民,能够保证国家认同的理念。但它不是来自于传统的阶级,也不是来自于传统的主义话语,更不是来自于权力的施加,这三个相加就是意识形态的信仰取向。

因此,这一"兜底的价值观念",配合国家哲学的中立性建构,应当是政治(国家)信仰的建构问题。其中,法律和权利的解释,包含了对法律和权利的信仰。可以说是信仰驱动的改革。所以,既要解决信仰问题,也要解决制度问题。要解决国家干部的"信仰危机",应该是用透明的"民主法治"观念做成"楔子",打入国家干部的心中,使他们牢记人民是国家主人,使他们明白贪污渎职损害人民利益是一种罪行,是必将受到法律制裁而绝无例外的。只有这样,干部中因"邪念纠结"而形成的"信仰危机"问题,才能够真正解决。②

表面上看,信仰问题似乎是一个意识形态的建设过程,以为抓紧思想品德的教育就似可见效了。然而,当代中国改革的特点是,以传统人文学者为主导,发起的一场又一场观念的变革。过去那种靠观念支撑的改革已经死亡了。接下来的中国改革,围绕的是法律和权利的实现,而不是观念和理论的讨论。对法律和权利的解释,是政府权力不断受到来自公民社会的挑战。③ 所以,执政党的信仰和国家信仰能否在宪政与法律层面分别建构,执政党的信仰能否与国家信仰在党章和宪法层面上予以不同的定义方式,而使国家信仰的建设与国家建设紧密联系。

马克思主义宗教观或者无神论的思想,无疑是执政党处理宗教信仰与社会公民信仰关系的基本原理,同时也是执政党重构信仰的理论基础。经

---

① 任剑涛:《中国:如何凝聚人心》,《瞭望东方周刊》,2011 年 4 月 18 日。
② 石天河:《对信仰危机的体会》,《书屋》,2011 年,第 4 期。
③ 蔡定剑遗稿:《政治体制改革的历史与现状》,《炎黄春秋》,2011 年,第 2 期。

典作家在论述社会主义政党与宗教关系的时候,曾经主张宗教信仰是公民私人的事情,只有革命政党的信仰才是公共的事情。如此强调,无意中或在实践中就把有神论和无神论在革命党国家中处于一种彼此对立的可能;无神论如作为执政党意识形态合法性基础的话,无形中就可能与宗教信仰有神论者处于一种可能对立的状态。

对此,学术界曾经提出有信仰分层的概念,在一个中国信仰的总体结构中分出有政治信仰、国家信仰、文化信仰、宗教信仰等层面。关键的是,这不同层次的信仰关系如何处理,使用法制的关系来处理,还是用领导人的文件、政策、说法来处理,或者是基于宪法的相关规定,这是有待于思考和研究、经由未来中国改革来回答的问题。可以这样认为,要完成从革命党到执政党的转变,信仰重构很重要、很全面,事关执政党的信仰建设、国家信仰建设,也同时事关中国社会的公共信仰以及文化之建设与繁荣。[①]

之所以如此讨论,这是因为,信仰最初乃是作为为社会关系的一种形式,只是人与人之关系的一种形式。所有的信仰与宗教信仰都是由社会形式转化出来的,而一旦宗教形式凝聚成形,又会对其赖以形成的母体 – 社会形式产生规导作用。社会作为人的互动关系,本身就带有宗教因素。因此,宗教信仰是一种社会关系的升华,是社会关系的超越形式。[②]可是,在国家与社会关系层面,如果权力关系大于、或强于社会交往关系,直接介入或构成了社会交往关系,那么,这种超越的社会关系就难以形成。人们就可能直接以权力关系作为超越关系来加以信奉。这种信仰方式虽然短期有效,但是,一经权力的转型,这种信仰危机依旧还会呈现出来。

从个体信仰到公民社会的信仰认同及其建构,指的是深入而持久地在时间与空间中(通过规则和资源而)建构的社会交往的连续性实践。它是一套关于行为和事件和规范模式,亦是一组普遍而抽象的认同体系。它依托在相应的制度层面,体现在组织结构之中,包含了意义、支配、合法化和促进社会结构转化的功能。从某种意义上讲,制度就是集体行动控制个人

---

① 李向平:《信仰重构:从革命党转变为执政党的重要机制》,《社会学家茶座》,2012 年第 3 辑,总第 44 辑;山东人民出版社,2012 年。

② G. 西美尔:《宗教社会学》,曹卫东译,上海人民出版社,2003 年,第 5 页。

行动的业务规则和运行中的机构,并由此构成了社会结构的基本框架,以及个人与社会群体行动、普遍性的价值观念、社会资源及其供求与分配之间的"过滤器"。①

因此,任何一个社会层面中的个体信仰者与共同体信仰,正式的信仰组织与非正式的信仰组织,无不需要这个"过滤器",使隶属于该体系的信仰和精神权利,建构为博弈均衡的"概要表征"或"共同信念",进而把信仰关系本身建构为一种共同信念,以及价值预期的制度化结果。②

这个过滤器如果是一个权力机构,那么,其信仰模式就会以权力的信仰为架构;如果这个过滤器是民族国家,那么,其信仰模式就会使民族国家;如果这个过滤器是一个团体,那么,这个信仰模式就可能是宗教组织。所以,一个由此而分化出来的信仰类型,由上而下,由下而上,官方的、民间的、宗教的、社会的……依据这种差异而划分出不同的信仰层次和认同方法,甚至是不同信仰的权力制约等级。这样就构成了一种经由象征权力建构起来的关系图式,有核心,有层次,先后上下地构成了中国人信仰认同的整体格局及其差异。

正是由于权力的信仰危机,出自于人们对权力的不信任。改革开放进程之中,官员们艰难自律,自律无缘,渐渐地失去了庶民百姓的信从与信奉,于是,上至高官,下至百姓,无不选择自己信任的神祇及其信仰方式。所以,对于这些官场巫术与官员信奉,无论私己的精神走私,还是假公济私的巫术般祭拜,这都是一种自我表白:他们手中的权力已经不再受人信用。

依中国人信仰传统及其信仰惯习,人们对领导、官员、统治者的信从,根源于他们人品道德的高尚,天人之际,替天行道,足可为天下典范;服从一人,如信一神。官员既是社会统治的权威,同时也是心目中卡里斯玛及其信仰中心,以保证他永远神圣而正确。然而,当这些官员们的道德行径出现差错,楷模失范,或者是因为官民之间的利益冲突,那么,其所内涵的信仰范式也就随之消失,其象征权力则同时衰落。因此,解决这种信仰危

① 道格拉斯·诺思:《经济史中的结构与变迁》,上海三联书店、上海人民出版社,1995年,第225页。
② 青木昌彦:《比较制度分析》,上海远东出版社,2001年版,第28页。

机之方法,就在于权力的民主化与理性化。舍此,别无他径。

五、民主法制建设的信仰动力

"宗教和政治之间的真正关系是非二元的,这种关系符合基于人类本质的因而归根结底基于实在结构的本质。现实问题也即宗教问题。关于人类终极的思考也是政治性的。政治与宗教不能彼此分离。没有一种宗教行为不同时属于政治行为。当今人类所有重大问题都既有政治性又有宗教性:饥饿、正义、生活方式、泛经济文化、资本主义、社会主义,如此等等。和平构成一个典型的例子,证明这一论断的真实性。依次观念,宗教的要素必须和超越者、超自然者、神圣者、超然者、涅槃、终极实在、永恒之物以及不可理解的内在之物有关。"①

为此,信仰与不同信仰间的认同方式,无论是国家特性的定义方式还是公民认同方式,它们既可揭示信仰与国家关系及其政治权力中社会运行结构的基本机制,同时亦包括和体现了国家政治秩序的内在运行机制和动力机制。就此国家特性和公民信仰认同之间的特殊关系而言,中国未来信仰的定义方式,既意味着公民个人信仰的身份界定,同时也将决定于执政党在公共信仰层面的定义方式。

政党、国家与信仰规范的关系,根本上表现为国家与公众崇拜和公众教育的关系。马克斯·韦伯曾把权力分为传统的、人格的与法理的三种形式,恰好,保罗·蒂里希也把国家权力分成三种象征形式,即魔鬼的、神圣的、世俗的。

第一是魔鬼的象征,它指出了国家毁灭一切的力量。一切精神价值都服从于国家,或者被它认可,或者被它排斥。它决定公众崇拜。"第二个象征把国家看成世间的上帝。国家是一个神性的象征。历史的意义,即世界精神在各民族精神中的实现,是在国家中产生,并通过国家表现出来的。因而,它是'世间的上帝'。一切神圣性都集中在国家身上。"第三个象征是

---

① 雷蒙·潘尼卡:《文化裁军——通向和平之路》,四川人民出版社,1999年,第62页。

"看守人国家"(watchman state),它通过自由主义而得到流行。一个极端的非宗教或非世俗的象征,代替了魔鬼与神圣的象征。国家不具有任何神圣化的意义。国家具有一种纯粹消极性的功能。这不需要任何神性的圣化,也不需要借助魔鬼的力量,而只需要足够的维护公正的力量。一切内在的力量都属于受它维护的社会。① 而信仰法律或基于法律的信仰,则是信仰国家与现实国家赖以存在的共同基础。这对权力与信仰两种关系正当化处理来说,都是十分关键的。

一般而言,现代民族国家具有两种类型。第一类把国家等同于主权,国家主权由个人权利让渡合成,而民族是个人的总和。这一国家类型,大多发生在现代性原发国家,其民族认同的建构,依靠的是主观的承认或契约;第二类是国家代表民族实体,主权只是国家的属性,并不依赖于人权。这一类民族国家只需工具理性和民族认同的建构,而这种认同构成,大多依靠的是文化、信仰、种族等客观认同符号。民族国家与社会公民之区隔的神圣性,大多是在象征维度上施行的,并且得到了信仰习性和权力象征化过程的保障,进而借助于"行政化"或"制度化",使信仰及其终极关怀始终位于政治和经济领域的核心位置,成为民族国家的信仰体系。

就是这样一种信仰体系,为包括政治活动在内的整个国家生活体制提供了一种神圣维度,赋予民族国家等权威以信仰上的正当性,使权力与统治过程具有了一种超验的目标。为此,民族国家建构起来的信仰体系,直接成为权力国家的信奉,把国家治理直接体现为一种对普遍的、超验的信仰实践,即从终极的、普遍现实的角度理解权力政治及其所有活动。这种信仰类型实质上等同于一种"世俗宗教",权力与国家被赋予神圣的、至高无上的性质,它把政府理论和信仰惯习进行画等号的解读,也可被称之为一种"信仰论政治"模式。②同时也被视为一种民族国家信仰,直接成为了

---

① 保罗·蒂利希:《政治期望》,四川人民出版社,1989年,第134、135页。

② 信仰论政治,来自一种完美的乐观主义宇宙观,其治理活动被理解是为人类完美(perfection)服务的,同时把国家治理理解成一种"无限制"活动,政府是全能的。这种说法只是关于政府目标在于"拯救"或"完美"的另一表达方式而已。与此相应的是怀疑论政治,统治被认为是一种特殊的活动,它与对人类完美的追求尤其格格不入。国家统治者的地位在这里是荣耀的、受人尊敬的,但不是崇高的。参欧克肖特《信念论政治与怀疑论政治》,张铭等译,上海译文出版社,2009年,第40、46页。

民族国家"政治正确"的象征权力及其标准。

目前中国国民的精神关怀状况是,虽有以政治教为基础的政治信仰,以及以私人欲求为核心的其他信仰,但前者公权力太强,后者也缺乏最大多数公民的认同,进而缺乏政治权力与公民社会的民主建设作为基础。正是由于权力独断的信仰危机,出自于人们对权力的不信任,因此,解决这种信仰危机之方法,表面上是政党国家信仰的建构,实质上还是政党国家权力的民主化与理性化建设。特别是信仰关系中有关法律和权利的解释,应当就包含了人们对法律和权利的信仰及其要求。所以,与信仰紧密相关的政治改革与民主建设,其核心问题应当是:执政党与国家权力究竟应该是民主化,还是基于信仰习惯的神圣化?而信仰及其实践关系,就其信仰社会学实质而言,也不仅仅是一种权力观念与信仰对象的问题,在其更深的层面,这是一种与信仰紧密相关的法律与权利如何实现的问题。

换言之,既要解决各个层面的"信仰焦虑"问题,也要解决信仰实践与信仰认同的建构方法问题。而解决公共权力层面的"信仰危机",应该用透明的"民主法治"观念。所以,中国信仰之最彻底的问题,乃是公共权力的信仰核心,是基于公共权力祛魅之后的理性化,对法律与宪政的信仰。

在一个秩序良好的社会之中,"没有任何个人或联合体所拥有的那种终极的目的和目标。"[1]为此,民主社会不是一个共同体或联合体,其意思是指"它受共享的完备性宗教学说、哲学学说和道德学说的支配。对于秩序良好社会的公共理性来讲,这一事实十分关键。"崇高的信仰构成,离不开一个好的社会:平等、公正、有序。这说明未来中国信仰转型的社会模式,实际上就是一种信仰与公共权力的特殊关系,以及处理这一特殊关系的特殊方法。依据信仰社会学的基本研究方法,不同的神圣观、超越观,导致并促使不同信仰的建构模式,甚至是不同内涵的权力观与国家观,也会主导或主宰了不同信仰类型的建构。解决国家政治层面之信仰危机的基本方法,是宪政法制;解决宗教层面合法性危机的基本方法,是多元共治;至于解决社会信仰缺失,则是信仰对话与信仰实践方式的民主与自由。正是在此层面上,那种单纯依靠信仰强化,并以之作为中国未来改革的某些

---

① 约翰·罗尔斯:《政治自由主义》,万俊人译,南京,译林出版社,2000年,第42-43页。

主张，必然会再度走入信仰危机或信仰焦虑的死胡同。

六、公民信仰与社会文化建设

改革开放 30 年以来，中国社会中的宗教信仰自由问题，已经从有没有宗教信仰自由的问题，变成了宗教信仰如何自由的问题，或者说从有无自由转变成多少自由、如何自由的问题，以及宗教信仰自由如何在法制社会之中得以实践的问题了。

个人层面的信仰自由，解决了个人的信仰问题，但并非等同于宗教的自由。私人性的信仰自由，指的是个人的精神与信仰层面，但不能完全包括个人信仰的生活实践与表达层面。个人信仰的实践与表达，实际上也不会局限于私人的范围了。因为公民个人的信仰不会总是局限于个人的脑袋之中，不能说出来，不能活出来。因此，宗教信仰自由原则的 30 年社会实践，能够告诉我们的是个人的信仰自由与社会的宗教自由，其实是两个不同却又紧密联系的两大层次，它们难以分隔，更不可能人为割裂。而宗教事务的依法管理，其本质就是在宗教信仰自由原则基础上对社会性宗教自由的一种最基本的定义方式。既强调了宗教信仰的社会性，同时也肯定了信仰宗教的个体性，从而能够将私人层面的信仰自由与公共社会层面宗教自由，在现代法制建设之中整合起来。

回顾 30 年前的 1982 年中共中央 19 号文件，这就需要我们重新理解文件与宪法规定的"宗教信仰自由"这一概念及其原则。如果仅仅是把宗教信仰之自由理解为或局限于公民之间私人的事情，那么，不同信仰之间如何能够体现信仰上的相互尊重呢？要不就把宗教信仰局限于为私人交往关系与信仰者的个体神秘认同之中。所以，不同信仰与宗教信仰与不同信仰之间如何尊重的问题，似乎还有一个信仰与宗教信仰社会实践的公共领域建构的问题。只有在宗教信仰被社会某一层次共享认同的基础上，宗教信仰才能成为社会、文化建构的重要资源之一。至于那种局限于私人认同、私下交往的宗教信仰方式，则很容易被秘密化、神秘化、巫术化，处于现代社会之边缘。这就是中国有了信仰、却又呈现信仰无用、信仰缺失的基本原因。

相对于个人崇拜、中国人处于被信仰的权力共同体而言,私人信仰的形成,实属社会进步的结果。它与1980年代以来个人主体性确立与自我的发现相互配合,具有人心解放、权力解构的一定作用。它拆解了那种一元、单极、带有象征权力独断特征的信仰结构。人们仅仅信奉自己。为此,私人的信仰可说是开启了一个个体主义新时代,一种更为私人化、情感化和更民间化的信仰方式。

然而,问题也出在这里。仅仅是私人或私人的信仰,或许会导致信仰本身所包含的公共性丧失,而信仰之公共性所赖以依托的社群或共同体缺失,会使一个社会信仰的公共性始终无法建构,导致一个社会公共信仰的缺失。在公私领域尚且无法界定的时代,私人信仰也无法再度提升为圣人信仰的前提下,私人信仰有可能演变出一套私人主义的意义模式。他们不期待自己的身份改变,甚至不期于与他人交往、互动,而是渐渐地把他们的私人信仰构成一种亚社会、亚文化生活方式,变异为一种仅仅关心自己利益、自我满足的精神关怀。

在打天下先得人心的传统社会,人心几乎等同于信仰以及对权力更替的信仰,私人信仰几乎不可能;而国民时代,民族国家如同世俗之神,私人信仰同样难构成。而整个20世纪以来,宗教被道德、美育、科学、哲学等"主义信仰"所替代,私人信仰依旧给人焦虑。而真正的私人信仰,只有在1980年代后的改革开放中,才得以渐渐呈现。特别是当信仰之公共性不能依托于自由社群之时,私人信仰便可能被推向了个人内在、单一的道德修养,最后未能为信仰之公共性提供孕育、滋生的土壤,变质为单纯的私人之事。

实际上,私人信仰是自然状态下的信仰方式,而公民信仰则是社会交往中的信仰方式,同时也是承载了私人信仰公共性与社会性的实践方式。私人信仰只有演进为公民信仰,才有可能构成良性互动的社会秩序。因个体的私人修持,只能净化自我,甚至连自我也无法净化。个体私我的关怀,缺乏终极。而终极的关怀形式,就在于神人、神圣信仰的公共互动之中。与此相反,当代中国为什么会频频出现"贪官信教"的权力困惑?即是因为这些官员们"信仰走私",这与他们的"权力走私",往往一脉相承、彼此推动。各人只信自己的,无法交往、难以认同,也不会彼此制约。

在这里,既有宗教的问题,亦有信仰层面的私人关系的限制。信仰的神圣性,必定出自于信仰的公共性与社群性。实际上,"没有法律的宗教,将失去其社会性和历史性,变成为纯属于个人的神秘体验。法律(解决纷争和通过权利、义务的分配创造合作纽带的程序)和宗教(对于生活的终极意义和目的的集体关切和献身)乃是人类经验两个不同的方面;但它们各自又都是对方的一个方面。它们一荣俱荣,一损俱损。"①宗教如此,信仰也是同样。缺乏法律共识的信仰,将失去其公共性与普遍性,变为特殊群体的象征权力构成;而以宪政建设为基础的信仰,才会建构一个公共的信仰平台,构成社会层面的公共信仰。当人们只信任自己的信仰,不信任私我之外的任何存在之时,最终将导致更为深层的另一种信仰危机、权力危机——我们的信仰如何被信任!? 什么才是值得信任的权力? 什么才是被认同的信仰方式?

就此而言,现代国家、社会文化的建设,乃是与公民信仰是相辅相成的。一种国家形态,必然会有一种信仰形态相与配合。权力至上的国家,私人信仰为其服从;而民主国家之需要,则是公民信仰。因此,一个人有信仰不难,难的是信仰那种能够交往、相互认同的信仰;一个国家要成为一个大国容易,而要建构一个有信仰的公民社会更难。

一个民主政治的社会文化,总是具有诸种宗教学说、哲学学说和道德学说相互对峙而又无法调和的多样性特征;因宗教的或哲学的完备性学说都包含着超验因素,因而是无法调和的。因此,未来中国信仰最基本的问题是:"什么样的原则和理想才是公民们平等共享终极政治权利、以使他们每一个人都能合乎理性地相互证明其政治决定的正当合理性呢?"②什么样的公共信仰才具有终极的神圣特征?

这就是说,无论未来中国信仰呈现何种形态,存在几种信仰模式,不同信仰之间整合构成的公共理性,应当是最最重要的,那才是民主社会公民的平等理性。正如存在各种属于宗教、大学和诸多其他市民社会联合体的

① 哈罗德·J.伯尔曼:《法律与宗教》,梁治平译,北京:三联书店,1991年,第95页。
② 约翰·罗尔斯:《政治自由主义》,万俊人译,南京译林出版社,2000年,第32页。

非公共理性一样。公共理性才是一个民主国家的基本特征。它是公民的理性,是那些共享平等公民身份的人的理性。他们的理性目标是公共善,此即政治正义观念对社会之基本制度结构所在。而这个能够形成不同信仰、价值观及其认同方式之"共同基础",即是约翰·罗尔斯说的"公共理性",即公民在有关宪法根本和基本正义问题的公共论坛上所使用的推理理性。①

诚然,这种公民信仰认同方式最能够建构一种以公共信仰为基本信念的中国行动逻辑。因为公民身份的定义及其认同系统的构成,既可认识现实社会中的信仰惯习,亦可认识信仰者如何在不同的社会成员中获得自己应有的权利和承担的责任与义务,从而以信仰表达及其公共规则达成公共理性秩序。因此,国家、社会乃至社会成员,大都能够确立、维护或消除、破坏某种固有的身份系统,使国家权力体系中的权威资源出现重新配置,促使某一部分社会成员获得相对比较优越、或比较弱势的地位。在这个意义上,公民信仰认同方式或国民阶层的"信仰"惯习,实际上意味着各种信仰资源的重新配置,以及公民信仰认同的途径和身份定义系统的建构和变化。它们往往伴随着国家权力的整合问题,在法律与宪政基础上,使作为公民个人权利的信仰成为公民个人权利作为制度正当性基本根据而重新定位。

人们常说,在经济发展的同时要给公民社会留一个生长的空间。依此,中国信仰层面的社会文化建构,其实就是公民信仰的成型。一个强大的国家不仅仅需要发达的经济,同时也需要有信仰的公民与公共的信仰。这是国民经济与社会文化健康发展的基础。

个中深意,正如我在《信仰但不认同—当代中国信仰的社会学诠释》②一书中指出的那样:"国人不知其异,以信仰就可安心立命。虽然它们的制度分割与实践取向,会给中国人带来人心安定的某些效果,但在信仰实践

---

① 约翰·罗尔斯:《政治自由主义》,万俊人译,南京译林出版社,2000 年,第 10 页。
② 李向平:《信仰但不认同—当代中国信仰的社会学诠释》,北京:社会科学文献出版社,2010年。

的现实里面,它们之间却有很多很深层的混淆与隔阂。"所以,对当代中国人而言,信仰也许已不是问题,但更关键的是如何信仰:如何实践自己的信仰,认同公共的信仰。

The Contemporary Social Uniqueness and Convergence of the Traditional Chinese Religion in Taiwan

Hsing-Kuang Chao

Introduction

Most Taiwanese their ancestors or themselves have migrated from mainland China to Taiwan some times in the last four hundred years. Their ancestors brought Chinese traditional religions, Buddhism, Taoism, and Popular (folk) religions (Popular religions thereafter) with them for comforting their spiritual needs during the settle down process. The fleeing of the Chinese Nationalist government from mainland China to Taiwan with many western religions (mainly Christian denominations) in 1950's, Taiwan have been a society with religious diversity and vitality. The raise of marsh law in 1987, the prosperity of new religious movements and the revival of different denominations of Han Buddhism indicate that religious market has been formed, and the religious organization identities among the believers of different religious groups have been diversified. (Kuo, 2001:29)

According to the data of Taiwan Social Chang Survey (TSCS), the percentage of Buddhists, Taoists and believers of Popular Religions in population is floating each year, but the percentage of Chinese traditional religious believers, the sum of Buddhists, Taoists, and Popular Religious believers, in population is around 75% in the last twenty years. Many scholars attribute this phenomenon to the syncretism nature of Chinese religions. Most of Chinese had difficulty to distinguish differences among Buddhism, Daoism, and Popular Religion in terms of faith, ritual, and deities worshiped in their daily life. For example, a Buddhist may go to ask Taoist and Popular Religions' gods for blessing when he or she encounters a trouble. One the other hand, a Taoist or a believer of Popular Religion may participate in Buddhist's meditation practicing in Buddhist temple regularly. Whether the three major traditional Chinese religions, Buddhism, Taoism, and Popular Religion, are three individual religions with different religiosities or they share a common religiosity but present different features?

Based on the data of the Survey of Religious Experience in Taiwan (REST), we try to explore whether the three traditional religions share the same religiosity or they are three different religions indeed. Following the purpose of this study, the primary questions we would like to ask in this study are: (1) what are religious experiences Taiwanese religious believer experienced most frequently; and (2) how the experiences are related to their religious identities, religious conceptions, and new life attitudes? Is there any difference between Taiwanese traditional religions and Christianity related to religious experiences, conceptions, and new life attitudes? Is there any commonality in religious experience, conceptions, and new life attitude among believers of different religious groups?

Analysis Data

In order to explore the religiosity, in terms of religious experience, conception and new life attitude, of the three Chinese traditional religions, we use the data of 2009 Religious Experience Survey in Taiwan (REST), which is a comprehensive and in-depth investigation of the topic of religious experience in Taiwan. REST used stratified multistage sampling to obtain a representative sample of adults aged 18 and above (born after 1990) in Taiwan. It has a total of 1,714 valid cases, of which 49.1% are males and nearly 85% of respondents are believers in a certain religion. Among these religious believers, 38.4 are believers of Folk Religions, 18.6% are Buddhists, 13.1% are Taoists, and 5% identity themselves are Christians (including Protestants and Catholics). To fulfill our study, we include respondents of these four groups as our analysis cases. The questionnaire of REST consists of 121 questions. The main part of the questionnaire is related to four kinds of religious experience: transcendental power, life philosophy, extraordinary dreams, and mystical vision or events. The survey also includes questions related to general religious beliefs and behaviors.

Measures

1. Religious Identity

In the SRET questionnaire, respondents were asked "What is your religion?" The respondent options were: "None," "Popular religion," "Buddhism," "Taoism," "I-Kuan Tao," "Catholicism," "Protestantism," "Buddhism-Taoism combined," and "Other." The main purpose of this study is to compare the varieties of religious experience, conception, and experience of new life attitude among respondents who were affiliated to different religious groups. Because of some groups are not large enough to compare statistically, we decide to combine Catholicism and Protestantism as "Christianity" and exclude other two groups "I-Kuan Tao" and "Buddhism-Taoism combined. ①" "None" is excluded for not fitting the purpose of this study.

2. Religious Experience of Power and Experience of Acquiring in a Flash New Understanding of Life

There are four dimensions of religious experiences listed in the REST questionnaire, including power, experience of acquiring in a flash new understanding of life, dreams, and mysterious. In order to examine the relations between different dimensions of religious experiences, we redefine power dimension of religious experience as "religious experience", and experience of acquiring in a flash new understanding of life dimension of religious experience as "new life attitude". Also, we record the two variable values as 1 = never, 2 = once

---

① I-Kuan Tao was established in China in Ching Dynasty and spread to Taiwan after the World War two. The doctrine of I-Kuan Tao incorporates Confucianism, Chinese-Buddhism, and Taoism and recognizes validity of Christianity and Islam as well. Before 1987, the raise of martial law, I-Kuan Tao was banded as an illegal secret society (religion). Many scholars identify I-Kua Tao as a new religious movement. The believers of Buddhism-Taoism combined proclaim the consistency of Buddhism and Taoism in the doctrine and practice. It is very common that Believers of Buddhism-Taoism combined practice Taoist ritual and Chart Buddhist sutra in their daily life. There is very few official institutes of Buddhism-Taoism combined.

or twice, 3 = sometimes, and 4 = frequently.

3. Religious Conception

The religious conception lists fourteen statements of religious faith, such as believing in gods, the power of ancestor worship, and Qigong, in the REST questionnaire. The purpose of the fourteen statements is to understand what people believe in these religious faith statements. We also record fourteen variables values as 1 = never, 2 = once or twice, 3 = sometimes, and 4 = frequently.

4. Core Religious Experience (CRE), Core New Life Attitude (CLT), Core Religious, Conception (CRC)

Using factor analysis statistics, we are able to sort respondents' major religious experiences, new life attitudes and religious conceptions according to religious identity. We label the major religious experiences, new life attitudes and religious conceptions of each religious group as core religious experience, core new life attitude and core religious conception.

5. Common Religious Experience (CMRE) and New Life Attitude (CMLT)

Based on factor analysis statistics, we are able to sort the common factors of religious experience and new life attitude which are most frequently experience by respondents affiliated to believers of all four religious groups, including Buddhism, Taoism, Popular religion, and Christianity.

6. Gap between Core and Common Religious Experience (GC-CRE) and Gap between Core and Common new Life Attitude (GC-CLT)

In order to examine our observation that how much Christian's religious experience and new life attitude are different to the religious experience and new life attitude of believers of other traditional Chinese religious groups. We created two variables that measure differences between core and common religious experience and between core and common new life attitude.

GCCRE = CRE-CORE GCCRE = CLT-GCCLT

7. Degree of Religiousness which indicate the strength of commitment to a specific religion are measured as 1 = do not believe at all, 2 = do not really believe, 3 = somewhat believe, 4 = believe, and 5 = completely believe.

8. Number of friends sharing one's faith refers to the density of respondents' social network within the religious institution. The variable are measured as 1 = no one, 2 = almost none of them, 3 = some of them, 4 = half and half, 5 = most of them.

9. Offering Rate. In order to examine the influence of religious experience, conception, and new life attitude on respondents' donation to the religious institution, offering rate was created to measure respondents' offering to the religious institution against respondents' family income. We expect that higher percentage of offering rate indicate higher religiousness of the respondent.

Findings

Core and common religious power experienced by believers of different religious groups

In order to explore the core religious power, religious conception, and new life attitude experienced by respondents of different religions, factor analyses were executed. We find that respondents' religious identity influence respondents' religious power(s) experienced. Among Christian respondents, they most frequently experience the power of God, Jesus, the Holy Spirit, or the Virgin Mary, and some of respondents also experience the power of fate or fortune.

Buddhists most frequently experience powers of the Buddha or Bodhisattva and Karma. Many Buddhists also experience the power of fate or fortune. Taoists often experience power of the Buddha or Bodhisattva and fate or fortune. Believers of Popular religion most frequently experience the power of the Buddha and Bodhisattva, Karma, and fate or fortune. (Table 1)

(Table 1)

Religious Experience Power	
CMRE	Fate or fortune; the Buddha or Bodhisattva (excluding Christian)
CRE	
Christianity	God, Jesus, the Holy Spirit, or the Virgin Mary
Buddhism	the Buddha or Bodhisattva Karma
Taoism	the Buddha or Bodhisattva
Popular Religion	the Buddha or Bodhisattva Karma

Table 1 shows that believers of all four religious groups experience power of fate or fortune. Believers of other there traditional religious groups also experience power of the Buddha and Bodhisattva. Both Buddhists and believers of popular religion are affected by the power of Karma. However, most Christians frequently experience the unique power of God, Jesus, the Holy Spirit, or the Virgin Mary. These results suggest that fate or fortune is the most common religious power affecting Taiwanese in their everyday life. For those who believe in traditional Chinese religions, the Buddha and Bodhisattva is the most common religious power to experience.

Core religious conceptions of believers of different religious groups

For exploration of core and common religious conceptions of different religious believers, we perform factor analyses to discover the core religious conceptions of each religious group. Christians believe two core conceptions: (1) there is a supreme God in the universe; and (2) gods, spirits, ghosts, and demons do exist. Buddhists most believe in the two conceptions: (1) there is reincarnation after death; and (2) spouses, relatives, and friends are preordained relations from a former life. Taoists prefer to believe in three core conceptions: (1) gods, spirits, ghosts, and demons do exist; (2) the good will be rewarded and the bad will be punished; and (3) a spiritual medium can exorcize evil spirits and cure illnesses. Believers of Popular religion believe in the existence of gods, spirits, and ghosts and other two core conceptions (1) Fengshui affects us and our family and (2) the dead without offerings will become ghosts. (Table 2).

The finds regarding to the core conceptions of believers of each religious group are very interesting. Believers of three religious groups, Christians, Taoists, and believers of popular religion, share the common conception in believing in the existence of gods, spirits and demons, in term of supernatural been(s). Most of Christians believe in the existence of a supreme God in the universe. Two core conceptions shared by most of Buddhists are "there is reincarnation after death" and "spouses, relatives, and friends are preordained relations from a former life."

Two conceptions "the good will be rewarded and the bad will be punished" and "a spiritual medium can exorcize evil spirits and cure illnesses" believed by Taoists imply that the existence of gods, spirits, and demons, in term of supernatural beeing. Believers of popular religion tend to believe in Fengshui and filial piety which are very common conceptions in the Chinese religious culture and are related to ancestor (spirits) worship. Basically, the finding show that believers of four religions believe in different type conceptions. Christian and Taoist tend to believe in the existence of supernatural been(s). Believers of Popular religion more focus on the interaction between ancestors' spirit and their descendants. Many Buddhists prefer not to believe in the existence of God or gods, spirits, and demons (supernatural been) and tend to believe in Darma in terms of reincarnation a non-personality power, but they do proclaim that they are affected by Buddha or Bodhisattva. This shows that we need to do more investigation on the different conception of the Buddha, Bodhisattva, gods, and spirits among Buddhists, Taoists, and believers of Popular religions. Whether in Han-Buddhism, Buddha is treated as a greater god.

(Table 2)

Religious Conception	
Christianity	Gods, spirits, ghosts, and demons do exist There is a supreme God in the universe
Buddhism	There is reincarnation after death Spouses, relatives, and friends are preordained relations from a former life
Taoism	Gods, spirits, ghosts, and demons do exist The good will be rewarded and the bad will be punished A spiritual medium can exorcize evil spirits and cure illnesses
Popular Religion	Gods, spirits, ghosts, and demons do exist Fengshui affects us and our family The dead without offerings will become ghosts

Core and common new life attitude understood by believers of different religious groups

Concerning the new life attitude, believers of all religious groups tend to feel that "detach myself from the world; just follow the natural course of things" is most common new life attitude grasped. However, in addition to the common new life attitude, Christians tend to feel "God arranges everything; follow God's will" as their new life attitude. Buddhists are like to grasp "nothing is permanent in life; don't be so rigid" and "good deeds will be rewarded; we must do good to merit future rewards" as their core new life attitude. Taoists have the same new life attitude as Buddhists in "good deeds will be rewarded; we must do good to merit future rewards." But, they feel "life and death are matters of fate and heaven disposes fame and fortune" is another important new life attitude understood. We also find that believers of popular religion keep the same core new life attitude as Buddhists in "nothing is permanent in life; don't be so rigid" and "good deeds will be rewarded; we must do good to merit future rewards".

（Table 3）

The most important common new life attitudes shared by majority believers of all religious groups are "detach myself from the world; just follow the natural course of things." We are able to find the new life attitude of "good deeds will be rewarded; we must do good to merit future rewards" is shared by many believers of religious groups excepting for Christians.

（Table 3）

Feeling of a Flash New Understanding of Life	
CMLT	Detach myself from the world; just follow the natural course of things
CLT	
Christianity	God arranges everything; follow God's will
Buddhism	Nothing is permanent in life; don't be so rigid Good deeds will be rewarded; we must do good to merit future rewards
Taoism	Nothing is permanent in life; don't be so rigid Life and death are matters of fate and heaven disposes fame and fortune
Popular Religion	Nothing is permanent in life; don't be so rigid Good deeds will be rewarded; we must do good to merit future rewards

Means and Gap of Core and Common Religious Experience, New Life Attitude, and Conception among Believers of Different Religious Groups

Table 4 shows means of core and common religious experience, life attitude and core conception, and the gaps between means of core and common religious experience, life attitude by religions. In the dimension of religious experience, Christianity has the highest mean in CRE and the lowest mean in CMRE, and the mean of CRE for popular religion almost the same as the mean of CMRE. For Christianity, the gap between CRE and CMRE is 1.8 and is statistically significant. The gap between CRE and CMRE of popular religion is very few as low as 0.03 and is no longer statistically significant. Gaps between CRE and CMRE of Buddhism and Taoism are statistically significant, but the gaps are minimized to 0.47 (Buddhism) and 0.58 (Taoism). This may reflect that in the dimension of religious experience,

(Table 4)

Mean Comparison in Religious Experience, New Life Attitude, and Conception							
	Religious Experience			Life Attitude			Conception
	CRE	CMRE	GCCRE	CLT	CMLT	GCCLT	CORE
Christian	3.47	1.67	1.8 ***	3.74	2.91	0.83 ***	3.17
Buddhist	2.67	2.20	0.47 ***	3.30	3.13	0.17	3.12
Taoist	2.71	2.13	0.58 *	2.87	2.83	0.04	3.03
Popular Religion	2.87	2.83	0.04	2.91	2.83	0.08	2.75

Christian shares a very different power experience with believers of other religious groups. Among believers of popular religious groups, there is no gap between their core and common religious experience.

In the new life attitude dimension, again, Christian show the highest mean score in feeling "God arranges everything; follow God's will." The gap between the mean score of core life attitude and the common life attitude is 0.83 and is statistically significant. On the other hand, the gap between the mean score of core life attitude and the common life attitude seems to get smaller in Buddhist, Taoist, and believers of popular religion. These findings indicate that Christian share a very different life attitude with believers of other traditional religious groups in Taiwan. For believers of Buddhism, Taoism, and popular religion, the frequency of feeling the core life attitude and the common life attitude are almost the same.

In the dimension of religious conception, we could not find any common conception for the religious groups in this study. But the data reveal that Christian, Taoist, and believers of popular religion believe in the existence of gods, spirits and demons. The conception of existence of gods, spirits, and demons is not Buddhists' major concern. Buddhist tend not believe in the conception of the existence of supernatural been. Generally, Christian holds the strongest core conception in comparison to believers of other religious groups.

Predicting the Life Attitude of Believers of different Religious Groups

In order to examine the influence of respondents' religiosity, in terms of religious experience, conception, and religiousness, on the new life attitude of different religious groups, we further used OSL regressions with control for other two commitment factors, the social networks in the institution and the offering rate. Table 5, 6, 7, and 8 analyses the influence of religious experience, conception, and religiousness on the new life attitude for Christian, Buddhist, Taoism, and believers of popular religion. Table 5 reveals what predicts the new life attitude for Christian. All of three variables, religious experience, conception, and religiousness in model 1 significantly influence on respondents' grasping the new life attitude. We add social networks variable to mode 1 and 2, and the result shows that all of four variables influence the grasp of new life attitude of Christian. Finally, we add offering rate to the equation. Social networks are the only one variable to influence respondents' new life attitude significantly. This shows that religiosity is important to impact on understanding Christian's new life attitude. But social network is more crucial in forester respondents' new life attitude among Christian.

(Table 5)
OSL Regression Predicting New Life Attitude for Chuistian

	Model1	Model2	Model3
Religious Experience	.230 *	.220 *	.181
Conception	.274 * *	.249 * *	.235
Religiousness	.285 * *	.236 * *	.099
Social Networks		.205 *	.266 *
Offering Rate			.036
N	83	78	78
R2	.377	.363	.409

Table 6 analyzes what predicts understanding the new life attitude for Buddhist. The results show that religious experience and conception are significantly influence on Buddhist's grasping the new life attitude. The coefficient indicates that religiousness affects very few respondents' new life attitude and it is not statistically significant. Social networks show no significant influence on respondents' new life attitude in model 2, so as offering rate in model 3. Religious experience and conception are two major variables, especially religious experience, to influence grasping the new life attitude among Buddhists. Social networks and offering do not show any significant influence on Buddhists' new life attitude. The influence of religion experience on life attitude are relative strong at 0.450 in model 1, 0.463 in model 2, and 0.416 in model 3. In contrast to Christian model, religious experience is the most crucial factor to impact on Buddhists' new life attitude.

(Table 6)

OSL Regression Predicting New Life Attitude for Budddhist

	Model1	Model2	Model3
Religious Experience	.450 * * *	.463 * * *	.416 * * *
Conception	.197 * * *	.236 * * *	.242 * *
Religiousness	− .002	− .055	.099
Social Networks		.080	.129
Offering Rate			.019
N	292	252	147
R2	.312	.337	.324

For Taoist, table 7 shows that, in all three models, religious experience and conception are significant variables to influence respondents' grasping the life attitude. Respondents' subjective religiousness does not affect their new life attitude significantly. In model 2, we control for respondents' social networks, and the influences of religious experience and conception on new life attitude remain significantly. But the influence of social networks on new life attitude is not significant. In model 3, we add offering rate as second control variable, the result shows that religious experience and conception still impact on respondents' life attitude, and the coefficient indicate that the influence of religious experience is stronger than the influence of conception on Taoists' life attitude. We can't find any influence of offering on respondents' new life attitude. Based on the statistics of table 6 and table 7, we find that religious experience is the most significant variable to forester the grasp of new life attitude among Buddhist and

Taoist.

(Table 7)

OSL Regression Predicting New Life Attitude for Taoist

	Model1	Model2	Model3
Religious Experience	.334 * * *	.370 * * *	.338 * * *
Conception	.262 * * *	.266 * * *	.331 * *
Religiousness	- .024	- .060	.014
Social Networks		.009	.010
Offering Rate			.058
N	212	181	105
R2	.221	.245	.279

For believers of popular religion, again, two major elements of religiosity, religious experience and conception, significantly influence on believers' understanding the new life attitude. In model one, we find that the influence of religious experience on grasping of the new life attitude is relative weak, but the coefficient of the influence of conception is extremely strong at 0.980. Again, in model 2, we control for respondents' social networks. In model 3, we add offering rate as anther control variable. The coefficient of the influence of religious conception on understanding the new life attitude remains at. 976. Table 8 indicates that, in all three models, two major factor on religiosity, religious experience and conception influence on respondents' life attitude. But, conception variable contribute most of influence on life attitude. Like our findings in table 6 and table 7, we can't detect any influence of personal subjective religiousness, social networks, and offering rate on life attitude of believers of popular religion.

（Table 8）

OSL Regression Predicting New Life Attitude for Popular Religion

	Model1	Model2	Model3
Religious Experience	.016 *	.016 *	.021 * * *
Conception	.980 * * *	.982 * * *	.976 * * *
Religiousness	.006	.004	.011
Social Networks		− .005	− .003
Offering Rate			.005
N	598	494	298
R2	.974	.979	.971

Summary and Discussion

In this study, we explore the core and common religious experience, conception, and new life attitude of different religious groups. We also try to find the association between religiosity, religious experience (power), conception, religiousness, social networks, and offering, and grasping the new life attitude of believers of different religious groups. Feeling the extraordinary power of "fate or fortune" is the most common power experienced by believers of all religious groups including Christian in Taiwan. But the powers of Buddha or Bodhisattva are often experienced by believers of other three traditional Chinese religions. Experiencing the power of Karma is common among Buddhist and believers of popular religion. Believers of the three traditional religions all experience the power of Buddha or Bodhisattva, but Christians believe in the power of God, Jesus, the Holy Spirit, and Virgin Mary. Taiwanese religious believers seem believing in the existence of supernatural beings including Buddha, Bodhisattva and gods or spiritual been. We further examine the table 2 respondents' religious conception. Christians, Taoists, and believers of popular religion, excepting Buddhists, believe that gods, spirits, and demons do exist. However, Buddhist tend to believe in a non-personal supernatural power called "Karma" or "reincarnation." We could not find a common religious conception for all religious groups. People believe in personal gods, spirits, or demons are most common phenomena in Taiwan. But Christians tend to believe in the existence of a supreme God in the universe, and Buddhists believe in a universe power called "Karma" which is in charge of reincarnation after death.

Table 3 regarding to understanding of new life attitude in some occasions, most of respondents from all religious groups most commonly grasp the life attitude of "detach myself from the world; just follow the nature course of thing." This is the most common life attitude of Taiwanese cross religious boundary. Believers of the three traditional religions feel that "nothing is permanent in life; don't be so rigid" is the most important life attitude when they encounter problems of life. In contrast with believers of traditional religions, Christians usually grasping a more positive attitude "God arranges everything; follow God's will." In general, Christians have very different religious experience, conception, and life attitude from other three traditional Chinese religions. But all religious believers share common elements of religiosity on religious experience, feeling the power of fate or fortune, and life attitude, understanding the need to detach oneself from the world and follow the natural course of things. Among believers of the three traditional Chinese religions, they share most of elements of religiosity of religious experience on power and life attitude on encountering life events. But they seems believe in relative different religious conceptions and practices.

Concerning the gap between CRE and CMRE and between CLT and CMLT, Christian group shows GCCRE is 1.8 and GCCLT is .83.

Both coefficients of GCCRE and CCLT are statistically significant. In the group of popular religion, both GCCRE and GCCLT are lower at 0.04 and .008, and are not statistically significant. We may conclude that there is no tension existence between CRE and CMRE of popular religion. Popular religion is the mainline religion, and Christianity hold a strong tension with popular religion in religious experience on power, life attitude and conception. Christianity occupies the marginal religious market in Taiwan. The major difference concerns with the imagination of supernatural being. However, we do find common factors in two religious experience dimensions. People cross religious boundary experience "fate or fortune" and feeling "detach myself from the world; just follow the natural course of things." We believe these factors are embedded in our traditional religious culture. Among the three traditional religions, Buddhists tend to believe in Karma as the power which influences their conception and life attitude. But Taoists and believers of popular religion tend to understand Buddha or Bodhisattva as gods or spirits. Although the different experience on power and conception are experienced, they tend to forester almost the same life attitude.

We examine the influence of religious experience, conception, and religiousness and other two commitment variables on respondents' grasping the new life attitude. We find that both religious experience and conception influence respondents' grasping the new life attitude for believers of all religious groups. Religiousness and social networks variables only influence on Christians' understanding the new life attitude but not on believers of other religious groups. What explains this different predicting power among different religious groups. First, perhaps Christianity is the marginal religious in Taiwan. As the minority, Christian shares a stronger organizational identity and takes their religion seriously. When a Christian proclaims the importance of his religion, his religiousness will be reflected in his life attitude. Second, Christianity is an institutionalized religion, and members are requested to participate in church activities regularly. Social networks in the church generate tremendous social capital to promote the solidarity of church members and forester strong life attitude which supported by the church. We also find that the conception is a stronger predictor than religious experience on Christian's life attitude. On the other hand, other three traditional religions are defused religion in general, both religious experience and conception are very important predictors of grasping the new life attitude. We are very interested to find that, one the one hand, religious experience is a more important predictor than religious conception on grasping the new life attitude among Buddhists and Taoists. One the other hand, religious conception is the most important factor to predict grasping the new life attitude among believers of popular religion in Taiwan.

In sum, it is very clear that Christianity is a very different religion, in terms of, Christian's religious experience, conception and life attitude, from other three traditional Chinese religions. Believers of three traditional religions share some elements of religiosity on religious experience and life attitude. But they show different conceptions on believing in personal gods, spirit, and non-personal power. Especially, believers of popular religions believe in the importance of the influence of ancestor spirit, and the conception becomes the most important predictor of grasping the new life attitude when encountering their life events. In this study, we are not easy to conclude the incorporation of three traditional religions in Taiwanese society.

Reference

Chao, Hsing-Kuang. 2004. Sociological perspective of church growth In

Taiwan: an application of the theory of new religious movements. In *Essays on Christian studies*. edited by the Graduate Institute of Religious Studies, Tung Hai University, 1 – 17. Taichung: Tung Hai University. (In Chinese)

——. 2006, "Conversion to Protestantism among Urban Immigrants in Taiwan." *Sociology of Religion*, 67(2):192 – 204.

Chen, Carolyn. 2008, *Getting Saved in America: Taiwanese Immigrants Converting to Evangelical Christianity and Buddhism*. Princeton University Press.

Chen, Hsinchih. 1995, The development of Taiwanese folk religion, 1683 – 1945. Ph. D. diss. , Department of Sociology, University of Washington.

Chiu, Hai-Yuan. 2006. *Religion, Occultism, and Social Change in Taiwan*. Taipei, Taiwan: Wu-Nan Publisher. (In Chinese).

——. 1997, "Religious Faith and Religious Attitudes among Taiwanese. " In *The Influences of Socio-Politic Factors on Religious Change in Taiwan*, 1 – 40. Taipei: Wu-Nan Publisher. (In Chinese)

——. 1986, "Religious Beliefs and Family Ideology." *Taiwan Academia Sinica Institute of Ethnology Research Journal*, 59:111 – 122. (In Chinese).

Hexham, Irving and Kalar Poewe, 1997, *New religion as global cultures: making the human sacred*. Boulder, COLO. : Westview Press.

Kao, Wen Parn, 2001, "Old or new religiosity?" a paper read at the Conference of Religion and Social Change, Institute of Sociology Academia Sinica, Taipei.

Lin, Pen Hsuan, 2001, "Religious Mobility and Geographic Mobility in Taiwan," Paper presented at the 11th Conference on the Taiwan Social Change Survey, Taiwan Academia Sinica, Taipei.

——. 2003, Media of faith transformation and self-conviction in the conversion process, In *Essays on faith, ritual and society*, edited by Institute of Ethnology, Academia Sinica, 547 – 581. Taipei: Institute of Ethnology, Academia Sinica.

Liu, Eric Y, 2009, "Beyond the West: Religiosity and the Sense of Mastery in Modern Taiwan," *Journal for the Scientific Study of Religion* 48 (4): 774 – 788.

Pas, Julian, 2003, "Stability and Change in Taiwan's Religious culture,"

Pp. 36 – 47 in *Religion in Modern Taiwan*: *Tradition and Innovation in a Changing Society*, Edited by P. Clart and C. B. Jones. Honolulu: University of Hawai'i Press.

Stark, Rodney, and Roger Finke, 2000, *Acts of faith*: *Explaining the human side of religion*, Berkeley, CA: University of California Press.

Su, Jennifer, 2006, "Every Tribe and Class: If These Missionaries Have Their Way, Millions of Taiwanese will No Longer be Too Embarrassed or Intimated to Go to Church," *Christianity Today*, 50(5):45 – 48.

Tamney, Joseph B. and Linda Hsueh-ling Chiang, 2002, *Modernization*, *Globalization*, *and Confucianism in Chinese Societies*, Praeger Publishers, Westport, Connecticut London.

Yang, C. K. 1961, *Religion in Chinese Society*, Berkeley and Los Angeles: University of California Press.

Yang, Fenggang, 2005, "Lost in the Market, Saved at McDonald's: Conversion to Christianity in Urban China," *Journal for the Scientific Study of Religion* 44 (4): 423 – 441.

Modalities of Doing Religion: Religious Diversity within Chinese Religious Culture

Adam Yuet Chau

The Very Idea of Religious Diversity or Religion Pluralism

Religious pluralism or religious diversity is defined as the co-existence of multiple religious traditions within one polity. As a concept it is rooted in the experience of Christianity's own internal differentiation into a multitude of different churches as well as its encounter with other religious traditions.

Before the modern era of secular liberalism and liberal, pro-pluralist religious policies in the West, the close ties between Christianity and the state (be it in the form of empires, kingdoms or states) resulted in two prominent forms of state-church relations. The more common form is the state's adoption of one form of Christianity (e. g. Roman Catholicism, Anglicanism) as state religion at the expense of other possible religious traditions. This one-state-one-religion situation came into being in Europe as a result of the Peace of Westphalia, which concluded long periods of religious wars. However, these states were fully aware of other, often neighboring states' adoption of other religions as state religions. Therefore one can say that in these situations even though religious diversity was not found within any one polity it was at least an ambient sensibility. Religious diversity was not an unknown object but was specifically rejected as an option for any one polity. In practice, however, individuals or communities of the so-called religious minorities always did exist even these single-religion polities, but they had to practise their religions very discretely or even underground. The other form of state-church religions is the state's explicit tolerance of multiple religious traditions within its territories, including the multitude of splinter Christian churches (e. g. as in some early modern European states and in the USA). This second form of pluralistic state-church relations gave rise to the modern form of liberal, pro-pluralist religious policies.

The other important historical root of the conception and ideology of religious pluralism and religious diversity is Christianity's encounter with other religious traditions. This encounter had many phases. But to make a long story short we can schematize this encounter into two phases. The first phase was characterized by Christian triumphalism, as Christianity spread to all corners of the world aided by colonial and imperial conquests. During this phase none of the other religious traditions were considered worthy equals of Christianity. The second phase was characterized by the ideology and practices of world religious pluralism. During this phase Christian leaders were forced to recognize many of the world's religious traditions as Christianity's equals (at least in structural and political terms if not in theological terms). For example, American Protestant leaders attempted to fight the threat of irreligiosity and secularism by joining forces with other religions and organized the Parliament of the World's Religions in 1893, which has continued even to this day to act as a platform for the recognition and promotion of world religious diversity.

Broadly speaking the above-mentioned paradigm of religious pluralism and inter-religious dialogue are the conceptual and intellectual framework (and one may say, baggage) that we bring to thinking about religious diversity in the Chinese context. Does such a framework apply in Chinese religious history? In what ways does it apply and in what ways does it not apply? Since I am an anthropologist rather than an intellectual historian, I will look at the issue of religious diversity in China from the perspective of ordinary people engaging in religious activities on the ground rather than religious elites engaging in high-power debates. Specifically, I will look at how religious diversity is *lived* through the consumption of religious services by religious consumers. China has always been a religiously diverse country, but this diversity is more evident as different "modalities of doing religion" (explained below) rather than as discrete confessional religions. For the vast majority of Chinese people historically and today, the presence of a wide variety of modalities of doing religion is simply a fact of their daily lives. However, "religious diversity" as a concept is alien to most Chinese people since their approach to religion is primarily instrumental and occasion-based (what can be called an efficacy-based religiosity) rather than confessionally-based, and their experience of religious diversity is embodied in the employment of different religious service providers on various occasions rather than abstract systems of religious doctrines and teachings. This paper will be divided into three parts. *First*, I will explicate what I have called "five modalities of doing religion" in China. *Second*, I examine one of the five modalities, the liturgical modality, in more detail since it is the most illustrative of how so much of religious life in China can be seen in terms of the provision and consumption of religious services. *Third*, I discuss the implications of such efficacy-based religiosity for our understanding of religious diversity.

Modalities of Doing Religion

In the long history of religious development in China, different ways of "doing religion" evolved and cohered into relatively easy-to-identify styles or "modalities."[①] These are relatively well-defined forms that different people can adopt and combine to deal with different concerns in life; however, the specific contents within these forms can vary widely. These modalities of "doing religion" are: (1) Discursive/scriptural, involving mostly the composition and use of texts; (2) Personal-cultivational, involving a long-term interest in cultivating and transforming oneself; (3) Liturgical, involving elaborate rit-

---

① For some of these discussions I have drawn upon some of my earlier work. See *Miraculous Response: Doing Popular Religion in Contemporary China*, Stanford University Press; "Modalities of Doing Religion," David A. Palmer, Glenn Shive and Philip Wickeri, eds. Chinese Religious Life (Oxford: Oxford University Press; 2011), pp. 67 – 84; "Modalities of Doing Religion and Ritual Polytropy: Evaluating the Religious Market Model from the Perspective of Chinese Religious History," *Religion* 41 (4) (2011) (special issue *Beyond the Religious Market Model*): pp. 547 – 568; "Efficacy, Not Confessionality: On Ritual Polytropy at Chinese Funerals," in Glenn Bowman, ed. , *Sharing the Sacra: the Politics and Pragmatics of Inter-communal Relations around Holy Places* (Oxford: Berghahn; 2012), pp. 79 – 96.

ual procedures conducted by ritual specialists; (4) Immediate-practical, aiming at quick results using simple ritual or magical techniques;
(5) Relational, emphasizing the relationship between humans and deities (or ancestors) as well as among humans in religious practices.
Even though these modalities of doing religion are also products of
conceptualization and schematization, I would like to argue that they
are far more "real" than conceptual fetishes such as "Buddhism,"
"Daoism," and "Confucianism." The Chinese people have engaged
with these modalities of doing religion in real practices, whereas no
one ever engages with "Buddhism" or "Daoism" because these exist
more as conceptual aggregates. Religious thinkers and scholars of religion have of course attempted to make various religious practices into
coherent wholes (including by giving them names such as "Buddhism" and "Daoism"), but such attempts at arriving at cognitive,
conceptual and sometimes institutional coherence have not had much
impact on how most people "do religion" on the ground, where they
don't care which deity belongs to which religion or which religious
tradition inspired which morality book. What happens on the ground
"religiously" is very much a congruence of local customs, historical
accidents, social environment, personal temperaments, configurations
of modalities of doing religion, and the makeup of the local ritual market (e. g. the availability of which kinds of ritual specialists to cater
for the need as well as to stimulate the need of which kinds of cli-
ents). Below I shall explicate in a little more detail each modality of
doing religion found in Chinese religious culture. One thing I need to
emphasize, however, is that these modalities are more or less ideal
types, and that they sometimes overlap (e. g. some actual religious

practices manifesting multiple modalities).

The Discursive/Scriptural Modality
of Doing Religion

People are attracted to this modality because of the allure of Confucian, Buddhist, Daoist and other "great texts" (classics, sutras,
scriptures, etc.). This modality often requires a high level of literacy
and a penchant for philosophical and "theological" thinking. Key
practices within this modality include compiling and editing scriptures
or discoursing about "the Way" (dao), or preaching, and its paradigmatic forms include reading, thinking about, discussing, deba-
ting, composing, translating, and commenting on religious texts. Also
included in this modality is the composing of morality books using
spirit writing and Chan/Zen masters' exegesis on gong'an (dharma
riddles). The products of this modality are usually textual (or at least
eventually appearing in textual forms) that range from a single religious tract to a whole set of scriptures and liturgical texts (e. g. the
so-called Buddhist Canon or Daoist Canon compiled under imperial
patronage). These texts form the basis of the classical "religious studies" approach to studying Chinese religions, which was derived from
Western religious/theological exegetical traditions. Because of this
textual bias, for a long time Chinese religious practices were understood in the West as exclusively this textually-transmitted esoteric
knowledge or, in the context of New Age or Orientalist consumption of
exotic texts, "Oriental wisdoms. "

The Personal-Cultivational Modality
of Doing Religion

Practices such as meditation, *qigong*, internal or outer alchemy, the cultivation of the "Daoist body", personal or group sutra chanting, the morning and evening recitation sessions in a Buddhist monastery, merit-conscious charitable acts (e. g. volunteering to accumulate karmic merit), and keeping a merit/demerit ledger belong to this modality. This modality presupposes a long-term interest in cultivating and transforming oneself (whether Buddhist, Daoist, Confucian or sectarian). The goals of this transformation and cultivation are different in each religious tradition: to become a so-called "immortal" (*xian*) in Daoism, to be reincarnated into a better life or to achieve nirvana in Buddhism, and to become a man of virtue or to be closer to sagehood (*sheng*) in Confucianism. But the shared element is the concern with one's own ontological status and destiny, something akin to a Foucaultian "care of the self." In other words, the practices in this modality provide "technologies of the self."

Within this modality of doing religion there are both elite and popular forms. For many, working on scriptures itself constitutes a form of self-cultivation. However, ordinary and even illiterate people can pursue personal-cultivational goals without esoteric knowledge or high literacy or much religious training. For example, illiterate peasants can practice self-cultivation by chanting "precious scrolls," which are in metered rhymes and often memorized. The simplest self-cultivation technique is the repeated utterance of the mantra *namo amituofo* (*namo amitabha*) thousands of times a day. Charismatic movements sometimes precipitate out of these personal-cultivational pursuits. The modern *qigong* movement also exemplifies the personal-cultivational modality of doing religion. When *qigong* practitioners perform daily regimented routines at home or in parks as instructed by their masters, they are engaged in the personal-cultivational modality of doing religion. The key words in this modality are "to cultivate" and "to craft" (oneself).

The Liturgical Modality of Doing Religion

This modality include practices such as imperial state rituals (e. g. the Grand Sacrifice), the Confucian rites, the Daoist rites of fasting and offering, exorcism (e. g. a Nuo ritual drama), sutra chanting rites, Daoist or Buddhist rituals for the universal salvation of souls, the Buddhist grand water and land dharma assemblies, and funeral rituals. Compared to the personalcultivational modality, practices in this modality aim at more immediate ritual intervention conducted in complex and highly symbolic forms, and are commissioned by and conducted for collective groups—be they families, clans, villages or neighborhoods, temple communities, or the state. This is the modality of the religious specialists (monks, Daoist priests, *fengshui* masters, Confucian ritual masters, spirit mediums, exorcistdancers, etc.) and often involves esoteric knowledge and elaborate ritual procedures. I will be discussing this modality in more detail below as I would argue that developments within this modality can best illustrate how Chinese religious culture is so prominently characterized by the provision and consumption of ritual services through the payment of fees.

The Immediate-Practical Modality
of Doing Religion

Practices in this modality also aim at more immediate results but compared to those in the liturgical modality they are more direct and involve shorter and simpler procedures. There is minimal ritual elaboration. Examples include divination (oracle rod, moon-shaped divination blocks, divination sticks, coins, etc.), getting divine medicine from a deity, using talismans (e. g. ingestion of talismanic water), consulting a spirit medium, calling back a stray soul, begging for rain, ritual cursing, or simply offering incense, etc. Because of its simplicity and low cost, this modality is the most frequently used by the common people (peasants, petty urbanites). The key concepts in this modality are "efficacy" (*ling*) (or miraculous power) and "to beseech for help." The practices included in this modality are usually called "magic" in the writings of those scholars who would not want to give them the dignity of the label "religion." Many of these simpler religious services are also provided by specialists for a fee, and they are much cheaper than the more elaborate rituals in the liturgical modality.

The Relational Modality of Doing Religion

This modality emphasizes the relationship between humans and deities (or ancestors) as well as relationships among worshippers. Examples are building temples, making offerings (i. e. feeding ancestors, deities, and ghosts), taking vows, spreading miracle stories (i.

e. testifying to the deities' efficacy), celebrating deities' birthdays at temple festivals, going on pilgrimage, imperial mountain journeys, establishing religious communities, and forming affiliations between temples and cult communities. This modality also emphasizes sociality, the bringing together of people through ritual events and festivals. Obviously the other modalities all exhibit relational and sociality aspects, but the making and maintaining of relations and the production and consumption of sociality seem to be at the foundation of those practices that I have grouped under this modality. The key concepts in this modality are "social comings and goings" (*laiwang*) and social relations (*guanxi*), or connectedness.

These modalities are frameworks for religious practice and action. They both restrain and enable people to express their religious imagination in words, images, sculptural and architectural forms, and actions. More importantly, these modalities lend religious specialists readily recognizable forms to adopt and practise, not unlike the ways in which the differentiation and consolidation of various literary genres such as the novel, the essay and poetry have facilitated their production and consumption as literary forms. At any one time in any locale of the vast late imperial Chinese empire—and to a some extent today as well in the larger Chinese world—all of these modalities of doing religion were in most probability available to be adopted by individuals or social groups, though factors such as class, gender, literacy level, accidents of birth and residence, position within different social networks, temperament, local convention and the configuration of various modalities might channel some people towards certain modalities and not others. Most peasants in China have traditionally adopted a combination of the relational and the immediate-practical modalities into their religiosity; sometimes they adopt the liturgical modality and hire religious specialists when the occasion requires them, such as funerals and communal exorcisms. Illiteracy and lack of leisure would preclude them from most of the discursive and personal-cultivational modalities. The traditional educated elite tended to adopt a combination of the discursive and the personal-cultivational modalities, but they too often needed the service of the liturgical specialists.

This *modalities framework* focuses our attention on the ways in which people "do religion" rather than their religious conceptions. Studying people's religious conceptions is important, but it yields a bewildering diversity, whose explanation often lies more in human imagination than social processes; on the other hand, there are only a limited number of forms (modalities) that permeate the Chinese religious landscape. The varieties of Chinese religious life-i. e. the reality of religious pluralism-have resulted from the elaboration of differences within these forms as well as the different configurations of various forms. The limited number of forms (modalities) and their lasting stability and versatility, no less than the great variety in the symbolic contents of the Chinese religious world, has been a great achievement in the history of world religious cultures.

Efficacy-Based Religiosity and Ritual Polytropy

One important implication of the modalities framework is that different modalities of doing religion might presuppose and produce different kinds of *religiosity* (defined simply as "ways of being religious"). In other words, we should speak of a diversity of religiosity in any particular religious culture, especially in places like China, where the prolonged interaction of different religious and sociopolitical forces have spawned a sheer plethora of religious practices. The various modalities of doing religion can cater to, and help consolidate, such radically different religiosities that the people adopting certain modalities might be quite estranged from or even hostile to some other modalities. For example, the religiosity of a Confucian literatus-official in late imperial times who was equally versed in Confucian classics, Buddhist sutras, and Daoist inner alchemy texts (i. e. the scriptural/discursive modality of doing religion) might be characterized by a constant introspection and a desire to proximate a sagely life, but he would sneer with impugnation at the kinds of pragmatic rituals the common people were engaged in to beseech divine help from local deities (i. e. the immediate-practical modality of doing religion). Indeed, he would more often than not try to suppress and prohibit all kinds of religious activities (say within his jurisdiction) in those modalities of doing religion that were alien (and perhaps therefore repugnant) to him. However, the kind of religiosity premised on efficacy, that of a deity or that of a ritual specialist, was the predominant religiosity among the majority of the Chinese, so in this paper I will focus on one of the modalities of doing religion that thrived on such religiosity: the liturgical modality of doing religion.

Most "Han" Chinese throughout China's long history have not had confessional religious identities, with the exception of very small pockets of groups claiming Muslim, Protestant, Catholic, Jewish and millenarian/sectarian identities. ①The overwhelming majority of Han Chinese would not call themselves Daoist, Buddhist, or Confucian. They enshrine Daoist, Buddhist, or other kinds of deities on their domestic altars alongside the tablets for their ancestors in a seemingly indiscriminate manner and they approach in a seemingly opportunistic manner deities or religious specialists of whichever persuasion to exorcize evil spirits, ward off bad fortune, produce a good marriage partner or a long-awaited male descendant, deliver good fortune and blessing for the family or cure for a difficult illness, find a lost cattle or motorcycle, or resolve a life dilemma. A person with a particularly difficult problem will go to a Daoist temple, then a Buddhist temple, then a spirit medium, and then even a Catholic church or a Muslim mosque if the problem is resistant to other interventions. To him or her what matters is not which religious tradition the particular temple or specialist is affiliated with but how efficacious (*ling*, *lingying*, *lingyan*) the deity or specialist is in responding to his or her requests. Typically, a person will make a vow promising that if the problem is solved he or she will bring offerings or money, help with the temple festival by contributing labor or materials, or spread the name of the deity far and wide. For temple festivals that hire opera troupes a devotee and supplicant can also promise to sponsor a number of opera performances. Depending on the extent of engagement over time one has with these various temples, deities, and specialists, one develops a network of more or less enduring and meaningful relationships with

---

① By "sectarian" I am referring to the mostly Buddhist-inspired millenarian cults that developed around charismatic leaders that demanded exclusivistic membership adherence. Their occurrence was sporadic in Chinese history and they were often targets of state crackdowns.

them which might be maintained for generations. Less efficacious deities and specialists are visited less often and are gradually dropped from the network, while newly discovered, more efficacious ones are added. The temples and specialists might, and do, vie with one another for clientele and donations, but they never take the form of one religious tradition as a whole (e. g. Buddhism) against another religious tradition as a whole (e. g. Daoism) except occasionally at the elite, discursive level and in competition for patronage by the dynastic court (again usually at the elite level). ①

In contrast to among the commoner majority, more or less coherent religious group identities did develop among the elite religious practitioners such as members of the Buddhist sangha, the Quanzhen Daoist monastic order, and Confucian academies. One key element all these three traditions shared was reliance on canonical texts; indeed, it is these texts that made them into so-called " Great Traditions. "②
These elite religious practitioners' main goal was self-cultivation and their penchant for textual exegesis and philosophical reflections necessarily attracted them to one another's textual and conceptual resources. As a result historically there was frequent and serious traffic-

---

① The form of competition may include Buddhist temples against Daoist temples, Daoist temples against spirit mediums, Buddhist temples against other Buddhist temples, Daoist temples against other Daoist temples, householder Daoist priests against other householder Daoist priests, spirit mediums against magical healers, etc.

② It goes without saying that different strands of socio-religious practices only gradually cohered into these distinct traditions through the efforts of a large number of people (usually elite religious practitioners who were far more interested in systematising and differentiating than the common people). Confucius did not found Confucianism, nor did Laozi Daoism, and Buddhism did not arrive in China in one flat-pack. By invoking the notion of "Great Traditions" I do not intend (nor did Robert Redfield in his original conception of the great and little traditions) to portray them as existing independently of less elite forms of religious practices.

king of people and ideas between these three Great Traditions. So at
the level of discourse and practice each of these three Great Traditions
became rather syncretistic. But one has to remember that the elite
members of these religious traditions with stronger sense of religious i-
dentities were a *very small minority*. And even these identities were
strictly speaking more akin to professional identities than confessional
identities, so a Confucian scholar-ritualist could learn to become a
Daoist priest in a process culminating in the Daoist ordination ritual,
which was more like additional professional accreditation than a state-
ment of religious conversion. In other words, one accrued more religious identities and "qualifications" rather than converting from one
to another.

Below the elite religious practitioners in term of level of sophistication there were all kinds of religious service providers such as *fengshui* masters, diviners, fortune-tellers, spirit mediums, magical healers, householder Daoist priests, Buddhist ritual masters, and Confucian ritualists who provided their specialist services for a fee or its e-
quivalent. There were also sectarian village-based volunteer ritualists
who provided ritual services to fellow sect members and other villagers
for free.

There is usually one kind of specialist for each occasion. For
finding the best site for houses and graves one needs a *fengshui* master; for divining one's luck and fortune one consults a fortune-teller;
for exorcising evil spirits one can hire a spirit medium or an exorcist.
But the one ritual occasion that is the most significant in the Chinese
world is the funeral, and it is what the Chinese do ritually at the funeral that will be used in this paper to illustrate their strongly efficacy-

based religiosity. Unlike standard funerals in most societies, where a religious specialist belonging to the same religious group as the deceased presides over the funeral, in China either Daoist priests or Buddhist monks perform the funeral ritual (following different liturgical programmes) depending on the availability of ritual specialists locally and locally salient conventional practice. [1] But what is most interesting is that rich people in late imperial and Republican times would hire as many groups of religious specialists as possible to accrue karmic merits and other spiritual benefits for the deceased (and, by association, his or her kin) as well as to assert the family's social status and prestige. These religious specialists could include groups (always groups) of Buddhist monks, Buddhist nuns, Daoist priests, Tibetan Buddhist lamas, and lay sectarian practitioners. In other words, the Chinese funeral exhibits the sharing of the same ritual event by groups of religious specialists belonging to different religious traditions. This condition can be called *ritual polytropy*. [2]

To the majority of the Chinese, it was the efficacy of the rituals (and the ritualists) that mattered, not one's religious identity (if that was even discernible). We can call this an *efficacy-based religiosity*, as opposed to the kind of *dharma-based religiosity* that characterizes the way people do religion in the Buddhist countries in south-

---

[1]   In Japan, the two major religious traditions Shinto and Buddhism have worked out an admirable division of labor (and, one may add, share of income), in which the Shinto priests are in charge of matters relating to life-stage rites of passage and marriage while the Buddhist monks take care of the funeral and after-death matters.

[2]   I have modified the expression first was first coined by Michael Carrithers, "On Polytropy: Or the Natural Condition of Spiritual Cosmopolitanism in India: The Digambar Jain Case." *Modern Asian Studies* 34/4 (2000): 831 – 61.

east Asia and in monotheistic religions. ① By hiring ritual specialists from different religious traditions only when one needs them obviates the necessity to adhere to any one of these traditions. One may speculate that had Western missionaries attempted to merely provide the Chinese with Catholic priests or Protestant ministers as yet another of the many troupes of ritualists and not force them to adopt the Christian confessional framework it would have been a lot easier for the Chinese to accept them; it would mean simply adding one more tradition (and form of efficacy) to the existing ritual polytropy. ② In a way we can already observe the tendency for the Chinese to use Christian rituals opportunistically as a sign of the incorporation of Christian liturgy and ritual efficacy into the general efficacy-oriented Chinese religious world (e. g. witness the popularity of getting married in a Christian church even if the couple is not Christian or is only nominally so and the attendance of the Catholic mass on Christmas Eve without being a Catholic).

But how did such a ritual polytropy come into being? To put it simply, the elite specialists of various religious traditions catered to the needs of a market for rituals by having invented and standardized various liturgical repertoires for various ritual occasions; indeed, one may even say that these ritual occasions (e. g. funerals, exorcisms) were largely constructed by these liturgical inventions. But the liturgical repertoires of one group of specialists as religious products were

---

① While drawing a contrast that is real, I am aware that there are a wide variety of "modalities of doing religion" in these other religious cultures as well.

② For a historical study of the "interweaving" of Chinese and Catholic funeral rituals, see Nicolas Standaert, *The Interweaving of Rituals: Funerals in the Cultural Exchange between China and Europe* (Seattle, WA: University of Washington Press; 2008).

susceptible to being pilfered or copied by other groups, and that was exactly what happened in China. For example, the Daoist funerary liturgy was in large part inspired and influenced by the Buddhist funerary liturgy, and the Buddhist "water and land dharma assembly" liturgy and the Daoist "universal salvation" liturgy have many elements in common. One consequence of such mutual borrowing of liturgical elements was the increasing convergence of liturgical goals and therefore the apparent mutual substitutability of rituals from different religious traditions. But there were also enough differences between the liturgical programmes of various religious traditions so that there was often a division of ritual labor or segmentation of the ritual market, so that everyone could make a living out of selling ritual services and no single ritual tradition could have a monopoly in the entire ritual market (though one ritual tradition might achieve prestige and dominance in a local ritual market). In fact, because most ritual specialists in China worked as householder ritual service providers and could hardly cater for a demand higher than what they could handle as a family troupe, there was little incentive in crowding out other providers (though of course there was plenty of competition for the more lucrative ritual jobs in one's catchment areas). [①] In most cases these various ritual specialists chose a more or less peaceful co-existence. Sometimes arrangements were made so that one family of ritualists would have a monopoly over a certain neighborhood or district, but such arrangements were more common between ritualists of the same

①　The most important reason for most ritual specialists to adopt the household idiom is to keep a low profile in order to dodge the attention of the state, which has not always friendly towards these ritual service providers. See Adam Yuet Chau, "Superstition Specialist Households?: The Household Idiom in Chinese Religious Practices," Minsu quyi (Journal of Chinese Ritual, Theatre, and Folklore) 153:157 – 202.

tradition providing the same liturgical programmes than between ritualists of different traditions, partly because of the division of ritual labor and segmentation of the ritual market mentioned above.

One important thing we have to keep in mind is the wide variation in the configuration of ritual markets in different regions and neighborhoods. In some places, especially rich urban areas, there would be a higher concentration of ritual specialists and therefore more competition for the more lucrative ritual jobs. On the other hand, in some other places, especially poorer rural regions, there is sometimes a dearth of ritual specialists so people had to make do with whomever they could find. In other words, there is a spectrum between, at one end, an extreme efficacy-maximising ritual polytropy with an abundance of many kinds of ritual specialists in the local ritual market and, at the other end, a sort of involuntary, making-do "monotropy" without the luxury of either choice or "efficacy maximization through ritualist-multiplication." We can speculate that one of the most important reasons behind the popularity of sectarianism in some parts of rural China was the fact that membership in these sectarian groups guaranteed free ritual services, which most of the people would not be able to pay for a professional ritual provider to do.

The Elaboration of the Liturgical Modality of Doing Religion Within Daoism and Buddhism

Here I will have space for a very brief explication of the ways in which the liturgical modality was elaborated within Daoism and Buddhism.

The early Daoist Church founded in the second century CE during the chaotic later days of the Han Dynasty, called the Way of the Heavenly Masters (*Tianshidao*), was one of the first sectarian groups trying to set their members apart from non-members through doctrinal elaboration (not "doctrinal difference" since it is hard to say that the non-members had any explicit doctrine). The founder, Zhang Daoling, claimed to have received revelations from Laozi and began teaching a millenarian message of self examination, sin absolution (through confession and rituals) and salvation from imminent apocalyptic disasters. The followers were called the "seed people" (*zhongmin*) who would repopulate the world when all the rest of humanity would have died in the disasters. The sect was based in an area in what is present-day Sichuan Province. The followers were divided into and administered through twenty four parishes, and the entire region became a theocratic state, with the Heavenly Master (*tianshi*) at its head. This was a membership-based religion, though it is not clear if they were actively proselytizing and recruiting new members. This state did not last long; it was taken over and absorbed by the Wei state and its members dispersed.

The parish organization did not survive except in some modified form among the Yao minority people in southwest China. Over the centuries afterwards, religious Daoism developed into various modalities identified above (i. e. the five modalities of doing religion). In the discursive/scriptural modality, elite Daoists produced, compiled, and systematized thousands of treatises and ritual manuals, culminating in the various versions of the imperially sponsored *Daoist Canon* (Daozang) (in imitation of the Buddhist Tripitaka). In the self-cultivational modality, numerous methods of achieving immortalhood (*xian*) were developed and practised, including making and ingesting potions (*dan*) and meditation (the so-called external and internal alchemy). The most prominent institution catering to, and perfecting, the self-cultivational modality is the Quanzhen school of monastic Daoism made up of celibate Daoist monastics. In the liturgical modality, elaborate liturgies were invented to cater to the need among the imperial court and the rich to sponsor and consume increasingly long and spectacular rituals, and to rival Buddhist liturgies. The elaboration of liturgy was closely connected to the flourishing of ritual manuals in the discursive/scriptural modality, as the overwhelming majority of Daoist texts were actually liturgical. In the immediate-practical modality, relatively simple exorcistic and healing techniques were invented to deal with simpler problems. Actually a whole new category of Daoist ritual specialists came into being, the ritual master (*fashi*) [distinctive from the Daoist priest (*daoshi*)], who engaged in simpler exorcistic and healing rituals, and sometimes working with spirit mediums[1]. A prominent expression of the relational modality was the lineage structure that many Daoist schools developed, especially the Quanzhen School, which created spiritual kinship based on lines of transmission. One may also argue that the hierarchical structure of the Daoist pantheon mimicking the imperial state hierarchy also resulted from structuring impulses derived from the relational modality of doing religion.

Obviously the vitality and long-term success of Daoism as a religious tradition depended on the ways in which these various modalities

---

① See Edward Davis, *Society and the Supernatural in Song China* (Honolulu: University of Hawaii Press; 2001).

of "doing Daoism" were elaborated. But among the five modalities, the liturgical modality stands out as the most important and relevant modality to the wider population (i. e. beyond the inner circle of Daoist monastics and elite practitioners, for whom the discursive/scriptural and self-cultivational modalities would have been more important). This is the case because the majority of Daoists in China's long history have been priests providing ritual service to customers for a fee. The customers do not need to be Daoists themselves (unlike for example in Abrahamic religions where the priest and the ritual congregation need to be co-religionists); in fact, there is hardly such a thing called non-priest/lay Daoists (except in the case of a minority of lay devotees who are engaged in the self-cultivational modality of doing Daoism). The priests were either household-based and transmits their ritual skills down the generations or managed small temples as celibate priests and trained a small number of disciples. There is a wide variety of regional ritual traditions with different liturgical manuals and ritual-musical styles, but in the late imperial period up to today the majority of Daoist priests have been in the Zhengyi tradition (which traces its origins to the original Daoist Church), whose symbolic head is the Zhang-surnamed Heavenly Master, based on the Longhushan (Dragon and Tiger Mountain) in present-day Jiangxi Province. [1]

Given the prevalent tendency in Chinese religious culture towards generating efficacy through rituals, Buddhism also "behaved" very differently in China compared to, say, in South Asia, Southeast Asia and Tibet, where one's religious identity as a Buddhist is much stron-

---

[1]   See Vincent Goossaert, "Bureaucratic Charisma: The Zhang Heavenly Master Institution and Court Taoists in Late-Qing China." *Asia Major* 3rd series, 17/2 (2004): 121 – 159.

ger. The attitude of the late imperial state towards religion was a crucial explanatory factor. Even though many emperors of various dynasties favored Buddhism during their reign, they stopped short of imposing Buddhism onto the general populace (as opposed to, for example, the case of sovereign-led, population-wide conversion to Christianity in Europe). In fact, many emperors and literati-officials perceived the expansion of Buddhist influence (e. g. in the form of large monasteries with many monks and large tax-exempt monastic estates) as a threat and launched attacks on the Buddhist establishment. There were waves of decrees confiscating monastic estates and forcefully laicising monks and nuns. As a result of these persistent attacks advocates of Buddhism in China never succeeded in converting the Chinese into the kind of *dharma-based religiosity* that more characterized people in Buddhist kingdoms in, for example, Thailand and Sri Lanka. One can say that Buddhism succeeded in penetrating into Chinese society not by making Chinese people into *dharma*-following lay believers but by providing ritual (primarily funerary) services to them, which could be understood as an "amicable" compromise. Such ritual penetration was so thorough that for most Chinese traditionally the Buddhist funerary ritual almost became the norm (though the Daoists and the sectarians developed their own funerary rituals and competed for ritual market share).

Conclusions: Implications for Our Understanding of Religious Pluralism

Religious rivalry in Chinese history did not take the form of competition between membership-based churches as it was common in societies with confessionally-based religiosity; rather, there was more typically competition *between* the different modalities of doing religion and especially *within* each modality of doing religion, especially the liturgical modality. Religious pluralism in China is not manifested as the co-existence of, and competition between, confession-and membership-based denominations and churches but rather primarily as the co-existence of, and competition between, various ritual service providers with different (though sometimes convergent) liturgical programmes. From the religious consumers' perspective, more differentiation in religious service provision (in terms of types of services and pricing) would mean a wider choice, which is always a good thing.

The Chinese case of religious diversity as I have presented it does present a challenge to our conception of religious pluralism. It is a somewhat messier kind of religious pluralism, with no readily identifiable religious leaders, religious organizations or systems of religious thought. But should we sacrifice true understanding for apparent clarity? The religious elite and modern state regulatory apparatus in China have an invested interest in constructing certain Chinese religious traditions in the image of monotheistic religions; however, such a construction is carried out at the expense of the vast majority of the providers and consumers of religious services in China, as it favors the discursive modality of doing religion and suppresses most of the practices encompassed by the other four modalities, many of which are labelled as superstition or counter-revolutionary sectarianism. The modern Chinese state recognizes and approves five major religions: Buddhism, Daoism, Protestantism, Catholicism and Islam. However, it is primarily the discursive modality within these religious traditions that is granted legitimacy. As a result, for example, the Daoist Association is completely dominated by the Quanzhen monastic Daoists since they can discourse much better than the Zhengyi ritualists, and on the national stage the Buddhists prevail over the Daoists thanks to, among other reasons, the superior Buddhist discursive apparatus. Not so incidentally, the religious-pluralism and inter-faith-dialogue paradigms in the liberal West also favors the discursive modality of doing religion, as all religious traditions have to meet the demand of coming up with reasoned and communicable discourse in order to even enter the dialogue with the much more theologically and discursively sophisticated Abrahamic traditions. The vast majority of the world's population who "do religion" in other ways are thus silenced. A true religious pluralism must acknowledge the full range of modalities of doing religion in all societies.

美国慈善公益的"上帝在场"

——以美国中镇为案例

高　卉

一、问题的提出与田野说明

中镇位于印第安纳州中部的特拉华县,是美国中西部最为普通的一座小城,因林德夫妇的《米德尔敦:当代美国文化研究》而一举成名,它的地理名称叫曼西(Muncie),中镇是曼西在学术文献中的称谓。

中镇目前有 14.3% 的家庭和 23.1% 的人口处于贫困线之下。其中 18 岁以下的人口占 24.2% ,65 岁以上人口的占 9.7% 。[①] 据官方报导,中镇的失业率近 20 年内急剧上升,由 1990 年的 5.0% 上升到 2010 年的 10.2% ,而印第安纳第二食物银行提供的数据为 40% 。工业衰落以及经济转型所锐减的就业机会,造成了远高于美国与印第安纳州的失业率和失业人口。

但是,中镇人并没有因贫困而乞讨,也没有因贫困而挨饿受冻。分布在艺术、文化、教育、环境以及健康等领域的众多的非营利组织,为人们提供着各式各样的公共服务。目前,中镇共有 1300 多家非营利组织(NPO),

---

① 参见 2010 United States Census。

其中有 7 家基金会、220 家教会、1000 多家慈善组织和一些行会①。在中镇做人类学田野调查的一年多时间里,我深深地沉迷于美国非营利组织所进行的公益事业里,尤其是宗教给人们带来的祥和、宁静的精神慰藉以及教会对贫穷者所提供的住房、食品、衣服和医疗等方面的物质救助。祛魅后的上帝在美国完成了世俗化过程,而再度着魅后,上帝不再是一个高高在上的神,而是走下了神坛,走向了人性与现实生活。

二、上帝的在场

多项研究成果表明,慈善与宗教有着千丝万缕的关联,宗教渗透到美国人的日常生活。据统计,有90%以上的美国人宣称相信上帝,有30万个教会和2千多个教派组织,参加宗教活动的美国人超过了参加美国其他任何组织活动的人数(Terry,1994)。中镇所处的印第安纳州有89%的人信教,其中新教徒占总数的67%,罗马天主教徒占20%,其他基督教派教徒占1%,其他宗教教徒占1%②。基督宗教是中镇最盛行的宗教,它分为天主教和新教,新教又包括卫理公会、教友会、浸礼会和路德会。此外,还有韩国教会和中国教会。那里的教会对每一个人都是开放的,人们入教时,一般会依据教会的名声、教会的风格、距离家的远近和家庭传统的宗教习惯等进行选择。闲暇时间,人们都喜欢去教堂,教会生活是他们最重要的社会生活方式。

早在 19 世纪,法国政论家托克维尔就在《论美国的民主》中指出,宗教在美国发挥着重大作用,宗教精神与自由精神如此完美地结合在一起,共同统治着这个国家。基督教对于很多美国人来说像呼吸一样的自然和重要③。雷雨田在《上帝与美国人》中,也认为:"上帝是美国文明的核心要素……大自总统选举、民权运动和文教事业,小至禁酒和戒烟运动,在美国历

---

① http://www.stats.indiana.edu
② 参见 http://baike.baidu.com/view/706548.htm。
③ 托克维尔:《论美国的民主》,董果良译,北京:商务印书馆. 2002。

史上的重要阶段和社会生活的各个领域,上帝似乎无所不在、无所不为"。①
米德更是把做一个基督徒和做一个"文明的人"、"诚实的人"或"值得尊敬
的市民"联结在了一起。

　　宗教与慈善关系紧密,并被亨利·艾伦·莫誉为慈善之母。基督教的
正义观、财富观以及罪富文化,使上帝成为公正与仁慈的化身,而人们只是
上帝的"管家"。自中世纪以来,基督教的神圣地位与慈善的合法地位得到
了奥古斯丁和阿奎那等神学家的大力支持,并不断制度化,如什一税的征
收。慈善已远非世俗意义上的接济与救助,而是神恩的结果,是最高贵的
神恩的渗透,是上帝的无条件的恩典,是完成个人救赎的重要路径。文艺
复兴以后,基督教开始由神圣走向世俗,而美国就是基督教世俗化的完美
转身的典型,上帝不再是彼岸的敬畏,而是此岸的人生,关照着贫困、公平
乃至生命的希望与意义。正如威尔·赫伯格(1960)所言,美国基督教的兴
起始终是伴随着世俗化的过程。在美国环境的影响下,历史上的犹太信仰
和基督教信仰作为部分被整合到美国生活方式所规定的更大的集体中。②
暗合着实用、理性、独立、自主与博爱的美国宗教,也使慈善不再是一种强
制性的诫令,而是个体自由、自愿、自决的选择,因为"每个人心里都有一个
上帝"。

　　美国雪城大学的亚瑟·C·布鲁克斯教授在《谁会真正关心慈善》的研
究中发现,宗教对人们慈善行为的影响十分重大。美国 2000 年的一次大规
模的全国性调查表明,81% 的美国人表示自己捐过善款,在捐款者中,宗教
信徒的比例高出世俗论者 25%。在同样是年收入为 4.9 万美元的家庭中,
宗教信徒每年的善款大约是世俗论者的 3.5 倍,两者对应的平均值为 2210
美元和 642 美元。美国南达科他州的人口与旧金山差不多,但面积是后者
的 1615 倍,旧金山拥有大学文凭的人口是南达科他州的两倍,年平均家庭
收入也高出南达科他州 78%。然而,这两个地方家庭的平均捐款几乎都是
1300 美元。实证研究的结果表明,是宗教导致了南达科他州的居民具有更
高的慈善水平。大约 50% 的南达科他州居民每周都去教堂,而在旧金山这

---

①　雷雨田:《上帝与美国人——基督教与美国社会》,上海:上海人民出版社,1994。

②　Herberg, w., Protestant, Catholic, Jew. Rev., &Company. 1960.

一比例只有14%。另外,49%的旧金山居民从不上教堂,而在南达科他州,这一比例只有10%。①

无论是神圣化的上帝还是世俗化的上帝,它对西方社会生活与慈善公益影响重大,而在美国尤其明显。20世纪后,在科技异化、理性膨胀、两次世界大战以及日益强化的工业主义、消费主义对世界生态圈以及人文意识的破坏等等一系列的现代性危机背景之下,传统哲学在本体论上的无能,更把人类置于实用主义与虚无主义的境况之中。一战后,西方学者对理性主义、科学思想由怀疑而产生失望,重新意识到了宗教拯救的需要。他们批判经验主义、实证主义,强调宗教价值与慈善公益的独特性,认为宗教本身具有一种不可消解的本质,不能根据除它自身之外的任何东西来解释。上帝的在场,使人们在理性的重压下获得了精神的相对自由与可能发展,使对生命的意义与财富的观念有了另维的理解,也有了基于宗教信仰基础之上的美国慈善。

三、免费的午餐

曦晨教会是我在中镇接触最早的慈善组织,它不仅为贫困者提供食品和衣物,还启动了"面包篮子"项目,为周围的居民提供免费的午餐。每周六10点-11点半曦晨教会会准时为居民提供免费午餐,就餐结束时还会根据家庭人口向就餐者分发可以带回去的食物。就餐一般在曦晨教堂里进行,每个房间的墙上不仅贴有教会的宗旨和规章制度,还写有"分享基督的福音,以耶稣的名字,在充满基督之爱的环境中提供热饭"、"不可忘记用爱心接待客旅,因为曾有接待客旅的,不知不觉接待了天使"等服务指南。开餐前,首先由牧师讲解10分钟的圣经,然后由一位志愿者带领大家祈祷。如果有人愿意,他也可以和大家一起分享自己的故事。

每年的7月16日,曦晨教会还将举办大型的社区露天餐会。餐会前一

---

① 布鲁克斯,亚瑟·C:《谁会真正关心慈善》,王青山译,北京:社会科学文献出版社社,2008。

周人们就开始忙碌,志愿者会分头去附近的小区挨家挨户的散发传单,介绍那天的活动,邀请他们参加,最后还会送一盏灯,并不忘告诉他们,上帝永远都会为他们照亮道路。

免费的午餐不仅仅限于教堂,有时还会送到穷人的家中。每逢感恩年、圣诞节等重大节日,教会都会派出志愿者亲自把食物送到穷人的家里,并向他们解释,这是上帝派他们来的。我曾参加过曦晨教会圣诞节前的"篮子食物"活动,接受食物的一家男主人隔着栏杆接过食物并与我们牵手做了祷告,感谢上帝给了他食物。接受食物的另一家女主人和我们聊起了家常,最后也是一起做祷告,感谢上帝,并祈祷上帝保佑他们的亲人平安,孩子健康。尤其让我震惊的是,在回去的路上遇到一辆急驶而过的救护车,与我同行的约翰立刻把车停靠在路边,和儿子一起,为救护车上的人做起了祷告:"天上的父呀,求你保佑救护车上的人平安,让他能够健康。"

在美国做志愿者的那些日子里,我深切地体会到了上帝不再是一个抽象的概念,而是一个有血有肉的生命实体。宗教也早就从教堂回到了日常生活,回到人的内心本性,它如此真切,如此温暖,如此朴实,如此感动。它唤起了人们内心深处的慈悲与善,不再是一种强制性的诚令,而是一种个人亲历的体验,一种从人的心灵深处散发出来的宁静,一种朴素的仁爱与关怀。

虽然,从表面上看,免费午餐的领取不需要任何理由和条件,只要人们填完自己的姓名、住址和家庭人数后,就可以享受到上帝的馈赠与关爱。但它的背后,是自中世纪以来,一直就没有停止过的是否需要附加条件的争议。无条件的捐助与有条件的捐助既反映出慈善理念与慈善目标的不同,也反映出工具理性对价值理性的反叛与冲击。

工具理性是法兰克福学派批判理论中的一个重要概念,它来源于马克斯·韦伯(Max Weber)所提出的合理性(rationality)概念。韦伯将合理性分为两种,即价值理性和工具理性。价值理性相信的是一定行为的无条件的价值,强调的是动机的纯正和选择正确的手段去实现自己意欲达到的目的,而不管其结果如何。工具理性是指行动只由追求功利的动机所驱使,行动借助理性达到自己需要的预期目的,行动者纯粹从效果最大化的角度考虑,而漠视人的情感和精神价值。①

慈善从价值理性看,人们相信每一个人都是上帝的子民,都被赋予平等尊重的权利,每个人对生活、健康、自由以及希望的基本需要都应得到尊重和满足,人们有义务与责任去关心那些生活窘迫的人,这种关心应是无条件的。但从工具理性看,人们对事物效率最大化的追逐,使他们在进行慈善活动时,不断地考量慈善行为所采用的手段与取得的成效,为取得事物的最大功效,可以忽视人的情感和精神价值,也可以通过精确计算附加条件。

这种冲突主要反映在对待穷人与贫穷的态度上。中世纪晚期,随着瘟疫、战争以及人口下降而引起的劳工价格的变化,社会对穷人的态度开始发生显著改变。昔日备受关爱的穷人开始为人们质疑、敌视,传统的不加区别的施舍开始为日益高涨的区别救助呼声所冲击。英国人菲茨伦夫在15世纪50年代写了大量关于贫穷的文章。他认为,财产即使在天堂里也会被发现,贫穷不是财富,而是一种罪孽的产物。在此基础上,他提出一种"劳动道德",即不劳动者不得食。

在教会内部,13世纪50年代巴黎神学院的威廉姆、英国的威克里夫、理查德·菲茨拉夫尔和罗拉德派,从《圣经》出发明确提出废除善功观念、救助真正穷人、驱逐那些身体健壮的流浪乞讨者的观点。罗拉德派指责那些人终日游手好闲、不劳而获,他们榨干了国家的财富,又窃取了真穷人应得的施舍。他们伪装起来乞讨,窃取了穷人们的施舍;他们假装放弃他们原本能够维生的世俗财物来骗取富人们的施舍。在严峻的形势下,教会所宣扬的一视同仁慈善施舍原则面临重大挑战与变革,这不是一个简单的变化,正如伊利亚德所言,为了信仰而理解的中世纪时代正在结束,为了理解而信仰的时代正在到来②。

原初无条件的救助不断受到质疑,社群主义者强调福利申请者的义务和权利。正如《负责任的社群主义》所宣称的"互惠性的观点是社群主义理解社会公平的核心"。在实践中,这意味着慈善受益是有条件的。个体的

① 韦伯,马克斯:《经济与社会》,林荣远译,北京:商务印书馆,2004。
② 伊利亚德,米尔恰:《神圣与世俗》,王建光译,北京:华夏出版社,2002。

权利必须基于特定条件的满足,这些条件涉及作为父母、邻居或者劳动力市场成员的行为。社群主义者支持条件化慈善,并以契约的名义表达出来,即如果慈善机构向受助者提供了服务,那么申领者也应该通过合理使用这些服务实践他们的义务。正如存在于米德尔敦人中的悖论:一方面,慈善必须帮助那些确实需要帮助的人,因为一条狗也不能活活饿死。但另一方面,他们又坚持不能让人轻易地吃到救济。①

　　免费的午餐并不免费,这尤其反映在制度化的慈善事业中。正如戴维·埃尔伍德(Davie Ellwood,1988)在《贫困救助》一书中所言,人道福利从未成为现实,因为有太多的怀疑和冲突嵌入该制度了。他建议,唯一可避免此类冲突的途径,是重新将福利定义为作为临时或过渡性的救助。现金津贴应做时间限定,在享受这一福利的时间限定内,福利申请者必须接受有条件的教育和培训。在现金津贴时效中止时,这部分人应该找到工作。如果还没能就业,他们将有义务为公共部门服务。

　　关于慈善理念与慈善目标的争论,也严重地影响着志愿者、管理者和受捐者的心理感受与个人尊严。在供应午餐时,志愿者在服务过程中,脸上始终都挂有温暖的笑容,以免让就餐者感到难堪。管理者也在不断地改善着他们的行为和态度,而受影响最大的依然是接受捐助的人。有一次,我和伊莎及她的女儿去超市,在付款时,伊莎现金结账,她天真的女儿一遍遍地提醒:"妈妈,妈妈,你有食物券。"但最后,伊莎还是执意用现金付账。后来伊莎给我说出当时的感觉:"我不想让别人知道我用食物券。当时女儿很大声的话语,真让我无处可逃。"詹姆斯也有同样的经历,他给我讲道:"如果一个人没有工作,没法付钱,这种感觉很糟糕。即使你工作只有很少的钱,但这是你挣的,是用你的肌肉、你的力气、你的头脑去工作挣的,这会让你感觉自己还可以、还有能力。当别人给你薪水时,你会很高兴。而只等着政府的帮助,尤其是帮助又很有限,不够用时,你只能去给政府一遍又一遍地证明:这些钱不够用,我真的找不到工作。每一个月你都要去政府那里证明多要一点帮助,这是很羞辱的,会让人觉得自己很卑微。"由于多

───────────

① 林德,罗伯特·S.林德,海伦·梅里尔·米德尔敦:《当代美国文化研究》,李银河译.北京:商务印书馆,1999。

年没有工作,他的精神一直很抑郁,我们可以看到,在"免费午餐"的背后,已经附加了多重条件,包括尊严和快乐。

正如兰德修女在一次演讲中所说:"我渴,不只是缺少饮水,而是渴望和平与正义;我饥饿,不只是缺少食物,而是需要爱和被爱,需要精神生命的粮食;我赤身露体,不只是需要衣服,更渴望人的尊严;我无栖身之所,不只是缺少陋室,更渴望他人的理解、支持,和被人理解的一份关怀。"

走向人性的上帝并不能解决世俗生活给人们带来的困惑,也无力应对制度性贫困对人所造成的苦难与压迫,但是上帝的光芒仍然是照亮人生苦难之旅的希望。

四、生命的希望

詹姆斯在《实用主义》一书中指出,超验意义上的上帝,被基督徒具体化为经验层面上的希望,它不再是本体论意义上的实体与存在物,而是一种信念,一种精神意志,引导着人们过一种有意义的生活。[①] 在此,上帝成为人类生活的希望与寄托。"世界上存在着有'希望'的意义,'有没有上帝'就等于说'有没有希望'"。

杰克就有着这样的经历,记得 2010 年 9 月他第一次去教堂的时候,不和任何人说话,但在 2011 年 2 月份,他开始变得健谈,饭后,他也会做一些打扫卫生的活,还会和别人开开玩笑。安吉拉这样回忆:"对,我们刚和他接触的时候,不知道他还会说话,因为那时他和谁都不说话,就安安静静的,神色忧郁。有一次,做完礼拜之后,我们带他去吃午饭,不知道为什么他非常喜欢那个地方,开始讲话,我们都惊呆了。因为在此之前,他一句话都没讲过。然后我们就说,哇,原来你会说话呀。然后我们问他从哪儿来的,才开始真正认识他。应该说,那以后他对这儿才有了归属感,才变得乐观。随后,我们就开始一点一点聊开了,到现在就相处得很好。因为人们多数会看不起那些拿救济金的人,但我们不同,我们只想让人们意识到他

---

① 威廉,詹姆士:《实用主义》,李步楼译,北京:商务印书馆,2011。

们很重要。上帝爱他们,我们也是,他们可以通过自己的努力改变生活,可以变得更好。"

阿尔伯特也是从教堂中获得意义与希望的。他一年前来到曦晨教会,最初,他沉默不言,留着很长的胡子,衣服也很脏,很远就能闻到身上的味道;慢慢的,他开始回应别人的问候。再后来,他与人交流的次数越来越多。2011年4月的一天,他突然走进安吉拉的办公室,拉起T恤的衣袖给我们看小臂上的伤痕,并告诉我们,他原本想过自杀的,只是因为今天午餐的时候,志愿者与他聊天,谈到了生命,也说到了很多开心的事,他才放弃了这个念头。阿尔伯特在3岁时被收养,14岁时离开家,一个人生活辗转流离,大多时间没有工作。18岁后申请了政府的食物和住房补助,虽然生活基本可以保证,但常感孤独。那次的聊天之后,阿尔伯特剃掉了胡子,衣服也变得干净了,成为晨星的志愿者,帮助清洁卫生,帮助修剪草坪,并开始积极找工作。

在田野中,屡屡会得到这样的回答,是宗教,让受助者恢复了信心,点燃了生的希望。在某种意义上讲,基督教之于慈善,不仅仅是财物的捐助,更是一种生命之意义的指引。

美国是一个流动性非常大的国家。有人戏言,美国人口中有三分之一的常住人口,三分之一正在搬家,三分之一准备搬家。工作的频繁变动与生存的巨大压力,使人们经常由一个熟悉的环境进入一个陌生的环境。原有的社会联系断裂,如何快速地融入新的社区生活,并与他人建立联系?教堂通常被认为是最普遍、最便捷的方式之一。数量众多的教堂为不同的社会群体提供了各自交流与沟通的场所,每周一次的礼拜活动和经常性的宗教节日庆典,使人们能够经常性地相遇,并逐步增进相互间的了解,从而扩大了社交网络。

教会作为一种特殊的社会组织,不仅可以为贫困者提供食物和钱财,更能从精神和感情上满足人们对生命意义、爱的需要。这种需求是人维持生命、参加社会生活的重要动力。许多人认为只有在宗教组织中才能找到生命的意义。"宗教可以为个人和群体提供一种身份的认同感和根基感"。宗教团体还能频繁地为个人提供群体的友谊和生活的意义。

教堂是人们最爱去的场所,它为具有相似背景和兴趣的人们创造了一个社会环境,使之得以组成各种小的团体。属于某个宗教团体意味着从属于一个社会关系的网络。参与宗教团体的社会活动,给其成员提供了得到其他宗教社区的认同的更多机会,遵守道德规范和与其他成员分享活动和资源。而因为他们参与社会服务的工作,许多成员就有了更多的与团体以外的人交往和工作的机会。

美国社会学家南希·安默曼认为教会是社会资本的源泉,是参与更大范围的社会秩序的重要途径。美国全国城市复兴委员会的威廉·高尔斯顿也认为,宗教组织是文明社会的支柱,它的社会服务涉及的人数超过了美国人口的一半以上,它对那些收入甚微、教育程度较低,也无意加入其他团体的人尤为重要。

毋庸置疑,宗教信仰的力量并非仅仅是教义对信仰者的外在指导和约束,还在于信仰本身与人们心灵的内在契合。社会的急剧转型与理性工具对人的无形控制,滋生了现实生存中的更多的迷惑与无奈,而仍具有神秘色彩、尚未被解释的上帝依然满足着人们的精神需求。不论是基于信仰的外在的上帝,还是发于个体的心中的上帝,上帝的在场让人们对基于正义和慈爱基础上的教会的慈善增添了更多的自觉与自愿色彩,这种"爱人如爱已"的最朴素的真情,体现在慈善活动中,更显得温暖和真情,并像"呼吸一样自然"。

结　语

理性与信仰是人们理解世界的两种不同方式,宗教弥补了理性所无法计算与测量的无限宇宙与人类心灵,与其共生的慈善公益不仅为贫穷者与无家可归者提供最基本的衣物、食品与住所,也唤起了人们内心深处的慈悲与善,点燃了生活的意义与希望。超验意义上的上帝,已被基督徒具体化为经验层面上的希望,它不再是本体论意义上的实体与存在物,而是一种信念,一种精神意志。在此,上帝成为人类生活的希望与寄托,这在后危机时代,显得尤其重要。

目前,慈善仍是人们在看到政府失灵、市场失灵之后所寄予的寻求解决社会之困与社会之难的最后的选择,并把慈善机构看成与政府和市场并行的第三部门。每个人慈善行为背后的动机与真相无法真正地去透析,但基于宗教信仰与公民责任的慈善仍是大多数人的选择。人需要某种精神的东西,一方面可以抵御拜物主义、消费主义对人们精神的冲击;另一方面也可以增添人生中许多的温情,比如慈善。上帝无疑是被反复证明了的属于那种精神的东西,虽然他仍在遭遇争议,但也依旧散发着迷人的光芒,这种光芒照耀着人生之旅,并赋予其意义;这种光芒也照耀着人性之善,滋生并发展着慈善。

On the Governance of Religion in Transitional Societies

Yunfeng Lu

China has witnessed the prosperity of religions, which could be illustrated by the widely practiced folk religion and the strong revival of Confucianism, Buddhism and Daoism, and especially by the tremendous growth of Protestantism. According to official statistics, there were 700 thousand Christians in 1949, and the number increased to 3 million in 1982 and 4. 5 million in 1988. In 1997, the number surged to 12 million, and a remarkable 23 million was reached in 2009. Despite the inaccuracy of these statistics, we can ensure that, Christianity is rising rapidly in China, which not only affects religious ecology in China, but also reshapes the map of Christianity around the world. In addition, the rapid and vigorous development of religion poses severe challenges to religious regulation in China. How could the state regulate religion effectively? This article tries to probe this question though comparing the governance of religion in the United State of America and Taiwan.

Four Models of Governance of Religion

Many people would think that belief is a matter of faith and personal affairs, which should not be regulated by the government. However, even in America, where religions are thought to be given the utmost freedom, restrictions are imposed on religious organizations. Federal government exerted much pressure on the Mormons who practiced polygamy, sending polygamy practitioners into prisons. Similar is the case for Amish, who rejected secular educational system. They are compelled to establish schools and send their children to schools under the pressure of federal government. In this sense, there is no absolute religious freedom, nor will any government permit freedom without restriction.

Sociologists devote much attention to promoting typologies of religious regulation. Finke (1997) classifies regulation into subsidy and suppression; Yang (2006) categorizes four religious markets according to the degree of regulation: totally prohibited (where there is no religion), monopoly (where only one religion is permitted), oligopoly (where few religions are allowed) and free religious market (where religious pluralism exists). In this article, I will categorize four patterns of religious governance based on the difference of governing body: theocracy, state religion, selective regulation by the state and governance by society.

The governing body for theocracy is religious leaders, and Israel in Old Testament Era is an example. Prophets at that time were regarded as the spokesmen of God. Not only did they administrate religious affairs, but also wielded power in politics even every social affair by the name of God. Under this pattern, politics and religion are entwined with each other without functional differentiation, and state is not an independent entity.

The pattern of state religion began to prevail after state became an independent agency. According to Wikipedia, "state religion is a religion officially endorsed by the state with a higher status compared to other religions". There are at least two versions of state religion in history. The first version is the state religion under the system which integrates religion and politics and people are forced to believe in the religion, such as the Roman Catholic in the Middle Age Europe and Islam in Taliban Afghanistan. We can call it the radical version of state religion. Under this system, state regime is seen as the mandatory agency of state church, responsible for promoting the state religion. On the other hand, the state religions directly affect the stability of political regimes because they wield tremendous political power in affecting and controlling the public. They can mobilize the public for rebellions, so do they have the power to prevent such rebellions. The second version is state religion under the separation of politics and religion. Some nations in Southeast Asia designate Buddhism as official religion (such as Thailand and Cambodia), while some European nations appoint certain denomination of Christianity as official religion (such is the case in the UK and Norway), and Arabic nations appoint Islam as official religion (such as Iran and Saudi Arabia). These nations proscribe certain religion as state religion with Constitution or other laws explicitly, but state religion can no longer dominate national policy and people's lives along with the evolving of modernity and the trend of politics – religion separation. Nonetheless, state religion still possesses higher status compared to other religions, and it remains to be the source of regime legitimacy. This version of state religion can be called mild state religion.

The third type of governance on religion is the state's selective regulation, which is the case of Ming and Qing dynasties in China (Ma and Han 1992). They officials treated religions from the perspective of political steady, classifying hem into different categories and keeping balance of the weak. In detail, secular regimes closely watched the religious groups' political ambition and potential capacity to rebel, and categorized religions into two kinds, namely 'orthodox' and 'heterodox'. Religious institutions inclined to rebel were listed as 'heterodox' which should be repressed. While the religions (such as Buddhism and Daoism) widely practiced are entitled with 'Orthodox' despite their difference from Confucianism. The Confucian officials adopted measures to support these orthodox religions to some extent, although the number of monks is restricted. Meanwhile, amalgamation is imposed intentionally by the state to avoid any exclusive religion from gaining dominance. Secular regime would impose restrictions or even conduct suppression in case any religious association expanded its power excessively. In this way, the balance of the weak could be well kept.

Governance by society can be found in contemporary America and Taiwan. In this case, societies act as the governing body. The state no longer supports or suppresses certain religions according to law, nor does it actively get involve in religious affairs like gathering intelligence on whether religious associations would be rebellious. If no one sues religious groups, the state would leave them alone. Society becomes the main force to conduct administration towards religion. Families, mass media and other related social associations will trigger their supervision first once religious figures are spotted to conduct immorally or controversy arises. Provided anyone file lawsuit, judiciary involvement is ensued, thus laws are utilized to regulate the behavior of religious associations.

In the following sections, I will probe the advantages and disadvantages of state religion, selective regulation by the state and governance by societies, based on the experience of the United States and Taiwan. I choose the two areas for comparative study because they switched religious regulation patterns when faced with social transformation. While contemporary China can draw upon the wisdom from their switch in religious governance.

The Governance of Religion in
United States of America

During the era of colony, the United States following the pattern of state religion, which means that secular regimes were seen as Compulsory agency of a particular religion and religion is the source of legitimacy. Under this pattern, only the official religion was supported while all other religions were repressed. This policy reflects the idea that only one religion reveals the truth, while the rest are illusive and thus should be suppressed.

Nine of the thirteen colonies in North America designated state religion, such as Anglican in Maryland and Virginia. Laws, taxation and other measures were adopted to suppress other denominations. In Massachusetts, Baptist Churches were explicitly prohibited and many people were put to trial or even sentenced due to heresy, blasphemy, or heathenism. Quakers might not exist in Massachusetts, and at least four Quaker adherents were hanged, and some children were sold to be slaves because their parents were members of the Quaker. In Virginia, all denominations except the Anglican Churches were banned from worship activities, and Anglican members absent from worship activities for three times would be punished for a six – month labor. Besides, adherents of Catholic and Quaker were prohibited from public posts.

Various denominations existed within Protestantism, jostling with each other for adherents. Nevertheless, these denominations could be united as one when opposing Catholic. Catholics were deprived of legal residence in eleven colonies, and anti – Catholic events occurred frequently. However, Protestantism and Catholic became alliance when they waged campaigns against Judaism. Nothing describes the situation better than ' a war of all against all '. Pioneers intended to pursue freedom of religious faith. They hoped to designate Protestantism as state religion with the power of secular regime, however they spoiled the ship for a half – penny worth of tar. It was true that some denominations enjoyed subsidy by the secular regime, but more denominations suffered from persecution. The religious disputes and conflicts on the New World were no less than that of Europe.

The situation was improved after American Independence. At that time, many denominations wished to become the state religion of the newly – established United State of America, but no one could be powerful to do so. Puritanism might be the most influential in Massachusetts, but it was no doubt a minority when all thirteen states were taken into consideration. Besides Puritanism, nearly every denomination hopelessly found that it was not capable of dominating the whole religious market of America. A wise choice under such circumstance was to compromise and accept current situation, thus avoiding persecution from any church that gains exclusive power. Therefore, the First Amendment clearly stipulated that the Congress shall not enact laws to designate state religion or prohibit freedom for religious faith. Only three states out of the primary thirteen states opposed to the stipulation, while the rest held no objection. Federal government adopted ' two – track system ' during the process of implementation. In 1833, the separation of politics and religion and religious tolerance were finally achieved in America, marked by the disestablishment of last state religion in Massachusetts. Today, whenever we talk about the separation of politics and religion, many would emphasize the wisdom by excellent leadership or the philosophical influence of Enlightenment. These factors undoubtedly could not be overlooked, but the

fundamental reason lies in the gaming of benefits between different religious associations. It is a result of conflicts and compromise. Along
with the enactment of the First Amendment, the religious regulation
pattern shifted from state religion to governance by society: government no longer interfere faith on specific matters while society become
the main governing strength. In detail, we can summarize at least
three characteristics of America's governance of religion.

Firstly, religious governance deals with the practice of controversial religious organizations, instead of doctrines. According to Star
and Finke (2000), there is tension between religious groups and the
surrounding society and most of religions keep the tension relatively
moderate. Very few religious bodies have very high tension or have
highly harmonious relationship with the society, which can be found
on the two tails of the normal distribution. We can draw two primary
conclusions from this distribution model. First, it's normal for religion to keep certain degree of tension with exterior society, as long as
tension is controlled to a certain extent. We can not expect religions
to be completely compatible with the secular world, because retaining
a certain degree of tension is destined due to the nature of religion.
Second, the targets of governance on religion are supposed to be sects
that keep high tension with the outside society. Federal government
targets behaviors of religious adherents, instead of their mind. We
can draw from the case of Mormons which gave up plural marriage
practice.

The primary adherents practiced polygamy due to religious reasons, but this practice went against American laws and customs, and
led to an escalated tension between Mormons and the federal government. In 1862, American Congress passed Morrill Anti – Bigamy
Act, which was considered by Mormons to violate the clause protec-
ting religious freedom proscribed in the First Amendment. Mormons

decided to challenge the law. Reynolds, the secretary of Brigham Young, admitted to the government that he married with two wives for fulfilling the religious duty, and was then sued by the court. In 1879, the Supreme Court concluded that Reynolds was sentenced for two years' imprisonment and a fine of 500 dollars. It's indicated in the case that religious freedom is confined to people's thoughts and minds, while religious behavior is subject to law. Although people are given the freedom to believe in whatever religion, it's not justified to violate commonly recognized behavioral norm or to disrupt social order with religious reasons. During the fight with Mormons, only those who entered into plural marriages were punished, while ordinary Mormons adherents without plural marriages need not to be responsible for their belief in polygamy doctrines.

Secondly, although the state lied on laws to regulate religions, the officials were very patient. Since Reynolds vs. United States case, American government enhanced its law enforcement effort toward polygamists. Polygamists, no matter how high their positions were in the Mormons, would be listed as wanted and sent into prison. Besides, the government mobilized the public to 'hunt' polygamists. These 'hunters' would track polygamists for a long time, and broke into the room when evidence was spotted. The 'hunters' got awards from the government, while church leaders with plural marriages were forced to go underground. These measures eventually compelled Mormons to officially renounce polygamy in 1890. Till then, the Morrill act had been formulated for nearly 30 years, and the long time span fully demonstrated the patience of American government. Utilizing the two weapons of law and patience, federal government successfully cultivated the Mormons, though failures existed in America in dealing with religions, notably the case of Waco siege. In 1990s, due to the lack of understanding and patience, Clinton government adopted tough measures and even resort to force when dealing with Branch Dravidians in Waco, resulting in the death of more than 100 innocent adherents. It's manifested, both in the successful experiences in dealing with the Mormons and the lessons drawn from the failure dealing with the Dravidians, that time and patience are the best tools to deals with controversial religious groups.

Last but not least, although America mainly rely on laws and social strength to enforce its religious regulation, it doesn't mean that American government neglect religions. On the contrary, it attaches great importance to religion and has explicit religious strategis. For America, it's only a primary goal to avoid sects or cults to make trouble, while the strategic goal is to strengthen the identity of America. Protestantism plays an important role in American society. While American constitution emphasizes equal treatment to all religions and designates no state religion, many institutions are designed to provide favorable conditions exclusively to Protestantism. No wonder Wikipedia names Protestantism as the 'implicit state religion' of America. Wikipedia does not exaggerate the fact. As Tocqueville said, there is no nation in the world like the United States where Christianity has so tremendous influence on people's mind and soul. Those protestants who were shipped to the new continent by May Flower considered themselves to be chosen by God, and America to be the land that God blessed. Although Protestantism is not given a supreme status in legislation, but is clearly printed on American dollar that 'in God we trust'; it's written in the national anthem that "God Bless America"; the oath of allegiance embodies following words that 'I pledge to bear faith and allegiance to the banner of the United States and the Republic it represents, a nation belonging to God '; the president of America must place his hand on Bible in his swearing in and God has to be mentioned in his inaugural speech. All of these show that Prot-

第三部分

◎ 多元信仰与文化建设

pose control by police and intelligence agencies. I will elaborate that subsidy and suppression——the two main methods of selective regulation by the sate, will both generate expected consequences, and lead to an actual anarchy of religious regulation.

By analyzing the religious situation in contemporary China, Yang (2006) argues that heavy regulation cannot effectively reduce religion but lead to the formation of three markets: a red market (officially permitted religions), a black market (officially banned religions), and a gray market (religions with an ambiguous legal status). This article also finds that restrictive regulation cannot muffle suppressed religions; instead, suppression tends to drive repressed religions to be innovative, adaptive and aggressive. Yiguan Dao is a good example. As scholars (Song 1983; Lin 1990) point out, Yiguan Dao was virtually the most innovative religious group on Taiwan during the period when the sect was suppressed. In a restricted religious economy, unlike the dominating religions which could utilize political power to strike rivals, Yiguan Dao had to actively update its services and develop innovations to attract and retain members. "Innovate or die," this is the situation which the sectarians faced. In order to survive, the sect had no choice but to innovate, both doctrinally and organizationally. Doctrinal innovations not only increase the otherworldly rewards but also create committed members. Organizational innovations are especially vital for the survival of suppressed religions. The organizational structure made the sect avoid detection, sustain morale and protect the existence of sectarian networks. The sustained sectarian networks later served as the vehicle of massive recruitment.

State suppression can not only increase the otherworldly rewards provided by the oppressed religions but also reduce the risk of such rewards. These unintended consequences make the conversion to suppressed sects become a reasonable choice: though the suppressed sectarians have to pay more costs and sacrifice more, they can gain more other – worldly rewards; sacrifices caused by suppression make religious promises more credible. This finding is helpful to understand the long – standing puzzle that why people would like to contribute their time, enthusiasm, money and even lives to a suppressed and stigmatized religious group. When addressing why people join sects, Chinese imperial officials always thought that the mass of sectarians were stupid, ignorant and gullible (Overmyer 1976). Officials used to call sectarians "stupid people" (Yumin) and they put "the constant emphasis on the 'ignorance' and 'confusion' of the people" (Overmyer 1976: 38). By contrast, this study shows that people convert to repressed sects at least partly because the suppression unintentionally increases both the other – worldly rewards and the certainty of such rewards by suppressed religious firms. In other words, state suppression makes the religious rewards more profitable and more dependable, so it is reasonable for people to convert to the suppressed religions. Also, suppression, along with sacrifice and social stigma, may act to filter out half – hearted members and overcome the free – rider problem.

Government campaigns against Yiguan Dao in Taiwan forced the sect to run secretly or even disband temporarily, but persecution did not cut its throat. On the contrary, the sect grew steadily and quickly during the period of suppression. Although we cannot get the sect's exact membership before 1987 due to its underground nature, the following estimations can give us a sense of its development in general. The statistics issued by the police department reported that the sect had about 50,000 followers in 1963 (Song 1983: 27). Its membership since then has skyrocketed, surpassing 324,000 in 1984, according to the data by the Taiwan social change survey 1. In 1989, two years after the sect gained its legal status, the Taiwan social change survey shows that 2.2 percent respondents, namely more than

443,000 were Yiguan Dao believers. Though these numbers are not quite precise, they indeed indicate that Yiguan Dao successfully developed from a small immigrant sect into one of most influential religious groups in Taiwan.

While the Kuomintang state failed to prevent the development of Yiguan Dao by means of repression, it produced lazy Buddhism through subsidy. The Buddhists played an active role in lobbying the state to suppress the sect. As the official representative for Buddhists in Taiwan, the Buddhist Association of the Republic of China (hereafter, BAROC) tried to utilize political forces to suppress its rivalries, including Yiguan Dao. Buddhists produced many pamphlets to attack Yiguan Dao, claiming that it is an offspring of the White Lotus Sect, a heterodoxy perceived by imperial officials (Overmyer 1976; Naquin 1985; ter Haar 1992). Since the White Lotus Sect was involved in the rebellion at the end of Yuan Dynasty, the Buddhist monks argued that Yiguan Dao must be rebellious in nature. These charges were readily accepted by the authoritarian state. Even when the Kuomintang state attempted to legalize Yiguan Dao in 1981, the Buddhist association still pressured the state to suppress the sect (Song 1983).

Since the early years of 1980s, Taiwan authorities gradually realized the disadvantages of its governance of religion and turned to start a thorough reform and this change began from Yiguan Dao for it was a main subject of political control to religion. Thus, the sect won its virtual freedom and played an important role in local election. In the year 1987, dozens of "legislator" who supported by Yiguan Dao proposed to lift the ban on the sect. In succession, other prohibitions to forbidden groups were repealed either. In 1989, Taiwan authorities revised "Civil Associations Act" and permits free registration of religious groups, which means the prohibitions on religions were completely lifted.

After that, a new religion fever raised in Taiwan, and various religions emerged. According to the dada from Taiwanese "Ministry of Interior", the number of registered religious groups rise from 78 (1986) to 1062 (2004) all across the island. This rise was followed by what is called "religious chaos", many religious figures were believed to take advantage of religion to make money, and Sung Chi – li was one of them. Sung Chi – li was born in 1948, Kaohsiung, Taiwan. He was once sentenced to three years in prison for violation of law of negotiable instrument in 1985. After release he began to promote the concepts of "Doppelg? nger" and "Dharmakāya – Self". In 1990, he founded his own religious group. Since then, "Sung Chi – li fever" heated up in the island, and his followers was several hundreds of thousand at the climax, including a senior figure in Taiwan's DPP, Frank Hsieh and his wife Yu Fang – chih.

But the controversy followed his popularity. In the followers' eyes, Sung was a Charismatic leader with superpower evidenced by photography Sung provided. More than that, he was "Yidam", "Universal Light Body", or a savior for his followers. Religious Association of Taiwan issued the challenge to Sung for he claimed himself with the magic power of "multiple – appearing". They even prepared an iron cage for the performance. Once succeed, Sung would got a villa which worth of 5 million NTD. But he rejected the invitation. The mass media began to discuss Sung's phenomenon negatively. Some of them even revealed that Sung sold his "lighting" photography at very high price, and the followers would pay 10 million NTD to meet Sung himself. Under the impetus of the media, Sung was accused in 1996 and was sentenced to be imprisoned for seven years. In 2008, considering there were no victims in this case, and there is no evidence to support the implementation of fraud, the high court ended this case with his acquittal.

From Sung's case, we can catch a glimpse of the measures Taiwan authorities dealing with religious disputes after the prohibitions on religions were lifted. First, the officials adopt a "de – political" perspective to treat religion. Second, the state is to take the attitude that "if no people sue religious figures, the state would let them be (民不举,官不究)". Non – government agencies, including families, the mass media and public opinion became the fresh troops to supervise religious figures, and the primary focuses are whether their behaviors violated customs and ethics or not. In Sung's case, disclosure from the media played an important role. The characteristic of Taiwan authorities in religious governance is "to place public opinion first, judiciary second". If it was policemen who were sent to monitor those "ambitious" sects in the past, currently it is "judicial institution" that took their place and became the main force to deal with religion. And it takes actions only after populace report and disclosure from media or pubic. The issues involved should be nothing to do with the faith itself. What the prosecution charged in Sung's case is mainly about "fraud", and the key to it is whether Sung's "multiple – appearing" photographies are photomontages, instead of his magic power. Sung was sentenced seven years in prison in first – instance judgment because the local court believed those photographies were photomontages.

Before 1989, intelligence units and policemen worked really hard to suppress religious groups in Taiwan. But such efforts failed and Yiguan Dao kept increasing in spite of suppression. It is difficult for the state to keep the policy and finally lift the repression on Yiguan Dao. Social forces, including families and the mass media, gradually take the place of policemen to regulate religious groups. The controversial religious figures may not be convicted, but their groups' development would be substantiality effected.

Discussion and conclusion

Through comparing the governance of religion in Taiwan Province and the United States, we could get the following conclusions. First, the transformation of religious governance model originated from the conversion of religious view. The United States changed from "state religion" to "society – oriented regulation". Meanwhile, Taiwan changed from "state – oriented selective regulation" to "society – oriented regulation". What behind the state religion model is a "exclusive and dominant" religious view, which tries to eliminate dissidents by force. But it caused religious conflicts and promoted religious persecution. "State – oriented regulation" reflects the religious view of "orthodoxy vs. heterodoxy", subsidizing some religious groups while repressing the others. But both subsidy and repression would lead to some unexpected consequences: while former creates lazy religious firms, the latter is helpful to religious growth.

Second, the social forces should replace policemen to govern religious groups. In current Taiwan, the society becomes the main force to supervise religion, and the state tried to "govern by non – interference". Although religious chaos occasionally happened in the island, they are controllable and religious groups play a positive and constructive role.

References

Finke, Roger. 1997. The consequence of religious competition. In Rational choice theory and religion: Summary and assessment, edited by Young, Lawrence A, 46 – 65. New York: Routledge.

Ma Xisha and Han Bingfang. 1992. Minjian Zongjiao Shi [A History of Chinese Popular religions]. Shanghai: Shanghai People Press.

Naquin, Susan. 1985. The transmission of White Lotus sectarianism in late imperial China. Pp. 255 – 291 in Popular culture in late imperial China, edited by Johnson Davis G, Andrew J. Nathan, and Rawski. Berkeley: University of California Press.

Overmyer, Daniel L. 1976. Folk Buddhist religion: Dissenting sects in late traditional

China. Cambridge, Mass.: Harvard University Press.

Song Guangyu. 1983. Tiandao goucheng [An investigation of the Celestial Way]. Taipei: Yuanyou Press.

——. 1990. Shiliu shiji yilai zhongguo minjian mimijiaopai de jiben jiegou (Chinese secret sects' organizational structure since the 16th century). In Renleixue yanjiu (Anthropological researches), edited by Xie Shizhong and Sun Baogang, 155 – 173, Taipei: Nantian Shuju.

Stark, Rodney, and Roger Finke. 2000. Acts of faith: Explaining the human side of religion, Berkeley: University of California Press.

Stark, Rodney, and Laurence R. Iannaccone. 1994. A supply – side reinterpretation of the

"secularization" of Europe. Journal for the Scientific Study of Religion 33: 230 – 52.

——. 1996. Recent Religious Declines in Quebec, Poland, and Netherlands: A Theory

Vindicated. Journal for the Scientific Study of Religion 35:265 – 71.

ter Haar, B. J. 1992. The white lotus teachings in Chinese religious history. Honolulu:

University of Hawaii Press

Wang Jianchuan, Zhou Yumin and Lin Meirong. 1997. Gaoxiongxian jiao-pai zongjiao

[Sects in Gaoxiong county]. Pressed by Gaoxiong county government.

Yang, Fenggang. 2006. "The Red, Black, and Gray Markets of Religion in China. "

Sociological Quarterly 47: 93 – 122.

1 The survey indicates that 1. 7 percent respondents worshiped the Eternal Venereal Mother. Although the Mother was commonly worshiped by many Chinese sects in history, the deity was mainly worshiped by the Yiguan Dao sectarians in the 1980s in Taiwan. Considering the fact that the sect was still "illegal" in 1984 and thus many sectarians did not want to reveal their religious identity, the virtual number of Yiguan Dao believers should be more than 324,000.

第三部分　多元信仰与文化建设

古典学的兴起和基督宗教
不同解经传统的形成

赵敦华

　　我们常说西方思想传统源于希腊,其实这个传统不是希腊罗马思想的自然延续,而是经历了与基督教思想相融合、蜕变的漫长过程。特别是在文艺复兴时期,新兴的古典学与宗教改革相结合,信义宗和改革宗形成了与天主教不同的解经传统。按照现代解释学,学术传统是以文本为中心的效果历史,这一历史起源于经典,传世于经典的评注、改造和转化。我们试从古典学与解经学相结合的角度,说明学术与信仰在西方的一个重要社会转型期的复杂关系,以期能对不同信仰传统与当代文化建设的联系有所启示。

一、古典学与解经学的最初结合

　　西方基督教世界自 13 世纪开始,亚里士多德哲学与神学相结合,把经院哲学推向了理性的高峰。人们由此看到了希腊哲学的魅力,但又缺乏全面了解希腊文化的途径。1453 年,奥斯曼帝国攻陷东罗马帝国首都君士坦丁堡,关闭了它的高等学府。一批学者携带古希腊罗马典籍流亡意大利,流亡的希腊学者带来的是西方人渴望已久的文化宝藏。人文主义者把古典文本作为榜样,开创了注释、整理古希腊和古典拉丁文本,以及圣经希伯来和希腊文本的古典学研究。

现在的古典学主要是对古希腊文和拉丁文的语文学（philology），基本不触及宗教信仰问题，但这门学科在诞生时却是一门专门针对中世纪"学问"（doctrine）的批判艺术（art），古典学创始人都有批判志趣和改革主张。比如，伊拉斯谟属于天主教内的人文主义改革派，他写了不少批评僧侣和经院哲学家的书，但他最重要的作品当属希腊文－拉丁文对照的《新约全本》。原来他只想用当时流利的拉丁文重新翻译圣经，但后来发现替代中世纪流行的通俗（Vulgate，武甘大）拉丁文圣经的最佳途径是用希腊文圣经勘定后者的错误。伊拉斯谟的《新约全书》共有5个版本。路德的德译本利用了第二版，早期的英译本，如丁道尔本、英王本依据第三版。伊拉斯谟的希腊文－拉丁文对照版被称作"标准版"（Textus Receptus）。其实，与同时期多语种的"康普顿斯圣经"（Biblia Complutensis）相比，伊拉斯谟的圣经内容（只有新约）和语种（没有旧约希伯来文和希腊文）均有缺憾，而且新约希腊文的来源也不全。只是康版为等待教皇批准而晚出几年（1522年发行），销路不大（600套，而爱版第一、二版销售3000册），更重要的是，伊版被德英译者当作原版，因而被"标准版"。

二、路德宗解经学的演变径路

路德的《圣经》德文本为宗教改革提供精神动力，故有"伊拉斯谟下蛋，路德孵鸡"之说。但这不是伊拉斯谟的本意。路德对罗马教会的激烈批判以及宗教改革派的激进行动引起人文主义改革派的不安。伊拉斯谟首先发难，与路德在自由意志问题上展开论战。他俩论战的意义已不限于具体的神学观点，而涉及到解经学的基本原则：圣经文字的意义是可疑的，还是确定无疑的？圣经的文字意义是否有待人的解释？圣经解释是否服从教会规定的信仰准则？伊拉斯谟认为圣经的文字是可疑的，需要通过解释才能明白圣经的启示。他引用早期教父安布罗斯、阿里索斯顿、哲罗姆、奥古斯丁和中世纪神学家的权威解释来确定圣经的言论。他批评路德说："你命令我们不应探究或接受除圣经外的任何东西，但你的命令只是要求我们承认你是圣经的惟一解释者,并谴责其他解释者。因此,如果我们允许你不是圣经的仆人,而是主的话,胜利就属于你了。"

路德在论战中直接诉诸圣经,很少旁征博引,但正如他所宣称的那样,他并不比对手缺少哲学和古典学知识:"他们是博士吗?我也是。他们是学者吗?我也是。他们是哲学家吗?我也是。他们是语文学者吗?我也是。他们是教师吗?我也是。他们写书吗?我也写。……我能运用他们的辩证法和哲学,且比他们所有人都运用得好。此外我还知道他们无一人懂的亚里士多德。……我这样说并不过分,因为我从小就受教育,一直运用他们的知识。我知道它的深浅,他们能做的一切,我都能做。"路德与伊拉斯谟之争不是信仰与学术的冲突,而出自对信仰与学术关系的不同立场,即对圣经信仰是否服从古典学术问题的不同回答。他没有把圣道与载道的福音书分开,圣道的启示与阅读福音书是一个里表一致的过程。他认为圣经文字的意义清晰明白,因此圣经传播的圣道才有直指人心的启示力量。他反对传统释经学者对圣经四重意义,即文字意义、类比意义、神秘意义、道德意义的区分,他只承认文字意义的真实性,强调圣经意义的清晰性使教育水准、语言能力不同的人有着同等的理解圣经和接受启示的机会。路德并不否认圣徒解释和神甫牧师宣讲圣经和教会规范信条的作用,但应该解释的只是文字意义,教会的信仰规范应以圣经为基础;教会不是挡拦在个人与上帝之间的障碍,而是支持信徒与上帝通过圣经直接交往的后盾。

路德去世之后,菲利浦·梅兰希顿(Phlip Melachthon)竭力弥合路德与人文主义的隔阂。他是维腾堡大学希腊语教授,对哲学与人文学科有深厚学术造诣。他从16世纪30年代起开始认识到,基督教应表现为真正的哲学,古代的复兴学科(studie renascentia)是创立系统神学的重要途径,亚里士多德的著作应得到尊重。路德宗神学院极其重视古典文字和知识的传授,在18、19世纪德意志民族崛起之时更是蔚然成风。神学家倾向于把圣经的文字意义与原初意义相等同,从"惟有圣经(sola scriptura)"走向"回到本源(ad fontes)"。他们热衷考察的"本源"问题有:圣经的作者是谁?圣经(特别是摩西五经和福音书)在成书之前是不是经历了一个口传阶段?这个阶段对圣经作者有何影响?他们所处的社会文化环境对圣经的写作有何影响？他们使用的语言和写作方法、风格有何特点？圣经的成书有没有一个编辑过程？编者是如何处理原始资料的？为什么要这样处理？圣经是如何保存、翻译和传播的？如何理解圣经不同版本的差异？如此等等。

"惟有信仰"（sola fide）和虔敬派（Pietism）净化灵魂和道德的主旨使他们相信，圣经的真正意义只与信仰和道德有关，圣经中历史记录只是当时的、外在的现象，可以而且应该接受批判的考察。虽然路德神学以"惟有圣经"著称，但耐人寻味的是，19 世纪后，圣经历史批评一直是德国路德宗神学院的显学。

三、天主教的解经传统

伊拉斯谟新编和新译的新约和康普顿斯圣经全本都得到教宗利奥十世的批准，伊拉斯谟并把他的新编本献给教宗。始料未及的是，宗教改革中流行的圣经新译本却成为新教与天主教之间激烈冲突的根源。首先是版本之争，新教使用的版本只承认旧约 39 卷为正典，而把拉丁通俗本旧约 46 卷中其他卷章当作外经。其次，新教否认教皇拥有解释圣经的权威，不承认罗马教廷的传经传统。

罗马教廷在宗教改革进程中首先阐明关于圣经正典和教廷传经的教义。1546 年 4 月，第四次特伦托主教会议颁布关于圣经正典的敕令，其中关键的一句是，凡不接受正典的全部之书包含在"老的武甘大本之中，以及主观故意蔑视此后传统者"，"让他被诅咒"（即革除教籍）。这个规定以武甘大本作为标准，确定正典的卷目，以及"此后传统"即天主教会传经传统的权威。

宗教改革后，罗马教廷多次在大公会宪章、教宗通谕和信函中多次阐明天主教的解经传统。本笃十六在 2008 年发布的牧函《主之道》可谓是最新的阐明。这些纲领性文件都恪守圣经是神圣启示，绝对无误，强调天主教会解经传经传统的权威性和教廷教导机构（Magisterrium）对圣经解释的指导作用。

随着时代的流转,天主教廷逐步强调从原初文字校勘、研究和翻译圣经的重要性,对历史批评方法也经历了从完全排拒到有条件肯定的转变。庇护十二于1943年9月30日发布通谕《圣神之默感》多次要求吸收"批评"的新成果。本笃十六最近牧函明确肯定:"历史批评解释和最近引入教会生活的其他文本解释是有益的",因为"拯救史不是神话学,而是真实的历史,应以严肃的方法从事历史研究"(第32条)。

四、加尔文对古典学研究的利用

加尔文和路德一样不承认教会有评判圣经意义的权威。他在《基督教要义》中明确地说:"认为评判圣经的大权是在乎教会、因此确定圣经的内容也以教会的旨意,这乃是非常错误的观念。"(1.7.2)但加尔文并未因此忽视古典知识,相反,他大量引用古代和中世纪经典作家解释圣经。加尔文把人类知识分为三类:"第一类包括民政、家事和其他一切文艺与科学;第二类包括对上帝和他旨意的认识,以及在我们生活中与这认识相配合的规律"(2.2.13);第三类"即那规范我们生活的规则,我们称之为义行的知识"(2.2.22)。这三类知识都有古典知识。

第一类知识指理性知识、文学、技艺等。加尔文说:"当我们看到真理之光在异教作家的著作表现出来,就要知道,人心虽已堕落,不如最初之完全无缺,但仍然禀赋有上帝所赐优异的天才。如果我们相信,上帝的圣灵是真理的惟一源泉,那么,不论真理在何处表现,我们都不能拒绝或藐视它。……我们读古人的著作只有赞叹敬佩;我们要敬佩他们,因为我们不得不承认它们确实优美。我们岂不当认为那受赞叹并被看为优美的都是出自上帝吗?……圣经上称为'属血气的人'既在研究世间的事物上表现了这么多的天才,我们就应该知道,在人性最优之点被剥夺以后,主还是给它留下许多美好的品性";即使异教作家也"将一切哲学、立法和有用的记忆,都归于他们的神。圣经上称为'属血气的人'既在研究世间的事物上表现了这么多的天才,我们就应该知道,在人性最优之点被剥夺以后,主还是给它留下许多美好的品性。"(2.2.15)加尔文以柏拉图为例说,虽然柏拉图把知识归于人的灵魂的回忆是错误的结论,但这可以证明:"人都禀赋有理性和知识。这虽然是普遍的幸福,然而每人都要把它看为上帝的特殊恩惠。"(2.2.14)(2.2.15)但他最后说,由于"最聪明的人"对上帝之爱的认识"比鼹鼠还更盲目",因此"他们的著作虽然偶然含有稀少真理,但其所包含的虚伪更不知有多少。"(2.2.18)

为什么异教徒崇拜"他们的神"而不知道上帝的爱和恩惠呢?这要回到《基督教要义》的开始。加尔文开宗明义地说,认识神是人类的自然的本能,"我们认为这一点是无可争辩的。"他赞成西塞罗在《论神性》中所说,"没有一个国家或民族,野蛮到不相信有一位神。即使在某方面与禽兽相去不远的人,总也保留着多少宗教意识"(1.3.1)。他并引用柏拉图的"灵魂至善"说和普鲁塔克的宗教观说明上帝在人心中撒下宗教的种子。但是,加尔文并不因此而赞扬人性的善良,他是要阐述保罗的那句话:"自从造天地以来,神的永能和神性是明明可知的,虽是眼不能见,但藉着所造之物就可以晓得,叫人无可推诿。"(罗马书 1:20)加尔文强调,人类堕落之后,充满着否认神的存在、亵渎神和崇拜假神偶像的罪恶。他说:"恶人一旦故意闭着自己的眼睛以后,上帝就叫他们心地昏暗,有眼而不能见,作为公义的报应"(1.4.2)。这就应了保罗的一句话:"他们既然故意不认识神,神就任凭他们存邪僻的心,行那些不合理的事"(罗马书 1:28)。加尔文列举柏拉图的"天球说"、斯多亚派编造的神的各种名称、"埃及人的神秘学"、伊壁鸠鲁派、罗马诗人卢克莱修、维吉尔蔑视神,以及古希腊吟唱诗人西蒙尼德斯的"未知的神"(1.5.4 – 12)等事例。他说:"人类卑劣的忘恩负义之心,就在这里表现出来了"(4),"他们亵渎神的真理可谓无所不用其极"(11)。

第三类"义行的知识"相当于哲学家所说的"实践理性"或通常说的道德良心。保罗说:"没有律法的外邦人若顺着本性行律法上的事,他们虽然没有律法,自己就是自己的律法。这是显出律法的功用刻在他们心里,他们的良心(syndersis,和合本译作'是非之心')同作见证,并且他们的思念互相较量,或以为是,或以为非。"(罗马书 2:15 – 16)加尔文通过对古希腊哲学家的良心观的剖析说明保罗给予的启示。他首先讨论柏拉图《普罗泰哥拉斯》中苏格拉底说的"无人有意做恶"的观点,他说,既然人有良心,但仍然犯罪,那么"一切罪行都由于无知的这句话,是不对的。"(2.2.22)

其次,加尔文讨论了公元 4 世纪的亚里士多德注释者特米斯丢在《论灵魂注》中的一个观点:"在抽象的事或在事物的本质上,人的知识不容易受骗;但在进一步考虑具体的事上,它就容易犯错误。"(2.2.23)比如,人都承认"不准杀人"是对的,但却认为谋杀仇人是对的;人都承认"不准奸淫"是对的,但自己犯了奸淫之事,却暗中得意。加尔文说,这种说法比较合理,但不适用所有情况,因为有些人犯罪"甚至不用道德的假面具,明知故犯,蓄意作恶。"他引用罗马诗人奥维德在《变形记》中美狄亚的话"我明知并赞同那更好的道路,却走上那坏的道路"(2.2.23),以此证明"犯罪的意念"(sensus peccati)并非出自对普遍原则的无知。

最后,加尔文采用了亚里士多德关于"不自制"(akrasia)与"放纵"(akolasia)的区分。亚里士多德的问题是:"一个人何以判断正确,却又不自制呢?"(1145b25)设"吃甜食不好"是正确判断,"吃甜食快乐"是感性意见,"甜食就在眼前"是当下感觉,"要吃甜食"是欲望(pathos)。"不自制"是感性意见在当下感觉面前服从欲望,而不服从理性,但事后仍承认理性规则;而"放纵"则是感性意见代替正确判断成为行为规则,追求感觉的呈现和欲望的满足。亚里士多德说,正如不发怒就打人比盛怒之下打人更坏,"放纵比不自制更坏"(1150a30),"放纵者从不后悔,坚持自己的选择,而不自制者则总是后悔的。"(1150b30)加尔文虽说亚里士多德的区分"是很对的",但他实际上把亚里士多德的问题转化为"人何以有良心,却又犯罪呢?"他用寥寥数语概括了亚里士多德在《尼科马可伦理学》第 7 卷中用10 章篇幅的区别和讨论。按照加尔文的解释,"不节制"是"思想失去具体的认识"而犯罪,事后尚知忏悔,良心犹存;而"放纵"则是良心丧失,"反倒坚持选择恶行。"(2.2.23)

五、古典学对中国学术的启示

我们现在读到的现代文本的圣经,是在古典学诞生之后,经历了长期的整理、翻译和评注的产物。随着中世纪沿用的拉丁文衰落,法、德、英文相继成为西方学术的主要语言。但古典希腊文和拉丁文始终是西方人文学术的基本语言;虽有现代西文的译本,古典学依然是研读圣经和神学经典的基本功;即使研究近现代神学,如不回溯古希腊和拉丁文本,终成无本之木,无源之水。历史上的新理论,无不是站在经典文本的肩膀之上,引经据典,批判总结,才写出传世经典。

从古典学到解释学的西学传统,对中国学术不乏启示和借鉴作用。如果说经学与古典学相媲美,那么中国古代的"汉学"和"宋学"之争,"小学"和"义理"的分殊,"我注六经"和"六经注我"的张力,也可视为现代解释学问题。近代以来,经学衰微,文本解释传统断裂,追求新的学术范式充满争论,如中西之争。没有文本依据的空疏之论,既无助于经典的新生,也未促成文本的创新。在新旧学术断裂之际,回顾征实有据的经学传统,借鉴从古典学到解释学的西学传统,建立以经典、文本为中心的学术范式,已成为当代中国学术的任务。

Chinese Moral Philosophy,
the Religious Enlightenment in Europe,
and a Global Ethic

Stewart J. Brown

The European Enlightenment of the late seventeenth and eighteenth centuries was a diverse cultural movement that changed perceptions of the nature and destiny of humankind, and of the foundations of individual and social ethics. It was, according to the intellectual historian, Jonathan Israel, a "revolution of the mind", bringing new conceptions of individual freedom, human capacity, and human progress. [1] It contributed significantly to the growth of democracy, equality under the law, human rights, free markets, universal education, individual autonomy, the separation of Church and state, and religious toleration. It was especially directed to achieving freedom from religious authority, whether the authority of the churches, the Bible or Christian tradition. For Enlightenment thinkers, humankind was at last entering the clear light of day, and putting behind it the dark night of superstition, credulity and ignorance. Thinkers of the Enlightenment believed that they were discovering universal truths—and

---

[1]　J. Israel, *A Revolution of the Mind: Radical Enlightenment and the Intellectual Origins of Modern Democracy* (Princeton: Princeton University Press, 2010).

ushering in a new understanding of the natural laws that shaped the physical universe and the social laws that shaped human nature and human cultures. Theirs was, they believed, a world movement that would lead to increased unity and harmony among all humankind.

Enlightenment thinkers sought a new grounding for morality. For centuries, most Europeans had believed that the foundations of morality were to be found in the Christian Scriptures, which for them were the direct, revealed word of God. In Scripture, it was believed, God had provided his human creatures with a complete set of moral laws and precepts, which, if obeyed, would ensure social harmony in this world and eternal salvation for individuals in the afterlife. While Christian thinkers recognised that ancient Greek or Roman ethical teachings had been precursors to Christian morality and had provided partial ethical truths, the teachings of the Christian Scriptures were believed to contain the purest ethical precepts and the only sound basis for a lasting social order. Enlightenment thinkers, however, questioned this notion. For them, individual and social ethics should be based, not on an infallible Scripture expressing the commands of God, but rather on observations of human psychology and of the harmonies of the natural world, or by following the innate sense of right and wrong in human conscience. For some Enlightenment thinkers, it was possible to live a moral life without any religious faith. They came to believe that people could act morally and unselfishly, without the threat of eternal punishment or the promise of eternal reward in a next life; they could value virtue for its own sake. This is not to say that the Enlightenment was opposed to religion. Most thinkers of the Enlightenment believed in God. They perceived of themselves as religious and adherents of the historic Christian faith. According to the historian, J. G. A. Pocock, the Enlightenment was "a product of re ligious debate and not merely a rebellion against it". [1] And yet, many thinkers of the Enlightenment came to accept that religious sanctions were not necessary for a moral society, and that a separation of Church and state was possible, and even beneficial. In post-Enlightenment Europe, Christianity became less about social authority, and more about individuals fulfilling their human potential and serving others.

As scholars have long been aware, Europe's growing awareness of China, and especially of Confucian thought, played a significant role in shaping the early European Enlightenment. Many Enlightenment thinkers came to admire China as an ancient, orderly, stable and humane society, with a social ethic that had developed independently of Christian influence. The existence of China's sophisticated civilisation raised serious questions about the need for Christian revelation to support a social ethic. For centuries, Europeans had believed that Christianity formed the one sound basis of morality, but the example of China's ancient culture suggested there were other possibilities and this in turn opened up new ethical horizons for Europeans. This paper will explore the vital influence of China, and especially Chinese moral philosophy, in helping to define the moral and religious thought of the European Enlightenment.

China and the Beginnings of the European Enlightenment

A sustained European awareness of Chinese moral philosophy began with the Jesuit missionaries who began working in China from the end of the sixteenth century. As part of their effort to convert the peo-

---

[1]　Quoted in D. Sorkin, *The Religious Enlightenment: Protestants, Jews, and Catholics from London to Vienna* (Princeton, 2008), p. 3.

ple of China to Catholic Christianity, the Jesuit missionary Matteo
Ricci (1552 – 1610) and his followers——including Nicolas Trigault
(1577 – 1628), Alvaro Semedo (1586 – 1658), Gabriel de Magal-
haes (1610 – 1677), and Martino Martini (1614 – 1661)——had
embraced a policy of "accommodation", by which they endeavoured
to accommodate Christianity to Chinese culture as part of their strategy
for converting the people of China. [1] The Jesuit missionaries arrived in
China with no intention of ever leaving; unless they were recalled to
Europe to promote the mission, they remained in China for the re-
mainder of their lives. In China, they adopted Chinese dress and customs, and developed connections with the imperial court. They studied the Chinese language, history, geography, manufactures, political
institutions, and culture, and, to enhance their understanding of Chinese morals, they translated the ancient Confucian texts into Latin. [2]
Through their studies, the Jesuit missionaries became convinced that
the ancient Confucian texts represented a form of natural religion,
which included a perception of the one true God, a sense of the preordained harmony of the universe, and knowledge of the social vir-
tues, including the social responsibilities to others, that were compatible with Christianity. It would be possible, the Jesuits believed, to
build upon this Confucian natural religion in order to form a Christian-
Confucian synthesis that would be the basis for a Chinese Christianity.
In their commentaries, to be sure, the Jesuits simplified the ancient
and complex Confucian teachings, and they largely ignored the later
influence of Buddhism and Taoism on Confucian thought——largely
because they viewed Buddhist and Taoist influences as corruptions of

---

[1] D. E. Mungelo, *Curious Land: Jesuit Accommodation and the Origins of Sinology* (Stuttgart: Franz Steiner, 1985).

[2] A. C. Ross, *A Vision Betrayed: The Jesuits in Japan and China*, 1542 – 1742 (Edinburgh: Edinburgh University Press, 1994), pp. 142 – 54.

the ancient Confucian teachings. None the less, their translations of the Confucian texts were often highly accurate and they proved effective in introducing the Confucian teachings to educated Europeans.

Jesuit translations of the Confucian texts began to be published in Europe from 1615. The most important and influential of these translations appeared in 1687 in Paris, under the title of *Confucius Sinarum Philosophus*. This was the work of seventeen Jesuit scholars assisted by several Chinese co-workers, and it was edited by the Flemish Jesuit, Philippe Couplet (1623 – 1693). The volume consisted of a lengthy introductory essay on Chinese culture; translations, with commentaries, of three of the Confucian Four Books; a short biography of Confucius; and a chronology of Chinese history. [①] Another collection, with three additional translated Confucian texts, was edited by the Jesuit Fran? ois Noel (1651 – 1729) and appeared in 1711 in Prague, under the title, *Sinensis imperii libri classici sex*. A further major compendium of the Confucian texts, edited with a commentary by the French Jesuit Jean-Baptiste Du Halde, was published in 1735. The publication of these Chinese texts aroused considerable interest among the European literati. For many, they provided evidence of a Chinese social ethic of great antiquity that was rooted in reason and human nature. The European literati found much to admire in the Confucian ethical teachings, including the ideal of loyalty and service to family, community and state, the insistence on the humane and compassionate treatment of others, the practice of virtue for its own sake (rather than for hope of reward in a future life), and the belief that state functionaries should be motivated by high philosophical principles. Late seventeenth and early eighteenth-century European thinkers, among them Isaac Vossius, Charles de Saint-vremond and Sir

---

① Mungelo, *Curious Land*, pp. 247 – 99.

William Temple, became convinced that ancient China had been a u-topia, which had been led by wise and virtuous philosopher-kings, who had ruled, under the guidance of learned Confucian literati, for the benefit of their people. ① This veneration of Chinese philosophy was paralleled by a growing European trade with China and a high de-mand for Chinese fine manufactures, including printed silk fabrics, porcelain vases and figurines, lacquered furnishings, and painted screens and wall hangings. China was becoming highly "fashionable" in Europe.

There was another aspect to this "China vogue" of the late sev-enteenth and early eighteenth century. The Jesuit histories of China, including Father Martino Martini's *Sinicae historiae decas prima* of 1658, portrayed China as a very ancient civilisation, with a continu-ous history dating from at least 3000 BC. European scholars indeed developed great respect for the accuracy of the Chinese historical re-cords, and were profoundly impressed with the antiquity of the Chi-nese imperial state. These historical accounts of Chinese antiquity, however, raised serious questions about the historical accuracy of Christian Scriptures. For according to the Bible, upon which Europe-ans based their understanding of world history, the world had been created in 4004 BC, and all human life, with the exception of Noah and his family who had found refuge on the ark, had been destroyed in a universal flood that occurred 1,656 years after the Creation, or in 2348 or 2349 BC. How did China fit into the universal history of hu-mankind as revealed by God in sacred Scripture? Some European

---

① A. H. Rowbotham, "The Impact of Confucianism on Seventeenth Century Europe", *Far Eastern Quarterly*, 4 (1945), pp. 224 – 42; W. W. Davis, "China, the Confucian Ideal, and the European Age of Enlightenment", *Journal of the History of Ideas*, 44 (1983), pp. 523 – 35; J. Israel, *Enlightenment Contested: Philosophy, Modernity, and the Emancipation of Man*, 1670 – 1752 (Oxford: Oxford Universi-ty Press, 2006), pp. 640 – 52; D. E. Mungelo, *The Great Encounter of China and the West* 1500 – 1800 (Lanham, Maryland: Rowman and Littlefield, 1999), pp. 59 – 74.

scholars, including the German Jesuit, Athanasius Kirchner (1602 – 1680) in his China monumentis qua sacris of 1667, argued that ancient China had been settled by Egyptians, and they claimed to see similarities between Egyptian hieroglyphs and Chinese characters. [①] Others maintained that after the flood Noah's ark had landed on the frontier of China and that the Chinese were descendents of Noah's sons. But still other thinkers, including the influential Dutch scholar, Isaac Vossius, a great admirer of the Chinese historical records, found such arguments to be unconvincing. The Chinese state, these scholars argued, had come into existence hundreds of years before the biblical flood, and there was no record that the Chinese civilisation had been destroyed by a universal deluge. Indeed, by the 1650s Vossius was arguing that the existence of China's ancient civilisation undermined the Bible's authority as a history of the world. [②] The accuracy of the Scriptural account of the creation of the world was already being challenged by new discoveries in natural science. Now, European thinkers increasingly questioned the historical truth of Scripture, and this in turn raised questions about claims that the Christian Scriptures were the revealed Word of God. The debates over the China's place in the biblical chronology were important in the growth of critical biblical scholarship and of scepticism about the exclusive truth-claims of Christianity. This, in turn, helped to open European minds to the value of other world civilisations and other world faiths.

---

① Mungelo, *Curious Land*, pp. 134 – 57, 177 – 79.

② E. J. Van Kley, 'Europe's "Discovery of China and the Writing of World History", *American Historical Review*, 76 (1971), pp. 358 – 85; T. Weststeijn, "Spinoza sinicus: An Asian Paragraph in the History of the Radical Enlightenment", *Journal of the History of Ideas*, 68 (2007), pp. 537 – 48; Israel, *Enlightenment Contested*, p. 640 – 41; R. Shackleton, "Asia as Seen by the French Enlightenment", in R. Iyer (ed.), *The Glass Curtain between Asia and Europe* (London: Oxford University Press, 1965), pp. 183 – 4.

Confucian Thought as Natural Religion

Many European thinkers were attracted to the favourable Jesuit portrayals of Chinese Confucianism as a form of natural religion, which included belief in one God and in universal moral truths that were revealed in nature and individual conscience. In their translations and commentaries, the Jesuits spread the view that Confucius had been the head of a religious movement, and had worked to restore and preserve ancient religious beliefs, in a similar manner to the ancient Hebrew prophets of the Christian Bible. [1] For several Jesuit scholars, most notably Joachim Bouvet (1656 – 1730), Confucianism was a form of *prisca theologia*, or Ancient Theology; for these scholars, Confucius had worked to restore the original truths that had been directly communicated by God to the first humans. Bouvet and his fellow Jesuit scholars, known as "Figurists", scoured the Confucian texts for images or expressions that represented vestiges of the Ancient Theology. Bouvet believed that this Ancient Theology formed the foundation for both Confucianism and Christianity, and that the Confucian texts, which predated the birth of Jesus Christ, contained anticipations of later Christian teachings. [2] For some Europeans, weary of the religious warfare of Protestant and Catholic since the Reformation (most recently the devastating Thirty Years' War of 1618 – 1648), the teachings of Confucius offered the prospect of discovering a universal religion that might unite all peoples and bring world peace. Isaac Vossius was attracted to the notion that Confucianism represented a "universal religion"; while the German Jesuit Athanasius

---

[1]　Rowbotham, "The Impact of Confucianism on Seventeenth Century Europe", pp. 227 – 8.

[2]　Mungelo, *Curious Land*, pp. 300 – 19.

Kircher argued in 1652 that Confucianism was a branch of the "one primeval religion" that had once united all humankind. [1]

The most prominent promoter of the view of Confucianism as a form of universal natural religion was the German philosopher and mathematician, Gottfried Wilhelm Leibniz (1646 – 1716), arguably the most important thinker of the early Enlightenment. [2] Attracted to the notion that Chinese civilisation might provide the key to world unity and harmony, Leibniz corresponded with leading Jesuit scholars of Confucianism from 1670, especially the Italian Jesuit missionary, Claude Philip Grimaldi. Leibniz began a serious study of Chinese history and culture from 1689, and he developed an impressive knowledge of Confucian thought. [3] He became committed to developing close cultural connections between Europe and China, believing that the two civilisations, at the opposite ends of the great Eurasian land mass, had much to contribute to one another, and to the world. In the preface to his book on China, the *Novissima Sinica* ("News from China") of 1697, Leibniz praised the high social morality of the Chinese people. The Chinese possessed, he insisted, a social ethic and notions of the one true God that were rooted in a natural religion revealed through reason. China's social morality, he further argued,

① Weststeijn, *Spinoza sinicus*, pp. 550 – 5.

② There is a rich and growing literature on Leibniz's engagement with China. See D. F. Lach, "Leibniz and China", *Journal of the History of Ideas*, 6 (1945), pp. 436 – 55; D. E. Mungelo, *Leibniz and Confucianism: The Search for Accord* (Honolulu: University Press of Hawaii, 1977); D. J. Cook and H. Rosemont, Jr., "The Pre-Established Harmony between Leibniz and Chinese Thought", *Journal of the History of Ideas*, 42 (1981), pp. 253 – 67; F. Perkins, "Virtue, Reason and Cultural Exchange: Leibniz's Praise of Chinese Morality", *Journal of the History of Ideas*, 63 (2002), pp. 447 – 64; F. Perkins, *Leibniz and China: A Commerce of Light* (Cambridge: Cambridge University Press, 2004).

③ Julia Ching and W. G. Oxtoby (eds.), *Moral Enlightenment: Leibniz and Wolff on China* (Nettetal: Steyler, 1992), pp. 23 – 6; Cook and Rosemont, Jr., "The Pre-Established Harmony between Leibniz and Chinese Thought", pp. 256 – 8; "Leibniz's works relating to China", see G. W. Leibniz, *Writings on China*, trans. and ed. by D. Cook and H. Rosemont, Jr. (Chicago, 1994).

was superior to that of the Europeans. Leibniz did, to be sure, believe that Europe's Christianity was intrinsically a superior religion; however, he also believed that Europe's Christianity had become corrupted by its sectarian divisions and religious warfare, and that the Christian social teachings were now largely ignored. As a result, he argued, the Chinese now "surpass us... in practical philosophy, that is, in the precepts of ethics and politics adapted to the present life and use of mortals". "Indeed", he added, "it is difficult to describe how beautifully all the laws of the Chinese, in contrast to those of other peoples, are directed to the achievement of public tranquillity and the established of social order."[1] He highlighted what he viewed as the most important elements of Chinese social ethics, including family devotion, mutual respect among social equals, an established set of social duties, politeness and good manners, calmness, neighbourliness and respect for customs. He was particularly impressed with the system of recruiting senior civil servants and political advisors through a system of open, competitive examinations. It was clear to him that Europe now needed to study the natural religion and moral philosophy of the Chinese. Moreover, Europe needed missionaries to come from China. "Certainly", he wrote, "the condition of our affairs, slipping as we are into ever greater corruption, seems to be such that we need missionaries from the Chinese who might teach us the use and practice of natural religion".[2] In one of his last works, the *Discourse on the Natural Theology of the Chinese* (1716), Leibniz developed his arguments that the ancient Chinese philosophers, including Confucius, had a sophisticated set of beliefs in God, the immortality of the human

---

[1] G. W. Leibniz, Preface to the *Novissima Sinica* (1697) in G. W. Leibniz, *Writings on China*, edited and translated by Daniel J. Cook and Henry Rosemont, Jr. (Chicago: Open Court, 1994), pp. 46 -7.

[2] Ibid. , p. 51.

soul, and rewards and punishments in an afterlife. [1]

　　Leibniz's openness to learning from Chinese culture was attractive, as was his hope that reason and natural religion might form the basis for the religious and moral unity of peoples and civilisations. His admiration for China's natural religion was taken up by other literati of the European Enlightenment, and most notably by the French deist *philosophe*, François-Marie Arouet, or Voltaire (1694 – 1778), one of Europe's most influential authors. [2] Educated by the Jesuits, Voltaire was well read in the Jesuit literature on China, including the works of Trigault, Samedo and Kirchner, and he largely accepted the Jesuits' idealized version of China. Deeply impressed with the antiquity of the Chinese imperial state, Voltaire portrayed the Chinese emperors as hard-working civil servants and philosopher-kings, who were advised by able, highly educated scholars of Confucianism and whose highest concern was the well-being of the people. Like Leibniz, Voltaire believed that the ancient Chinese, especially Confucius, had been monotheists, whose religion had included adoration of the Supreme Being, a high regard for social virtue, and toleration of other faiths. Voltaire venerated Confucius and kept a picture of the Chinese sage on the wall of his private library at Ferney. Of Confucius, Voltaire wrote, "I have read his books with attention, I have made extracts from them; I found that they spoke only of the purest morality. . . . He appeals only to virtue, he preaches no miracles, there is nothing in them of ridiculous allegory." [3] Of the natural religion of the Confucian literati, Voltaire wrote in 1756: "The religion of their

---

　　[1]　G. W. Leibnz, "Discourse on the Natural Theology of the Chinese" (1716), in Ching and Oxtoby (eds.), *Moral Enlightenment: Leibniz and Wolff on China*, pp. 87 – 141.

　　[2]　A. H. Rowbotham, "Voltaire, Sinophile", *Proceedings of the Modern Language Association*, 47 (1932), pp. 1050 – 65.

　　[3]　Quoted in A. Reichwein, *China and Europe: Intellectual and Artistic Contacts in the Eighteenth Century*, English translation by J. C. Powell (London: Kegan Paul, 1925), p. 89.

learned men was never dishonoured by fables, nor stained with quarrels or civil wars". [1] Other European thinkers shared this admiration for China's natural religion and social ethics. In 1731, the English author Eustace Budgell praised Confucius's "sublime Notions of *Moral Virtue*". [2] For the English author, Sir William Temple, China's Confucian literati "adore the spirit of the world, which they hold to be eternal; and this without temples, idols, or priests". [3]

However, the claims of such Enlightened European literati that China had a superior system of social ethics based solely on natural religion raised serious questions about Europe's Christianity, which Europeans believed had been revealed by God in the sacred Scriptures. If China's natural religion was sufficient to maintain social morality and preserve the Chinese imperial state for over 4,000 years, was there a real need for revealed religion, including sacred Scriptures, priests and churches? Leibniz had argued that Europe's Christian religion had once been superior to China's natural religion, but that it had been corrupted by religious conflict. However, if revealed religion could be so corrupted, was not the ancient natural religion of China superior to the Christianity of Europe?

Social Ethics without Religion

Leibniz maintained that China had a highly effective social morality based on natural religion; that is, a conception of the goodness of God gained through rational contemplation of the natural world. How-

---

[1] Voltaire, *Essai sur les moeurs et l'esprit des nations* (1756), quoted in J. D. Spence, *The Chan's Great Continent: China in Western Minds* (New York: W. W. Norton, 1998), p. 98.

[2] E. Leites, "Confucianism in Eighteenth-Century England: Natural Morality and Social Reform", *Philosophy East and West*, 28 (1978), p. 149.

[3] Sir William Temple, "Of Heroic Virtue", *Miscellanies, In Four Essays* (Glasgow: Robert Urie, 1761), p. 143.

ever, another leading German philosopher and academic went further, and argued that the Chinese example showed that a civilisation could have an effective moral system without any religious belief. This, in turn, led to one of the most celebrated controversies of the Enlightenment era.

Christian Wolff was a highly respected German mathematician and philosopher, and a professor at the University of Halle in the Kingdom of Prussia. He had come to take an interest in Chinese social ethics, in part through reading the translated Confucian texts, edited by the Jesuit Fran? ois Noel, which appeared in 1711 in Prague. [1] In 1721, Wolff gave a public lecture on the practical philosophy of the Chinese at the University of Halle, in which he argued that the ancient Chinese had developed a highly sophisticated social ethic without any religious foundation. [2] Confucius, he maintained, was not a creative thinker, but had rather worked to restore the ancient Chinese moral teachings. The ancient Chinese, Wolff further argued, had no conception of God, no sense of a divinely ordained universal order, and thus no natural religion. "The ancient Chinese", he insisted, "... knew no Author of the Universe, and had no natural religion, even less a revealed one. Only the strength of nature-free from every religion-could conduct them to the exercise of virtue." [3] Wolff may

① Ching and Oxtoby (eds.), *Moral Enlightenment: Leibniz and Wolff on China*, p. 14.

② For accounts of the episode, see D. F. Lach, "The Sinophilism of Christian Wolff (1679 – 1754)", *Journal of the History of Ideas*, 14 (1953), pp. 561 – 74; M. Larrimore, 'Orientalism and Antivoluntarism in the History of Ethics: On Christian Wolff's "Oratio de Sinarum Philosophia Practica"', *Journal of Religious Ethics*, 28 (2000), pp. 189 – 219; Julia Ching, "Christian Wolff and China: The Autonomy of Morality", *Synthesis Philosophica*, 7 (1989), pp. 241 – 8; R. B. Louden, '"What Does Heaven Say?": Christian Wolff and Western Interpretations of *Confucian Ethics*', in B. W. Van Norden, *Confucius and the Analects: New Essays* (New York: Oxford University Press, 2002), pp. 73 – 93

③ Christian Wolff, "Discourse on the Practical Philosophy of the Chinese", in Ching and Oxtoby (eds.), *Moral Enlightenment: Leibniz and Wolff on China*, pp. 162 – 4.

have misunderstood the Confucian texts (and much depends on the multiple meanings of *tiān*, or "Heaven", as the word appears in the *Analects*). [1] None the less, he argued boldly that the ancient Chinese example showed that it was possible to have a social morality based solely on the powers of human nature, without any religious sanction. "I do not see", he insisted, "how anyone could deny that such strength of nature exists effectively for the practice of virtue and for flight from vice. And the Chinese... have palpably proved by their example that one can make great use of such strength with success." [2] They achieved a highly moral society, not by appeals to God and the promise of future rewards and punishments in an afterlife, but through the education of the innate human powers. "The Chinese took therefore as the first principle, that one should carefully cultivate his reason, in order to reach a distinct knowledge of good and evil and therefore become virtuous by choice and not from fear of a superior or hope for recompense." [3] For the Chinese, Wolff insisted, virtue was its own reward: "the Chinese are given to good works because they realized intimately the intrinsic goodness of such actions". [4]

His lecture roused a storm of controversy. Conservative Christian thinkers at the University of Halle immediately denounced the lecture as an attack on the Christian faith, and their denunciations were taken up by Christian writers across Germany. However, other thinkers defended Wolff's notion that it was possible to have a virtuous, non-Christian, even atheistic society. It has been estimated that the heated controversy surrounding Wolff's lecture generated some two hun-

---

[1]   Louden, "What Does Heaven Say?": Christian Wolff and Western Interpretations of Confucian Ethics', pp. 77 – 81.

[2]   Wolff, "Discourse on the Practical Philosophy of the Chinese", p. 167.

[3]   Ibid. , p. 173.

[4]   Ibid. , p. 180.

dred polemical books. In 1723, the King of Prussia, Frederick William I, became convinced that Wolff's lecture had been an assault directed at both the Christian religion and the Christian foundations of morality, and that Wolff was subversive of all social order. He ordered Wolff to leave his territories within forty-eight hours or be put to death. Wolff left Prussian territory, and was immediately offered a teaching position at the University of Marburg in the neighbouring state of Hesse. For much of Enlightened Europe, he had now become a martyr for truth, and his views on Chinese social ethics, and the possibility of a social ethics without religious belief, stimulated great interest. He received widespread expressions of support, including a pension from the Russian Tsar Peter the Great.

Wolff continued to write on Chinese social ethics. In 1726, he published the text of his 1721 lecture on the practical philosophy of the Chinese, now with extensive notes in which he expanded and defended his various points. [①] In 1730, he published a lengthy work on Chinese political philosophy, under the title, *On the Philosopher King and the Ruling Philosopher*. In this work, he argued that the ancient Chinese emperors had been models of the enlightened monarch, ruling in the spirit of philosophical reflection and receiving guidance from philosophically trained civil servants. For this reason, the Chinese state which they established nearly 3,000 years before Christ continued to thrive. According to Wolff, "the first three emperors, Fu-hsi, Shen-nung and the Yellow Emperor, established that model of government which after so many thousands of years still excels all other models in the world and is continuing to flourish while other monarchies

---

① For an English translation of the 1726 text, including most of the explanatory notes, see Ching and Oxtoby (eds.), *Moral Enlightenment: Leibniz and Wolff on China*, pp. 143 – 86.

and kingdoms have had their downfall and dissolution. "[1] Wolff clearly hoped that European monarchs would follow the Chinese model. In 1740, meanwhile, a new Prussian monarch, Frederick II, came to the throne, and one of his first acts was to reverse the act of his father and invite Wolff back to his professorship at the University of Halle. This was widely viewed as a major victory for Enlightened humanism.

Following the Wolff affair, members of the Enlightened European literati increasingly argued that religion was not necessary to social ethics, and that people could act morally without the prospect of eternal punishment or reward in a next life. "To learn the true principles of morality", the French philosophe, Baron d' Holbach would later argue, "men have no need of theology, of revelation, or gods: they have need only of reason". [2] Writing in 1799, the young German theologian, Friedrich Schleiermacher, claimed that cultured people no longer believed that religion was necessary "for maintaining justice and order in the world". [3] Such attitudes helped to open the minds of Europeans to the value of non-Christian cultures outside of Europe. Educated Europeans found they could learn from the social ethics of non-Christian societies. An example of this was the Scottish Protestant clergyman and historian, William Robertson, who in 1793 published a highly favourable account of the non-Christian social ethics of India. [4]

The growing belief that it was possible to have social morality

---

① Christian Wolff, "On the Philosopher King and the Ruling Philosopher", Ching and Oxtoby (eds.), *Moral Enlightenment: Leibniz and Wolff on China*, p. 193.

② Quoted in Louden, ' "What Does Heaven Say?": Christian Wolff and Western Interpretations of Confucian Ethics', p. 81.

③ Friedrich Schleiermacher, *On Religion: Speeches to its Cultured Despisers* (1799), English translation by John Oman (New York: Harper, 1958), p. 18.

④ S. J. Brown, "William Robertson, Early Orientalism, and the *Historical Disquisition* on India of 1791", *Scottish Historical Review*, 88 (2009), pp. 289 – 312.

without religious sanctions could also have a liberating effect for European religion. For centuries, Europeans had believed that religion was necessary for the maintenance of ethics and social order. Church and state, they had believed, must be united and impose order on the people. This is in turn had led to the corruption of religious faith through an unhealthy association with political power. However, in the later eighteenth and early nineteenth centuries, Christian belief in much of Europe became less linked to social control and political power, and the churches became less entangled with political authority. In part through the influence of such later Enlightenment thinkers as Moses Mendelssohn, Jean-Jacques Rousseau and Friedrich Schleiermacher, religion began to become more a matter of the fulfilment of human potential through personal reverence, love, humility and service to others.

The influence of the Confucian traditions on the European Enlightenment should not be exaggerated. Many leading Enlightened European literati took no interest in China or Confucian thought, and many other European thinkers were highly negative about Chinese moral culture, believing the Chinese imperial state to be based on cruelty and oppression. Enlightened Europeans who were negative about Chinese philosophy and morality included such figures as Montesquieu, Rousseau, Kant, Herder and Hegel. The celebrated German philosopher, Immanuel Kant, lectured on Chinese history and philosophy at the University of K? nigsberg, but he did not believe that Europe had anything to learn from China. "Philosophy", he asserted, "is not to be found in the whole Orient.... a concept of virtue and morality never entered the heads of the Chinese."[1] European

---

[1]　Quoted in Julia Ching, "Chinese Ethics and Kant", *Philosophy East and West*, 28 (1978), p. 169.

interest in China and Confucian thought, moreover, began to wane after about 1750, in part because Europeans were growing weary of the 'China vogue' and Confucius and Chinese philosophy were no longer "fashionable". None the less, Europe's discovery of the ancient Chinese learning and the Confucian texts in the seventeenth and early eighteenth centuries had contributed to an emerging willingness on the part of at least some educated Europeans to learn from other, non-Christian cultures, and through the influence of Leibniz and Wolff helped to shape visions of world harmony and of a global ethics that was not bound to any one religious tradition.

万里路　数百年

——联结中欧的《马可·波罗圣经》

[意]阿尔贝托·梅洛尼

这是一颗蒙尘的宝珠,一条绵延的丝线,这是一幅幸免于破碎的画卷,是一枚轻浅的印记,却在跨越海陆、联结中欧的漫漫长路上清晰可鉴。这座墨写的桥梁,一头是腓特烈二世的欧洲、路易十四的欧洲,一头是蒙古可汗和清朝的帝王;一头是 12 世纪的神学,一头是 21 世纪的今天。这是一次国际合作研究的盛事,足以重整学术界,足以挑战"企业无法获得文化盛誉回报"的观念。这就是独一无二的《马可·波罗圣经》。

这个名字随这本 16.5 厘米长、11 厘米宽的圣经一起,于 1685 年 12 月被收入托斯卡纳大公爵科西莫三世的图书馆藏书目录。这部手抄而成的圣经,被写在薄如蝉翼的羊皮纸上,很可能是在 13 世纪 30 年代的最后几年中制成的;它原产于法国北部地区,游历过中国,最后停留在佛罗伦萨。其时,耶稣会士柏应理从那遥远的东方返回欧洲,为礼仪之争中的耶稣会立场辩护:对于礼敬皇帝、礼敬祖先,西班牙的方济各会士认为这是不可容忍的偶像崇拜行为,应予以禁止;而圣依纳爵的追随者则从罗明坚神父和利玛窦神父开始就依循一条开放思路,从文化角度予之理解、尊重和爱;他们对中国所怀的同样的爱,驱使他们去学习这个国家的语言和文化。

柏应理从佛兰德地区游历到了路易十四的宫廷,随后去往罗马,英诺森十一世的教廷:这位教皇出身于奥德斯卡奇家族,曾被雕塑大家贝尼尼漫画调侃。当柏应理返回巴黎,督促王室印刷所最终印成儒家典籍译本前,给托斯卡纳大公留下了一批书籍,其中就有这部"马可·波罗圣经"。这个名字所指示的并非此书的所有者,而无疑是在指示书籍年代:不能否定马可·波罗本人可能曾见过这部圣经,或曾与这部以木盒装载、黄丝绸包裹的书籍擦肩而过。但更合理的推测是,这部圣经在罗马教宗向东方派遣身负政治-外交使命的传教士期间,经他人之手到达了蒙古可汗的宫廷。

最早是热那亚籍教宗英诺森四世从里昂派出了年老的方济各会士若望·柏郎嘉宾(Giovanni da Pian del Carpine)。他去朝觐可汗,为的是将这位君主争取为打击伊斯兰教的同盟者:这位史上最为强大的征服者麾下的军队,曾犹如刀刃切开黄油般横驱直入欧洲斯拉夫地区。柏郎嘉宾于 1245 年春季启程,虽然最终并未达到预期目的,却仍被视作具有决定性意义(可汗的回函今日仍原样保存在梵蒂冈档案馆中)。此后又有多位商人、多明我会士和方济各会士前往,如隆如美(André de Longjumeau)、阿思凌(Ascelino da Cremona)、帕尔玛的若望(Giovanni da Parma)、鲁不鲁克(Gugliemo di Rubruck)、克雷蒙那的巴托罗缪(Bartolomeo da Cremona)。他们在 13 世纪末踏着马可·波罗描绘过的道路,或是沿着取道不同、却同样险恶的路线,到达了成吉思汗和忽必烈治下的中国。在 13 世纪下半叶的某次旅途里,也可能是在此后的某次旅途(后又有孟高维诺、鄂多立克等传教士受命东去,直至教宗若望二十二世时期才中止)中,这部轻便小巧的便携式圣经来到了中国。

随后,它被一位不知名的主人保管着:这位主人大概为书中的精巧整齐的手写体、标题边的彩色卷涡纹样装饰和细致的注释所吸引,而这些特点在当时巴黎生产的手抄神学书籍中本是寻常;今天,这些书籍又成为了我们的研究对象。

我们不知道元朝时期,乃至在朱元璋在 1368 年攻克北京城建立明朝以后,这部圣经曾于何时辗转何处。柏应理将之命名为《马可·波罗圣经》,显然没有提及携带此书的方济各会士可能是谁:这时已是四百年后,耶稣会士正与方济各会士争论不休;但这名字已明示出从那位威尼斯旅行家以来延续至利玛窦弟子身上的深厚历史积累。我们也不知道,是谁将此书裹进一幅黄丝绸,直至今日还照样保存在佛罗伦萨的图书馆里:这块织料的颜色在中国宫廷之外是被禁止使用的,于是或可推测,保存这中欧文化往来的不寻常见证物的人,大概是来自上流社会;或许,是当它在美第奇劳伦佐图书馆被记录入档时——连同它的传奇和历史——有人将它如此装饰。随后它在这图书馆被珍藏了3个世纪。

20世纪30年代的耶稣会学者在研究本修会在明清中国的受挫史时,对此书很感兴趣;中世纪史家施泽尼亚(Boles? aw Szcze? niak)也曾留意到此书,并在1957年发表了一篇论述"14世纪的方济各会圣经"的文章。2001年,耶稣会为纪念已故的中世纪拉丁史家雷奥那蒂(Claudio Leonardi)召开国际学术会议,其研究就专注于13世纪的便携式圣经,这正是马可·波罗圣经所处的时期。2008年,美第奇劳伦佐图书馆工作人员乔万娜·饶(Giovanna Rao)将此书放在同类收藏里一同展出。正如雅典大学拜占庭史家纳内蒂(Andrea Nanetti)所说,在博洛尼亚宗教学研究所(Fondazione per le scienze religiose di Bologna)的研究活动中,在意大利百科全书中心(Istituto della Enciclopedia Italiana)阿玛托主任(Giuliano Amato)的慷慨协作之下,这部圣经开始了一段新的旅程。

马可·波罗圣经历经修复、拍照,在圣经专家佛罗伦萨贝托里大主教(Giuseppe Betori)召开的会议中被多方研究,此后又在2012年1月意大利总统纳波里塔诺(Giorgio Napolitano)访问博洛尼亚宗教学研究所时,得到了总统的赞许。如今我们得以完全地认识这部圣经,要归功于多位出色的历史学、语言学、抄本学及神学学者的不懈付出。而诸多机构和企业曾给予或将要给予该项文化事业的丰厚支持,则保证了来自于圣经的智慧得以在学术界流传,乃至进入大众视野。

如今,这部圣经不再仅是丝绸包裹,却配备上了学术研究成果和百科全书中心制作复本的先进技术,成为了文化和科技的见证。它已准备启程,从台伯河出发,穿越沙漠,翻山越岭,直抵它曾度过漫长岁月的东方,而包括意大利总理马里奥蒙迪在内的所有合作参与这项研究的欧洲和中国权威机构,都相信这次对话有着重大的价值和深远的意义。

这部圣经告诉我们,各个文化、各个大陆和各个传统之间的关系史,不是以日计数、而是以百年计的历史;这些关系既简单又复杂,必然遭遇变迁和演化,受到侵蚀和震荡,但这一切都无法斩断所有的牵连,无法抹去所有的印迹,无法摧毁那纤细而纯净的桥梁。

以"道"的思想实现和谐与幸福

〔日〕蜂屋邦夫

　　创造一个诸种文明和谐共处、全人类共同繁荣的世界,这是今天所有人共同的理念目标,然而现实情况却与之相隔千里。其主要原因在于,相互冲突的国家利益、狭隘的国家主义、缺乏包容精神的排他性宗教、只追求利润的经济行为、由不理解和排斥其他民族及其他人种而产生的民族主义及人种情绪等等。

　　在这种情况下,我们要如何才能实现一个让各种文明和谐共处、全人类繁荣幸福的世界呢? 我认为仍然只有一个办法,即研究过去长期而庞大复杂的人类历史、从各方面进行彻底通透的分析从而导出经验教训。这次的会议也是以此问题意识为基础的,而我除了立足于自己的研究领域别无他法,因此我将在研究古代中国各家思想的基础上来思考这个问题。

　　特别是春秋战国时期的中国社会与今天世界的情况颇为相似,那么生活在那个时代的人们是如何建构整个中国世界的和平与秩序的呢,我想弄清这一点具有非常重要的现实意义。只是我们还需要注意以下几点:虽然在春秋战国时代各国针锋相对,但是至少到春秋为止人们尚有隶属周王朝的意识和天下的概念;即使到了战国时代华夏世界观依然存在,人们怀有天下即将获得统一的预测或期待;人们意识到语言或文字上多少存在共通之处;人们还认识到,华夏和夷狄之间的人种对立并不是那么激烈,通过文化浸透和人种同化作用华夏世界是无限延展的等等。

上述几点与今天世界各种对立的实际情况并不相符,尽管如此,我依然认为春秋战国时代旨在统一的思想成就直到今天仍未失去其意义,因为这一思想成就中包含对普遍人性的洞察。

我想将其中对普遍人性的洞察凝聚为"道"的观念。"道"之一字源于中国,它包含着各种时代及地域特色,然而通过中国文化的传播它至少成为了东亚世界的共同观念。下面我想分析一下"道"的观念。

一、"道"的意义和儒家思想

"道"原本和西方的"way"及"Weg"一样是道路的意思。东汉许慎的《说文解字》中说,"道,所行道也。从辵从首。一达谓之道"(卷二下 辵部),其中对"路"的解释也是"道也。从足从各"(卷二下 足部),它是会意字,和道的意思一样。东汉刘熙的《释名》中说,"道一达曰道路。道,蹈也。路,露也。言人所践蹈而露见也"(释道第六),也就是说,道路就是人走过露出土的地方。

这些是东汉字典中的解释,可知"道"本来就是道路的意思。然而,它的意思逐渐发生了变化:先是指人们必经之处;而后意为行为准则,如道德、道术、道理、道统等词表现出的那样;后来又发展到广泛包含事物规律以至宇宙万物之原理及本体的意思。

在春秋战国思想史上具有重要意义的两个学派就是儒家和道家,因此我首先概述一下儒家的道的观念,它主要是指人类社会的实践道德。如"先王之道斯为美"(《论语·学而》)所说的那样,儒家所谓的道就是古代帝王制定并实践了的道德(据朱子的解释)。其实质内容是习惯上的礼文化传统,是在礼的基础上建立起来的上下身份秩序。《尚书·洪范》中说,礼的基本原则洪范九畴是上天赐予实践道的王者的。

孔子将道作为人类社会的最高理想,他说"道不行,乘桴浮于海"(《论语·公冶长》)、"志于道,据于德,依于仁"(《论语·述而》)。这就是说,道是行为准则,德是道的具体行为显现,仁是道德之根本。他对道的热衷可以从"朝闻道,夕死可矣"或"参乎,吾道一以贯之哉"(《论语·里仁》)等句中很好地体现出来。

　　孟子对"先王之道"作了更具体的充实,他认为实行仁义从而获得民心并和平治理天下的人才是得先王之道的王者,所谓"得道者多助,失道者寡助"(《孟子·公孙丑下》)。具体来说,此道即是人生来具备的仁义礼智"四德"和君臣、父子、兄弟、夫妇、朋友关系的"五伦",如"仁义礼智非由外铄我也。我固有之也"(《孟子·告子上》)。无论是孔子还是孟子,他们都认为道首先是由内在的觉悟唤起的东西。

　　荀子对道作了进一步的具体解释,他将道理解为实践意义上的礼,是"道德之极"(《荀子·劝学》)。他主张无论是修身还是治理国家都要遵循礼,如"礼者所以正身也"(《荀子·脩心》)、"为政不以礼,政不行矣"(《荀子·大略》)。《礼记》在此荀子学的基础上提出"道德仁义,非礼不成"(《曲礼上》)。可以说,荀子的"礼"是春秋战国末期对实践道德的道作出的一个结论。

　　由此可知,儒家的道与其说是一种普遍性的道德,其本质却是在礼的基础上建立的上下身份秩序。下面这段被认为是战国时期的言论清楚地表明了这一点,"天下有道,则礼乐征伐自天子出。天下无道,则礼乐征伐自诸侯出。自诸侯出,盖十世希不失矣。自大夫出,五世希不失矣。陪臣执国命,三世希不失矣。天下有道,则政不在大夫。天下有道,则庶人不议"(《论语·季氏》)。

　　然而,在春秋战国时代,孔子以后的确有人在探寻什么是与为政者相符的道德性内容,犹如"君子之德风也。小人之德草也。草上之风必偃"(《论语·颜渊》)一句表明的那样,当时人们讨论的除了王道以外还有圣人之道、君子之道等,这也是事实。像这样赋予政治以显著的道德性是儒家作出的贡献,从此以后中国的政治理念是以为政者的道德为支柱的,即便是名义上的,这也值得我们特书一笔。

二、道家的道的思想

　　(一)老子

儒家的道的观念重在政治和道德问题，与此相对，道家的道主要指天地万物生成的本源，道德的本质也完全存在于造化的自然原理。老子最早提出这一点，他说"有物混成，先天地生。寂兮寥兮，独立不改，周行而不殆，可以为天下母。吾不知其名，字之曰道。强为之名曰大"（《老子》第二十五章）。这段文字给人以类似于讨论宇宙起源的现代天文学的印象①。

第四十章中说"天下万物生于有，有生于无。反者道之动，弱者道之用"，所谓"弱"（柔弱）是指没有丝毫勉强却切实运行的状态；所谓"反"（回归根本）是指，从动植物等自然界万物年年岁岁生生流转然后到安静休息的运行方式中，他领悟到一定有个源头（无）使这些活动得以成立，那就是根本，而我们全都来自那个根本并要回到那里。他承认其中存在着可称为平静的必然性的东西（常）而非乱七八糟的偶然，因此他用道来表达。故而老子的道是存在于一切现象根源的永恒实体，如同第二十五章"人法地、地法天、天法道、道法自然"说的那样，老子通过长期不懈地观察天地之大从而得出了这样的构想。

我们说的站在观察者的立场上是指老子具备所谓的自然科学家的眼光。《老子》中有多处是否定"欲"的，而否定"欲"是指要采取客观的立场，例如第一章的"常无欲以观其妙"即是如此。老子从这种客观立场出发论述了天地自然及万物的生成，如第四十二章的"道生一，一生二，二生三，三生万物。万物负阴而抱阳，冲气以为和"等。我认为在春秋战国时代只有老子的思想中包含宇宙论的构想，这应该归功于他所谓自然科学家的一面。当然，尽管那只是一种直观而非科学。

老子从客观的角度出发观察天地自然，他获得了各种各样的发现。在老子的眼中，最重要的莫过于天地自然世界成立于一种玄妙的平衡之上。在第七十七章中相对于人道有一句话叫"天之道，损有余而补不足"，这正好体现了天的绝妙平衡。这种和谐的思想正是他从客观立场对天地自然进行观察的结果。

这还与老子为何尊重"一"的问题有关。第三十九章表达了这样一种与天地万物有关的思想，例如天既有晴天也有雨天，若全是晴天就会造成

① 下文对《老子》的解释均源于拙著《老子》（岩波文库），岩波书店，2008年12月。

旱魃,天就会裂掉,换言之,天的本质是晴即"清",不过"清"只有和非"清"的状态完美混合、保持平衡才能永久存在下去。纷繁多样的现象互相配合保持均衡,天地万物不失其本质,老子用"一"来表达这种概括或平衡的意思。第十四章说"视之不见,名曰夷。听之不闻名曰希。搏之不得,名曰微。此三者不可致诘,故混而为一",此处的"一"也是概括的意思,"道"原本就有着如此无限的内容。这种"一"的思想也是和谐思想的重要方面。

这种"一"的思想还是调和二元对立的思想,是排除极端的思想。第二章中在"有无相生"之后列举了难易、长短等相对的概念组,这些对立项例如高低是以高的概念为基础的,只要牢记这一点就不会被相对的价值对立牵着走。于是它得出圣人不拘泥于此而"处无为之事、行不言之教"的结论。

由此看来,老子的目标是将所有文化都还原为白纸状态然后遵循自然的大道,而儒家所谓的王道及实践性的人道只不过是人为的、相对的道而已。这种思想体现在第十八章的"大道废,有仁义。智慧出,有大伪。六亲不和,有孝慈。国家昏乱,有忠臣"、第三十八章的"故失道而后德,失德而后仁,失仁而后义,失义而后礼。夫礼者,忠信之薄,而乱之首。前识者,道之华,而愚之始"等处。

而排除极端思想这一点体现在如第二十九章的"圣人去甚、去奢、去泰"一句中,还有第三十九章也说王侯一直拥有最高权力是非常危险的。在《老子》一书中,如第九章表现出来的避免自盈自满的思想也非常引人注目,可以说这种思想是将通过观察天地自然得出的"道"的思想运用到安身处世的"德"上的结果。这种避免自盈自满的思想即使在现代也具有非常深刻的意义。

老子还认为天地自然本身不会走极端,一旦到达极限就会反向回归本元。第十六章说"夫物芸芸,各复归其根"、第二十五章说"大曰逝,逝曰远,远曰反"、第三十四章说"万物归焉(=道)而不为主",这些都是说万物最终都会回归到"道"这一根本。

老子通过对天地自然的观察得出的一个奇特思想,那就是对无限大的发现。第四十一章中有一段由此而发的独特警句,"大方无隅,大器晚(=免)成,大音希声,大象无形"。的确,它打破了人们局限于常规的思维方式,解放了人们被缠绕在日常繁琐中的心灵 ①。

总之,老子认为道派生天地万物,所谓遵循道的生存方式就是无欲恬淡、清静柔弱、无为的生活方式。道既是外在的客观法则,也是人内在的道德原理。严格区分内外之别是近现代的合理主义思想,而这种合理主义思想在现实国际形势中的对立面前几乎无可奈何,虑及此,老子的道的思想不是更值得我们重新探讨和评价吗?

老子的思想中还包括一个独特的政策论,即希望大者自重、以及尊重小者的讨论。例如第六十一章说"大国者下流,天下之交,天下之牝。牝常以静胜牡,以静为下。故大国以下小国,则取小国。小国以下大国,则取(于)大国。……夫两者各得其所欲,大者宜为下",此外第八十章提到"小国寡民"。

只是,小国寡民的理想世界获得实现的结果就是自给自足的小规模封闭性农村社会,我们承认老子身上存在许多以这种理念为首的极端反文明的思想。从本次"全体繁荣"的主题来看这的确存在着问题,那么我们该如何调和老子的反文明论和今天的文明之间的矛盾呢,要解决这个问题就还需要我们作进一步的探讨。

(二)老子思想的展开

我想举两个例子来说明老子思想对后世的影响,一是它对 12 世纪在金国统治下的华北产生的全真教的影响,一是它对俄罗斯大文豪列夫·托尔斯泰(Lev Tolstoy)的影响。

1. 王重阳和老子

全真教是由王重阳(1112－1170)初创、其弟子马丹阳及丘长春扩大并确立起来的。丘长春受到蒙古成吉思汗的尊重并获得在蒙古势力范围布教的权利,于是全真教在元代有了长足发展,后来与正一教旗鼓相当直至今日。从中国的信仰和社会的问题角度来看它是个极为重要的宗教②。

王重阳在《望蓬莱·醴泉觅钱》中咏道"能下手。便晓这元元。为甚得

---

① 请参考拙稿《老子的自然,大和无限的思想》,钦伟刚译,收录于盖建民编:《开拓者的足迹卿希泰先生八十寿辰纪念文集》,四川出版集团,巴蜀书社,2010 年 8 月。

② 请参考拙著《金代道教研究－王重阳与马丹阳－》,钦伟刚译,海外道教学译丛,中国社会科学出版社,2007 年 6 月。

通三一法。都缘悟彻五千言。立起本根源"(《重阳全真集》卷4),说其修行以《老子》为基础。"元元"即玄玄,此据《老子》第一章;而"三一法"当为锻炼精气神、统一为一气的意思,许是源自《老子》第四十二章。王重阳在领悟内丹术之前喜读《老子》,《老子》的道理存在于王重阳的思想最深处。

将王重阳大力推往道教内丹术方向的是某道士传授的内丹术口诀,因此王重阳在入道之初无疑十分专心于内丹术的实践。但是,他一边勤于修炼内丹术,一边怀揣身体不过火风地水四假之集合的想法,要使尘土般的凡胎达到真实的状态,就必须依靠极其抽象的观念。这种观念不就是道家逍遥坦荡的心理状态、尤其是老子的道的理论吗?

王重阳还在《醴泉觅钱》中咏道"真大道。能结坎和离。认取五行不到处。须知父母未生时。此理勿难知"(同前),说"道"与"五行不到处"和"父母未生时"有关。简单说来,"五行不到处"是指天地得以成立的根本之道,"父母未生时"是意为本来面貌的禅语 ①,还是指根本之道。

像这样,王重阳通过透彻理解《老子》之道而假定一切现象的背后都存在一个元初的根源性实体。王重阳的道教相信那个根源性的道是实际存在的,通过他亲身感受那个道还贯彻于自己体内而使宗教得以成立。那个自己体内的道就是"本来真性"。

"重阳祖师修仙了性秘诀"(收于《晋真人语录》)虽然还不能被确定是王重阳的真迹,但它非常准确地表述了王重阳的教义。读了这份资料就会发现,其中有非常之多的部分都与《老子》的语句有关。这些《老子》的内容有:例如"大道"玄妙、无言无情,用语言难以理解;人的自处方式应该是柔弱谦下、先人后己、冲和无为,如此还能长生久视等等。由此可知,王重阳引用《老子》的范围包括道的根源性及超语言性、无争谦下的生存方式、尊重无为等等。

对于道士来说最终目标就是成仙,而王重阳的成仙思想是建立在坚信道的根源性的基础上的。道是开天辟地之前(五行不到处、父母未生时)就已有的本源性存在,因此是超越时代和地域的普遍性存在,而成仙就是在

---

① 《碧岩录》卷三,第二十一则"智门莲花荷叶"。北宋圆悟的《评唱》中有"父母未生时如何"一句。

这种固有的普遍性中释放自己。

由于人的身体具备天地之理,因此修行就是发现人自身中的天地之理。这就要放弃作为、让身体回到根本的状态,放弃作为就是任其自然(处于真实的状态)。让身体顺其自然就是让心顺其自然,其极致就是"病即教他病,死即教他死"①的境界,这些自然状态中伴随着"抱道"的内涵。我认为这种想法直到今日仍然具有一定的价值。

2. 托尔斯泰和老子

托尔斯泰(1828-1910)从1878年开始对老子产生兴趣,尤其是1884年之后甚至要将法文译本的《老子》翻译成俄语,由此可见其热衷程度。在他用自己的方式翻译完法文译本后的第二年、即1885年9月,他写了一篇题为《傻瓜伊凡》的民间故事,并于10月完稿。收录这则故事的民间故事集中共有14篇,其他故事都有清晰的来源(原典),唯独《傻瓜伊凡》的出处无法明确②。我个人以为其源泉是老子思想。当然,《傻瓜伊凡》中除了老子思想以外还有许多其他思想,不过我认为构成其核心的是老子的思想ⅰ③。

伊凡王国的人民都是些除了流汗务农别无所长的傻瓜,但是只要强调与农民协调一致和泛劳动主义,就不需要所谓"王国"的"统治"形态。这种"统治"和人民的状态用老子的语言来说就是,伊凡王"处无为之事……万物(万民)作焉而不辞"(第二章)、"圣人无常心,以百姓心为心"(第四十九章),国王(我)和人民的关系就是"我无为而民自化。我好静而民自正。我无事而民自富。我无欲而民自朴"(第五十七章),而人民就是"民莫之令而自均"(第三十二章)。

伊凡王国曾遭到他国的侵略,但王国的人们放任他们的侵略行为任其掠夺,终于到最后侵略军们丧失了劲头而撤军。可以说这种应对与托尔斯泰理解的老子的不抵抗和平主义(第八章、第六十一章、第八十一章)完全

---

① 《长春丘真人寄西州道友书》(《真仙直指语录》卷上):祖师云"无为道者,先舍家而后舍身。病即教他病,死即教他死。至死一著,抱道而亡,任从天断"。

② 见《民间故事与少年物语》的译者解说,该作品收于《托尔斯泰全集》13,中村白叶译,河出书房新社,1973年。

③ 请参考拙稿《〈傻瓜伊凡〉和老子》(上、中、下),载于《UP》第176-178期,1987年6月-8月,东京大学出版会。曹章祺译,载于《孔子研究》总第二十二期,1991年第二期,1991年6月,孔子基金会。

相符。

从 1894 年到 1895 年期间,托尔斯泰协助一位名叫小西增太郎(1861 –
1939)的日本人翻译《老子》并谈论了许多意见①。托尔斯泰想象中的老子
是个完全否定军事行为的绝对和平主义者,可是《老子》中也有"兵者不祥
之器,非君子之器。不得已而用之,恬淡为上……"(第三十一章)等语句,
而托尔斯泰则激动地说,"老子这般人物是不可能说这种话的,这部分绝对
是后人添加的"。托尔斯泰只将与绝对和平相关的部分提取出来看做老子
的思想。

此外,《傻瓜伊凡》中还出现了拒绝使用头脑工作的思想,说那完全是
不尊重"愚"的生存方式的行为。这是老子极富特色的思想,在第二十章、
第四十八章、第六十五章等处都有体现。

托尔斯泰这种不抵抗的绝对和平主义思想还对圣雄甘地(Mohandas
K. Gandhi,1869 – 1948)产生了影响。他在南非居住了二十几年,1910 年
代在约翰内斯堡近郊建立了共同农场,这是非暴力不合作运动(Satya-graha
Movement)的一环,他们实践了自给自足的平等主义生活。他对托尔斯泰
的思想产生了共鸣,从而将自己的农场命名为"托尔斯泰农场",并给托尔
斯泰写了信。当然他的思想基础受到印度宗教及历史等影响,但他的非暴
力思想的直接依据却被认为是托尔斯泰的和平思想。

由此可知,此处存在一条内容为老子 – 托尔斯泰 – 甘地的联系链条。
假使我们现在将老子的思想直接运用于现实,不知道它对严峻的世界形势
是否管用。但是,正是在战乱及敌对不止、环境恶化、大量的人们苦于饥饿
和疾病的现代,可以说老子的思想才更加具有意义。

(二)庄子

庄子也将道理解为宇宙的本源,"自本自根,未有天地,自古以固存,神
鬼神帝,生天生地"(《庄子·大宗师》)。

道是超出人的智力所能理解的范围的,《庄子·应帝王》中的一则寓言象征
性地说明了这一点,"南海之帝为儵,北海之帝为忽,中央之帝为浑沌。儵与忽,

---

① 请参考小西增太郎写的自叙传《我谈托尔斯泰》(『Tolstoyを語る』),岩波书店,1936 年 10
月。

时相与遇于浑沌之地。浑沌待之甚善。儵与忽，谋报浑沌之德，曰：'人皆有七窍，以视听食息，此独无有。尝试凿之。'日凿一窍，七日而浑沌死"。庄子一面继承了老子的道的思想，同时在语言表达上体现出独特的创意。

道是宇宙本源，因而无处不在。关于道之所在的问题，东郭子提问说"所谓道恶乎在"，庄子答曰"无所不在"，东郭子进一步追问，庄子接着答曰"在蝼蚁"，后来又回答说在稊稗及瓦甓中，最后回答说在屎溺中（《庄子·知北游》）。东郭子对其答案无语了，庄子于是告诉他"汝唯莫必，无乎逃物，至道若是"。庄子特意使用粗俗的表达是为了打破世人的常规，这与后来禅的问答有相通之处。

《庄子》中反复提到道是无法用常识及语言来把握的，《庄子·天地》中的寓言就象征性地说明了这一点，"黄帝游乎赤水之北，登乎昆仑之丘而南望，还归，遗其玄珠。使知索之而不得，使离朱索之而不得，是喫诟索之而不得也。乃使象罔，象罔得之。黄帝曰，'异哉，象罔乃可以得之乎'"。玄珠是对道的比喻，知、离朱、喫诟分别是对智慧、眼睛、善辩的拟人，象罔是无形之物，比喻无心。

庄子不太关心老子说的统治之术，而很看重通过遵道达到精神解脱的一面。《庄子·大宗师》中说"古之真人，不知说生，不知恶死……不以心捐（＝捐）道，不以人助天"，说明人心和天地自然的活动一样自由、不受感情约束。《庄子·人间世》说"乘物以游心，托不得已，以养中"，这是说遵照天地自然的旨意（不得已。即道）解放心灵，培养中正的境界。这些都表达了自我意识消失、一切归于道之世界的意思，同时《庄子·齐物论》中又说"天地与我并生，而万物与我为一"，意思是只要抛开对立及常识并站在天的立场上，万物就能与我成为一体，即我的意识反而扩展得大如天地。

庄子这种道的观念是在彻底分析自我存在的基础上展开来的，因此他深刻的人性观即使到现在仍然是值得我们汲取的思想源泉之一。

结束语

在本次发表中我认为，研究中国春秋战国时代的思想将有助于提供一种方法,这种方法是为了实现一个让各种文明和谐共处、全人类繁荣幸福的世界。在此我主要举出了老子的"道"的思想,而道至少是东亚共通的概念,通过重新确认我们共同拥有道的思想的事实,也许能够找到某个共鸣之处。

儒家的道具体是指建立在礼的基础上的上下身份秩序。但是,也的确有人探寻了什么是与为政者相符的道德性内容,而为政治赋予道德性这点是儒家作出的贡献。

老子所说的道是指天地万物生成的本源和原理,道德的本质不外乎这一原理。道既是外在的客观法则,同时也是人内在的道德原理。

老子通过长期观察天地之大从而得出了这种构想。他从这种观察出发建构了以下思想,如天地自然在一种玄妙的平衡上得以成立、让事物停留在"一"的状态而不是追根究底、调和对立并排除极端等等。

遵循道的生存方式就是一种无欲恬淡、清静柔弱、无为的生存方式,由此他希望大者自重、尊重小者,并以小国寡民的社会为理想。我们还需要留意老子身上这种反文明的思想。

接着我简单谈论了王重阳的全真教和托尔斯泰对老子的理解,以此说明老子思想的展开情况。王重阳确信根源之道具有超越性和实在性,他的成仙思想是建立在这种基础上的。托尔斯泰将老子的思想理解为绝对的和平反战主义,并创作了《傻瓜伊凡》的民间故事。此外,和平反战的思想还对甘地产生了影响,老子 - 托尔斯泰 - 甘地这条线索的思想传承在世界史上都留下了足迹。

最后我提到了庄子的道的观念,庄子的言论是在彻底分析自我存在的基础上展开的,因此他对世人的深刻观察即使到现在仍是值得我们汲取的思想源泉之一。

（翻译：刘丽娇）

"文道之神"的诞生

——日本学术之神菅原道真思想的历史意义

[日]吉原浩人

　　菅原道真(845－903)在日本广为人知。文章道出身的道真在平安前期已经破格晋升至"从二位右大臣兼右大将"。我们可以从《菅家文草》、《菅家后草》中收藏的诗文以及《日本三代实录》、《类聚国史》的编纂得知他的绚丽文采。

　　但是,为日本所熟知的菅原道真形象毋宁说是在全国各地的天满宫所供奉的"天神"。日本人对其"学问之神"的形象笃信之至,在中考、高考之际,或到天满宫参拜,或在绘马匾上写祈祷文,抑或在此购买护身符带入考场来祈求考试合格。换而言之,菅原道真在日本的地位与孔子在中国的地位异曲同工。孔子在中国乃至世界各地的文庙(孔子庙)被供奉,作为圣人被敬仰。在儒教中孔子被神化,有专门为孔子举行的祭祀,名为释奠。在中国的前近代时期,孔子庙被称为圣庙;在日本提到圣庙,则是指祭奠菅原道真的太宰天满宫、北野天满宫、吉祥院天满宫等。

　　虽说都是学术之父,但菅原道真与孔子最大的差异在于菅原道真在左迁至九州太宰府后死于非命,在其逝世后 20 年左右才被奉为神。这是因为,当时平安京接连发生雷电和疫病等灾害,人们猜想是道真的冤魂在作祟,为平息其怨灵,则在京城外的北野这个地方将其供奉。也就是说,道真作为神被敬仰的直接原因与孔子不同;道真被供奉并非是出于其在思想和学术方面成就显著。

　　菅原道真的"文道之祖"之称，始于986年庆滋保胤对道真的评价"文道之祖，诗境之主"。1009年，大江匡衡在此基础上有称之为"文道之大祖，风月之本主"。这一表达在镰仓时代初期创作的《北野天神缘起》的抬头被引用为"追根溯源，其为文道之大祖，风月之本主"，这样道真在日本作为"学问之神"的形象不久便广为人之。

　　不过，"文道"这个词，到底是什么意思呢。实际上，在中国唐代以前，"文道"这个词很少被使用。即便是对日本思想和文学都具有巨大影响的白居易的作品中也仅出现一次而已。

　　我认为"文道"一词包含有日本独特的文化意义。在这次发表中，我想就"文道"这一概念，查找中日文献，并对其在两国文献中的不同含义进行比较。另外，我想就"神"这一概念进行溯源，比较中国的"神"和日本的"神道"，肃清两者在天神信仰方面各自的含义。

一、日本的学制与释奠的祭祀

　　日本平安时代（794—1185）的实职官员培养是在大学寮里进行的，而大学寮是参考奈良时代（710—794）中国唐朝的学制而设立的。这种培养制度相当于唐朝的国子监制度，主要学习中国的经典、史书，也就是三史十三经、《文选》以及日本的律令制。根据《延喜式》第二十卷《大学寮》中记载，《礼记》、《春秋左氏传》、《周礼》、《仪礼》、《毛诗》、《律》、《令》、《周易》、《尚书》、《论语》、《孝经》、《史记》、《汉书》、《后汉书》、《文选》被列为大经，而《春秋公羊传》、《春秋穀梁传》、《孙子》等其他著书则被列为小经。①

　　大学寮开设了明经、纪传、明法、算道等课程。在奈良时代，明经道相对受到重视，而从平安初期开始，纪传道开始逐渐兴盛，俗称文章道。这是

————

　　① 桃裕行『桃裕行著作集』第一卷「上代学制の研究〔修訂版〕」（思文閣出版，1994，初出1947）など参照。

因为文章道通过文章生考试的选拔,只募集少量的学生(文章生),他们通过学习,能够作为实职官员撰写公文书,或是为达官显贵们代写私人的表、奏折以及愿文等等,这在当时被看作是出人头地的一条捷径。文章生经过再次选拔,成为文章得业生,并参加令制中最高级别的职称考试——方略试,通过这个考试的文章道出身的官员被称作儒家或者儒士。作为最高级知识分子的儒家们有着强烈的支撑整个国家思想的主人公意识,并承担着撰写高水准文章的责任和义务。儒家中的最高层被称为文章博士,作为指导者统率着整个儒门。

在二月和八月的上丁之日(农历每月上旬的丁日)举行的"释奠"是为隶属大学寮各道官员的上任而举办的最重要的仪式。《延喜式》第二十卷《大学寮》中,用超过半数的篇幅记载了"释奠"的流程。虽说是祭奠孔子以及以颜回为首的九贤弟子的仪式,但执行者却是王卿官员以及大学寮的工作人员,与僧侣和神官毫无干系。"释奠"原本是中国古代的宗教仪式,传入日本后其宗教性被淡化,主要以讨论会和宴请为中心。关于"释奠"的情形首次记载于《续日本纪》大宝元年(701)二月条。另外,在《藤氏家传》下卷《武智麻吕传》中,引用了庆云二年(705)二月释奠中写给孔子的祭文。也就是说,自奈良时代开始,日本与中国一样定期举办"释奠",讲孔子供奉为学问之祖。[①]

二、菅原道真与天神信仰的概要

菅原道真(845-963)就是在上述学制中脱颖而出,被选拔为文章博士的,闪耀在日本平安时代文化史上的一颗璀璨的文曲星。他主持了《日本三代实录》、《类聚国史》等国史的编纂,撰写了《菅家文草》、《菅家后草》等诗集。另外,他还积极参与国家政治,并被破格选拔为从二位右大臣兼右大将,这对于一个出身于平安时代纪传道的学者来说,已是至高无上的荣

---

① 吉原浩人「院政期の思想—江家における累葉儒家意識と系譜の捏造—」(佐藤弘夫編『日本思想史講座 1 —古代』、ぺりかん社、2012)。

誉了。

　　菅原道真的祖父清公（770－842）曾在中国留学，被选为文章博士，继而提拔为从三位。他创办了文章院，设立了专门为纪传道学生准备的宿舍兼教室。后来，这些宿舍及教室分为东西两曹，菅原氏掌管东曹，大江氏掌管西曹，东西曹主的任命均采取世袭制。道真的父亲是善（812－880）亦由文章博士提拔为从三位参议。也就是说，菅原家祖孙三代都曾攀上学儒阶层的顶峰，甚至荣升为贵族、公卿。

　　然而，菅原道真之所以在日本声名远扬，并非因为他是平安时代最优秀的文章家，而是因为他死后，被供奉为神。将历史人物菅原道真供奉为神的信仰，在日本被称为天神信仰。这起源于菅原道真被当时的左大臣藤原时平一派诬告，于昌泰四年（901）被贬为太宰权帅，流放至九州太宰府，并于延喜三年（903）在住所死于非命。自此以后，参与诬告道真的贵族们相继离奇死亡，天变地异，人们唯恐是道真的怨灵作祟，便将其供奉为御灵神。

　　"天神"一词原本是与"地祇"相对应，日文训读读作"Amatsukami·Kunitsukami"。在日本，"天神"（天津神）指的是在高天原居住的神，或者是从高天原降临的神，"地祇"（国津神）指的是在地上居住的神。天神与地祇合称神祇，而天皇被看作是天津神的子孙，因此，天神、地祇是为了把日本八百万神统一编入大系而人为造出的概念。由此可见，天神并非是一个固有名词。然而，自从菅原道真被供奉为"大富天神"以及"火雷天神"①，"天神"一词一般特指道真。

　　在天神信仰的土壤中，曾经兴盛过御灵信仰。含冤而死的冤魂导致瘟疫、天变地异以及妖魔鬼怪的出没，通过祭祀这些怨灵可以达到辟邪的作用。御灵信仰便是这样一种信仰。在奈良时代，同日而薨的井上内亲王、他户亲王母子的怨念尤为强烈，于是人们修建了御灵社以及附属的神宫寺，以此抚慰他们的灵魂。贞观五年（863），崇道天皇（早良亲王）、伊予亲

① 道真の薨去は延喜三年（903）二月二十五日であるが、平安後期に編纂さた『扶桑略記』同年四月二十日条に、「前右大臣菅原朝臣、詔賜本職、兼増一階。并棄去昌泰四年正月二十五日宣命、令燒却之。勅号大富天神」とある。『新訂増補国史大系』では、この部分を『梅城録』により「火雷天神」と校訂する。そのため、研究者がどちらを採るかにより、二種の表記が存する。

王、橘逸势等六处举行了祭祀活动,在京都神泉苑也常年经营着盛大的御灵会。自此以后,当宫中妖魔鬼怪出没或是瘟疫流行时,便举行诵经、悔过法要或是向名神献币等活动来抚慰怨灵。①

道真的死于非命后二十年,即延喜二十三年(923),藤原时平的侄子(妹妹的儿子)保明亲王去世,年仅二十一岁。《日本纪略》延喜二十三年三月二十一日条有如下记载。

是日也,依皇太子卧病,大赦天下。子刻,皇太子保明亲王薨,年二十一。天下庶人莫不悲泣,其声如雷。举世云,菅帅灵魂宿忿所为也。

也就是说,举国人民都认为,保明亲王的英年早逝应归咎于曾任太宰权帅的菅原道真的"灵魂宿忿"。于是,延喜八年(908)藤原菅根的去世,翌年藤原时平于三十九岁英年早逝,以及前前后后的数次瘟疫、旱魃都使人们把矛头指向了道真,认为是他的怨恨在作祟。于是,延喜二十三年四月,道真左迁的诏书被收回,恢复了其声誉。但是,道真的怨恨并没有因此而消失,延长八年(930)六月,藤原清贯在宫中清凉殿被雷电击中而死,紧接着九月醍醐天皇驾崩。接二连三的离奇事件使得人们对道真的怨灵愈加恐惧。在这种气氛中,天庆五年(942)人们认为道真将灵魂托宣至多治比文子,于是在平安京右近马场修建了北野社。在太宰府道真的庙所中也建造了安乐寺,并在菅原家的氏寺——吉祥院祭祀道真的灵魂。由于这一系列宗教场所的修建,道真信仰迅速发展起来,民间盛行着供奉道真的肖像画、雕刻品等活动。尤其是与道真有着密切关系的场所被称为"圣庙",在平安时代中期,主要有以下三处圣庙。②

太宰府·安乐寺 = 安乐寺圣庙,现在的太宰府天满宫

洛外·北野社 = 北野圣庙,现在的北野天满宫

洛外·吉祥院 = 吉祥院圣庙,现在的吉祥院天满宫

---

① 御霊信仰と天神信仰については、民衆宗教史叢書第四巻『天神信仰』(雄山閣、1983)、真壁俊信『天神信仰の基礎的研究』(近藤出版社、1984)、上田正昭『天満天神—御霊から学問へ』(筑摩書房、1988)、真壁俊信『天神信仰史の研究』(続群書類従完成会、1994)、村山修一『天神御霊信仰』(塙書房、1996)、河音能平『天神信仰の成立—日本における古代から中世の移行—』(塙書房、2003)、真壁俊信『天神信仰と先哲』(太宰府天満宮文化研究所、2005)、竹居明男編『北野天神縁起を読む』(吉川弘文館、2008)など参照。

② 中世には、道真の本貫である河内道明寺も聖廟と呼ばた。

这三处圣庙都是僧职高于神职的神宫寺。北野社在创建初期,对外公开的称呼是北野寺,但实际上也叫做北野宫寺。宫寺是指主要由僧侣创建并运营的庙社,它既是神社,也是寺院,是一种特殊的形态。①

另外,在当时出现的《日藏梦记》一书中,道真成为了"日本太政威德天",而醍醐天皇却下了地狱。这在当时引起了极大的轰动。到了镰仓初期,绘卷的名作《北野天神缘起》出版,它的复制版广泛传播,为鼓吹天神信仰起到了非常重要的作用。平安后期,道真又被当作十一面观音的垂迹神,于是天神信仰又与观音信仰以及净土信仰结合在一起,甚至人们信仰他是通往极乐净土的指引者。另外,将道真本人供奉为阿弥陀、毗沙门天、大圣欢喜天、辩才天等。如今,将菅原道真作为祭神供奉的神社有天神社、天满宫、菅原神社、北野神社、老松神社等共一万两千多处。

三、作为"文道之大祖"的天神

如上所述,菅原道真著文无数,掌管私塾"菅家廊下",其门下英才辈出。人们给予菅原道真天下第一文人的褒奖不仅仅局限于平安时代,而是贯穿了整个日本历史。因此,如今道真作为学问之神被供奉是情理之中。②但是,从上述考察可以看出,最初人们供奉道真缘起于他的怨灵作祟,是作为御灵神供奉的。

那么,从何时开始,又是通过何人之手,使得天神摇身一变,成为学问之神的呢?令人意外的是,关于此方面的研究至今凤毛麟角,笔者试图探索供奉"文道之大祖"的滥觞。

---

① 宫寺には、別当? 検校? 長吏などと呼ばる長官が置か、世襲妻帯を許さた僧侶が勤め、神職はその下位に置かた。宫寺の代表的な存在としては、石清水八幡宮護国寺? 祇園感神院(現八坂神社)、あるいは修験系の熊野? 白山などがある。こらはかつて、本質的には寺院であったが、明治初年の神仏分離によって仏教色が一掃さた。

② 学問の神としての菅原道真の性格については、以下のような研究がある。久保田収「学問の神」(『菅原道真と太宰府天満宮』上巻、吉川弘文館、1975)、長沼賢海「天満天神の信仰の変遷」(村山修一編『天神信仰』、雄山閣出版、1983、初出1918)、林家辰三郎「天神信仰の遍歴」(同前、初出1977)、同「天神信仰の展開—御霊から学問の神へ—」(上田正昭編『天満天神 御霊から学問神へ』、筑摩書房、1988)。

　　天神之所以成为如今的学问之神,其决定性的一环是镰仓初期成书的《北野天神缘起》第一段,将菅原道真称为"文道之大祖"。

　　追其本源,文道之大祖,风月之本主……

　　这里出现的"文道之大祖,风月之本主"一文至今为止被无数次引用,从而确立了天神"文道之祖"的地位。这一说法的直接出处是宽弘六年(1009),向北野天神祈祷疾病痊愈的大江匡衡(952－1012)在《北野天神供御币并种种物文》(《本朝文萃》第十三卷)中的说法。

　　右天满自在神,或盐梅于天下,辅导一人,或日月于天上,照临万民。就中文道之大祖,风月之本主也。

　　可以看出,《北野天神缘起》中的引用将上文前后顺序进行了互换。而大江匡房参考的典故是宽和二年(986)庆滋保胤(?－1002)为举办北野庙前《法华经》作文会而撰写的《赛菅丞相庙愿文》(《本朝文萃》第十三卷)。

　　其一愿曰,就天满天神庙,会文士、献诗篇。以其天神为文道之祖、诗境之主也。

　　由此看出,正是由于庆滋保胤将天神称作"文道之祖",才有了道真的"学问之神"之称。

四、"圣庙文学"的产生

　　上述作品的作者庆滋保胤、大江匡衡是活跃在平安中期,出身于纪传道的贵族阶层。当时藤原摄关家成为日本权力的中心,也称作摄关期。太政大臣藤原道长(966－1027)手下活跃着紫式部、清少纳言等女性文学家,是日本文化发展史上非常重要的时期。此外,由于菅原道真的建议而终止遣唐使制度以来,日本与中国大陆文化交流也几乎完全停止。然而,随着宋朝一统江山,两国的商人又开始新的往来,带来了最新的情报和两国的文物。①

　　平安时代的圣庙中产生了许许多多的诗词和和歌,但是散文主要有以下诗序、愿文、祭文、告文等。

　　1. 大江以言《三月尽日陪吉祥院圣庙同赋古庙春方暮》(《本朝文萃》第十卷《诗序三·圣庙》、《本朝丽藻》下卷)

　　2. 高阶积善《七言九月尽日侍北野庙各分一字》(《本朝文萃》第十卷《诗序三·圣庙》、《本朝丽藻》下卷)

　　3. 源相亲《初冬陪菅丞相庙同赋篱菊有残花诗序》(《本朝文萃》第十一卷《诗序四·草》)

　　4. 庆滋保胤《赛菅丞相庙愿文》(《本朝文萃》第十三卷《愿文上·神祠修缮》)

　　5. 大江匡衡《北野天神供御币并种种物文》(《本朝文萃》第十三卷《祭文在供物》、《朝野群载》第二卷)

　　6. 藤原敦基《七言春陪吉祥院圣庙同赋樱花残古社诗一首》(《本朝续文萃》第八卷《诗序上·圣庙》)

　　7. 大江匡房《七言秋日陪安乐寺圣庙同赋神德契暇年诗一首》(《本朝文萃》第八卷《诗序上·圣庙》)

　　8. 大江匡房《七言早春内宴陪安乐寺圣庙同赋春来悦多诗一首》(《本朝续文萃》第八卷《诗序上·时节》)

　　9. 大江匡房《七言三月三日陪安乐寺圣庙同赋栾流叶胜游诗一首》(《本朝续文萃》第八卷《诗序上·时节》)

　　10. 藤原明衡《九日陪圣庙听讲法华经诗一首》(《本朝续文萃》第八卷《诗序上·法会》·《三十五文集》)

---

　　①　この時期の日宋間の交流については、木宮泰彦『日華文化交流史』(冨山房、1955)、『塚本善隆著作集』第七巻「浄土宗史? 美術篇」(大東出版社、1975)、木宮之彦『入宋僧奝然の研究—主としてその随身品と将来品—』(鹿島出版会、1983)、『西岡虎之助著作集』第三巻「文化史の研究Ⅰ」(三一書房、1984)、木宮之彦『日宋文化交流史—主として北宋を中心に—』(鹿島出版会、1987)、上川通夫『日本中世仏教形成史論』(校倉書房、2007)など。また、吉原浩人「慶滋保胤「奝然上人入唐時為母修善願文」考」(林雅彦? 小池淳一編『唱導文化の比較研究』、岩田書院、2011)、同「慶滋保胤の奝然入宋餞別詩序—白居易? 元稹詩文との交響—」(河野貴美子? 王勇編『東アジアの漢籍遺産—奈良を中心として』、勉誠出版、2012)参照。

11. 大江匡房《于安乐寺被供养大般若经愿文》(《江都督纳言愿文集》第三卷)

12. 大江匡房《安乐寺内满愿寺愿文》(《江都督纳言愿文集》第三卷)

13. 大江匡房《北野》(《三十五文集》)

按照不同圣庙分类,得出以下结论。

安乐寺圣庙……3、7、8、9、11、12

北野圣庙……2、4、5、10、13

吉祥院圣庙……1、6

文人们经常聚集于这些圣庙中,举行作文会或法会等。在这样的场合创作出的汉室和和歌,我想把它们成为"圣庙文学"。在关于天神信仰史的研究中,缺乏对圣庙文学综合研究的视点,因此今后笔者将尝试通过为每一部作品做注释,以小见大,勾勒出天神信仰的整体架构。①

上述作品中,现存的最古老的作品是3,创作于康保元年(964)。其次是宽和二年(986)创作的4、长保元年(999)的1、宽弘元年(1004)的2、宽弘六年(1009)的5。

五、劝学会的影响

上述作者当中,庆滋保胤、大江以言、大江匡衡、高阶积善四位是日本思想史上著名的劝学会的参与者。劝学会是应和四年(964)成立的法会。每年三月和九月的十五日,天台宗的僧侣和大学北堂的学生,二十人为一组在佛寺集结,作为现当二世之友,互相交流佛法与文道。成立劝学会的意图正在于此,加上天台宗的精英和纪传道的年轻知识分子也都争先恐后地参加,因此,劝学会对日本佛教史、思想史、文学史的发展产生了极其重

---

① この研究については、以下の科研費を得ており、本稿はこの成果の一部である。平成23~26年度日本学術振興会科学研究費補助金基盤研究（C）「「聖廟文学」の思想—平安朝文人貴族の天神信仰—」、課題番号23520108。

要的影响,关于劝学会的研究也屡见不鲜。①

　　在劝学会,僧侣们每天清晨讲诵《法华经》,傍晚念诵南无阿弥陀佛,一直到翌日破晓,不停吟咏赞佛之诗,而这些诗歌均被收入寺中保管。这种说法源于白居易晚年曾将自己的文集收入了洛阳香山寺。也就是说,劝学会除了是以《法华经》为基础的天台宗教学、净土宗念佛为主要形式外,白居易的诗文也对其产生了重要的影响。白居易在《香山寺白氏洛中集记》(《白氏文集》第七十卷)中曾经这样说。

　　我有本愿,愿以今生世俗文字之业,狂言绮语之过,转为将来世世赞佛乘之因,转法轮之缘也。

　　其中,狂言奇语之过,转为将来世世赞佛乘之因这句话,对日本的文人产生了很大的影响。作为官僚阶层的儒者们,靠撰写四六骈俪文维持生计。骈俪文要求必须有典可考,文章形式也要以《文选》为模版,并以华丽的辞藻装点。但是这种作文方法在信奉佛祖、祈求来世平安的场合,就显得有些无病呻吟,违背了佛教的基本教义,即必须抱有执着之心。

　　白居易在《六讚偈序》(《白氏文集》第七十卷)中有如下说法:

　　乐天常有愿,愿以今生世俗文笔之因,翻为来世讚佛乘转法轮之缘也。(中略)故作六偈,跪唱于佛法僧前,欲以起因发缘,为来世张本也。

　　在这里,白居易赞颂了佛法僧三宝以及众生,并祈请六首忏悔、发愿的偈文能够为来世张本。也就是说,用狂言绮语装饰诗文虽然只会加深前世留下的烦恼之业,但亦可戏剧性得转化为来世通往往生极乐的善根。

　　平安中期,出身于纪传道的日本学者们,为白居易的这种思想所倾倒。白居易晚年以净土信仰为轴心,对《法华经》的思想也有很深的理解。大学北堂的学生们以白居易的佛教信仰为基础,学习他的行文思想,便是劝学会创立的初衷。

　　法会的日子定在每月十五日,也就是象征佛祖圆满悟道的满月之日。因此,劝学会使用的诗文,都是尽可能从《法华经》及其注释、净土经典、《涅

---

　　① 勧学会の研究は、桃裕行著作集1『上代学制の研究〔修訂版〕』(思文閣出版、1994、初出1947)、小原仁『文人貴族の系譜』(吉川弘文館、1987)、後藤昭雄『平安朝漢文文献の研究』(吉川弘文館、1993)ほか数多い。

槃经》以及白居易的作品中选出更多词汇,以此为行文规范。这种现象曾经隐约可见,而笔者通过对劝学会的诗文逐字逐句的研究,能够更加清晰地证明这一点。①

另外,虽然与本文主题相去稍远,不做详细叙述,但是藤原明衡(989 - 1066)、藤原敦基(1046 - 1106)、大江匡房(1041 - 1111)等都是平安中期到后期的主流儒者。当然,他们的汉文学作品都收到了白居易的影响。另外,劝学会也断断续续地维持到了平安后期。也就是说,在至今为止的日本思想史研究中,将劝学会与"圣庙文学"结合起来进行论述的观念并不存在,但是今后,有必要将其作为一种思想运动重新把握。

六、"文道之祖""文道之大祖"全文

以上述内容为前提,笔者试图考察被供奉为神的菅原道真是如何被冠以"文道之祖"、"文道之大祖"之名的。首先,我将引用两篇曾经出现过这两个词语的文章全文。文章 A 是宽和二年(986)庆滋保胤在北野圣庙前为祈请《法华经》作文会的举办而撰写的愿文,B 是宽弘六年(1009)大江匡衡在北野圣庙前奉上的祭文。

A 庆滋保胤"赛菅丞相庙愿文"(《本朝文萃》第十三卷)

沙弥某前白佛言。往年为荣分,为声名,祈庙社,祈佛法,有日矣。遂其大成,徙于微官,是天之工也,是神之福也。其一愿曰,就天满天神庙,会文士,献诗篇。以其天神为文道之祖、诗境之主也。某暮年出家,一旦求道。今老沙弥,无便营风月之赛,此一乘教,有心展香花之筵。嗟呼花言绮语之游,何益于神道,希有难解之法,可期其佛身。当此时也,一神有庆,众生赖之。功德无边,普及一切,敬白。

---

① 以上は、吉原浩人「慶滋保胤勧学会詩序考―白居易との関連を中心に―」(吉原浩人？王勇編『海を渡る天台文化』、2008)、同「紀斉名勧学会詩序訳註」(『早稲田大学大学院文学研究科紀要』第五五輯第一分冊、2010)、同「紀斉名勧学会詩序考―十五日開筵の意義と白居易の仏教思想―」(『水門―言葉と歴史―』第二二号、勉誠出版、2010)、同「高階積善勧学会詩序考―白居易詩文と天台教学の受容―」(高松寿夫？儁雪艶編『古代日本文学と白居易』、勉誠出版、2010)などにおいて明らかにした。関連する論文？訳註も約十本執筆している。

宽和二年七月二十日

B 大江匡衡《北野天神供御币并种种物文》(《本朝文萃》第十三卷、《朝野群载》第二卷)

献上

御币上纸百贴供物二长柜中折柜

色纸绘马三疋走马十列

右天满自在天神,或盐梅于天下,辅导一人,或日月于天上,照临万民。就中文道之大祖、风月之本主也。翰林之人,尤可夙夜勤劳。而性愚事剧,思以涉年。爰露命半徂,无益噬脐,风情欲隐,不如倾首。昔彭祖七百载,已悔杖晚而早衰,今小子六十余,犹恨趋朝以不几。万死也,一生也,只仰神眷而已。匡衡病中,右笔伏地,敬白。

宽弘九年六月二十五日

正四位下行式部大辅兼文章博士丹波守大江朝臣匡衡敬白

首先,请看文章 A 的下划线部分,其中有"以其天神为文道之祖、诗境之主也"的叙述。另外,在文章 B 的下划线部分,也有"右天满自在天神,或盐梅于天下,辅导一人,或日月于天上,照临万民。就中文道之大祖、风月之本主也"这样的叙述。

七、"文道"一词的使用

在日文中使用的所有汉语词汇,都需要在中国的文献中查找出处。但是令人感到意外的是,"文道"一词在中国的文献中却鲜有发现。在白居易的《赋赋》(《白氏文集》第二十一卷)中,有这样的说法:

我国家恐文道寝衰,颂声凌迟,乃举多士,命有司,酌遗风于三代,明变雅于一时。

在这部作品中,白居易用"赋"这种华丽的文体叙述历史,并分析了这段历史的政治作用。国家"文道"式微,唯恐为太平盛世歌功颂德的民声消失,于是启用优秀的文人,任命为官员,汲取夏、殷、周三代遗风,凸显《诗经》中可以见到的"变雅"。在这里,非常重要的一点是,国家意识到"文道"的衰退。但是,在三史十三经以及其他中国古典名著中却难以见到"文道"一词。虽然在《全唐文》以及其他十三经注释雷的书籍中能够偶尔见到,但是,在平安时代的知识分子经常参照的汉学书籍中却无法见到"文道"一词。

那么,在日本"文道"一词究竟是如何出现的?最初此词见于天长四年(827)编纂的《经国集》第二十卷中收录的《延历二十年二月二十六日监视》一文:

问,摸阳而立文道,写阴而树武略。所以揖让之君,干戈之帝,是依世革。寔用斯绪,康时庇俗,庶听捐指。

这是延历二十年(801)对策文的全文。在开头部分,"文道"与"武略"相对应。

但是从那以后,直到平安中期,"文道"一词再未出现。源为宪(? - 1011)在永观二年(984)为尊子内亲王撰写的《三宝绘》下卷第十四篇《比睿坂本劝学会》中,有如下的说法。

クレノ春、スエノ秋ノ望ヲソノ日ニ定テ、経ヲ講ジ、仏ヲ念ズル事ヲ其勤トセム。コノ世、後ノ世ニ、ナガキ友トシテ、法ノ道、文ノ道ヲタガヒニアヒスゝメナラハム。

此文虽说不是汉文,但"法之道"和"文之道"相互呼应。这段话最能准确把握劝学会的特点,因此是劝学会研究不可或缺的宝贵资料。作者源为宪也是劝学会的成员,也是一名德高望重的文人。"法之道"指佛教,僧侣们与"文之道"进行互动,便是劝学会的本质。

平安中期关于"文道"一词的用法,在以下《本朝文萃》中可以见到。

C 大江匡衡《请持家鸿慈因准先例兼任辩官左右卫门权佐大学头等申他官替状》(第六卷)

以儒学为业,以风月为资。贫而乐道,未兼温官,贱而嗜文,难耐寒苦(中略)去秋遇重阳之宴,誇文道之已兴,今春贱朝拜之仪,感圣代之复旧。

D 大江匡衡《请殊蒙天恩依检非违使劳兼任越前尾张国主阙状》(第六卷)

去年之秋除目,文道成业之人多进,今年之春叙位,乱阶不次之赏不见。

E 大江匡衡《请特蒙天恩因准先例兼任备中介阙状》(第六卷)

右匡衡,伏见当时之政化,莫不延喜之旧风。文道渐兴,赏罚分明。天下幸甚,祝尧者多。爰匡衡业书籍而贫,携风月而老。(中略)因之今虽被兴文道,曾无尚儒尊师。

F 大江匡衡《请特蒙恬裁召问诸儒决是非今月十七日文章生试判违例不稳杂事状》(第七卷)

然则时栋诗已免瑕瑾。吹毛之求,还为文道之蠹害。

G 庆滋保胤《春日于右监门藤将军践能州源刺史赴任劝醉惜别》(第九卷)

右监门藤将军,花下移榻,月前命觞,践源能州。重文道也。

H 大江匡衡《为右近中将源宣方四十九日愿文》(第十四卷)

居武官而威风远扇,嗜文道而词露自鲜。

文章 C 有正历四年(993)正月十一日的日期标记,D 为长德二年(996)正月十五日,E 为长德二年四月二日,F 为长德三年七月二十日,H 为长德四年十月十二日。G 没有日期,但是源顺(911 – 983)被任命为能登守时在天元二年(979)正月。

由于篇幅所限,不能对每部作品进行详细说明,但是其中除了庆滋保胤的一篇,大江匡衡的五篇之外,《本朝文萃》中的其他作者均为使用过"文道"一词。也就是说,在现存的平安中期的汉文学作品当中,积极使用"文道"一词的作家只有这两位。当然,也有必要将刚才介绍的《三宝绘》的作者源为宪也算在内。

如果将上述内容按照时间顺利整理,会得出以下结论。最初是在天元二年(979)的正月,庆滋保胤为源顺赴任能登守的送别会诗序上,使用了"文道"一词。其次,是永观二年(984),源为宪在《三宝绘》中,为与"法之道"相互呼应,而使用了"文之道"一说。而在宽和二年(986),庆滋保胤将菅原道真称为"文道之祖",正历四年(993)以后,大江黄衡在官位叙任的申请书中,为了强调自己所创下的业绩而使用了"文道"一词。另外,文章 H 中源宣方四十九日忌愿文中,有赞扬宣方的文字,即虽为"武官"却精通"文道"。最后,在宽弘六年(1009),匡衡称赞菅原道真为"文道之大祖"。

庆滋保胤、源为宪与大江匡衡均为劝学会成员。除了这三位之外,劝学会的其他大学寮出身的文人贵族也喜欢使用一些只有他们之间才能通用的生僻词汇。① "文道"一词在汉语中并不常用,但是文人同好之间为了共享作品信息,却广泛使用该词。宽弘八年(1012)七月十七日,大江匡衡去世时,藤原实资(957–1046)在日记《小右记》中这样写到:

> 昨夕丹波守匡衡卒,当时名儒,无人比肩,文道灭亡。

实资是高居从一位右大臣的达官显贵,虽然他不是纪传道出身,但是他的阅历与见识却广泛受到好评。实资将匡衡的死看做是"文道"的灭亡,这说明"文道"一词在当时已被广泛使用。自此以后,一直到平安后期,也能在一些作品中偶尔见到该词。

那么,纪传道也俗称"文章道"。然而,在公文书中几乎完全无法见到将纪传道成为"文章道"的例子。该词在中文著作中很少见到,但是在《通典》第二十一卷《职官三·中书省·舍人》中,有以下的说法

> 自永淳以来,天下文章道盛,台阁髦彦,无不以文章达。故中书舍人为文士之极任,朝廷之盛选,诸官莫比焉。

在日本文献中,"文章道"仅在《本朝文萃》中菅原文时的《封事三条,一请不废失鸿胪馆怀远人励文士事》(第二卷)出现过一次。

> 昔子贡欲去告朔之饩羊,仲尼不许。以为羊在犹所以识其礼也。今陈不废此馆者,盖亦为文章道焉。

菅原文时(899–981)是道真之孙,作为文章博士,曾经指导过庆滋保胤和大江匡衡。天历十一年(957)上奏的《封事三条》中,有反对废止接待外国使节的鸿胪馆一条。该条由于叙述了文学的重要性而闻名,因此保胤和匡衡也理应拜读过。

保胤开始使用"文道"一词的时候,或许同时注意到了白居易的《赋赋》和文时的《封事》。因此,平安中期以前很少出现的"文道"一词,经历了上述过程,成为文人间喜闻乐道的词语。

---

① これについては、上記勧学会関連論文の註釈において明らかにした。

八、"文道"的成立

如上所述,"文道"一词虽然在中国文献中非常罕见,但是如庆滋保胤、大江匡衡这样的平安中期纪传道出身的文人,由于尊崇白居易,因其《赋赋》一作受到启发,逐渐得到普及。那么,"文道"又是如何成为作为天神被供奉的菅原道真的代名词呢?

首先,我们必须考察"～道"这种说法的来历。或许,我们第一个想到的是诸如"儒道"、"佛道"、"神道"等表示思想、宗教的概念。在这种情况下,"道"意味着"道法"、"道术"。①"医道"中的"道"也曾经代表同样的概念。

但是"文道"一词,是超越这个范畴的。这里的"道",指的是某个集团共同确立的某个专门的行为方法。进一步来讲,这里的"道"所指的是一条通往高超的技能,甚至是优秀的人格之道。例如"武道"、"艺道"、"茶道"、"香道"等,若非经过长年累月的严酷修行是无法达到最高境界的。这个关于"道"的概念,是日本平安末期到镰仓时代、室町时代确立,到了近现代,这种概念也经常通过文化逆输出流传到中国。

"文道"便是成立于平安中期的这些概念的先驱者。这里的"道"的概念的成立于门族意识息息相关。在古代日本,职位的继承多为世袭制,但是当该职业高度专业化时,多以秘密的家传和口传为主,因此罕有记载。

但是,在书香门第之家,一家之主执掌作诗撰文之事,因此,从保存下来的作品当中,能够追溯到长年积淀下来的累叶的家族意识。如前所述,在日本,菅原氏和大江氏曾经分别执掌文章院的东西两曹,文人们必须在其中某一家学习儒学。在这里,累叶和起家的区别就出现了。累叶指的是

---

① この概念については近年、小林正美「東晉？南朝における「佛教」？「道教」の称呼の成立と貴族社会」(中国社会科学院歴史研究所？財団法人東方学会『魏晉南北朝における貴族制の形成と三教？文学―歴史学？思想史？文学の連携による―』、汲古書院、2011)により整理されている。神道の概念については、吉原浩人「日本古代における「神道」の語の受容と展開」(ルチア？ドルチェ、三橋正編『「神仏習合」再考』、勉誠出版近刊)を参照されたい。

将学问之事世世代代世袭下来的家族关系,而起家是指,不一定要出身于学问之家,只要有足够的学识,也能够被录用的文人们。

累叶的家族意识在大江氏家族中体现的尤为明显。大江朝纲(886 – 957)在延喜十九年(919)迎接渤海使到任之时,曾经作诗如下:

　　江家昔有忘年契 莫怪鸿胪暂比踪

这里"忘年契"指的是,贞观十四年(872)渤海时节来朝之时,朝纲的祖父音人曾经作为参议参加了接待工作,以此为契机,大江家世世代代都与渤海国交往甚深。使用"江家"一词最为频繁的莫过于大江匡衡。宽宏三年(1006),他向一条天皇讲述《老子》之时所赋之诗的长诗题中,曾经这样说道(《江吏部集》中卷):

　　顷年以累代侍读之苗胤,以尚书一部十三卷,毛诗一部二十卷,文选一部六十卷,及礼记、文集。侍圣主御读。皆是莫不润色鸿业,吹萤王道之典文。又近侍老子道德经御读。(中略)于是江氏之为体,一家相传历李部官之任,十代次第为萝图帝王之师,有以哉。就中祖父江纳言,以老子经奉授延喜天历二代明主,今以不佞之身侍至尊之读。江家之才德可谓光古今。

江家之所以作为世世代代以侍读为业的苗裔,得以向一条天皇讲述中国古典,是因为他们通过家传世袭历任式部官,十代人都曾任天子之师。可以说,江家的才德光耀古今。江家人认为,为天皇侍读这种莫大的名誉,是祖先世世代代积累的德行,他们以此为荣。

另外,江家之所以有如此成就,也得益于白居易之恩。接到一条天皇为《白氏文集》七十卷加点的旨意的诗题中,有如下说法(《江吏部集》中卷):

　　近日蒙纶命,点文集七十卷。夫江家之为江家,白乐天之恩也。

文章接着叙述了大江千古·维时父子为醍醐天皇、维时·齐光父子为村上天皇、齐光、定基父子为圆融天皇侍读《白氏文集》的例子,由此,白居易的诗文在日本受到的重视程度可见一斑。另外,从匡衡的诗文中,可以窥见到强烈的家门意识。①

---

① 大江氏の累代意識については、吉原浩人「院政期の思想—江家における累葉儒家意識と系譜の捏造—」(佐藤弘夫編『日本思想史講座１—古代』、ぺりかん社、2012)について詳しく論じた。

那么,庆滋保胤的情况又如何呢? 保胤是阴阳家贺茂忠行的次子。哥哥保宪是历法博士、天文博士,弟弟保远是阴阳博士,兄弟几个都继承了父业,而保胤成为了文章博士,与弟弟保章一起在大学寮学习文章道,选择成为菅原道真之孙文时门下的弟子。庆滋一姓是贺茂的训读,是新创造出的姓氏。虽说自己选择了学问之路,但由于是起家出身,从五位下大内记已是最高官阶,于宽和二年(986)出家为僧,法号寂心。后来远渡大宋在杭州出家的寂照(大江定基)就是他的弟子。保胤虽说是靠自己创下了学问之家的家业,并没有累叶意识,但是正因为如此,他以曾师从菅原道真的门派菅家廊下而感到自豪。

我认为,正因为有了累叶意识或者说同门意识,"文道"一词才得以在平安中期得到广泛的传播。它的直接出处是白居易的《赋赋》,但是是摄关期的劝学会成员首次使用,才逐渐传播开来。

九、被供奉为神的孔子和白居易

菅原道真到处被供奉为天神之时,是作为御灵神被供奉的。当一个真实存在过的人被供奉为神时,是为了抚慰其因为死于非命而充满怨恨的灵魂,并避免他的怨念转化为引起灾害瘟疫的神威,而是转化为保护居民和通行者的力量。这种概念上的神并不是日本独有的。比如,中国古代的伍子胥就是一个典型的例子。他协助吴王夫差打败了越王勾践,但是因不堪谗言而被迫自杀。他的遗体被夫差投入长江,但是吴人为了表达对他的怜悯,为他建立了祠堂。之后,作为水上交通的保护神,在中国各地都修建了伍子胥庙。

另外,在中国有这样一种传统,即把在精于学问和文章之道的人供奉为神。孔子不仅在中国,乃至在世界各地都被供奉在孔子庙中,被尊崇为圣者。在儒学中,孔子更是被神格化,以释奠之名受到祭祀。而在日本,同样有每年两次的释奠活动。

不仅如此,白居易也被供奉为神。长保四年(1002)成书的《政事要略》第六十一卷《纠弹杂事》中,有以下文字。

　　白居易云云,白居易字乐天太原人也。或言,其先秦将武安君白起后也。父钦通建三云,兼解文章。媵姿梁氏女,合唹之后,为几有娠。先是梁氏梦与一大夫对语亲昵,共习笔墨。语曰,我是天帝之孙也。感渠神慧,来做配定。今降文星,拟为儿息。梁氏既而怀孕。静居一室,心执端直。十一月间,披经阅传。诞生之时,忽闻钟鼓之乐从天降来,铿锵之响彻于屋宇。(中略)或曰,古则宝应菩萨下他世间,号曰伏羲,吉祥菩萨为女娲。中叶则摩诃迦叶为老子,儒童菩萨为孔丘。今时文殊利菩萨为乐天。又曰,岁星为曼倩,文曲星为乐天焉。

　　这里引用的《白居易传》是唯一一篇佚文,即使在中国也已经失传的来历不明的传记。关于白居易的出身,有如下的第一种说法。白居易的母亲梁氏在梦中与一名大夫亲密交谈。两人共同作诗之后,这名大夫自称是天帝的资讯,感叹于梁氏的聪慧,并想与她共度余生,于是化为文曲星下凡,与她生儿育女。于是梁氏怀孕,期间阅读了经典与传记,白居易诞生时钟鼓乐队从天而降,在家中声乐大作。另外,还有第二种说法,在某一本书中有这样的记载,宝应菩萨降临世间号伏羲,吉祥菩萨化身为女娲。到了中叶,摩诃迦叶化身为老子,儒童菩萨为孔子。到了现代,文殊菩萨化身为白乐天。另外,还有岁星化身为曼倩也就是东方朔,文曲星化身为白乐天之说。

　　也就是说,有白居易是文曲星或者是文殊菩萨的化身这两种说法。关于这种说法在日本的普及这里不再赘述。① 也有人说,这篇《白居易传》的佚文有可能是在日本流传的伪作,但是我认为,这或许是在中国的唐末到宋初期间完成的作品。

---

　　① 2010 年 9 月 25 日、「神として祀られる白居易—平安朝文人貴族の精神的基盤—」と題し,北京師範大学文芸学研究中心他主催「多元視野下的中国文学思想」国際学術研討会 において、基調講演を行った。日本語論文は同題で、河野貴美子? 張哲俊編『東アジア世界と中国文化—文学? 思想にみる伝播と再創—』(勉誠出版、2012)に公表した。

十、结　语

在日本的平安时代中期,孔子在大学寮中被尊崇为学问之祖。而白居易以其佛教信仰为背景,成为了文人贵族的精神支柱。二者都是真实存在的人物,也都被供奉为神。而菅原道真成为"文道之祖"、"文道之大祖"正是以此为背景。

在菅原道真之前,日本并不存在学问之神、文章之神。另外在整个平安时代,也没有其他儒者被供奉为神。只有道真受到了这样的待遇,是因为"文道"一词本身包含着强烈的家族意识。菅原道真是菅原氏的祖宗,并执掌了菅家廊下,培养了超越门阀氏族的优秀门徒。具备了文人受到尊敬的两个必须的条件。于是,新的"文道之神"诞生了。

虽说是作为已经拥有强大神威的御灵神的天神,这里如果加上了"文道"的要素,再受到万人敬仰,那么,也不难理解为何现在天神信仰如此兴盛了。

基督宗教信仰对于社会秩序的意义

黄保罗

本文将通过对社会秩序（social order）和宗教信仰（religious faith）这两个概念的分析，集中探讨宗教信仰，特别是一神论的基督教上帝信仰对于社会秩序的意义。

一、什么是社会秩序（social order）和
基督宗教信仰（Christian faith）

社会秩序是秩序的一种，根据《辞海》，"秩，常也；秩序，常度也，指人或事物所在的位置，含有整齐守规则之意。"就字面意义而言，秩序乃指有组织地安排各构成部分以求达到正常的运转或良好的外观状态，一致性、连续性和确定性是其主要特点，是"无序"的对立面。秩序可以分为自然秩序（natural order）和社会秩序（social order）。

自然秩序表示自然界各要素之间的有序状态，其本身形成的原因，可作多种理解，但其深层原因仍是未解的奥秘。这种秩序及其规律多是自然科学研究的对象。

社会秩序表示人类社会各构成要素之间的有序状态，涉及人与人、人与自然、人与超自然之间的经济、政治、生态环境、伦理道德和人神关系等多方面的秩序内涵，核心要素是人。这种秩序是经济学、政治学、社会学、

哲学、伦理学、神学等社会科学和宗教学的研究对象。本文所说的秩序主要是社会秩序,也可称为公共秩序(public order);它是为维护社会公共生活所必需的秩序。这又有刚性与弹性之分。刚性的社会秩序,包括社会各阶级、阶层在内的各种社会群体的组织形式,由法律、行政法规、国家机关、企业事业单位和社会团体的规章制度等各种强制性规则所确定的社会管理秩序、生产秩序、工作秩序、交通秩序和公共场所秩序等。① 而弹性的社会秩序则是指由血缘、地域、经济、宗教、文化等因素构成的特殊社会群体组织形式,是由风俗习惯和道德规则等约定俗成的弹性规则约定俗成。

中国古代思想家们提出的"治",就表示社会的有序状态的维护与巩固,"乱"则表示社会秩序的破坏之无序状态。就社会秩序所达到的结果而言,它最起码可以分为等级秩序与平等秩序两个次类。等级秩序可能如金字塔形状,从上到下,虽不平等,却各就各位;也可能如同心圆形状,从里到外,层层扩展,虽有内外之别,却也和谐有序。平等秩序则明显体现为一视同仁、大家拥有同等地位。中国社会的秩序,传统上被认为属于等级类型;而目前全球化范围内占主流的倾向,则是平等型的秩序。所以,在今天的汉语语境中讨论社会秩序,本文提倡的是平等秩序。平等秩序比等级秩序的合理性与优越性何在,如何处理平等秩序中的等级关系等,都是可以详细讨论的话题,限于篇幅,本文对此阙如,权且以平等秩序作为立足点来展开信仰对社会秩序的意义之讨论。

界定清楚秩序的内涵之后,需要讨论的是,如何才能获得和维持社会的平等秩序,宗教信仰特别是上帝信仰和神圣律法信仰对这种秩序能产生什么影响呢? 为了论述上帝信仰对社会的平等秩序发生的影响,我们需要首先界定什么是信仰和宗教信仰?

"信仰"作为名词,可表示"相信"(belief)、"确信"(conviction)或"信

---

① 遵守公共秩序是公民的基本义务之一。从国际视角而言,公共秩序是一个弹性条款,因为国内公共秩序与国际公共秩序有所不同。外国公法的适用情况是,目前几乎所有的统一冲突法公约都规定有公共秩序保留条款。中国《民法通则》中有条款全面规定了公共秩序保留制度。国际私法上的公共秩序,主要是指法院在依自己的冲突规范本应适用某一外国法作准据法时,因其适用的结果与法院国的重大利益、基本政策、基本道德观念或法律的基本原则相抵触,而拒绝或排除适用该外国法的一种保留制度。因此它有时又被称为"公共秩序保留"。公共秩序制度,在国际私法中又被称为"安全阀"制度。

任、信念"(faith)等;作为动词,它是"相信"(to believe in)。因此,我们可界定信仰是对某人或某种主张、主义、宗教等的相信和尊敬以至于以之为自己的榜样或准则。信仰的本质是相信其正确,甚至宁愿相信其正确,不在于其是否真实。所以,很难界定信仰所谓的真假,信仰是对人生观、价值观和世界观等的选择和持有。信仰可分成多种类型,如宗教信仰与非宗教信仰、政治信仰与非政治信仰、有神论信仰与无神论信仰、一神论信仰和多神论信仰等。本文特别从宗教信仰(religious faith)和非宗教信仰(non-religious faith)这种分类法来讨论宗教信仰对于社会秩序的影响,因为汉语学界中,宗教信仰,特别是基督教一神论上帝信仰(faith of monotheist God)对于社会秩序的意义研究不够,有待加强。

以当代西方欧美社会为例,我们可以发现其社会秩序得以维持的三个根本途径。正如法国社会学家莫里斯·古德利尔(Maurice Godelier)在他著名的演讲《西方会成为人类的普世模式吗?》中指出,现代西方建立在自由市场的资本主义(capitalism)经济、议会民主制(representative democracy)和基督教(Christianity)三个轴心之上:以资本主义自由贸易为核心的经济关系模式、以普选和代议制为核心的民主政治模式、与以基督教为核心的精神生活形式;即:经济生活的生产与流通方式、政治生活的组织形式、而精神生活的个人皈依形式和意义建立形式。①这成了西方现、当代的核心价值观,是希腊传统、启蒙运动/理性主义/社会进化论、和犹太教/基督教的混合产物。这三个路径可否直接移植到汉语语境中来呢? 为了说明这个问题,笔者将上述的经济和政治模式称为西学中的人学传统,而基督教则被称为西学中的神学传统;本文将以宗教信仰对社会秩序的影响为探索目标,通过论述它对于经济秩序、政治和法律秩序的影响来研究上帝信仰对于社会秩序的意义。

---

① Maurice Godelier, *Wird der Westen das universale Modell der Menschheit*? Wien: Picus Verlag, 1991). Yang Xusheng (杨煦生), "The Transcendental Dimension of the Age of Disenchantment: The Paradox of Religion in the Contemporary Context of China", in *International Journal of Sino-Western Studies*, No. 1, Helsinki: Nordic Forum of Sino-Western Studies, 2011:27 – 38.

二、自由市场的资本主义经济这一匹脱缰野马
在器物层面对于社会秩序的影响

从社会的器物层面而言,自由市场经济像一匹渴望随私意到处奔驰的野马,既促进了欧美社会的经济发展和物质繁荣,又为社会带来了贪婪自私和冷酷无情的痛苦。经济秩序的获得和维持,需要私利与道德的平衡;由此可见,这匹野马需要刚性的法律束缚和弹性的信仰约束(后者就体现出宗教信仰的意义)。

一方面,由于人的自私性能够产生生产和发展的动力,资本主义自由市场经济就变成了一只"看不见的手"(the invisible hand)来维持着经济秩序。18 世纪大多数受过教育的人都相信,只有统治者的精心筹划才能使一个社会免于混乱与贫困,但亚当斯密斯(Adam Smith,1723 - 1790)不同意当时的这种流行观点。他虽没有发明"经济学的思维方式",但他比前人更广泛地发展这一思想,且首次将之运用于对社会变革和社会协作的综合分析。他的观点似乎可以总结为:人类享用的各种服务和产品,都需经过复杂而互相关联的生产活动才能产生,这种自由市场表面看似混乱而毫无拘束,实际上却是由一只被称为"看不见的手"所指引,将会引导市场生产出正确的产品数量和种类。通过这只手,社会协作过程将不仅在政府(统治者)关注缺席时能起作用,甚至当政府的政策错误时,这个过程也能消除错误政策的后果。[①] 他关于自由市场的资本主义经济的论述,至今仍然有极大的说服力,欧美的经济发展和繁荣,主要得益于这匹追逐利益的野马;它

① 亚当斯密斯(Adam Smith):《国民财富的性质和原因的研究》(An Inquiry into the Nature and Causes of the Wealth of Nations),简称《国富论》,1776。Smith, A., 1976a, The Wealth of Nations edited by R. H. Campbell and A. S. Skinner, The Glasgow edition of the Works and Correspondence of Adam Smith, vol. 2a, p.456. Smith, A., 1980, The Glasgow edition of the Works and Correspondence of Adam Smith, vol. 3, p. 49, edited by W. P. D. Wightman and J. C. Bryce, Oxford: Claredon Press. Smith, A., 1976b, The Glasgow edition of the Works and Correspondence of Adam Smith, vol. 1, p.184 -5, edited by D. D. Raphael and A. L. Macfie, Oxford: Claredon Press. Smith, A., 1976b, ibid, vol. 2a, p.456, edited by R. H. Cambell and A. S. Skinner, Oxford: Claredon Press.

的疯狂奔驰变成了人民追求发展的动力,从十八世纪至今的二百多年,人类社会的发展速度和变化幅度之空前巨大就充分说明了这匹野马的力量,而中国过去三十年的经济发展更是这匹野马的生动说明。国内所谓的右派思想和自由主义者们在经济问题上所提倡的主要就是要发挥这匹野马的力量。

但是,另一方面,自由市场经济这匹资本主义野马,在为人类社会带来祝福的同时,也带来了空前的灾难与危机。生态环境的破坏、资源的枯竭、核武器的威胁、婚姻的危机、家庭的破碎、大量单亲儿童的出现,特别是道德沦丧和人心贪婪等等,使得市场经济这匹资本主义野马所到之处,传统的文明和世外桃源的朴实都几乎消失殆尽;它不仅引起文化冲突,更使人类面临着意义缺乏和对未来的担忧而陷入亘古未有的空前疑惑和恐惧之中。其实,写作了《国富论》强调"看不见的手"对经济秩序发挥积极影响的斯密斯,在 1759 年又发表《道德情操论》强调对他人同情的道德情操之重要性,特别是在自由市场那只"看不见的手"无法运作的领域,[①]如伦理道德、思想精神等弹性社会秩序中。

那么,以平等的社会秩序为特征的欧美社会是如何利用和约束这匹资本主义野马的呢?

三、由民主政治制定的法律这条套马缰绳和管制利维坦的 笼子在制度层面对于社会秩序的影响

为了维持社会秩序,特别是制度层面的秩序,法律在欧美社会就往往被用来当作管理工具。为了更好地说明,通过民主政治制定的法律如何得以成为束缚资本主义野马的缰绳,我们需要比较一下等级制和平等制的社会秩序一般是如何获得和维持的。

等级制的社会秩序是靠强权手段或精英统治获得和维持的。首先,这

---

① Smith, Adam (2002) [1759]. Knud Haakonssen. ed. *The Theory of Moral Sentiments*. Cambridge University Press. P. XV. Buchan, James (2006). *The Authentic Adam Smith: His Life and Ideas*. W. W. Norton & Company. p. 12

种统治需要一种政治理念作为理论基础,即为什么某个统治者有理由获得统治权?中国古代社会的主要理论根据是"天命"说,即某人/家族的品德和爱民行为符合上天的旨意,因此,其德配道,被苍天赋予统治万民的使命。从夏、商、周到秦始皇以来的各朝帝王获得和维持社会秩序统治权的理论根据基本都是这个天命观,它已经成为中国人的一种信仰,对社会秩序产生了极大的影响。这与古代欧洲的"君权神授"几乎一致,强调被上帝、苍天等超自然力量的拣选和委任,带有强烈的宗教信仰色彩,一神论和多神论都可以发挥影响。其次,统治者需要强权甚至暴力来夺取、获得和维持统治权,从而也面临着被暴力剥夺统治权的危险。第三,至于等级制的社会秩序的维持,中国封建社会靠的主要是法家和儒家思想,法家强调严厉的惩罚,儒家强调三纲五常等伦理性的说教。近现代以前的欧洲则主要靠基督教的伦理体系。

平等的社会政治秩序现在已经逐渐在全世界代替了不平等的等级秩序,最起码在观念上,这已经成为价值观的主流。自从辛亥革命以来,中国的政治理念就由封建王朝时代的"真龙天子降世"变成了"以民为本"的代表人民利益的"共和国"(Republic of China 中华民国 1911–1949,People's Republic of China 中华人民共和国 1949–),其基本含义就是,国家和政府是公共的,而不是私人的,国家和政府应当为公共利益而努力,而不应当为私人利益。另外,国家各级政权机关的领导人不是继承的,不是世袭的,也不是命定的,而是由自由公正的选举产生的。因而,公正而自由的选举,是判断一个国家是否真正实行共和政治的又一基本准则。欧洲自近代以来,中国自现当代以来,传统的等级制的社会秩序观念逐渐被平等制的社会秩序观所代替,而且这种共和的秩序观已几乎成为全球化的普世性信念,广为众人接受,有的地区虽然没有如此的制度,但人们却心向往之。

欧洲统治者获得统治权的理论根基不再是上帝的"君权神授",中国统治者获得统治权的理论根基不再是"真龙天子的天命",二者统治权得以获得和建立的理论根基都是为了人民的利益和大众的平等。但是,怎样才能维持这种平等的秩序呢?

就经济秩序而言,如前所述,自由市场经济的资本主义不仅是欧美的轴心,而且正在向包括中国在内的全世界推延,虽然其局限性为人类带来的灾难被越来越多的学者所批判。

在政治和法律的制度领域,欧美流行的代表议会制的民主则几乎成为全世界追求的获得和维持政治秩序的保证。中国官方虽不接受如此的观点,但也面临着如何面对和迎战的问题。

在代表制的民主体系形成之前,托马斯·霍布斯(Thomas Hobbes,1588－1679)①在 17 世纪就用协作精神为核心的社会契约论来解释社会秩序的起源。他认为,独立的个人为了摆脱“人自为战”的混乱状态,相互缔结契约。因为人们都致力于自我保护和个人满足,因而只有强力(或源于强力的威胁)能使人们避免不断地互相攻击。他的假设似乎是:人们只要能不对别人进行人身攻击,也不侵犯他人财产,然后,那些能产生工业、农业、知识和艺术的积极协作就会自然而然地产生。如果没有协作,最糟糕的是人们将不断处于暴力死亡的恐惧和危险中,人的生活将孤独、贫困、卑污、残忍而短寿。他于 1651 年出版了以怪兽 Leviathan 命名的著作——《利维坦》,意在用以比喻一个强大的国家,借此论证君权至上,反对“君权神授”。据说在上帝造人之后,人请求上帝:“上帝啊,我们太弱小了。请你再创造一个英雄吧,让他保护我们”。上帝说:“英雄在保护你们的同时,也会欺压你们、吃你们”。后来人们为了抵御各种外来的风险,自己创造了一个利维坦这个能让他们有归属感的庞然大物——政府,但政府这个利维坦(Leviathan)有双面的性格。它由人组成,也由人来运作,因此也就具有了人性的那种半神半兽的品质,它在保护人的同时,又在吃人。所以,就有了人类社会的最高理想就是把利维坦关进笼子里一说。民主和法制就拥有了将利维坦关起来的“笼子”功能。这为后来的民主制度的政治和法律秩序的确立指出了协作和契约精神的重要性。

---

① Thomas Hobbes. *Leviathan-Revised Edition*, eds. A. P. Martinich and Brian Battiste. Peterborough, ON: Broadview Press, 2010.《利维坦》第二部分主要描述:自然状态中人们不幸的生活中都享有“生而平等”的自然权利,又都有渴望和平和安定生活的共同要求,于是出于人的理性,人们相互间同意订立契约,放弃各人的自然权利,把它托付给某一个人或一个由多人组成的集体,这个人或集体能把大家的意志化为一个意志,能把大家的人格统一为一个人格;大家则服从他的 意志,服从他的判断。

经过英国经验主义者洛克(John Locke, 1632 – 1704)①的发展,现代民主制度的基石在法国思想家让－雅克·卢梭(Jean-Jacques Rousseau,1712–1778)那里得到奠定;后者于 1762 年写成强调主权在民之思想的《社会契约论》(法语: *Du Contrat Social*,又译为《民约论》,或称《政治权利原理》)。他强调,在参与政治的过程中,只有每个人同等地放弃全部天然自由,转让给整个集体,人类才能得到平等的契约自由。人民根据个人意志投票产生公共意志。如果主权者走向公共意志的反面,那么社会契约就遭到破坏;人民有权决定和变更政府形式和执政者的权力,包括用起义的手段推翻违反契约的统治者。它深刻地影响了欧洲君主绝对权力的被废以及 18 世纪末北美殖民地摆脱英帝国统治而建立民主制度,其思想在美国的《独立宣言》和法国的《人权宣言》及两国的宪法均得到体现。②

这种以民为本的思想,在欧洲首先以反基督教的姿态出现,后来经过法国大百科全书学派、启蒙运动、法国大革命、美国独立运动等,最终在欧美奠定了决定性的地位,并且作为西方文化和西方价值观的一个部分向全世界推广,获得了普世性的影响,但与非西方文化圈及后殖民主义等思想意识之间却持续不断地发生冲突与矛盾。比如目前的中国官方就不认可如此的政治理念与模式。这也说明,就目前的实然状况而言,这种政治理念有其局限性。

民主议会制在社会秩序的管理上,是主要通过法律秩序的制定和实行来维持社会秩序的,这就需要公义性作为其根基。但是,欧美现在流行的民主制度来源于卢梭的社会契约论。这既不是霍布斯所说的有绝对权力的“利维坦”,也不是洛克所说的只有有限权力的政府,而是集强制力和自由的权利于一身的“公共意志”。通过民主政治及法律途径,公共意志成为了努力套住自由市场经济这匹野马的缰绳,成了试图将“利维坦”关起来的笼子。但这条绳索和这个笼子有效吗?

---

①　洛克不同意霍布斯要求人们转让生命权之外的一切权利,认为除财产权的判决权和执行权之外,一切自然的权利都不可转让。另外,洛克把统治者定为契约的另一方,人民有推翻不履行契约的暴君的权利。因此,他主张三权分立与宗教宽容。洛克:《政府论》,下篇,叶启芳等译,商务印书馆,1963 年,第 57 – 58 页。赵敦华 2001:《西方哲学简史》,北京大学出版社,第 252 – 253 页。

②　卢梭著、何兆武译:《社会契约论》(第三卷),北京:商务印书馆,2004 年。

　　为了束缚自由市场资本主义经济的消极性以至于社会秩序不会混乱，以公共意志为核心追求的民主政治，主要努力通过法律的手段来维持确保社会秩序和经济秩序等的有条不紊。① 通过选举追求公共意志的民主制度，现在则是欧美世界的主要体制，它一般被看成是人类社会令人不满意的制度中最令人满意的制度。其优点是考虑了如何克服人的自私性之消极影响，体现了共和、平等与多数人利益等因素。虽然民主制度与基督教信仰中的天赋人权、平等自由、博爱和法律等思想密切相关。

　　但人的自私性和局限性与公共意志之间的张力迫使人们询问：公共意志是否可能和可靠？卢梭声称，一个完美社会是为人民的"公共意志"（公意）所控制的；公意时指全体定约人的公共人格，使他们的人身和意志的"道义共同体"，是"每一个成员作为整体的不可分的一部分。"②虽然他未定义如何达成这个目标，但他建议由公民团体组成的代议机构作为立法者，通过讨论来产生公共意志。公意是不可摧毁的，通过投票来表达。③

　　这里需要指出的是，公意是一个抽象的概念而非集合概念，也就是说，公意不等于众意，不等于所有的个别意志的综合。虽可通过投票的方式来获得，但每个投票人不但代表自己及其团体的利益，而且代表和反映"公义"，相信公共意志不仅代表特定社团或国家甚至全人类的共同利益，而且能够帮助实现上述的共同利益。因此，如赵敦华总结所云："公意是没有相互矛盾的个人利益，它是在扣除众意中相异部分之后所剩下的相同部分。

---

　　① 世上主要存在着三种政府形式：民主制，即由全体或大部分人民治理；贵族制，由少数人所治理；国君制，由一人治理。严格意义而言，真正的民主从来就不曾有过，而且永远也不会有。贵族制：可以是自然的、选举的与世袭的。第一种只适于纯朴的民族；第三种是一切政府之中最坏的一种。第二种则是最好的；它才是严格说来的贵族制。国君制：没有比国君制更有活力的政府；但这种政府也具有很大的危险；如果其前进的方向不是公共福祉，就转化为对国家的损害。君主们倾向于追逐绝对的权力，大臣们只是阴谋家。结构单一的政府是最好的；实际上，政府都是混合形式的，都或多或少地借鉴了其他形式。参考卢梭著、何兆武译2004：《社会契约论》（第三卷），北京：商务印书馆。

　　② 北京大学西方哲学教研室编：《西方哲学原著选读》，下卷，北京：商务印书馆，1982 年，第72 页。

　　③ 卢梭著、何兆武译：《社会契约论》，北京：商务印书馆，2004 年："主权者除了立法权力之外便没有任何别的力量，所以只能依靠法律而行动；而法律又只不过是公意的正式表示，所以唯有当人民集合起来的时候，主权者才能行动。"（第三卷第十二章）。立法权力是属于人民的，而且只能是属于人民的。"（第三卷第一章）。

公意永远以公共利益为出发点和归宿,因此永远是公正的,不会犯错误。"①

　　但如今欧美民主政治的总体现实,则是以摆脱上帝的"少数服从多数"的投票决定的。这使得"众意"中的最强大者变成了"公意",使得"民粹"变成"民主",因为其理论根基是排斥或脱离上帝信仰的理性乐观主义,相信人类自己知道而且能够为人类本身谋求最好最大的利益。这种依靠人本身以民主投票寻求公意的体制,没有充分考虑整个社团、社会、国家或人类都有陷入自私、盲目、错误或无奈的可能性,过分盲目乐观地推崇理性主义和科学主义,造成了很多弊端。虽然美国等国家的议会仍然以手按圣经的方式发誓,但监督的方式还是主要依靠"少数服从多数"的民主投票,上帝信仰的约束力在限于个人内心世界,其在公共领域的表现受到了越来越多的限制。这种欧美启蒙运动以来的主要思维方式被历史证明:(民主制以政治和法律体现出来的)公共意志,在束缚资本主义脱缰野马和限制利维坦的消极性上有一定的成效,对于腐败、不公平等的治理也有一定的优势;但在人的精神、道德等弹性秩序领域却没有多少效用,因为它在人神关系等宗教领域会打破权威观念,会加深人的精神危机和心理恐惧以至于产生绝望。但是,在没有上帝信仰的国家与地区,投票式的民主制度则有危险变成完全不顾公平正义的"少数服从多数"为核心的民粹主义。所以,汉语学界探讨政治和法律秩序如何得以维持时,我们若能从上帝信仰对民主制度的影响进行分析,当能获得一定的洞见。探讨如何获得以"公义"为基础的"公意",并分析少数服从多数的民主投票方式、宗教信仰与乐观理性主义的角色,将会有重大启发意义。如果不做如此的区分,国内的自由主义与保守主义、西化与本土化之争,就会失去许多核心关注点。

　　通过法律手段去追求的刚性经济和政治秩序,需要公义性、合理性和权威性的约束,而弹性社会秩序领域则需要人的自觉性或上帝感召的神圣性。以利益追逐为动力,脱缰的野马在自由市场经济中可能会受到一只"看不见的手"所引导,带有一定的秩序性;以政治管束和法律制约为前提,脱缰的野马和吃人的利维坦在社会的公共领域中也可能受到契约与协作的引导,带有一定的秩序性;但触及伦理道德等弹性领域,无论是经济领域

―――――――――

① 赵敦华:《西方哲学简史》,北京:北京大学出版社,2001 年,第 282 页。

的"看不见之手"还是政治和法律上的"缚马缰绳"及"关利维坦之笼",都会失去其效力。而宗教信仰则可能通过神圣性来唤醒人的主观自觉性,在弹性秩序的维持上发挥重要影响。

四、基督宗教信仰这颗救心丸在精神
层面对于社会秩序的影响

资本主义脱缰野马为社会带来物质繁荣的同时也带来了自己贪婪的危机,利维坦在给人民带来保护的同时也对人民进行了欺压和伤害,民主法制虽能一定程度上束缚这匹野马和利维坦,却无法约束其心灵的弹性世界,因此,弹性社会秩序的维持很难离开宗教信仰,因为道德根基的确立与宗教信仰关系密切。① 没有宗教信仰,道德情操难以找到安身根基。康德三大批判的《判断力批判》要回答的问题就是:如果要真正能做到有道德,我们就必须假设有上帝的存在,假设生命结束后并不是一切都结束了。② 伏尔泰则从道德得以建立的视角说:"即使没有上帝,也要创造一个上帝"。③ 这种论述到底是出于纯粹的实用主义如传统中国的"神道设教"以吓唬小人一样,还是出于信仰? 学者有不同的意见,但明确的是,若没有上

---

① 边沁的功利主义虽以最大幸福作为道德的根基,但其对幸福的界定还是以人的理性为基础的,因此很难面对康德的批评。

② Kant says, as an idea of pure reason, "we do not have the slightest ground to assume in an absolute manner... the object of this idea", (Kant, *Critique of Pure Reason*, A685/B713), but adds that the idea of God cannot be separated from the relation of happiness with morality as the "ideal of the supreme good". The foundation of this connection is an intelligible moral world, and "is necessary from the practical point of view" (Kant, Critique of Pure Reason, A810/B838). In the *Jäsche Logic* (1800) he wrote "One cannot provide objective reality for any theoretical idea, or prove it, except for the idea of freedom, because this is the condition of the moral law, whose reality is an axiom. The reality of the idea of God can only be proved by means of this idea, and hence only with a practical purpose, i. e., to act as though (*als ob*) there is a God, and hence only for this purpose" (9:93, trans. J. Michael Young, *Lectures on Logic*, p.? 590 –91).

③ Voltaire: "If God did not exist, it would be necessary to invent him." [Originally, "Si Dieu n' existait pas, il faudrait l'inventer.", [[q:Voltaire]]], *Épître à l' Auteur du Livre des Trois Imposteurs* (1770 – 11 – 10)].

帝信仰,道德的根基难以确立,道德的规则难以获得能力施行出来,将是人类社会面临的重大挑战。[①]因为道德秩序的维持,有极大的弹性,许多领域都是强制性的法律和政治手段无法管辖的,宗教信仰的功能不容小觑,欧美社会之所以没有被资本主义市场经济这匹野马拖垮和变疯,也没有被利维坦吃掉,很大程度上得益于宗教信仰所起的平衡作用。这对目前的汉语学界关于道德秩序的讨论,有很大的借鉴参考意义。

概而言之,欧美的社会秩序得以维持的第一轴心是自由市场的资本主义这批野马,其优点是调动人的积极性,缺点是自私、贪婪和冷酷。第二轴心是通过民主而体现公共意志的政治和法律,其优点是努力在经济和公共社会领域克服人的自私性,其缺点是在人的私人领域和道德精神领域的无能为力。而基督教则是欧美社会的救心丸,平时不一定服用,但在关键时刻起到救命的作用,不但信徒依赖它,而且西方的文化认同在根本上也离不开它,它是欧美社会秩序得以维持的第三个轴心。

将此三个轴心与当代汉语的语境结合,我们可以反思下述几个问题:

首先,宗教信仰,特别是一神论的上帝信仰,是社会秩序得以确立的根基,最起码欧美社会是如此。[②]而佛教、道教等中国宗教之所以没有提升中国人的道德水准,就是因为这些宗教的教条,没有涉及到道德与责任——特别是这种道德与责任又是宣扬这种宗教的人自己也须对别人履行的,因而中国宗教信仰的功利性、多神论和不虔诚使得这些宗教没有与国家及其成员发生社会秩序意义上的关系,而只是集中于人的自私性功利。一神论的上帝信仰,在处理好排他性的问题时,能为社会秩序的确立奠定根基。在探讨中国社会应该是什么样以及怎样才能保持其秩序时,可以参考上帝信仰对欧美社会的积极影响。

其次,上帝信仰可以帮助汉语学界更好地思考法的问题。从立法目

①　根据卢克莱修等人的古典无神论,功利主义一直也被用来作为道德伦理建立的根基。边沁的最大幸福(功利)原则将此发展到顶峰,但笔者在下文论述政治和法律秩序时,将会通过说明社会公共意志的有限性来论证功利主义在伦理道德的确立与实行上的局限。

②　卢梭说:宗教是国家的基础,在任何时候都在公民的生活中占主要地位。每个公民都应该有一个宗教,宗教可以使他们热爱自己的责任,这件事却是对国家很有重要关系的。参考卢梭著、何兆武译:《社会契约论》(第四卷),北京:商务印书馆,2004年。

标、立法者、监督者、法的本质、适用范围、效力和特点等七个方面来探讨，我们可以看出基督教上帝信仰前提下的西学中人学传统之法、西学中神学传统之法和中国传统之法的异同。

	传统中国	西学传统的神学（犹太教/基督教）	西学传统的人学（古希腊、启蒙以来至今）
立法目标	一部分人统治另一部分人（孟子：劳心者治人，劳力者治于人）	上帝统治所有人	人类自我统治
立法者	劳心者	上帝	公共意志的代表者
监督者	劳心者和国家机器	上帝和教会	国家机器
法的本质	实现劳心者意志的工具性统治手段	实现上帝意志的神圣的义务、让人知道自己犯罪的事实、绝望中寻求上帝他力的拯救	实现公共意志的工具性秩序准则
适用范围	所有领域（刚性秩序、弹性秩序）	所有领域（刚性秩序、弹性秩序）	刚性秩序中的公共领域
法的效力	只对一部分人生效	对所有人生效	对所有人的部分领域生效
法的特点	变通性和功利性	神圣性	契约性

　　汉语学界有必要注意，西学中存在着既相互联系又充满矛盾冲突的神学和人学这两个次传统。基督教是一种纯精神的宗教；基督徒的祖国是不属于这个世界的。基督徒以一种深沉的、决不计较自己的成败得失的心情在尽自己的责任。这使得它能够冲破形而下的所有束缚，对人类社会的所有事情都保持一种改进的开放态度。西学中人学传统的法带有强烈的普遍性，在刚性的社会秩序中对所有人都能起到一定的作用，但在弹性社会秩序中的影响就很有限；而其神学传统的神圣性则不仅能协助法在普遍性上发生影响，而且特别能在弹性社会秩序中发挥作用；可是，中国传统的法既缺乏普遍性（只对劳力者产生约束）又缺乏神圣性（功利性将之变成一个技术性的统治手段而随当权者之意随便伸缩），因此，在刚性和弹性社会秩序中的作用都非常有限。

　　第三，以自由市场为中心的资本主义经济的"看不见的手"不一定能束缚住四处狂奔的自私野马,以启蒙运动倡导的人类理性为根基的民主法制这个"笼子"虽能在一定程度上套住自私野马和利维坦的身体却无法套住它们的灵魂,因此,西学中的自由经济和民主制度,一方面,在欧美社会之内面临许多精神领域中无能为力的尴尬,引起后现代解构主义的批判;另一方面,它在中国等非西方地区和国家遇到当地的传统文化与政治力量的反对,引起了后殖民主义和许多第三世界文化保守主义的批判。在当代的汉语语境中,如何将后殖民主义对于西学中的自私野马河利维坦的解构性批评与后现代主义对启蒙理性的解构性批评转变成为一种建构性的思路,使后现代主义的建构性与中国复兴传统文化的国学热结合起来迎接全球化的挑战,将是重建中国社会秩序的重要思路。[①]笔者认为核心是要矫正西学中的人学传统(特别是启蒙运动以来过分强调理性和科学)和中学国学传统中作为统治手段的法缺乏普遍性和神圣性的弊端。西学中人学传统的弊端已经遭到了解构性后现代主义的强烈批判,但人学迷失的根基在于其对基督教信仰的背叛,却在西方的后现代主义批判中并没有得到足够的重视,在汉语学界的后现代引介(除去汉语神学外)中对此的关注更是凤毛麟角。在此基础上,现在中国的复兴传统之国学热,若能兼顾中国传统中刚性秩序之法的不平等性需要克服以及神学思想需要发扬的话,我们就有可能建构性地为中国甚至世界社会秩序的重建找到一条出路;但现在出现的狭隘民族主义倾向及其对基督教等上帝信仰的排斥,则可能会一则重蹈西学中的人学只强调理性的弊端,二则陷入第三世界后殖民文化保守主义的报复性苦毒的情绪宣泄之中,从而丧失反省西学中的人学之大好时机、葬送中国国学重生的可能性。

总结而言,资本主义野马对于器物层面的社会有积极的贡献,但其唯利是图的本性却为社会秩序带来极大的挑战。高效有力的利维坦对于社会秩序的维持有积极贡献,但其吃人的自私本性却同样伤害社会与人民,特别是在非平等制的社会里。民主法制像一条绳索对约束人性自私的资本主义野马和利维坦的外在表现从制度上发挥有一定的约束果效,但却无

---

① 参考汤一介:《启蒙在中国的艰难历程》,载凤凰网《大学问》第七期,2012 年 1 月 6 日,http://news.ifeng.com/opinion/lecture/special/tangyijie/。

法在心灵、道德等弹性层面发挥作用。宗教信仰可为道德的确立提供根基,象救心丸一样引导人的行为脱离死亡(注重灵性的基督宗教则比佛道等更能提升人的道德水准,增加神圣性,而不只是为了自己私利得到满足)。如此的三个轴心共同运作,才能对社会秩序的稳定发挥积极影响。前两个轴心是西学中的人学传统,而后一个轴心则是西学中的神学传统。这两个传统既相互联系有充满矛盾,这种合作与张力为欧美社会带来了活力。

多元宗教和谐与冲突[①]

张桥贵

随着全球化时代的到来,不同宗教之间的相遇、交流与互动将更加频繁,如何引导多元宗教和谐共处将是我们面对的一个重要课题。多元宗教信仰和谐共处是两种以上宗教在交往相处过程中,持续动态的互益共存状态。不在同一空间、时间和人口范围存在的宗教不存在宗教和谐共处的关系。宗教和谐作为一种特定的宗教关系类型,首先必须要有某一类型的宗教作为载体,其次是作为载体的宗教之间能够相互接触交往。当两个及以上类型的宗教在同一的时间空间与人群中,具有实实在在互动的关系发生时,才可以谈论宗教和谐。

宗教中大量关于和谐、非暴力的智慧,不仅应该成为宗教间和谐共处的行动指南,更应该在人类生活的各个领域进行推广。思考和谐就是要学会和谐的思考并和谐的行动。在当代中国,我们正经历着深刻的经济转轨、社会转型,但与之相适应的心灵转向尚待完善。多宗教和谐共处的宝贵经验,能够为心灵转向提供有益的和谐智慧资源。在社会治理与文化建设中,我们既要研究以社会和谐为前提的宗教和谐,更要建构以宗教和谐为基础的社会和谐。

宗教和谐在本质上是一种社会关系。宗教和谐关系不能在真空中绝

① 本文系张桥贵主持的国家社会科学基金重点项目"云南边疆民族地区多元宗教和谐相处的经验和对策研究"的阶段性成果,项目编号11AZJ002。

缘存在,必须有其明确的对象、载体、内容与过程机制。宗教以特定的人群为界限,任何以普世性相标榜的宗教,也不能掌握全世界的所有人口,只能是影响范围相对较大而已。所以随着人群的交往,宗教之间的相遇成为必然,在全球化的时代更是不可避免。人类社会越发展,宗教间的传播交流就越发达。宗教和谐不是宗教融合,宗教融合是将差异抹平并取消一方独立存在权利的行为。宗教和谐带来的是多元宗教平衡互补、共同发展的勃勃生机。宗教和谐既是一种过程,又是一种目的,还是一种文化传统。自客观而言,是一种现象与状态;自主观而言,是一种理念和理想。不可否认经过潘尼卡、尼特等诸多重量级学者的研究与提倡,"宗教对话"也蔚然具有学科的规模,但其中不适合中国宗教国情的地方也不在少数。对话只是达成和谐的一种手段,手段在特定情景下的有效与否仍然值得认真研究。我们可以说,宗教对话为了宗教和谐,而不会反过来说宗教和谐为了宗教对话。

从宗教自身发展来看,对宗教资源的争夺,归根结底是对宗教信徒的争夺,能否合理解决信徒的宗教身份归属问题,是宗教冲突与和谐的内在分野,也是宗教与世俗社会关系好坏的重要标准。中国宗教之所呈现和谐局面,与各大宗教允许信徒在身份上同时兼容有关。

没有共同的特点与规律,在理论上宗教就不成其为一个整体性概念;没有宽容的精神与态度,在现实中宗教就不能和谐相处。没有交流就难以理解,没有理解就难以尊重,没有尊重就难以和谐。就宗教发展的整体趋势而言,多元化是一个必然的趋势:向内是宗教因社会的发展而不断增加维度,呈现多维化态势;向外是宗教因人类交往的增加而不断相遇交流,乃至在同一人群、地域和时间中相处,呈现多样化态势。

从辩证的角度来看,冲突中蕴含着和谐的因素,和谐中也蕴含着冲突的因素,二者的区别在于哪一方面的因素占据主导地位。和谐不是从来如此的,是在与冲突因素相协调的过程中发展起来的。事物的和谐状态并非一成不变,促成和谐的努力也不可能一劳永逸。宗教冲突或融合的目的导向是一教独存,而宗教和谐的目的导向是多教共存。研究和谐,就必然要正视冲突。冲突是两个或两个以上主体在特定利益基础上的直接或间接性对抗。冲突并不必然具有破坏性,在可以控制的规模、范围和水平上的冲突,为了特定的目标而发生,往往具有潜在的建设性。冲突所围绕的利益和矛盾的消解,必然在更高的阶段产生新的关系类型——和谐。

越是在神灵观念上秉持多元化的民族,宗教之间的冲突就越可能减少,宗教之间的关系就越可能呈现和谐状态。相反,越是在神灵观念上推行一元化的民族,也就是说信奉一元至上神宗教的民族,宗教之间的冲突就越可能增多,宗教和谐的神学基础就越薄弱。

一

和谐虽有共同的精神、原则与规律,但和谐状态的达成却没有一成不变的途径与手段,在结果上也表现出丰富多样的模态。宗教和谐在本质上是一种社会关系,宗教和谐关系不能在真空中绝缘存在,必须有其明确的对象、载体、内容与过程机制。宗教以特定的人群为界限,任何以普世性相标榜的宗教,也不能掌握全世界的所有人口,只能是影响范围相对较大而已。所以随着人群的交往,宗教之间的相遇成为必然,在全球化的时代更是不可避免。人类社会越发展,宗教间的传播交流就越发达。宗教和谐不是宗教融合,宗教融合是将差异抹平并取消一方独立存在权利的行为。宗教和谐带来的是多元宗教平衡互补、共同发展的勃勃生机。宗教和谐既是一种过程,又是一种目的,还是一种文化传统。自客观而言,是一种现象与状态;自主观而言,是一种理念和理想。不可否认经过潘尼卡、尼特等诸多重量级学者的研究与提倡,"宗教对话"也蔚然具有学科的规模,但其中不适合中国宗教情况的地方也不在少数。对话只是达成和谐的一种手段,手段在特定情景下的有效与否仍然值得认真研究。我们可以说,宗教对话为了宗教和谐,而不会反过来说宗教和谐为了宗教对话。

从宗教自身发展来看,对宗教资源的争夺,归根结底是对宗教信徒的争夺,能否合理解决信徒的宗教身份归属问题,是宗教冲突与和谐的内在分野,也是宗教与世俗社会关系好坏的重要标准。中国宗教之所以呈现和谐局面,与各大宗教允许信徒在身份上同时兼容有关。作为中国宗教和谐相处的典型省份云南省,在云南多宗教和谐共处的客观现象中,我们常常看到的是信徒身份的叠合,即是说允许一个人同时信仰多种宗教,成为多个宗教的教徒;神灵体系的叠合,即是说允许一个宗教同时吸纳其他宗教的神灵体系,这种吸纳可能带有一定的主次结构。活动场所的叠合,即是说允许一个宗教活动场所为多个宗教所共用,这实际是神灵体系叠合与教徒身份叠合的必然要求。

从宗教和谐的变量关系而言,地域空间越小、人口规模越小、互动程度越强的宗教之间和谐关系的研究就越具有典型性。宗教关系和宗教交往归根结底是人的关系和人的交往。以常识言之,如果多元宗教信仰能够和谐的存在于家庭之内,必然也能和谐存在于社区之内。

二

没有共同的特点与规律,在理论上宗教就不成其为一个整体性概念;没有宽容的精神与态度,在现实中宗教就不能和谐相处。对于宗教和谐的研究,首先应在整体性的基础上突出比较性,其次应在多元性的基础上强调互动性,再次还应在多维基础上强调一致性。因而宗教和谐关系具有多元性、有限性、开放性、动态性等特征,和谐是有限的、有条件的、暂时的。多元性是内在前提,没有两种及以上不同类型宗教的存在,且实际发生交往互动的情况,就不会衍生所谓的和谐。特定地域和人群中现有的宗教关系结构总是伴随新的宗教相遇而发生变化,需要持续不断的寻求差异互补基础上的共赢,一旦断裂则和谐关系很可能向冲突关系转化。开放性、动态性是从和谐关系的结构与过程方面分析的,从结果与功能的角度看,宗教和谐还具有平衡性与稳定性。宗教生存与延续的基础在于不断获取信徒,信徒的流失既可能是因老信徒去世而自然性发生的,也可能是因老信徒改教而人为性发生的,还可能是因为各种原因无法补充新信徒而发生的。所以历史上时常所见为了获取足够数量的信徒,各宗教之间采取极端的方式,强迫本宗教信徒留在教内,强迫他宗教信徒改信本宗。中国历史上释道关系紧张时期,冲突的重要根据即是如此,两教皆发展出了自成体系的护教理论,并相互攻击对方。但中国宗教最终通过包容信徒同时信奉多种宗教而和平地解决了对信徒身份的争夺,从而为三教合一打下了资源性的基础。随着护教理论的发展,中国宗教最终也发展出了正视对方长处、兼美通融的三教合一理论,比如主张"以儒治世,以佛修心,以道养身"就是典型。而不能包容多元信徒身份,又不能尊重其他宗教信仰,正视其他宗教优点的宗教,具有严重的狭隘性、排他性,为了争夺信徒在手段上会达到无所不用其极的地步,不仅有理论上的护教,还会有武力上的护教。

宗教是以特定神圣观念整合起来的一种特殊人类共同体,因而"神"的本质是和谐而不是分裂。问题在于,作为诸宗教之母的"神"之间千差万别,现存的"神学"皆以本宗教立场进行护教式辩论,忽视了对"神"之为"神"的共同本质的探讨。护教的策略目标和行动逻辑往往从两个方面入手:向内,稳定已有信徒群体,力争不使其流失,又可分为宗教垄断、宗教裁判、武力惩罚等硬措施和宗教感化、辩论对话等软措施。向外,传播扩展以争取新教徒,其方式也有硬措施与软措施之分。如果新教徒同时又是其他宗教徒,冲突在理论上就难免发生。所以一个社会中特定宗教徒的数量越多、影响越大,则与外宗教相遇时冲突发生的可能性就越大,这也要求我们研究宗教和谐关系必须限于一定时间、地域、人群水平之上。宗教之间如果和谐共处,需要信仰政策上的相宜,信仰理性上的相通,信仰伦理上的相合,信仰身份上的相容,信仰背景上的相符,信仰结构上的相类,信仰功能上的相补,信仰思维上的相近,信仰情感上的相惜。只要某一方面情况不妙,就很有可能导致宗教冲突。宗教和谐需要具备太多的因素和条件,其有限性是非常突出的。而宗教冲突往往只需要一个方面的因素或条件为导火索,就足以引爆冲突的炸药包。除了上述信仰方面的因素外,现实社会中对生存资源的争夺,对教理教义的不同解释,触犯宗教禁忌的行为,甚至一句伤害对方的粗话,都可以引发不同信教群体之间或信仰同一宗教的群体内部爆发所谓的宗教冲突。

用多元形容宗教,强调的是宗教相遇的场域性、宗教关系的整体性、宗教地位的平等性、宗教互动的结构性和宗教交往的动态性。和谐是在现实关系的无秩序状态中,通过物质性、精神性和行动性资源的支撑转化而达到秩序化存在的结构与规则的整合过程,同时运用结构化的手段将各种价值理念乃至虚幻想象植入一套特定的教义体系中,并对教徒发挥支配性的作用。在此转化、整合与植入的过程中，自我中心主义是必须克服的思想阻碍。一个宗教抬高自己，必然要贬抑他教，就不能做到彼此尊重与功能互补。因此我们必须将和谐视为一种精神理念、思维模式并内化为信徒的行动准则，然后才能通过信徒这一宗教最为重要的载体之间的和谐，推动宗教间的和谐共处。即是说，宗教的内在和谐、外在和谐、共在和谐是有机统一的"和谐整体"。就终极性而言，特定地域内的宗教和谐，必然要表现为信徒群体和信徒个人之间的和谐。宗教虽有高下，但不能以高压下；虽有主次，但不能以主欺次；虽有强弱，但不能以强凌弱；虽有先后，但不能以先驱后；虽有左右，但不能以左攻右；虽有内外，但不能以内排外；虽有我他，但不能以我逐他。破除高级宗教、主导宗教、强势宗教、本土宗教对后进宗教、次要宗教、弱势宗教、外来宗教的压制、支配、驱逐态度和行为，使二者形成共赢互补结构有机统一体的过程，就是宗教和谐的过程，其最终结果的外显化就是多宗教和谐共处状态。

假设两类宗教没有直接交往，彼此虽"老死不相往来"但却相安无事，这种平静不是和谐。没有交流就难以理解，没有理解就难以尊重，没有尊重就难以和谐。纵观历史上和现实中的宗教冲突，往往都是由于信徒之间互不理解尊重，因直接交往的小事而引起并扩大升级。信徒各自所属的宗教组织或社会网络，可以将冲突在更大的范围内迅速传播。秉持和谐思维和行动逻辑，则宗教融合可发展为宗教和谐；如果秉持冲突思维和行动逻辑，则宗教融合可发展为宗教冲突。所以，在宗教互动关系谱系上，宗教融合处于中性状态。

就人类宗教发展史的一般规律而言，某一地域或人群中最初往往只有一种特定宗教，随着交往传播范围的扩大，其他宗教逐渐进入。相应地产生冲突、和谐、融合三种可能结果。就宗教发展的整体趋势而言，多元化是一个必然的趋势：向内是宗教因社会的发展而不断增加维度，呈现多维化态势；向外是宗教因人类交往的增加而不断相遇交流，乃至在同一人群、地域和时间中相处，呈现多样化态势。宗教和谐相处是二元及以上宗教之间可能关系中的一种，并且能与其他类型的宗教关系动态转化。其他可能的宗教关系主要是宗教冲突和宗教融合，前者包括宗教战争、宗教排斥等子关系类型，后者包括宗教置换、宗教消解等子关系类型。同样，宗教和谐也包括宗教对话、宗教和平等子关系类型。对于宗教和谐的理解,一定要具有宏观的视野、动态的思维和多元的理论。多宗教共存都没有可能性,何来多宗教和谐?

<h1 style="text-align:center">三</h1>

宗教冲突往往是走向宗教和谐的必由之路,可以说没有宗教冲突就没有宗教和谐。宗教冲突是长期的,宗教之间发生矛盾是必然的,宗教通过冲突达到相知相识而磨合,通过取长补短而健全,通过磨合而理顺进一步发展的环境,并取得广泛的社会认可和信众基础。自然的、适度的、可控的、良性的宗教冲突是宗教走向成熟的基础,是宗教之间关系走向和谐的过程,具有建设性的价值和意义。宗教创建之初,在教理教义、组织机构、礼仪系统等方面往往还不完善,需要借助其他宗教文化中积极有利的因素来使自己得到不断地完善和健全。宗教冲突使宗教本身的弱点和不足得到充分的暴露,并往往成为对手攻击的把柄,使其找到改进的方向和目标,从而主动地或被动地修正自己的不足,弥补自己的弱点。

宗教冲突或融合的主要目的导向是一教独存,而宗教和谐的目的导向是多教共存。研究和谐,就必然要正视冲突。冲突是两个或两个以上主体在特定利益基础上的直接或间接性对抗。冲突并不必然具有破坏性,在可以控制的规模、范围和水平上的冲突,为了特定的目标而发生,往往具有潜在的建设性。冲突所围绕的利益和矛盾的消解,必然在更高的阶段产生新的关系类型——和谐。

不同宗教信仰群体之间的冲突,能增强同一宗教信仰群体内部的凝聚力。如往昔云南佤族部落成年男子以偷袭的方式砍取周边民族的人头来祭神的猎头祭谷仪式,使佤族同周边被猎头民族的关系处于一种紧张状态,这种情况却增强了本民族内部的凝聚力,如有谁被本民族驱逐出村寨,那这个人往往只有死路一条。

宗教冲突并不必然会导致灾难性的结果,适度的宗教冲突往往是先进的宗教文化替代后进的宗教文化的必由之路。云南省贡山独龙族怒族自治县丙中洛乡的傈僳族、怒族、藏族、独龙族信教群众分别信奉原始宗教、藏传佛教、天主教,有不少同一家庭内部的成员分别信奉不同的宗教,目前各宗教之间和睦相处,但在历史上是曾经发生过宗教冲突的,一种外来宗教的传入难免会与原有的宗教之间发生冲突。对于后进民族来说,放弃原始落后的传统宗教文化,去接受并屈从于较为现代先进的外来宗教文化,这种选择本身就像一个新生命的诞生一样,乃是一个阵痛的过程。这种选择本身也会使某些人因此而丧失既得的地位和利益,在一定范围内引发宗教之间的冲突,也是在所难免的。但其往往能带来民族文化的新生,直接带动社会生产力的巨大进步和发展。因此,我们不必将所有的宗教冲突都视为洪水猛兽,有些宗教冲突的发生乃是宗教发展的客观结果和内在需要,面对这类宗教冲突不必如临大敌,而是要积极加以引导。我们要反对和防止的是一些人别有用心地制造宗教冲突,并将事态扩大化。

从理想类型的关系分析,和谐应该是宗教关系的常态。但是现实世界以其无数事例告诉我们,宗教冲突是客观存在的事实。即使我们目前看到的宗教和谐状态,几乎都是经历宗教冲突而转化过来。我们找不到没有宗教存在的民族,同样也找不出在宗教相遇过程中,从来没有发生过冲突的民族。在云南宗教历史上,并非没有宗教冲突。如今被视为多民族、多宗教和谐共处示范区的云南省贡山独龙族怒族自治县丙中洛乡历史上曾多次发生过宗教之间的冲突,首先是藏传佛教传入之初发生了喇嘛残害当地原始宗教巫师的事件,此后,天主教传入的过程中亦引发司铎与喇嘛和当地民众之间的冲突。

18世纪的清朝乾隆初年,四川藏区的德格喇嘛寺杜建功活佛到云南省福贡县传教,最终没能打开局面而被迫转移到贡山县的丙中洛传教。藏传佛教传入贡山县丙中洛的怒族、傈僳族和独龙族聚居区,先后在丙中洛建盖了藏传佛教的寺院飞来寺和普化寺,打破了长久以来原始宗教一统天下的局面。当地原始宗教与藏传佛教之间最大的冲突发生在喇嘛寺的第四任治寺喇嘛兰雀治格治理期间。兰雀治格喇嘛在继位期间努力将当地藏传佛教的发展推到了顶峰,但不久便开始走向衰落。兰雀治格喇嘛在任期内通过大兴土木,还请来大批汉族、白族工匠,强行用摊派钱粮,抽人拉夫及向民间募捐集资的方法,花了7年时间,于1783年在飞来寺南边兴建了规模更大的普化寺。普化寺最兴盛的时期,仅出家住寺的喇嘛就多达百余人,寺院拥有水田一百五十多亩,风景林三十亩,牛马各一百多头(匹),绵羊千余只。不久,喇嘛寺里爆发了一种恶性的传染病,兰雀治格和许多喇嘛都患了此病。为了消除病灾,喇嘛们将当地的九名巫师全部招来杀牲祭鬼,巫师们使尽浑身解数都未能解除病灾。喇嘛们便将巫师处死,九个巫师中仅有名叫昆楚的巫师逃脱,昆楚迅速到维西厅告状。经审讯判决,普化寺被罚了一筒黄金,作为八个巫师的偿命金,普化寺的资产因此损失大半,因此大伤元气,从此走向衰落。从表面上看,恶性传染病的流行和爆发是引发冲突事件的直接原因,这次冲突事件对藏传佛教本身带来了沉重打击,便因此产生许多负面的影响,如喇嘛对病灾无能为力,而请巫师做法事,这种情况就极大地影响了藏传佛教在当地的声誉。

1888 年,四川康定教区派遣法国天主教司铎任安守(I. Leuefieq)前往西藏的察隅地区传教,在政教合一的藏族地区传教必然会与当地喇嘛寺产生矛盾和冲突,任安守被喇嘛驱逐出藏区,而转到与察隅交界的云南省贡山县丙中洛传教。从而使当地宗教形成了原始宗教、藏传佛教和天主教三教鼎立的局面。天主教在丙中洛的传播和发展过程中,由于采用不正当的手段争夺信众和地盘,非法干预当地少数民族的传统宗教活动,破坏当地的宗教信仰自由,引诱逼迫村民改信天主教等原因,与当地民众和喇嘛寺发生冲突,并最终引发了当地反天主教的白汉洛教案。此后传入的基督教会充分吸取天主教的教训,与当地的原始宗教、藏传佛教和天主教之间注重保持友好的合作姿态,没有引发大的冲突,并在当地得到迅速的发展,形成后来居上的局面。

近代基督教传入云南以后,曾多次与当地传统宗教信仰发生冲突,这种冲突在当今的许多地区仍然存在,只是这种适度的小范围冲突并不足以影响到整体上和谐共处的大局面。如近期红河哈尼族彝族自治州部分哈尼族内部基督教的传入引发了哈尼族家庭内部、亲戚之间和村寨内部诸多矛盾和冲突。由于同一家庭内部,夫妻双方信教的一方每周礼拜天都要去教堂或活动点做礼拜而不能下地干活,另一方则还要下地做农活,长此以往难免引起另一方的不满。有时也会出现丈夫不给晚上去做礼拜而晚归的妻子开门的情况。

同一家庭内部信奉了基督教的与不信奉基督教的亲属之间,在老人去世时是按传统的方式来安葬或是按基督教会的方式规则举办葬礼,基督教徒与非基督教徒各持一端,信奉基督教的子女担心老人不按教会的方式举行葬礼,来世就再也不能与去世的父母相聚;而不信奉基督教的子女则担心,不按传统的方式安葬去世的父母,老人就回不到老祖宗的聚集地而成为孤魂。双方都出于孝心,却从而引发兄弟姊妹之间的冲突等等,仍难免发生。由于信奉基督教的哈尼族清明节不去上坟祭祖,也会引起亲戚对他们不孝行为的不满。

按民族历史文化传统,哈尼族村寨举行大型的挖水井、维修村寨水源、开挖水渠、修桥补路、建盖集体活动场所等大型集体活动,往往要杀牲祭祀。已信奉基督教的哈尼族以不参加"封建迷信活动"为由,不参加以上的集体公益活动。个别已改信基督教的哈尼族信徒私自跑到长久以来被视为神圣不可侵犯的神山去砍伐供奉为村寨保护神的"竜树",用以建盖基督教徒的聚会场所,这种挑衅行为激起当地未改信基督教哈尼族群众的愤慨。哈尼族群众曾对这些基督教徒采取了断水断电,没收土地林地,甚至要把基督徒驱逐出村寨等处罚。如果放弃传统文化,一味接受外来基督教,现在可能早已不是多宗教和谐共存,而是基督教一教独大,传统宗教被消除殆尽的局面。所以,宗教必须秉持自己文化的独立精神,在求同的基础上做到存异,而不是无原则的消除差异。

宗教冲突的根本原因可以归结为两个方面。第一,没能正确对待相互之间的差异;第二,没能正确处理相互之间的利益问题。如果两类宗教信徒能够通过宗教性理解彼此之间千差万别的宗教行为,而不是采取偏激的对立态度否定和贬抑另一方,宗教之间则会倾向于和谐相处。宗教的原初精神不是排斥,而是整合,宗教在原始社会的凝聚团结中扮演神圣旗帜的作用。但是人类创造出来的宗教却不能越过人群的界限整合他者。如果宗教的传播具有世界性,但是宗教的精神却不具有世界性,不能容纳不同的信仰体系,在世俗力量和利益的推动下,必然导致冲突。研究宗教冲突,就是为了批判将宗教差异扩大化的不良习惯,将其根源和生存土壤一并拔掉,从正向的维度努力,化干戈为玉帛,转冲突为和谐。

越是在神灵观念上秉持多元化的民族,宗教之间的冲突就越可能减少,宗教之间的关系就越可能呈现和谐状态。相反,越是在神灵观念上推行一元化的民族,也就是说信奉一元至上神宗教的民族,宗教之间的冲突就越可能增多,宗教和谐的神学基础就越薄弱。

如果异教徒之间能够通婚,不仅有人口再生产的统计学意义,更能使不同的宗教也有了"联姻"的性质,从而再生产出新型的宗教信徒,为宗教和谐共处奠定人口学的基础。凡是宗教和谐的地区,信徒在选择信仰对象上都有很大程度的自由,反之则不然。

总之,在云南多宗教和谐共处的客观现象中,我们常常看到的是信徒身份的叠合,即是说允许一个人同时信仰多种宗教,成为多种宗教的教徒;神灵体系的叠合,即是说允许一个宗教同时吸纳其他宗教的神灵体系,这种吸纳可能带有一定的主次结构。活动场所的叠合,即是说允许一个宗教活动场所为多个宗教所共用,这实际是神灵体系叠合与教徒身份叠合的必然要求。

从辩证的角度来看,宗教冲突中蕴含着和谐的因素,宗教和谐中也蕴含着冲突的因素,二者的区别在于哪一方面的因素占据主导地位。和谐不是从来如此的,是在与冲突因素相协调的过程中发展起来的。多元宗教的和谐状态并非一成不变,促成和谐的努力也不可能一劳永逸。

从历史看信仰传统与文化建设

陶飞亚

　　文化建设是当下中国政府的重要议程之一。在文化建设中,必然会碰到如何处理信仰传统的问题。① 要恰当处理信仰传统,首先取决于对这种传统的基本认识和价值判断。值得提出的是,近代以来的中国,"传统"与"现代","信仰"与"文化"常常处于对立的状态,信仰传统长期被排斥在大众文化之外。改革开放以来,情况有了很大的改善,但信仰传统基本上还是局限在各自的寺庙教堂的圈子内,是一种信仰者群体内自我循环的小众文化和一些宗教研究知识分子的研究对象。说到底宗教话题还是被看成比较敏感的问题。② 那么,造成这种现象的原因在哪里? 它与文化建设有什么关系? 以往已经对此也有一些探讨,但通常把问题局限于当代因素而忽视其产生的历史根源,同时对宗教来说也较多地忽视了宗教附属事业对宗教核心价值相关性的重要意义。因此,本文将在这两个维度上来探讨宗教与文化建议的关系问题。

　　首先,在中国人的文化视野中,宗教仅仅有一席之地,而不像西方世界那样宗教一度笼罩一切。如果把宗教划分为核心价值和附属事业的话,那

---

　　① 本文在此讨论的信仰传统指的是宗教,文化则指世俗的社会文化。
　　② 卓新平:《宗教不脱敏 难以完成社会和谐构建》,"宗教在当代中国新文化的构建中仍处于边缘,人们对文化是否应涵括宗教内容也慎之又慎、极为敏感。中国改革开放的历程,正是人们在经济上'脱贫'、文化上'脱愚'和精神上'脱敏'的过程。如果宗教不能达到真正'脱敏',中国社会的和谐构建则很难完成。"2011 – 6 – 7 12:47:30 来源:凤凰网。

么一般来说,中国人看到的更多是宗教的附属部分,特别是非信仰群体更多的是从附属事业来接触和判断宗教的。

比如,人们会比较多的肯定宗教的慈善事业。宗教和传统的慈善有许多的共同的东西,乐施好善、悲天悯人、扶危济困都是宗教和慈善共同的东西。不同的宗教也都把施善和回报作为达致宗教的其他层次的途径之一。从这个意义上讲,宗教与慈善是同源的,或者说灵犀相通。西方扶弱济贫的传统主要源于《圣经》的教导,伊斯兰教"敬主行善"的观念也强调施恩于人。就中国的史实来看,佛教传入中国,带来了布施的概念,转化为后来的救济观念。① 大规模的慈善活动在政府、家族、行会之外,往往都由宗教团体提供。宗教慈善活动可能是唯一持久和经常性的慈善活动,同时这又是与世俗社会最经常地发生接触的地方。

再如,人们也会欣赏宗教的建筑文化。宗教建筑以其独特的风格已经成为重要的人文景观。在中国社会中,除了京都大邑的皇家建筑之外,保存的最好最多和历史最悠久的就是宗教建筑了。佛教寺庙、道教宫观、伊斯兰教清真寺、天主教和基督新教的教堂,以其独特的精神气质和建筑风格,成为各种宗教的空间符号,一方面在人世间彰显了宗教的精神感召力,一方面也展现了宗教创造的人文历史景观,成为今天许多名胜圣地的引以自豪的文化核心。宗教建筑是世界上最优秀的建筑遗存,往往会被列为世界文化遗产,被看作全人类共同的财富,受全世界人民的爱护和拥护和欣赏。

最后,宗教的艺术文化也较易为大众所接受。中国宗教在雕塑、绘画、音乐、戏剧等方面均有丰厚的文化资源。在中国的宗教艺术中,尤其值得注意的是宗教文化特有的石窟艺术,它集建筑、绘画、雕塑于一身,保存了大量古代的艺术珍品。我国现存的石窟遗迹约有 120 多处,其中最负盛名的有敦煌石窟、云冈石窟、龙门石窟、大足石窟、麦积山石窟等。伴随着基督教而来的西洋绘画雕塑艺术,也极大地丰富了中国绘画雕塑传统。佛教的输入,更是对中国戏曲的发展起了重要的作用。中国古代最早的正式剧

① 刘培峰:宗教与慈善从同一个站台出发的列车或走向同一站点的不同交通工具?〔来源:中国民族宗教网 | 发布日期:2012－03－03〕

场,就是佛教的寺庙,在此之前则多是露天或野地里开演。尤其是唐代寺院中的俗讲发达,本来始自以说唱佛经故事的方式传播佛教经文,但后来演化成百戏杂陈的戏场和变场,为中国戏曲的发展在文学和表演上铺平了道路。宗教文学在世界文学史上有极其重要的地位和影响。佛教文学的代表性著作自然就是佛经。除了宗教说教性质外,佛经中也包含有许多民间故事和传说,这些故事和传说早在释迦牟尼传教时就被用来宣传佛教教义,广为流传。佛经中这些故事和传说,对中国文学的发展有深刻和影响,中国的变文、小说、传奇和戏曲都曾从中吸取素材,一些著名的神怪小说如《西游记》、《封神演义》、《聊斋志异》,甚至《红楼梦》等,也明显受到宗教思想和宗教文学的影响。

　　毫无疑问,上述现象归根到底是与宗教信仰相联系的,但是其跨越"世俗"和"神圣"两界的特点,使得即使是非宗教信仰者也能理解和欣赏其所彰显的慈善行为、建筑艺术和审美情趣。但是,对于仅仅为宗教信仰者所践行的宗教思想和行为,也即是核心的宗教文化,情况就不那么简单了。所有宗教的核心文化可以简单地概括为有神论、灵魂不灭、神人关系和神主宰的赏善罚恶。①但这种思想在中国传统文化中并没有像在犹太文化和伊斯兰文化中那里受到绝对的肯定。孔子一系列的"未知生焉知死"、"敬鬼神而远之"的思想,深深地印铸在中国人的心灵中,使得不可知论影响到中国人思想习惯。赖德烈(Kenneth S. Latourette)曾经总结说:"华人首先不是一个具有丰富神秘体验的民族。他们当中有过一些神秘主义者,而为绝大多数人来说,神秘的东西并不是没有吸引力。然而,神秘主义远远不如在印度深厚,而像希伯来人的大先知和《圣经.诗篇》的作者那样的神秘精神也缺乏——希伯来人的特征是结合高尚的神秘体验和对个体及社会正义的激情。那些形成华夏本地宗教方面最有影响的人物主要是学者、管理者、哲学家和政治家。为(原文如此)他们来说,正义不是来自一种激发人的神秘体验,而是在于对社会的谨慎关注,对家庭和社会的义务感,对整体人民利益的纯正关切,对来世幸福的渴望或对改善自己的愿望。"②冯友

---

① 佛在中国大众文化中也是被看做神,甚至是最高一级的神。
② 赖德烈:《基督教在华传教史》,雷立柏等译,香港,道风书社,2009 年,第 22 页。

兰也说过中国人"和别国相比，一向是最不关心宗教的。"①这种宗教观在漫长的岁月中成为民族心理的积淀，造成中国有组织宗教的信仰人群总是社会中的少数群体。特别是当这宗教活动与其附属事业完全脱离，纯粹进入思辨领域时，人们对宗教的疏离感就会更加明显。

其次是五四以来的取消宗教或反宗教思想对后来的国人的宗教观产生了深刻影响。早在1915年陈独秀就大声疾呼要以科学取代宗教："在昔蒙昧之世，当今浅化之民，有想象而无科学。宗教美文，皆想象时代之产物。近代欧洲之所以优越他族者，科学之兴，其功不在人权说下，若舟车之有两轮焉。今且日新月异，举凡一事之兴，一物之细，罔不诉之科学法则，以定其得失从违；其效将使人间思想云为，一遵理性，而迷信斩焉，而无知妄作之风息焉。"②蔡元培则声称要美育代宗教："鉴激刺感情之弊，而专尚陶养感情之术，则莫如舍宗教而易以纯粹之美育。纯粹之美育，所以吾人之感情，使有高尚纯洁之习惯，而使人我之见、利己损人之思念，以渐消沮者也。盖以美为普遍性，决无人我差别之见能参入其中。"③陈讲的科学主义和蔡宣扬的美育代宗教，确实影响了许多人的宗教观念，但后来最值得注意的是国民党人张振振的看法：

> 我们站在党的立场上面讲，可以说宗教一方面的好处，我们党里都包括了。我们做党员的，毕生致全力于党的建设还来不及，那里来有闲工夫去管教不教的问题呢！以耶教来说，摩西是脱希伯来民族于埃及之厄的一个民族革命的导师，耶稣是反抗罗马之侵略的打倒帝国主义的先锋，他们提倡的又是自由平等博爱；但是，我们党的唯一的领导者中山先生的精神，更来得伟大精深，为摩西耶稣所不能比拟！中山先生的自由平等博爱的学说，更非粗浅的教义所能望及！我们只有把全部的聪明才慧献给党，不管什么教不教，而在党之下更不应该使教有具体的组织。说是

---

①　冯友兰：《中国哲学简史》，第6页。

②　陈独秀：《敬告青年》(1915年9月15日)，《独秀文存》，合肥：安徽人民出版社，1987年，第8-9页。

③　蔡元培：《以美育代宗教说——在北京神州学会演说词》(1917年4月8日)，高平叔编：《蔡元培全集》第三卷，北京：中华书局，1984年，第32-34页。

他们努力为劳苦民众谋幸福,难道我们党不是努力为劳苦民众谋
幸福的吗?他们宣传的是上帝,上帝是唯一的尊者。我们的总理
岂不是在上帝之下呢?况且他们是欺骗劳苦民众,并不是真正为
民众谋幸福![1]

张的名气自然不可与陈独秀蔡元培相提并论,但他把宗教思想简单化
和宗教组织政治化则反映了当时流行的看法。显然,五四以来新文化运动
开始的对宗教的批判最后走向了简单化和激进主义。其原因一是由于俄
国革命中反宗教和文化激进主义的示范和影响;二是对马克思主义宗教观
的片面理解;三是信仰传统虚无主义的影响。强势的世俗文化精英行使文
化话语权,宗教无论在国民革命还是共产主义革命运动中都是被批判的对
象。不过这种对宗教的批判多数还只限于思想的交锋,正如鲁珍晞(J.
Lutz)所说的是"纸上的战争",宗教的附属事业依然存在,至少这些事业在
依然维持着宗教在世俗社会中的一些体面。

新中国成立以后,执政党对在待宗教方面制定了正确的路线是显而易
见的。但是在传统和新思想影响下,正确的东西反而变得很脆弱,不断地
受到其自身的干扰,甚至主管宗教者都想建设无宗教县。理论和实际行动
之间始终有强大的张力。就连一直追随基督教三自爱国会领袖吴耀宗在
1957 年的报告中写道:"在以马克思主义和无神论为领导思想的新中国,基
督徒,特别是年青的一代,处处都受到影响和限制,这样基督教是否有发展
的可能,甚至有无维持现状的可能? 即使宗教信仰是自由的,新中国的环
境是不是把这个信仰自由的政策打了一个折扣?"吴还谈到"整个社会生活
的进步和宗教之间的矛盾。信徒感到整个社会的空气对他们的'压力'很
大,'许多教徒不愿说出自己的身份,怕被扣上落后帽子,怕自己的前途受
影响'。"[2]这还是在 1957 年之前中国社会最平稳时的情况,此后随"左倾"
思想的盛行,宗教在社会上的地位每况愈下了。

---

① 张振振:《我的宗教观》,《民国日报》,1928 年 2 月 12 日,《觉悟》版。
② 《关于今后基督教工作的一些意见》(1957 年 2 月),1 - 2,上海市档案馆藏,B22 - 1 - 71 -
8。转自邢福增编:《大时代的宗教信仰——吴耀宗与二十世纪中国基督教》,香港,基督教中国文
化研究社 2011 年版,第 504 页。

　　实际上新中国建立之后,除了不断的政治运动对宗教处境产生了负面影响,或许还有一个重要的导致宗教边缘化的原因还在于宗教组织的结构性变化。前面我们谈到了宗教附属事业是民众认识宗教在尘世之善的重要途径。但在1950年代一系列改造运动中基督教附属的大中小学校、医院、慈善机构等都被融入到国有体制之中,这当然为这些国有事业的进一步发展提供了新的动力。但是这些附属事业被剥离时是伴随着宗教负面化的批判运动的。这就不仅使得宗教之树枝蔓全无,变成了无法在社会公共生活中彰显自己实际善行的"裸教",使附着于这些机构的宗教精英"皮之不存毛将焉附",结果使得宗教团体趋向底层化。文化上的低水准也使其在尊重读书的中国社会地位下降。不仅如此,宗教场所的关停并转以及对此前教会慈善事业攻其一端不及其余的做法,也使得宗教事业负面印象变得根深蒂固。当时最有影响力的电影小说也为铸造宗教负面形象出力不少。如电影《古刹钟声》、《地下航线》、《林海雪原》等出现的宗教人物形象无不是反面人物。到"文革"时要破四旧时,都不必专门提到宗教,因为宗教已经被破的差不多了。

　　改革开放后,党的宗教理论和政策发生的深刻的变化。社会上对宗教看法逐渐在改变。但改革开放前30年宗教逐步负面化的影响还是很深的。对宗教问题的梳理往往在宗教界或有限的学术界展开,社会对宗教了解也很有限。直到数年以前,还有硕士生博士生对老师说家长反对其从事宗教研究。高校如此何况基层社会。宗教的附属事业依然凋零,宗教依然基本是"裸教"。今年已经出台民间组织办慈善事业的规定,但有些宗教没有或者短时期内也不可能重新建立起高水准的附属事业。相应的,宗教精英数量少,缺乏社会影响力。总起来说,在过去的文化建设中,宗教的身份并不分明,许多人都在觉得宗教很敏感,这就谈不上去发挥其积极作用了。因此,如果在新一轮文化建设中,宗教也能有所贡献的话,从历史的梳理中需要认识几个基本问题。

　　首先,要真正地实事求是的认识宗教,最主要的找出其对世俗文化的补充性。正如波士顿大学教授克利夫特(Peter Kreeft)所说的,"所有这些宗教都包含了一套道德法则,尽管在理论问题上如上帝的本质上彼此有分歧,但在实际问题上,例如人应该如何度过一生并没有很大的差别。"中国的各种传统宗教都强调道德实践,强调精神追求和行为实践紧密结合。所谓"举头三尺有神明",实际上是通过信仰神明的存在,能对人赏善罚恶,最后落到"善有善报,恶有恶报"这种最通俗的说教上。由此来影响人们自觉遵循道德的规则。在这里宗教的道德律发挥了人间的法律所不能起到的约束人们内心的作用。各种传统宗教还重视精神修养,由于宗教都有关于另一个世界的盼望,使得信徒在可以以彼岸世界的盼望来平衡此岸生活的跌宕起伏,因此能在世俗生活中淡泊名利,保持平和的心态。宗教教义还视谦卑和忍让为必要的修养。宗教都强调与人为善的伦理关系,以及重精神、轻物质名利,崇尚适度克制人性的贪欲。① 这些宗教道德不仅与社会公共道德主张在形式和内容上有共通之处,而且通过宗教戒律体现在信徒的行动中,成为信徒外在的一种身份特征。笔者曾经向一位有世代宗教背景的教授朋友请教过"信徒的道德水准比一般人怎么样?"得到的回答是很难一概而论。他认为新近入教者的道德水平可能是参差不齐的,与社会大众并无二致。不过,因为宗教组织生活中的无利可图和反而要求信徒经常奉献金钱和时间,所以有些人会离开。那么,一个人如果一直留在某个宗教组织里,他就有一种比较纯粹精神的追求,这些人的道德水准可能会高一点。美国杨百翰大学教授 Brett G. Scharffs 引用的数据从另外角度证明在美国各州中,信仰宗教人口比例最高的州也往往是慈善捐款最多的州。例如犹他州有95%人口是宗教信仰者,该州的人均捐献达到了其年收入的10.6%。② 因此,尽管宗教不等于道德,宗教的道德律只能对一部分人产生有限的作用,但当社会出现法律管不着而有赖人心自律的诸多消极现象时,宗教道德约束具有训诫和警示意义,有助于补充、矫正当前社会关系中

---

① 比如,道教讲尊道贵德、慈爱和同,要求信徒行善积德、济世利人,佛教主张众善奉行、庄严国土、利乐有情、普度众生,伊斯兰教主张孝敬父母、亲爱邻人、诚实公正、宽容团结,天主教和基督教提倡缔造和平,要求信徒爱人如己、服务人群,多做善功等。佛教称"贪、瞋、痴"是一切烦恼之源,讲求"苦、集、灭、道"四圣谛,只有放弃过分追求世俗的物质享受,才能解脱烦恼。道教追求精神的复归,以清静自然的人生,达到与自然的和谐共出。宗教教义提倡平等待人。佛教讲求众生平等,基督宗教提出上帝面前人人平等,伊斯兰教主张人与人皆兄弟。

② 12Source and Map: *How America Gives*, The Chronicle of Philanthropy, http://philanthropy.com/article/FaithGiving/133611/. Other data from the 2008 Pew Forum on Religion & Public Life, *U. S. Religious Landscape Survey* and the Gallup *Religiosity by State* 2011 survey.

的一些缺憾,有助于提高公民文明素质,强化公民的道德责任感,促进社会稳定和谐发展。实际上,在当今世界上许多地区和国家,尤其是所谓强势文化国家如欧洲北美,信仰传统和世俗文化之间的包容与渗透是普遍现象。罗伯特贝拉(Robert N. Bellah)致力诊断美国的社会及道德生态危机,提出靠美国历史中形成的宗教和公民传统来克服这些危机,宗教与世俗文化熔铸一炉成为凝聚国民精神的文化资本,引起社会广泛关注。①

其次,要在世界历史经验中反思五四以来的宗教政治化的看法。把宗教思想等同于政治思想,把人们的宗教倾向看成是政治倾向其实是一种简单化的做法。宗教的核心关注的是如何突破人的能力和生命的有限性,在与神圣力量的结合中而达致超越的无限性。在实际的社会生活历史中,信仰者是有多种社会形态的,对待政治的态度并不完全与宗教信仰画等号的。在宗教信仰与科学领域各自遵循不同的认识逻辑,但实际的人并不是信仰宗教就一定是与科学精神对立的。这样的多样化的例子简直比比皆是。毋庸讳言宗教中是有迷信的,但迷信不等于宗教,宗教最后落脚点是形成一个共信共行的"道德社群",而这对任何一个社会都有积极的意义。所以,中国历史上亘古以来就有"神道设教"的思想,尽管这里有统治者维护自身利益的功利主义,但在一定的条件下是有益于社会道德的。就像哲学家康德承认无论是经验还是理性都无法证明上帝的存在。但是他认为,为了维护道德的缘故,我们必须假设上帝与灵魂的存在。他把这些信仰称为"实践的设准",即一个无法证明的假设,但为了实践的缘故该假设必须成立。② 而在中国的传统文化是大量地吸收信仰传统的资源,为维护传统社会的价值观。所以中国有"佛教见性,道教保命,儒教明伦,纲常是正。……毋患多歧,各有所施。要在圆融,一以贯之。三教一体,九流一源,百家一理,万法一门"的三教合一的说法。③ 在某种意义上,这三者都被看成

---

① 贝拉(Robert N. Bellah),《"公民宗教"与社会冲突》,《二十一世纪》网络版,2003 年 3 月号。

② http://baike.baidu.com/view/3899.htm

③ 明心见性是要在觉性中来成就。而觉性必须要在人类世间来达成,让自己体证生存的辛酸过程,在酸甜苦辣中去印证自己生存的一切取向,更让自己在生存中不会脱离人世间的群居社会。觉性是了知天地万物的根本源。生活的过程就是让自己明了"觉性的根本源"。若脱离生存的取向过程,摈弃了生活的润生过程,就难有真实的生存经验去作内心世界的滋润资粮。

中国文化基本的组成部分的。其实,在世界近代历史中,新兴的资产阶级也曾无情的批判宗教,政教之间发生过激烈的冲突。例如法国大革命对宗教的摧毁,德国俾斯麦对天主教发动的"文化斗争",都在使得社会和教会付出沉重代价之后,宗教依然存在下来以满足社会的特定的需要。"文革"浩劫之后中国宗教的复兴实际上也是这种世界经验的并不完全相似的重演。因此正如哈佛大学教授桑德尔指出的"意识到生活的不同层面,像我们讨论的健康、教育、法律、家庭生活、公民生活,可能会由不同的价值支配,具有多元的价值观。而历史上专制的例子,多是由于提出了单一的至高的宗教观或意识形态,却忽略了社会生活的多元性却忽略了社会生活的多元性,以及不同的价值目的可能管辖着不同的社会领域。"①

　　最后,要看到宗教的外在和附属的事业与维护和谐社会的一致性。托克维尔(Charles Alexis de Tocqueville)曾说,尽管宗教注重个人虔诚,但它仍能把人们拉向公共世界领域。但在中国的公共世界领域,却很少能看到宗教在发挥作用。因此在去除宗教负面化的过程中,要给宗教一些空间。例如宗教是否可以有自己的一些附属事业。随着中国社会的老龄化时代的到来,是否可以借鉴西方和香港的做法推动宗教界参与到这方面的社会建设中来。以香港为例,截至 2007 年 12 月,获香港税务机关认可的免税慈善组织为数共 5123,其中仅以"推广宗教"名义申报的慈善机构就达 1773,占到总数的三分之一强。②以基督教为例,2010 年共营办 7 家医院、17 家诊所和 107 家综合社会福利机构,这些社会福利机构在各区提供多种服务,计有社区(家庭及青少年)服务中心逾 109 个、儿童院 11 所、老人服务机构? 中心? 院舍共 169 所、服务弱智、残疾、吸毒等人士的康复中心 59 间。③再如

---

　　①　http://v.163.com/special/sandel2012/

　　②　具体参见香港法律改革委员会慈善小组委员会的《慈善组织》咨询文件摘要,http://www.hkreform.gov.hk/tc/docs/charities_sc.pdf.必须指出的是,在 5123 家慈善组织中,上述的 1773 家宗教慈善机构是被归为"推广宗教"的慈善宗旨类别,余下的被归为"济贫"(1037)、"促进教育"(1790)及"其他"(523)这三大慈善宗旨类别,而这三大类别中的诸多慈善组织亦为香港各大宗教团体所创办,故由香港宗教团体举办经营的慈善组织数目实际上并不只有 1773 家,而是应该超出这一数目。有兴趣者可参考香港税务局有关截至 2011 年 8 月 31 日的"获豁免缴税的慈善机构及慈善信托的名单",http://www.ird.gov.hk/chi/pdf/c_s88list.pdf.

　　③　香港年报 2010,宗教与风俗,http://www.yearbook.gov.hk/2010/tc/pdf/C18.pdf.

香港的道教组织也非常重视社会公益事务,在教育方面在香港开办共四十多所中小学、幼稚园外,还资助各大学和专上学院举办课程,还在内地的贫困山区捐建希望工程学校,解决青少年上学困难。[①]以便使其能有实际的途径来体现宗教的善和道德,而不仅仅是捐钱而已。同时,适当开放和引导网络传媒、书报杂志等正面宣传信仰传统与社会主义社会相适应的成果,消除片面、狭隘、错误的观念和认知,大众媒体、广播影视以及文艺舞台,要为信仰传统中的积极的社会实践性内容提供更大空间,使宗教文化积极健康的道德规范及心理慰藉功能得以发挥。

---

①　香港年报 2010,宗教与风俗,http://www.yearbook.gov.hk/2010/tc/pdf/C18.pdf。

中国宗教要为中华文化建设作贡献

王晓朝

中国共产党第十七届六中全会审议通过了《中共中央关于深化文化体制改革、推动社会主义文化大发展大繁荣若干重大问题的决定》。公报指出:"当今世界正处在大发展大变革大调整时期,文化在综合国力竞争中的地位和作用更加凸显,维护国家文化安全任务更加艰巨,增强国家文化软实力、中华文化国际影响力要求更加紧迫。当代中国进入了全面建设小康社会的关键时期和深化改革开放、加快转变经济发展方式的攻坚时期,文化越来越成为民族凝聚力和创造力的重要源泉、越来越成为综合国力竞争的重要因素、越来越成为经济社会发展的重要支撑,丰富精神文化生活越来越成为我国人民的热切愿望。"这就引发了一个重要议题:中国宗教是否应当为中华文化建设作贡献?如果答案是肯定的,那么中国宗教在中华文化建设中应当如何作贡献?

一、外来宗教的本土化

中国国务院新闻办1997年发表的《中国的宗教信仰自由状况》白皮书在讲到中国宗教现状时明确指出:"中国是个多宗教的国家。中国宗教徒信奉的主要有佛教、道教、伊斯兰教、天主教和基督教。中国公民可以自由地选择、表达自己的信仰和表明宗教身份。""在漫长的历史发展中,中国各宗教文化已成为中国传统思想文化的一部分。中国的宗教徒有爱国爱教的传统。中国政府支持和鼓励宗教界团结信教群众积极参加国家的建设。""在中国,各种宗教地位平等,和谐共处,未发生过宗教纷争:信教的与不信教的公民之间也彼此尊重,团结和睦。这既是由于源远流长的中国传统思想文化中兼容、宽容等精神的影响,更是因为中华人民共和国成立后,中国政府制定和实施了宗教信仰自由政策,建立起了符合国情的政教关系。"①看了这样的论断,任何人都可以确信,中国政府坚定地认为,佛教、伊斯兰教、天主教和基督教在传入中国并与中国文化相融合以后已经是中国的宗教了,佛教文化、伊斯兰教文化、天主教文化和基督教文化已经是中国传统思想文化的重要组成部分。

但是,中国政府这样的论断在现实生活中尚未成为社会大众的共识。由于对宗教基础知识的缺乏,把伊斯兰教、天主教、基督教视为"洋教"的观点依然根深蒂固,在社会舆论中有很大市场。例如,去年网络上有一篇署名为"村长兼书记"的文章——《我为什么激烈反对基督教在中国的传播》。作者说:"基督教是西方文明对异教徒进行掠夺和屠杀的开路先锋。刚开始他们是派出牧师来进行诱骗,诱骗不成就组建十字军图穷匕见。中国近代史上有好些战争都是和牧师的名字联系在一起的。所以我说,西方人信仰基督教情有可原,中国人信仰基督教并且传播基督教的,罪无可恕。"②如果这位作者真的是"村长兼书记",那么他一定不了解中国共产党自改革开放以来有关宗教工作的方针、路线和政策。如果要他在他管辖的这个村里宣传和贯彻党的宗教政策,他一定会以阶级斗争为纲,把天主教和基督教的教会和信徒视为"二毛子"和"走狗"、"阶级敌人",作为斗争对象来讨伐,而不可能有什么"和谐"与"合作"。

再比如,中国内地高等院校里大批行政人员和教师也有这样的模糊认识。一大批政治思想工作者对宗教基础知识知之甚少,他们不懂得马克思主义的宗教理论,不知道中国共产党和政府现行的宗教政策,不知道如何

① 见国家宗教事务局网站对中国宗教概况的介绍,http://www.sara.gov.cn/gb/zgzj/index.html

② http://military.club.china.com/data/thread/1011/2521/50/49/3_1.html

对待少数在校大学生的宗教信仰,不知道如何处理国际文化交流中的相关宗教问题。他们的脑海里但凡浮现出"宗教"二字,必将之与"迷信"和"反动"画等号,若提起"基督教"或"天主教",亦必视之为"洋教",与"帝国主义的侵略"、"间谍"挂钩。他们不知道这个世界上不仅有外国的基督教和天主教,还有中国的基督教和天主教。

佛教、伊斯兰教、天主教和基督教这些宗教到底是中国的,还是外国的?这是一个看似简单,却不容易回答好的问题。学术界对这个问题虽然已有长期讨论,但时有不同的声音发出。在中国当下现实生活中,不同的人对这个问题也有不同的理解和认识。对这个问题的认识是思考中国宗教在中华文化建设中的地位和作用的前提,值得我们进一步探究。

一般说来,研究宗教的学者对这个问题的认识要比民众深刻一些,但我们也时不时地可以看到有些学者在走回头路,在思想上搞"以阶级斗争为纲"。一说起"儒道佛"就一股脑儿视为中华传统文化的精华与瑰宝,一说起天主教和基督教,那就是"西方人的宗教"、"洋教"。还有的学者认为现在研究佛教和道教保险,研究天主教和基督教危险,因为现在整个社会就这么看问题。哪怕你天天在那里烧香、开光和算命,也没人管,而你要是在那里认真研究基督教和天主教,就会招来怀疑的眼光。

伊斯兰教、基督教和天主教到底是中国的,还是外国的?宗教学界在以往的研究中已经从学理上讲清了这个问题。这个问题的实质是外来宗教本土化、中国化的问题。佛教是外来的,它在中国已有 2000 多年的历史。伊斯兰教于公元 7 世纪传入中国。天主教自公元 7 世纪起几度传入中国,1840 年鸦片战争后大规模传入。基督教于公元 19 世纪初传入中国,并在鸦片战争后大规模传入。道教不是外来的,它是中国土生土长的宗教,已有 1700 多年历史,但它发展到今天,也在走出国门,走向世界。中国现有这五种主要宗教从起源上说,除道教外,其他均为外来宗教。但当它们在中国大地上扎下根来、与中国文化融为一体以后,我们还要将它们视为外国的宗教吗?宗教传播可以与帝国主义侵略画等号吗?社会上的一般民众搞不清这个问题,做宗教学研究的学者也搞不清吗?

历史为我们提供了可资借鉴的经验,中国宗教现状为我们提供反思的基础。得益于改革开放以来中国共产党的宗教政策,中国宗教的发展迎来了她的"黄金时期"。"据中国天主教爱国会和中国天主教主教团统计,我国有天主教徒550万人,这个数字包括了受天主教地下势力影响的教徒。我国天主教的一个重要特点是教徒家庭世代相传,稳定性比较强。尽管天主教徒数量的增长速度不能与基督教信徒数量的增长速度相提并论,但与新中国建立初期的300万名天主教徒相比,也有了较大幅度的增长。"①"据中国基督教三自爱国运动委员会和中国基督教协会统计,基督教信教人数为1600万人,与新中国建立初期的70万人相比,增长十分迅速。这个统计数字不包括那些不经政府登记批准开放的教堂(活动点)的基督徒,因此基督徒的实际数量比这个统计数字要大。"②据此估计,2009年中国基督徒人数约为2100万,比1949年时增长了五倍。"得益于国家的发展和进步,中国教会近二十年来的兴旺成了今日基督教世界最令人瞩目的事情。"③如果我们把兴旺的中国教会和中国基督徒都视为"西方的"、"外国的"、"洋教"、"洋奴","特务"、"间谍",我们还怎么去创建和谐社会?

要解决全社会对中国基督教和中国天主教的模糊认识,就要从"基督宗教是中国的"这一观点入手。以往学界曾经讨论过"接受基督教"的问题。在具体语境中,"接受基督教"这一短语有三重含义:一是指个人信仰的皈依;二是指经由某些知识分子,导致社会群体、民族、国家把基督教的教义、思想体系作为文化要素接纳到民族文化精神体系之中;三是全社会各个层面的接受。这在当今中国已经不是希望,不是理想,而是现实。自1949年新中国成立以来,基督宗教就已经是受宪法和法律保护的宗教。"文革"期间,基督宗教虽然也受到打击,但没有在中国社会"失落",更没有根绝。"文革"之后,随着政府恢复宗教信仰自由政策,基督教信仰再次成为供人们自由选择的多种宗教信仰之一,中国教会的活动从总体上说亦趋于正常。所以我们可以说中国社会已经全面接受了基督宗教。

王作安先生在第二届"基督宗教在当代中国的社会作用及其影响"高

---

① 王作安:《我国宗教状况的新变化》,金泽、邱永辉主编《宗教蓝皮书2008》,北京:社会科学文献出版社,2009年,第71页。

② 王作安:《我国宗教状况的新变化》,金泽、邱永辉主编《宗教蓝皮书2008》,北京:社会科学文献出版社,2009年,第71页。

③ 王艾明著:《神学:教会在思考》,北京:宗教文化出版社,2010年,第180页。

级论坛讲话时指出:"基督宗教作为一个外来户,有一个在中国安家落户、落地生根的问题,也就是要适应中国社会,融会中国文化,走中国化道路。与同样是外来的佛教、伊斯兰教相比较,基督宗教在与中国文化的结合上相对滞后一些,需要更加努力。"陈泽民先生说:"从整个社会的层面上来说,中国基督教和基督徒如何真正与广大人民认同,如何最大限度地避免和杜绝片面的、狭隘的、消极的观念,如何能够在中国社会建设与发展中发挥有效的作用,这些问题都需要在神学上进行探索。"①他们的讲话从不同角度指出了基督教和天主教在本土化和中国化方面存在的问题和努力的方向。我相信,随着时间的推移,中国社会一定会完全接受基督教和天主教,中国民众终有一天提起基督教和天主教会像提起道教、佛教、伊斯兰教一样自然。

二、文化自党与文化自信

中国共产党十七届六中全会公报指出:"建设社会主义文化强国,就是要着力推动社会主义先进文化更加深入人心,推动社会主义精神文明和物质文明全面发展,不断开创全民族文化创造活力持续迸发、社会文化生活更加丰富多彩、人民基本文化权益得到更好保障、人民思想道德素质和科学文化素质全面提高的新局面,建设中华民族共有精神家园,为人类文明进步做出更大贡献。"公报对文化体制改革、推动中华文化大发展大繁荣作了纲领性的部署,首次提出要建设"文化强国"。这是 2007 年中国共产党十七大以来,"文化"命题首次成为中央全会的议题,也是继 1996 年党的十四届六中全会讨论思想道德和文化建设问题之后,中央决策层再一次集中探讨文化课题。

改革开放以来,宗教学界经过数十年的研究,对宗教与文化的关系问题作出了系统完整的解释。然而,由于中国是一个无神论的大国,要让全

① 陈泽民:《再论神学是教会在思考:中国教会神学建设的任务》,王艾明著:《神学:教会在思考》,北京:宗教文化出版社,2010 年,序,第 3 页。

社会都知道宗教的重要性不是一件易事。

中华文化建设的范围很广,内容很丰富。历史和现实告诉我们,每一种具有牢固的精神根基和历史传统的文化体系都不会从根本上被其他文化所取代,但是随着时代的变化,任何一种有着悠久历史传统的文化体系都不可能不发生变化。中国学术界普遍承认,中国社会正处在一个深刻的转型时期,它的文化也必将发生深刻的转变。当代中国文化建设是这种转型阶段的建设,而不是"光复"中国某一时代的传统文化。

一种有着悠久历史的文化就其核心内容而言,是不能加以简单替换的。我们应当把中外文化的交流、碰撞、融合的结果定位于文化转型与更新。文化转型是一个历史过程,它不是外来文化与本有文化之间的简单取代,而是通过外来文化与本有文化之间的冲突与调和实施重组,从而产生新型文化。异质文化之间的融合是可能的,这不仅是世界各大文化体系成形的历史告诉我们的事实,而且也是世界文化发展的大趋势。

无论如何看待当代中国文化发展的趋势,都不能抹去其开放性的特点。"对外开放作为一项不可动摇的基本国策,不仅适用于物质文明建设,而且适用于精神文明建设。"①当今一切有价值的文化成果,早已跨越国界,成为世界的文化,成为全人类的文化成果。中国的优秀传统文化需要发扬,外国的优秀文化成果也要吸取。中华文化建设也要面向世界,以开放的心态主动吸取外国各个时期创造的优秀成果,促进中国传统文化的更新,进而创造当代的中华文化。这是中国文化建设事业本身的要求,不但是中华文化建设不可缺少的内容,也是中国宗教不可推卸的历史责任。

党的十七届六中全会公报指出:"以改革创新为动力,发展面向现代化、面向世界、面向未来的,民族的科学的大众的社会主义文化,培养高度的文化自觉和文化自信,提高全民族文明素质,增强国家文化软实力。"所谓文化上的"自觉和自信"我理解是一种文化心态。它要求人们自觉地认识到自己固有文化、传统文化的优势和短处,也要正确认识到外来文化的长处与短处,要正确认识外国文化,既不要仰视也不要俯视,而是要平等的交流与对话;要正确理解传统文化,既不要盲目自大,也不要过分自卑;要

---

① 中共中央:《关于社会主义精神文明建设指导方针的建议》,人民出版社,1987年,第7页。

正确看待中国文化在全球文化中的地位和作用,以当代中华文化中的优秀成分为基础,吸收一切外来的优秀文化,体现时代性,保证民族性。

王艾明先生最近说:"中国教会的文献表明,自 1977 年开始,教会生活开始复苏,法律保障正常宗教活动成为现实。经过'文革'的灾难,教会与国家一样变得更加清醒。可以说从 1840 年第一个丧权辱国的不平等条约'南京条约'作为整个近代中国史悲哀的碑记,到'文革'的结束,一个多世纪的混乱和战祸使得民心思定和百废待兴成了整个民族的大趋势。教会的复兴和重建顺应了这个历史方向。茅屋时期的特征就是中国基督教继续走与中国人民、中国革命和中国文化和解之路。让圣经真理和基督信仰通过善良淳朴的信徒美好的言行来赢得国家的放心和社会的敬意。至此,中国基督教原来具有的'洋人'和'不平等条约'及外国传教士等外部特征完全消解和淡出。"①我相信,中国各主要宗教在积极参与中华文化建设的过程中,一定能进一步增强"文化自觉"和"文化自信",坚信中国化了的基督教和天主教能够更好地适应中国社会,自觉地成为国家的"软实力"的一部分,成为中华文化建设的一支生力军。

三、中国宗教与国家文化安全

自从改革开放以来,中国各主要宗教已经为中国宗教事业的健康发展做出了重要的贡献,同时也为中华文化建设出了力。几十年来,他们积极发展同世界各宗教和平组织的友好往来,共同促进和维护世界和平。希望工程、温暖工程、扶贫工程、公民道德建设、救助社会弱势人群、帮助聋哑残障人士、临终关怀、保护环境,这些社会工程都有宗教团体的身影。许多宗教团体还积极推进宗教间对话,努力消除宗教间的冲突。

十七届六中全会公报指出:"当今世界正处在大发展大变革大调整时期,文化在综合国力竞争中的地位和作用更加凸显,维护国家文化安全任务更加艰巨。"有学者在解读文件时指出:"强调文化安全是近年大势所趋。

---

① 王艾明著:《神学:教会在思考》,北京:宗教文化出版社,2010 年,序,第 180 页。

国家文化安全包括两方面：一方面，在文化竞争中是否具有自主性和竞争力；另一方面，在多种价值观中能否形成核心价值观的能力。""当今的冲突不再是军事进犯或意识形态冲突，而是文化和文明的冲突。现在的'文化帝国主义'不是传统帝国主义的军事入侵占领领土，而是一种文化的渗透，即价值观、思想、理论等的渗透。文化安全说到底就是要保持文化主体性，不能让外来的价值观消解了自己的文化，对自身文化前进方向要有清醒的认识，保留主体性和话语权。""现在维护国家文化安全任务重大。目前存在几个问题：首先，改革开放以来，部分西方国家和对中国持不同意见的势力和力量，对中国提出了'松土工程'，试图用西方宗教文化给我国社会主义文化'松土'。"

　　上述这些解读有可取的一面，也有很不到位的一面，其中最大的问题是以中外关系绝对对立和斗争的单向性思维来解读"中国文化安全"，忘记了当今中国与外国、中国文化与外国文化之间的关系不仅有对立和斗争的一面，还有和谐与合作的一面。如果把中国社会改革开放以来所发生的中外文化大规模交流均视为"文化帝国主义"的表现，那么我们又该如何定义中国近年来在世界各地办孔子学院？"357 所孔子学院遍全球，1 亿外国人热衷学汉语。""作为推广汉语教育与传播中国文化的重要平台，从 2004 年全球首家孔子学院在韩国成立以来，建设孔子学院的步伐越来越快，在国外的影响力也越来越大。"①如果按照上述专家的解读模式，我们是否也要将我们国家开展的和平的文化传播定义为"文化帝国主义"和"文化侵略"？

　　上述专家之所以对"国家文化安全"作出这样的解读，根本原因在于他不懂宗教。他把改革开放以来部分西方国家和敌视中国的势力利用西方宗教文化来对中国"松土"说成是当前维护国家文化安全的首要问题，但他可能没有想到，中国同样也可以用中国的宗教文化来松一松西方国家的"土"，可以用中国的宗教文化起到维护国家文化安全的作用。中国的佛教、道教、伊斯兰教、基督教和天主教是搞和谐的宗教，自改革开放以来就在维护世界和平方面做了大量工作。所以，中国不仅要为全世界提供印刷得最精美的宗教文化经典，而且也要向全世界提供中国化的宗教思想精

---

① 人民网 2011 年 11 月 28 日新闻报道。

华。

　　改革开放以来,中国宗教所展开的种种对外文化交流活动对维护中国的"文化安全"起了积极的作用,而不是在削弱或瓦解中国的"文化安全"。例如,2011 年 9 月 28 日,中国教会圣经事工展在华盛顿开幕。《国际在线》报道说:"在全球化的进程中,中美两国的交流合作越来越密切,而双方的宗教交流则是其中独特的一环。为了帮助美国更好地了解中国基督教发展情况,中国教会圣经事工展当地时间 28 日在华盛顿开幕。与会嘉宾表示,此次展览为他们提供了了解中国的另一个视角。""在悠扬的歌唱声中,中国教会圣经事工展在华盛顿拉开了帷幕。此次展览由中国基督教三自爱国运动委员会、中国基督教协会主办,主要通过图片、文字、实物以及圣经题材的艺术作品,回顾圣经在中国传播和翻译的历史,反映改革开放以来圣经的印刷、出版和发行事工,展现通过圣经事工给中国教会各个方面带来的各种变化,为希望了解中国的美国宗教界打开了一个窗口。中国国家宗教事务局局长王作安在开幕式上表示:'中国教会圣经事工展能够再次来到这里,是中美两国教会爱心人士共同努力的结果。在军舰、战机、导弹的消息充斥我们耳目的时候,两国教会在这里架起心灵沟通的桥梁,探讨如何用爱来诠释这个世界,让人感到非常难得。《圣经》把两国教会联系起来,爱让两国人民愿意彼此倾听和了解,这就是这次圣经事工展的意义。'"[1]

　　上述专家的解读还有一个更大的问题,这就是把社会主义核心价值观、价值体系与其他价值观、价值体系的关系视为完全异质的和敌对的,却不懂得任何一种价值体系都有一个形成与发展的历史过程,隶属于不同的价值体系的价值观具有同质性和相容性。这位专家说"不能让外来的价值观消解了自己的文化",那么马克思主义的价值观也是外来的,我们也不能让它消解"自己的文化"吗? 这个"自己的文化"又是什么呢?

　　众所周知,建设社会主义核心价值体系的战略任务是在中国共产党的十六届六中全会上提出来的。全会通过的《决定》指出:"马克思主义指导思想,中国特色社会主义共同理想,以爱国主义为核心的民族精神和以改

---

① 国际在线,2011 年 9 月 29 日新闻稿。

革创新为核心的时代精神,社会主义荣辱观,构成社会主义核心价值体系的基本内容。"这样一个价值体系的基本内容,决不能简单地用"外来的"和"内生的"来划分,也决不能把这些基本内容与其他价值观的关系理解为"对立"或"排他"。这一价值体系要以马克思主义理论为指导,要符合人类社会发展的历史趋势和时代要求,要深深地植根于中华社会的历史背景、历史进程和中华民族的优秀文化根基,它的基本内容必定也应是中华民族的全体成员所共同认可、共同奉行、共同选择的。全会的《决定》还说:"坚持以社会主义核心价值体系引领社会思潮,尊重差异,包容多样,最大限度地形成社会思想共识。"社会和谐是中国特色社会主义的本质属性,是国家富强、民族振兴、人民幸福的重要保证,建设富强、民主、文明、和谐的社会主义现代化国家是全国各族人民的共同理想,构建和谐社会是全体中国人民的共同价值追求。所以,"求同存异,兼容并包"才是建设社会主义核心价值体系的真精神,才是建设社会主义核心价值体系的正确道路。

中国共产党第十七届六中全会向全党和全国人民发出了建设中华文化的号召,这也是中国各宗教的一次历史性机遇。中国各宗教有责任也有义务积极参加中华文化建设,要以建设者的姿态,增强"文化自觉"和"文化自信",为中华文化的繁荣,为国家的文化安全作贡献。